LIBRARY
DISCARD

INTERPRETING AUTOMOTIVE SYSTEMS

INTERPRETING AUTOMOTIVE SYSTEMS

HARRY G. HILL

VAN NOSTRAND REINHOLD COMPANY
NEW YORK   CINCINNATI   ATLANTA   DALLAS   SAN FRANCISCO
LONDON   TORONTO   MELBOURNE

Van Nostrand Reinhold Company Regional Offices:
New York   Cincinnati   Atlanta   Dallas   San Francisco

Van Nostrand Reinhold Company International Offices:
London   Toronto   Melbourne

Copyright © 1977 by Litton Educational Publishing, Inc.

Library of Congress Catalog Card Number: 76-50041
ISBN 0-442-23419-8

All rights reserved. No part of this work covered by the copyright hereon may be reproduced or used in any form or by any means — graphic, electronic, or mechanical, including photocopying, recording, taping, or information storage and retrieval systems — without permission of the publisher.

Manufactured in the United States of America

Published by Van Nostrand Reinhold Company
450 West 33rd Street, New York, N.Y. 10001

Published simultaneously in Canada by Van Nostrand Reinhold Ltd.

15 14 13 12 11 10 9 8 7 6 5 4 3 2 1

Library of Congress Cataloging in Publication Data

Hill, Harry G
  Interpreting automotive systems.

  Includes index.
  1. Automobiles.   I. Title.
TL145.H54   629.2'5   76-50041
ISBN 0-442-23419-8

Preface

Each year the automobile seemingly becomes more complicated. The operation of the automobile as a whole is easier to understand if the components are studied individually through the use of numerous illustrations showing the structure of the components and their use in conjunction with other components of a particular system. *Interpreting Automotive Systems* is designed to help the reader accomplish this learning task with a back-to-basics approach. Automotive systems are separated into component assemblies so the reader will find it easier to gain an understanding of the way component parts function, how they are assembled, and where they are located in the system.

Interpreting Automotive Systems has numerous labeled exploded views to show the location of the basic parts and the relationship of adjacent parts. The section on automotive terms defines the component operation and location as simply as possible.

A major feature of this text is the review material. The Pictorial Review section requires the student to label the names of the component parts of an assembly. The view used in this section is a different one from that used for the labeled assembly. A cutaway rather than an exploded view is used here.

The Summary Review consists of multiple-choice, matching and completion questions. The answers to these questions may be found in the labeled figures or in the automotive terms section.

The Reference Review section is designed for the more advanced reader. The answers usually are not found in this workbook. Automotive shop service manuals, reference texts or work experience will be needed to answer these questions correctly.

The latest technological advances in the automotive field are incorporated in this classroom-tested material. Topics included are electronic ignition, electronic fuel injection and emission control devices. Other than an interest in learning about the automobile, special prerequisites are not required of the student before this text can be used.

Contents

SECTION 1 ENGINES

Unit 1	Reciprocating Engines	1
Unit 2	Engine Measurements	7
Unit 3	Crankshaft Assembly	13
Unit 4	Piston Assembly	19
Unit 5	Camshaft Assembly	25
Unit 6	Valves and Valve Trains	31
Unit 7	Rotary (Wankel) Engine	37

SECTION 2 FUEL SYSTEMS

Unit 8	Carburetors	44
Unit 9	Carburetor Systems	50
Unit 10	Fuel Supply Systems	57
Unit 11	Electronic Fuel Injection	63

SECTION 3 ELECTRICAL SYSTEMS

Unit 12	Electrical Circuits and Symbols	70
Unit 13	Conventional Ignition System	76
Unit 14	Conventional Distributors	82
Unit 15	Spark Plugs	88
Unit 16	Electronic Ignition System	94
Unit 17	Wiring Diagrams	102
Unit 18	Batteries	108
Unit 19	Alternators	114
Unit 20	Starting Systems	120

SECTION 4 EMISSION CONTROLS

Unit 21	Positive Crankcase Ventilation	128
Unit 22	Carburetor Emission Controls	135
Unit 23	Distributor Control Systems	141
Unit 24	Air Injection System	147
Unit 25	Evaporative Controls	153
Unit 26	Exhaust System Controls	159

SECTION 5 BRAKE SYSTEMS

Unit 27	Drum Brakes	167
Unit 28	Disc Brakes	174
Unit 29	Master Cylinder and Line Controls	180
Unit 30	Power Brakes	186

SECTION 6 SUSPENSION AND STEERING

Unit 31	Front Suspension	192
Unit 32	Rear Suspension	200
Unit 33	Shock Absorbers	207
Unit 34	Wheel Alignment Angles	213
Unit 35	Tires	219
Unit 36	Wheel Balancing	227
Unit 37	Standard Steering and Linkage	233
Unit 38	Power Steering	240

SECTION 7 LUBRICATION

| Unit 39 | Engine Lubrication Systems | 247 |
| Unit 40 | Chassis Lubrication | 255 |

SECTION 8 POWER TRAIN

Unit 41	Clutches	262
Unit 42	Standard Transmissions	269
Unit 43	Automatic Transmissions – Torque Converter	276
Unit 44	Automatic Transmissions – Hydraulic Control Systems	282
Unit 45	Automatic Transmissions – Planetary Gears	291
Unit 46	Drive Lines	297
Unit 47	Rear Axle Assembly	303
Unit 48	Conventional Differentials	308
Unit 49	Limited-slip Differentials	314

SECTION 9 AIR CONDITIONING AND COOLING

Unit 50	Air Conditioning Principles	319
Unit 51	Air Conditioning Systems	326
Unit 52	Cooling System	335
Index		345

SECTION 1 Engines

UNIT 1 RECIPROCATING ENGINES

RELATED AUTOMOTIVE TERMS

Block: Main casting of the engine that contains the cylinders; often made of cast iron.

Compression Pressure: Highest pressure developed during the compression stroke. May be checked with a compression gauge.

Cooling Method: Method used to remove excess heat from an engine. *Liquid cooling* systems use internal passages in the block and head, while *air cooling* systems have external fins on the block and head.

Cycle: A series of repeated events such as the intake, compression, power, and exhaust strokes of an engine.

Cylinder: The round hole(s) inside an engine block which provide space for the reciprocating piston(s).

Cylinder Arrangement: The way cylinders are placed in an engine, such as *in-line* (cylinders in a row), *V* (cylinders in two banks or rows at an angle to each other), or *flat* (pancake design).

Cylinder Numbering: The order in which the cylinders are numbered. Cylinder number one may be on either side of a V engine at the front. On in-line engines, the cylinders are numbered starting with one at the front.

Cylinder Combustion Pressure: Pressure in the cylinder from expanding gases immediately after mixture is ignited; about four times higher than compression pressure.

External Combustion Engine: An engine that burns the air-fuel mixture in a chamber outside the engine cylinder, such as a steam engine or a Stirling engine.

Firing Order: The order in which the cylinders deliver power strokes.

Fuel Burned: Type of fuel used; usually gasoline, diesel fuel oil, or LPG (liquefied petroleum gas).

Internal Combustion Engine: An engine that burns the air-fuel mixture in a chamber inside the engine cylinder, such as a conventional reciprocating engine or a rotary engine.

Number of Cylinders: The total number of cylinders (1, 2, 4, 6, or 8) contained in an engine.

Reciprocating: Back-and-forth (rectilinear) motion, such as the motion of a piston in a cylinder.

Rotary: Turning motion around an axis.

Stratified-charge Engine: An engine in which each cylinder has two combustion chambers connected by a small passage. The smaller prechamber contains the spark plug and receives a rich mixture. The main chamber receives a lean mixture which is ignited by the flame front from the prechamber.

Valve Arrangement: The way valves are placed in an engine, such as *I-head* (valves-in-head) or *L-head* (valves-in-block).

Section 1 Engines

1. Air cleaner
2. Vacuum motor
3. Intake manifold
4. Pushrod
5. Rocker arm
6. Valve
7. Cylinder head
8. Spark plug
9. Piston
10. Piston pin
11. Connecting rod
12. Hydraulic lifter
13. Crankshaft
14. Oil pan
15. Engine block
16. Exhaust manifold
17. PCV valve
18. Carburetor

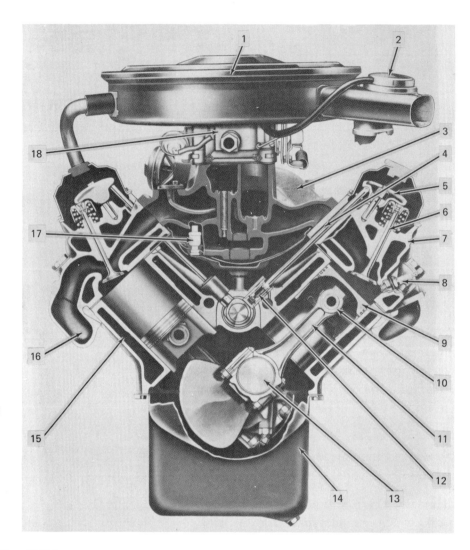

Fig. 1-1. Reciprocating V-8 Engine

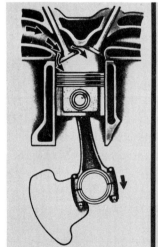 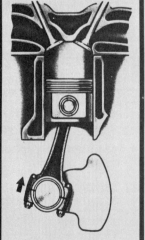 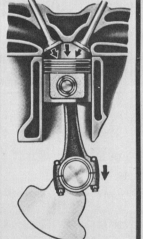 

Intake Stroke   **Compression Stroke**   **Power Stroke**   **Exhaust Stroke**

Fig. 1-2

Unit 1 Reciprocating Engines

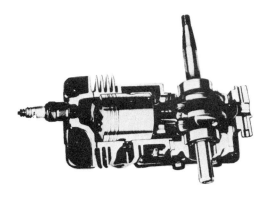

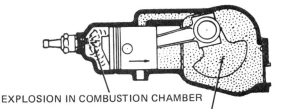

B
POWER STROKE
When the piston is near the end of its stroke, the mixture is ignited. The resulting explosion of the air-gasoline and oil mixture drives the piston back, compressing the awaiting charge in the crankcase.

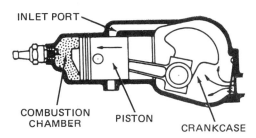

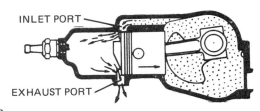

A
COMPRESSION STROKE
Here a charge of fuel is being drawn into the crankcase from the carburetor. As the piston moves forward, a partial vacuum is created in the airtight crankcase and as the piston continues its movement, the inlet port is uncovered. The charge of fuel rushes in to fill the vacuum.

C
EXHAUST STROKE
Continuing its movement, the piston uncovers the exhaust port, permitting the burnt charge to escape. At the same time, the inlet port is uncovered and the new fuel rushes into the cylinder. With the forward stroke of the piston, the entire cycle of operation is repeated.

Fig 1-3. Two-cycle Engine Principles

In the following exercises, indicate the best answer by inserting in the blank the appropriate number, letter, word(s), or calculation, as required.

PICTORIAL REVIEW

A. Identify the components of the reciprocating engine in figure 1-4 by writing the component names in the blanks.

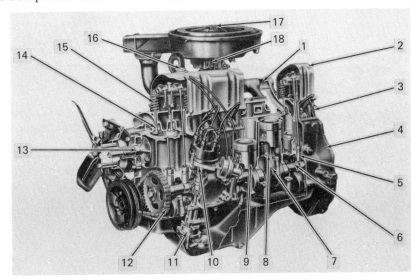

Fig. 1-4. Six-cylinder Engine

Section 1 Engines

1. _____ 10. _____
2. _____ 11. _____
3. _____ 12. _____
4. _____ 13. _____
5. _____ 14. _____
6. _____ 15. _____
7. _____ 16. _____
8. _____ 17. _____
9. _____ 18. _____

B. The complete cylinder firing order shown in figure 1-5 is _____.

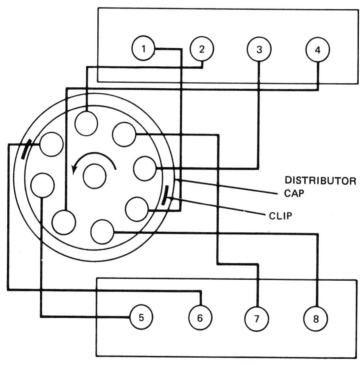

Fig 1-5. Reciprocating Engine Firing Order

SUMMARY REVIEW

____ 1. The word reciprocating means

    a. rotary.   c. in and out.
    b. revolving.   d. back and forth.

____ 2. The number of crankshaft revolutions required to produce four complete power strokes in a one-cylinder, four-cycle engine is

    a. two.   c. six.
    b. four.   d. eight.

Unit 1 Reciprocating Engines

____ 3. The piston is driven downward on the power stroke by
   a. the compression-stroke pressure.
   b. heat.
   c. the crankshaft.
   d. expanding gases.

____ 4. An internal combustion engine burns the air-fuel mixture in the
   a. cylinder.
   b. piston.
   c. combustion chamber.
   d. exhaust manifold.

____ 5. Compression pressure is developed when the
   a. piston moves down.
   b. piston moves up.
   c. valves are open.
   d. piston is at the beginning of the compression stroke.

6. Circle the word that describes the piston motion and valve position for each stroke of a four-cycle engine.

STROKE	PISTON MOTION	INTAKE VALVE	EXHAUST VALVE
a. Intake	up *or* down	closed *or* open	closed *or* open
b. Compression	up *or* down	closed *or* open	closed *or* open
c. Power	up *or* down	closed *or* open	closed *or* open
d. Exhaust	up *or* down	closed *or* open	closed *or* open

7. The valves are located in the _____ on an I-head engine and in the _____ on an L-head engine.

8. Three different fuels used with four-cycle engines are _____, _____, and _____.

9. The intake manifold attaches to the _____.

10. Insert the correct numbers of the matching terms or definitions in the blanks.
   a. ____ V-cylinder arrangement
   b. ____ in-line cylinder arrangement
   c. ____ flat cylinder arrangement
   d. ____ conventional four-cycle engine
   e. ____ Stirling engine

   1. external combustion engine
   2. cylinders in two angled banks
   3. pancake design
   4. internal combustion engine
   5. cylinders in a row

Section 1 Engines

REFERENCE REVIEW

_____ 1. Immediately after the air-fuel mixture is ignited in the combustion chamber, the cylinder pressure is

    a. the same as the compression pressure.
    b. slightly more than the compression pressure.
    c. several times greater than the compression pressure.
    d. less than the compression pressure.

_____ 2. Most one-cylinder, four-cycle engines have

    a. one valve.
    b. an I-head design.
    c. an L-head design.
    d. liquid cooling.

_____ 3. Which stroke(s) are partially or fully completed during the downward piston stroke in two-cycle engines?

    a. intake
    b. power
    c. exhaust
    d. all of these

4. Most small engines feature _____ cooling, while the majority of multiple-cylinder engines are cooled by _____.

5. Name three common applications for two-cycle engines.

    a. _____
    b. _____
    c. _____

6. The air-fuel mixture in a two-cycle engine is drawn into the crankcase when the piston is moving _____ and forced into the combustion chamber when the piston is moving _____.

7. Briefly describe firing order. _____
_____

8. Is high crankshaft rpm (revolutions per minute) easier to obtain with a *two-* or *four-*cycle engine? _____

9. Name four types of engines, other than the reciprocating engine, that may be major power sources for motor vehicles in the future.

    a. _____
    b. _____
    c. _____
    d. _____

_____ 10. Most multiple-cylinder engines have

    a. an I-head design.
    b. an L-head design.
    c. air cooling.
    d. one valve per cylinder.

UNIT 2 ENGINE MEASUREMENTS

RELATED AUTOMOTIVE TERMS

BDC (Bottom Dead Center): Piston position at bottom of stroke.

Bhp (Brake Horsepower): A measurement of horsepower (hp) delivered at the engine crankshaft. A *Prony brake* or an engine *dynamometer* is used to determine the brake horsepower: bhp = ihp – fhp.

Bore: The diameter of an engine cylinder.

Chassis Dynamometer: A device used to measure *net* horsepower delivered at the drive wheels.

CID (Cubic-inch Displacement): The volume of space displaced by the piston as it moves from BDC to TDC. Metric displacements are given in cubic centimeters, cc or cm^3 (preferred by international metric conference) or liters (l).

Clearance Volume: Total volume measurement above a piston at TDC, including the combustion chamber area.

Combustion Chamber: Area above a piston at TDC, primarily distinguished in a recessed cylinder head.

Compression Ratio: A measurement of how much the air-fuel mixture is compressed inside an engine. For example, when a mixture is compressed to 1/8 of its original volume, the compression ratio is 8 to 1.

Engine Dynamometer: Device to measure engine horsepower at the flywheel.

Fhp (Friction Horsepower): Engine horsepower losses due to friction from such sources as the engine, transmission, and drive train.

Hp (Horsepower): A measurement of engine power output, usually related to the rpm.

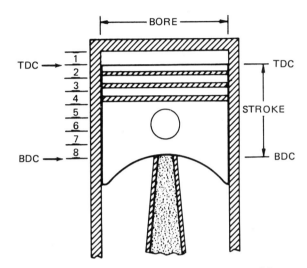

Fig 2-1. Reciprocating Engine Measurement of Bore, Stroke and Compression Ratio of 8 to 1 1

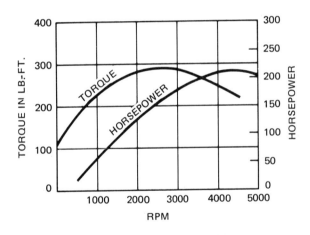

Fig 2-2. Relationship of Torque and Horsepower to Engine Speed (rpm)

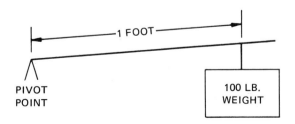

Torque = Force (100 lb.) x Distance (1 ft.) = 100 lb.-ft.

Fig. 2-3. Applied Torque of 100 lb.-ft.

Section 1 Engines

Ihp (Indicated Horsepower): A measurement of power developed by the combustion processes in the cylinders; ihp does not consider friction. Determining the indicated horsepower requires special indicating devices attached to engine.

Rpm (Revolutions per Minute): Rate of speed of a rotating part such as a crankshaft.

SAE or AMA (Rated) Horsepower: Rating methods sometimes used for vehicle taxing or licensing purposes.

Stroke: Distance traveled by the piston from TDC to BDC.

TDC (Top Dead Center): Piston position at top of stroke.

Torque: Measurement of the turning effect produced by a force acting perpendicular to an axis. The applied torque, which may or may not result in motion, is commonly measured in pound-feet (lb.-ft.), meter-kilograms (m-kg), or meter kilopounds (m-kp).*

*Use for force only.

Fig 2-4. Chassis Dynamometer

Total Volume: Volume of space in the cylinder and combustion chamber above the piston at BDC.

Volumetric Efficiency: A percentage ratio, varying with the engine rpm, between the quantity of air-fuel mixture actually entering a cylinder compared to what can enter under ideal conditions.

In the following exercises, indicate the best answer by inserting in the blank the appropriate number, letter, word(s), or calculation, as required.

PICTORIAL REVIEW

A. Plot and draw a single torque curve on the graph to show:

100 lb.-ft. at 500 rpm
300 lb.-ft. at 1500 rpm
350 lb.-ft. at 2500 rpm
250 lb.-ft. at 3500 rpm

Fig 2-5. Relationship of Torque to Rpm

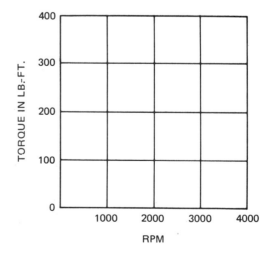

Unit 2 Engine Measurements

B. Plot and draw a single horsepower curve on the graph to show:

25 hp at 500 rpm
75 hp at 1500 rpm
125 hp at 2500 rpm
160 hp at 3500 rpm
150 hp at 3800 rpm

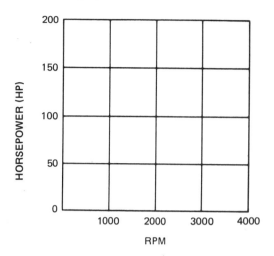

Fig 2-6. Relationship of Horsepower to Rpm

C. The compression ratio in figure 2-7 is _____ to _____.

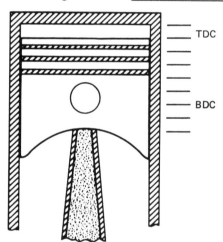

Fig 2-7. Compression Ratio

D. Compute the horsepower required to move the object in figure 2-8 the distance shown in 20 seconds. Show your work. Use the formula:

$$hp = \frac{\text{force or weight (lb)} \times \text{distance (ft)}}{\text{time (sec)} \times 550}$$

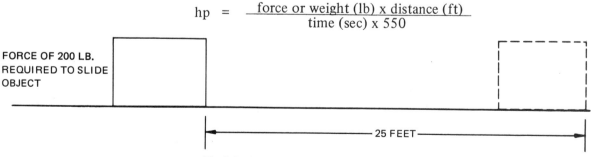

Fig 2-8. Horsepower Calculation

Section 1 Engines

SUMMARY REVIEW

_____ 1. The bore of an engine is a measurement of
   a. engine diameter.
   b. piston diameter.
   c. cylinder diameter.
   d. crankshaft size.

_____ 2. The stroke of an engine is a measurement of
   a. piston travel.
   b. piston length.
   c. piston diameter.
   d. cylinder length.

_____ 3. A chassis dynamometer measures
   a. cubic inch displacement.
   b. volumetric efficiency.
   c. net horsepower at drive wheels.
   d. indicated horsepower.

_____ 4. Torque is a measurement of
   a. twisting force.
   b. linear motion.
   c. rectilinear motion.
   d. twisting motion.

_____ 5. Engine torque increases
   a. constantly with engine speed.
   b. until the highest available rpm is reached.
   c. depending on the method of measurement.
   d. to a certain engine rpm and then decreases.

_____ 6. Torque applied to an automotive rear axle may
   a. result in wheel motion.
   b. may not result in wheel motion.
   c. either a or b.
   d. neither a nor b.

7. Write the complete names for the following abbreviations:
   a. TDC _____
   b. BDC _____
   c. CID _____
   d. bhp _____
   e. fhp _____
   f. cc _____
   g. rpm _____
   h. lb.-ft. _____

8. Metric cylinder displacement is measured in _____ or _____.

9. Describe what is meant by compression ratio. _____

10. The bhp of an engine having an ihp rating of 150 and an fhp of 30 is _____ .

10

11. How many pound-feet of torque are available if a 100-pound force is applied to the end of a 2-foot lever? _____

12. Insert the correct numbers of the matching terms or definitions in the blanks.
    a. ____ measures engine hp at flywheel
    b. ____ requirement to obtain indicated hp
    c. ____ measured by Prony brake
    d. ____ friction horsepower
    e. ____ measures net hp delivered at drive wheels
    f. ____ rating method sometimes used for licensing

    1. chassis dynamometer
    2. usually less than ihp
    3. engine dynamometer
    4. bhp
    5. AMA-rated hp
    6. special devices attached to engine

REFERENCE REVIEW

____ 1. Engine torque is concerned with the twisting effort resulting from
   a. flywheel momentum.
   b. compression pressure.
   c. internal engine friction.
   d. piston and rod force on the crankshaft.

____ 2. Engine torque increases up to the point where the
   a. volumetric efficiency is highest.
   b. rpm is highest.
   c. combustion efficiency is highest.
   d. none of these.

____ 3. A shorter piston stroke results in
   a. slower piston speed.
   b. increased piston and cylinder wear.
   c. faster piston speed.
   d. decreased camshaft revolutions.

____ 4. If an engine has a volumetric efficiency of 75 percent at 3400 rpm, the air-fuel mixture
   a. is 75 percent mixed.
   b. fills 75 percent of the cylinder.
   c. is 75 percent burned.
   d. all of these.

5. Write a formula for calculating the total piston CID of an engine.
   _____

6. Calculate the CID of an 8-cylinder engine that has a 4-inch bore and 3 1/2-inch stroke. Show your work.

Section 1 Engines

7. What is the compression ratio of an engine having a total volume above the piston at BDC of 48 cubic inches and a total volume above the piston at TDC of 6 cubic inches. Show your work.

8. Calculate the horsepower required to lift an engine block weighing 650 pounds a distance of 6 feet in 7 seconds. Show your work.

UNIT 3 CRANKSHAFT ASSEMBLY

RELATED AUTOMOTIVE TERMS

Balancing: Process of proportioning weight or force equally on all sides of an object. Most crankshafts are balanced both statically (at rest) and dynamically (in motion).

Conformability: Ability of bearing to reshape itself to fit better around the crankshaft.

Counterweight: Weight that is cast opposite each offset connecting-rod journal to provide the necessary balance.

Crankshaft: Revolving engine part, mounted in the lower portion of the block (crankcase) that, along with the connecting rods, changes reciprocating piston motion into more useful rotary motion.

Crankshaft End-play: Specified crankshaft endwise motion controlled by *side flanges* on one main bearing.

Crankshaft Main Journals: That part of the crankshaft, ground round and polished smooth, around which the closely-fitted main bearings surround the journals and support the crankshaft.

Crankshaft Oil Passage: Hole drilled through the crankshaft to allow oil to flow from the main bearings to the connecting-rod bearings.

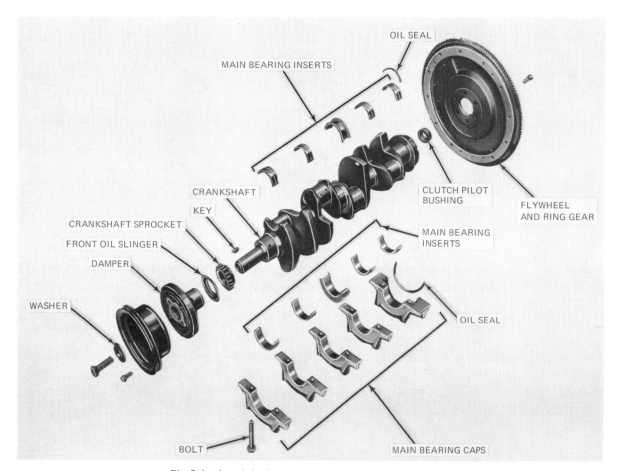

Fig 3-1. Crankshaft and Related Parts, Exploded View

Section 1 Engines

Embedability: Ability of a bearing to permit small dirt particles to sink into the bearing surface, thereby avoiding certain crankshaft scratches.

Fatigue Strength: Ability of a bearing or other metal part to withstand repeated stresses.

Flywheel: Heavy round wheel mounted at rear of crankshaft. Acts to absorb energy on power stroke(s) and return energy on other stroke(s). Also serves as a place to mount starter ring gear and to transfer power to the clutch or torque converter.

Journal Size: Finished diameter of a crankshaft journal. May be *standard* size on a new crankshaft or 0.010 or 0.020 inch *undersize*

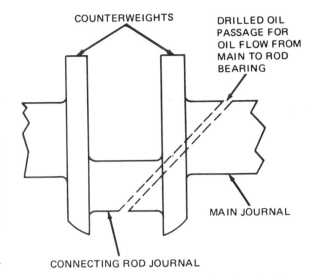

Fig 3-2. Portion of Crankshaft Showing Sections and Drilled Oil Passage

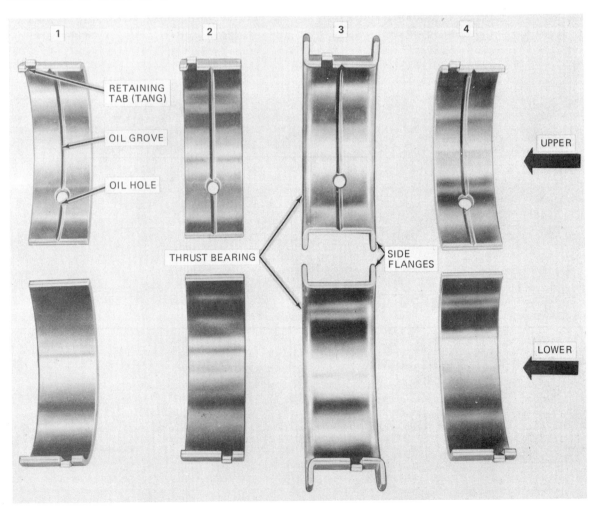

Fig 3-3. Set of Main Bearings

Unit 3 Crankshaft Assembly

on a reground crankshaft, requiring a matching undersize bearing.

Load-carrying Capacity (of a bearing): Ability of a bearing to withstand heavy loads from downward piston thrusts. Certain bearings are rated as high as 10,000 psi.

Main Bearings: The bearings that support the revolving crankshaft in the block.

Main Bearing Material: Metal used in bearing construction. Bearings are usually multi-layered, including a steel backing for rigidity with a *running surface* of babbitt, copper alloy, or aluminum alloy.

Momentum: The tendency of a moving object, such as a flywheel, to remain in motion.

Oil Clearance: The small space between the main bearing and crankshaft journal, usually 0.001 to 0.003 inch (about 0.025 to 0.076 mm). Lubricating oil circulates through this clearance.

Precision Insert Bearing: A bearing manufactured to fit an exact, specified crankshaft size.

Vibration Damper (Harmonic Balancer): A device designed to dampen or reduce crankshaft torsional (twisting) vibrations that might otherwise cause crankshaft cracks or breakage.

In the following exercises, indicate the best answer by inserting in the blank the appropriate number, letter, word(s), or calculation, as required.

PICTORIAL REVIEW

A. Name the numbered components in the crankshaft assembly in figure 3-4.

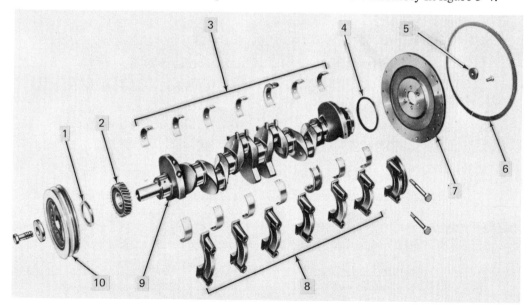

Fig 3-4. Crankshaft and Related Parts

1. _____
2. _____
3. _____
4. _____
5. _____
6. _____
7. _____
8. _____
9. _____
10. _____

Section 1 Engines

B. Identify the lettered sections of the vibration damper in figure 3-5 by placing the correct letter in each blank.

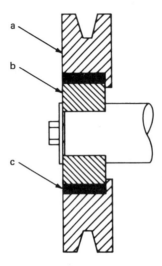

Fig 3-5. Cross Section of a Vibration Damper

1. ____ damper hub

2. ____ damper flywheel

3. ____ rubber layer

SUMMARY REVIEW

____ 1. The crankshaft along with the connecting rods change

    a. revolving motion to back-and-forth motion.
    b. rotary motion to rectilinear motion.
    c. torsional vibrations to twisting motion.
    d. rectilinear motion to rotary motion.

____ 2. The crankshaft counterweight(s) are located opposite the

    a. main bearings.
    b. vibration damper.
    c. connecting-rod journal.
    d. main-bearing journal.

____ 3. Oil holes drilled in the crankshaft supply oil to the

    a. rod bearings.
    b. counterweights.
    c. entire engine.
    d. main bearings.

____ 4. Conformability refers to the ability of a main bearing to

    a. withstand stress.
    b. avoid corrosion.
    c. hold dirt particles.
    d. reshape itself somewhat.

____ 5. A main bearing that fits an *undersize* crankshaft is known as a(n)

    a. undersize bearing.
    b. oversize bearing.
    c. standard bearing.
    d. standard oversize bearing.

____ 6. The function of a flywheel is to
   a. cause overlapping power strokes.
   b. dampen torsional vibration.
   c. support the crankshaft.
   d. absorb and return energy.

7. List three purposes of a flywheel:
   a. _____
   b. _____
   c. _____

8. Name three materials (metals) used in the construction of the running surface of main bearings.
   a. _____ b. _____ c. _____

9. Crankshaft end-thrust is controlled by a main bearing that features
   _____

10. A vibration damper may also be known as a(n) _____

11. Insert the correct numbers of the matching terms or definitions in the blanks.
    a. ____ momentum
    b. ____ fatigue strength
    c. ____ load-carrying capacity
    d. ____ precision insert
    e. ____ embedability
    f. ____ static balance
    g. ____ dynamic balance

    1. balance in motion
    2. withstand repeated stress
    3. ability to withstand pressure
    4. balance at rest
    5. exact size bearing
    6. tendency to remain in motion
    7. ability to accept small particles.

REFERENCE REVIEW

____ 1. A crankshaft bearing labeled *undersize* has a thickness that is
   a. unknown.
   b. the same as the original bearing size.
   c. less than the original bearing size.
   d. more than the original bearing size.

____ 2. The piston stroke is determined by the
   a. connecting-rod length.
   b. connecting-rod crankpin offset.
   c. crankshaft length.
   d. main bearing location.

Section 1 Engines

_____ 3. The number of main bearings in most V-8 engines is

    a. four.   c. six.
    b. five.   d. eight.

_____ 4. Crankshafts are manufactured from

    a. forged or cast alloy steel.   c. gray iron.
    b. cast iron.   d. tungsten steel.

_____ 5. The locating tangs on the upper and lower main bearing inserts are positioned in the engine

    a. toward the front.   c. on opposite sides.
    b. toward the back.   d. on the same side.

_____ 6. The amount of motion allowed between the outer and inner metal sections of the vibration damper is

    a. slight.   c. considerable.
    b. none.   d. adjustable.

_____ 7. The flywheel is attached to the crankshaft by

    a. fine-thread cap screws.   c. coarse-thread cap screws.
    b. rivets.   d. welding.

8. Main bearings are mechanically kept from revolving in their bores by _____ .

9. Does a *four-* or *eight-*cylinder engine usually need a heavier flywheel? _____

UNIT 4 PISTON ASSEMBLY

RELATED AUTOMOTIVE TERMS

Blow-by: Leakage of compressed air-fuel mixture or burned gases from the combustion chamber, past the piston and rings, and into the crankcase.

Cam-ground Piston: A piston ground oval or elliptical in shape as a way to compensate for expansion caused by heat.

Compression Ring: Piston ring that seals pressure during the compression and power strokes. There are usually two compression rings per piston.

Connecting Rod: Part used to attach the piston pin to the crankshaft rod journal.

Connecting-rod Cap: Lower bolt-on portion of the connecting rod.

Full-floating Pin: A piston pin that is allowed to move in both the piston and the connecting rod. In this arrangement, the piston pin is held in position by snap rings located in grooves in the piston boss.

Oil Ring: Piston ring that scrapes oil from the cylinder wall, to control cylinder wall lubrication, and prevent excessive oil loss past the piston and into the combustion chamber. There is usually one oil ring per piston.

Oil-squirt Hole: Small hole located near the lower end of the connecting rod, providing a lubrication path to the cylinders and camshaft.

Piston: Engine part that reciprocates in the cylinder and transfers the force of the expanding gases via the piston pin and connecting rod to the crankshaft.

Piston Boss: Part of the piston which supports the piston pin.

Piston Markings: Marks on a piston which are used to identify piston oversize and the front of the piston.

Piston Material: Metal used in piston construction, usually cast or forged alloy aluminum.

Piston Pin: Round precision-ground part (usually hollow), which attaches the piston to the connecting rod.

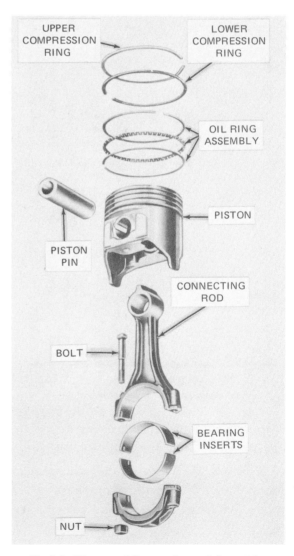

Fig 4-1. Piston and Connecting-rod Assembly

Section 1 Engines

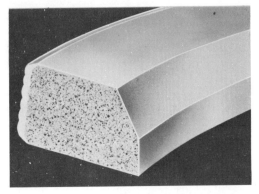
Beveled-type, Chrome-faced Compression Ring

Molybdenum-filled Compression Ring

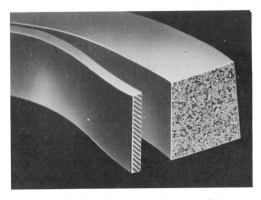
Expander-type Second Compression Ring

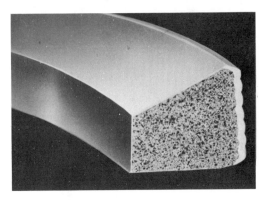
Keystone-shape, Heavy-duty Compression Ring

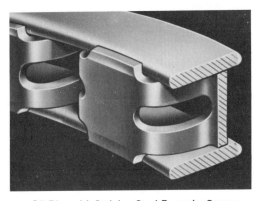
Oil Ring with Stainless Steel Expander-Spacer and Chrome-faced Steel Segments (Rails)

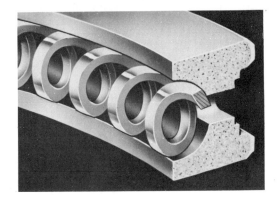
Heavy-duty Oil Ring

Fig 4-2. Compression- and Oil-ring Sectional Views

Piston-pin Bushing: Bushing pressed into the upper end of the connecting rod when free-floating pins are used.

Piston Skirt: Lower part of piston which makes contact with the cylinder wall.

Piston-skirt Clearance: Allowable space between the piston skirt and cylinder wall, usually 0.001 to 0.002 inch (about 0.025 to 0.051 mm) at room temperature.

Piston Slap: Noise made by undersize or loose piston skirt making contact with the cylinder wall.

Piston Temperature: Temperature of the piston at different areas, varying from over

450°F (232.2°C) at the top of the head to 200°F (93.3°C) near the bottom of the skirt.

Press Fit: Generally, the fitting together of parts by pressure. In one type of piston-pin arrangement currently in wide use, the pin is kept in its proper position by pressing it into the connecting rod.

Ring Expander: A flexible spring steel part placed behind certain rings to increase ring pressure on the cylinder wall.

Ring Gap: Gap between the ends of a piston ring installed in the cylinder; the gap is often 0.004 inch (about 0.1 mm) for each inch (25.4 mm) of cylinder diameter.

Ring Grooves: Grooves machined around the piston head to support the rings.

Ring Land: Projecting metal between the ring grooves on the piston.

Ring Ridge: That portion of the cylinder wall above the upper limit of ring travel in a worn cylinder.

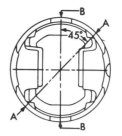
THE ELLIPTICAL SHAPE OF THE PISTON SKIRT SHOULD BE .010 TO .012 IN. LESS AT DIAMETER (A) THAN ACROSS THE THRUST FACES AT DIAMETER (B). MEASUREMENT IS MADE 1/8 IN. BELOW LOWER RING GROVE

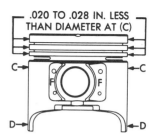
DIAMETERS AT (C) AND (D) CAN BE EQUAL OR DIAMETER AT (D) CAN BE .0015 IN. GREATER THAN (C)

Fig 4-3. Piston Measurements

Rod Bearing: Split bearing in the lower end of the connecting rod which surrounds the crankshaft rod journal.

Rod Press Fit: Term used to describe the interference fit of a piston pin in certain connecting rods.

Scored Piston: Term used to define deep, vertical scratches on the piston skirt.

In the following exercises, indicate the best answer by inserting in the blanks the appropriate number, letter, word(s), or calculation, as required.

PICTORIAL REVIEW

A. Identify the numbered piston assembly components in figure 4-4 by writing their correct names in the blanks.

1. _____
2. _____
3. _____
4. _____
5. _____
6. _____
7. _____
8. _____
9. _____
10. _____

Fig 4-4. Piston and Connecting-rod Assembly

Section 1 Engines

SUMMARY REVIEW

_____ 1. Piston diameter at the *lands* is about _____ than at the *skirt*.
  a. 0.025 inch more
  b. 0.002 inch more
  c. 0.002 inch less
  d. none of these.

_____ 2. The *greatest* diameter of a cam-ground piston is
  a. 45 degrees from the axis of the piston pin.
  b. 90 degrees from the axis of the piston pin.
  c. at the piston pin.
  d. at the piston land.

_____ 3. Clearance between an automotive piston skirt and cylinder wall is close to
  a. 0.002 inch.
  b. 0.004 inch.
  c. 0.010 inch.
  d. 1 inch.

_____ 4. Most compression rings are manufactured from
  a. high-carbon steel.
  b. cast iron.
  c. chrome.
  d. tungsten steel.

_____ 5. Piston pins are usually retained in place by lock rings or a
  a. bolt.
  b. cap screw.
  c. press fit.
  d. locknut.

_____ 6. The connecting rod attaches to the crankshaft and
  a. engine block.
  b. piston.
  c. piston pin.
  d. main bearing.

7. Briefly describe a cam-ground piston. _____
_____

8. The number of rings on an automotive piston is usually _____ compression and _____ oil rings.

9. Insert the correct numbers of the matching terms or definitions in the blanks.
  a. ____ blow-by
  b. ____ piston material
  c. ____ ring gap
  d. ____ ring land
  e. ____ amount of piston ellipse
  f. ____ may be located in top of rod
  g. ____ oil ring
  h. ____ amount of piston skirt clearance

  1. space between the ends of a ring installed in the cylinder
  2. about 0.010 inch
  3. pin bushing
  4. escape of confined gases
  5. about 0.002 inch
  6. bottom ring
  7. aluminum alloy
  8. metal projection between ring grooves.

Unit 4 Piston Assembly

REFERENCE REVIEW

___ 1. The front of a piston may be identified by the word *front* or a
   a. notch.
   b. hole.
   c. number.
   d. all of these.

___ 2. Oversize pistons are available for engine cylinders that are
   a. rehoned.
   b. rebored.
   c. tapered.
   d. out-of-round.

___ 3. The outside corner groove on an installed compression ring should usually be positioned.
   a. toward the piston pin
   b. inward
   c. upward
   d. downward

___ 4. The upper compression ring is often plated with
   a. steel.
   b. aluminum.
   c. cast iron.
   d. chrome.

___ 5. The top compression ring is the most abused piston ring because
   a. some abrasives enter the cylinder with the air.
   b. it becomes the hottest during operation.
   c. it receives the least lubrication.
   d. all of the above.

___ 6. An oil ring functions by allowing oil to flow through the ring and then through the piston
   a. holes or slots.
   b. lands.
   c. compression grooves.
   d. pin.

___ 7. Most automotive oil rings are manufactured from
   a. steel.
   b. cast iron.
   c. chrome.
   d. molybdenum.

___ 8. On the compression stroke, the rings are pressed tightest against what part of their groove?
   a. inner part
   b. outer part
   c. top
   d. bottom

___ 9. A connecting rod that is slightly bent when placed on an alignment checking device should be
   a. straightened hot.
   b. straightened cold.
   c. always replaced.
   d. left as is.

___ 10. Connecting rod bearings may be checked for proper oil clearance by using
   a. a torque wrench.
   b. lubricating oil.
   c. a plastigage.
   d. a leak detector.

23

Section 1 Engines

11. Underline the item(s) that may break if the ring ridge is not removed on a used engine.

    a. piston ring(s)
    b. piston skirt
    c. piston land(s)
    d. piston pin boss

12. What part of a piston ring may have chrome plating? _____

13. Define the two main functions for which a scraper-compression ring is designed.

    a. _____   b. _____

14. What is the proper oil clearance for the connecting-rod bearing of an automotive engine? _____

15. Used pistons having a worn top-ring groove may have the groove machined wider, after which a(n) _____ must be installed above the new ring.

UNIT 5   CAMSHAFT ASSEMBLY

RELATED AUTOMOTIVE TERMS

Cam Base Circle: That part of the camshaft in contact with the valve lifter when the valve is closed.

Cam (Lobe): The projecting part on a rotating shaft which changes rotary motion to reciprocating motion.

Cam-lobe Face and Nose Taper: Amount of slant (approximately a 0.002 inch, or 0.051 mm, change) designed across the cam face (contacting surface) from the cam front edge to the cam rear edge. This shape matches the convex lifter face, thereby promoting lifter rotation.

Cam-lobe Grind: Term referring to the shape of a cam, including the valve opening and closing ramps.

Cam-lobe Lift: Amount of rectilinear, or straight-line, motion transferred to the valve lifter by the cam lobe.

Camshaft: Engine part having cams or lobes which are used to operate the valve mechanism.

Camshaft Bearings: The bearings located in the cylinder block that support the camshaft.

Camshaft Sprocket (or Gear): Driven sprocket (or gear) bolted to the front of the camshaft.

Crankshaft Sprocket (or Gear): The small sprocket (or gear) at the front of the crankshaft that drives the timing chain and/or camshaft gear.

DOHC (Dual Overhead Camshaft): Term used to describe an engine having two camshafts over (above) each cylinder head.

Fuel Pump Eccentric: A V-8 engine part, usually bolted to the front of the camshaft, that is used to operate the fuel pump.

Initial Lubrication: Application of special lubricant to the camshaft before installation.

OHC (Overhead Camshaft): Term used to describe a camshaft located over (above) each cylinder head.

Rear Camshaft Plug: Plug driven in the rear of the block behind the camshaft to contain the oil supplied to the rear camshaft bearing.

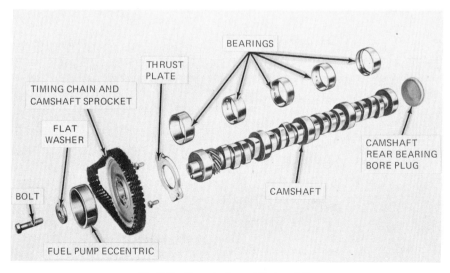

Fig 5-1. Camshaft and Related Parts

Section 1 Engines

Timing Chain: Drive chain that connects the crankshaft and camshaft sprockets.

Timing-chain Slack: Amount of sidewise motion in the timing chain between the sprockets; maximum slack is 1/2 inch (12.7 mm).

Valve Overlap: Period at the end of the exhaust stroke and at the beginning of the intake stroke when the intake and exhaust valves are partially open at the same time.

Valve Timing: The actual opening and closing of the valves in relationship to the number of degrees of crankshaft rotation.

Worn Cam: A cam that has lost its original shape, including height, during operation.

Fig 5-2. Timing Gears and Chain (Showing Alignment of Timing Marks)

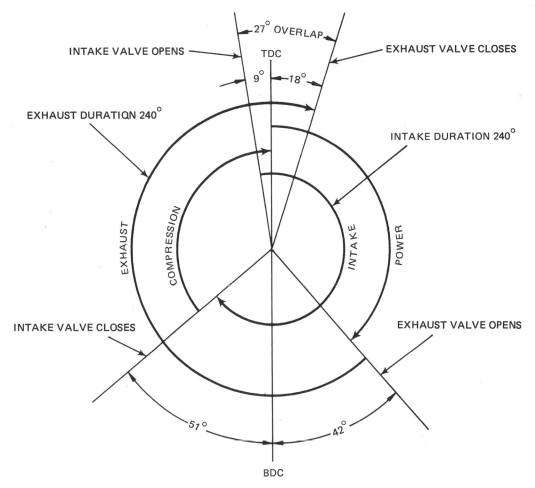

Fig 5-3. Valve Timing Diagram for a Six-cylinder Engine

Unit 5 Camshaft Assembly

In the following exercises, indicate the best answer by inserting in the blanks the appropriate number, letter, word(s), or calculation, as required.

PICTORIAL REVIEW

A. Draw a complete valve timing diagram to show the intake valve opening at 10° BTDC (before top dead center) and closing at 35° ABDC (after bottom dead center), and the exhaust valve opening at 35° BBDC (before bottom dead center) and closing at 10° ATDC (after top dead center).

Fig 5-4. Valve Timing

B. Identify the cam sections by inserting the correct letter from figure 5-5 in each blank.

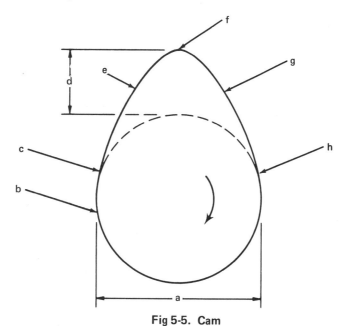

Fig 5-5. Cam

1. ___ base circle (heel)
2. ___ opening ramp
3. ___ closing ramp
4. ___ cam nose

5. ___ height of lift
6. ___ heel diameter
7. ___ valve starts to open
8. ___ valve closes

Section 1 Engines

SUMMARY REVIEW

___ 1. How many camshafts are there in a V-8 engine having a DOHC?

    a. one
    b. two
    c. three
    d. four

___ 2. Cam-lobe lift refers to the

    a. distance the valve lifter moves.
    b. diameter of camshaft.
    c. camshaft contour.
    d. distance from the cam nose to the base circle.

___ 3. Valve overlap is a term describing the time when

    a. one valve is open and the other is closed.
    b. both valves are closed.
    c. both valves are partly open.
    d. the valves are open too long.

___ 4. The maximum allowable sidewise slack on an installed timing chain is

    a. 1/4 inch.
    b. 1/2 inch.
    c. 3/4 inch.
    d. 1 inch.

___ 5. Before installing a new camshaft, it should be

    a. hardened.
    b. aligned.
    c. balanced.
    d. lubricated.

___ 6. The proper crankshaft-to-camshaft timing relationship is obtained by

    a. having the proper engine assembly.
    b. rotating the distributor.
    c. changing the valve timing.
    d. aligning the vibration damper mark and timing pointer.

___ 7. If the exhaust valve is fully open, the intake valve

    a. has just closed.
    b. is ready to open soon.
    c. is starting to open.
    d. none of these.

___ 8. The exhaust valve usually begins opening

    a. at TDC.
    b. before TDC.
    c. before BDC.
    d. at BDC.

___ 9. Part(s) mounted on the front of a V-8 engine camshaft include

    a. the fuel pump eccentric.
    b. the timing chain.
    c. the crankshaft sprocket.
    d. all of these.

___ 10. The purpose of the rear camshaft plug is to retain the

    a. camshaft.
    b. timing.
    c. oil.
    d. water.

11. One edge of the cam-lobe nose is usually _____ inch(es) higher than the other edge.

12. The nose of a cam lobe is usually slightly tapered to promote _____.

13. Insert the correct numbers of the matching terms or definitions in the blanks.

   a. ____ cam-lobe face and nose taper
   b. ____ valve timing
   c. ____ cam base circle
   d. ____ cam lobe
   e. ____ ramp
   f. ____ timing chain

   1. camshaft section contacting lifter when valve is closed
   2. connects cam lobe to base circle
   3. matches shape of lifter face
   4. valve opening and closing relationship
   5. connects camshaft and crankshaft sprockets
   6. camshaft section contacting lifter when valve is open

REFERENCE REVIEW

____ 1. The camshaft lobe contour designed for hydraulic lifters compared to that designed for mechanical lifters is
   a. the same.
   b. different.
   c. lower.
   d. slower opening.

____ 2. The camshaft bearing running surface usually is composed of
   a. babbitt.
   b. aluminum.
   c. steel.
   d. copper alloy.

____ 3. Valve overlap for a high-performance engine is usually _____ the overlap for a standard engine.
   a. the same as
   b. greater than
   c. less than
   d. retarded more than

____ 4. Greater volumetric efficiency may be obtained with a
   a. higher engine speed.
   b. cam having a high lift.
   c. cam having a low lift.
   d. larger camshaft gear.

____ 5. The purpose of valve overlap is to
   a. improve low-speed torque.
   b. allow smoother idling.
   c. increase valve life.
   d. allow more time to fill and empty the cylinder.

____ 6. If a new camshaft is installed, new _____ should also be installed.
   a. pushrods
   b. valves
   c. rocker arms
   d. lifters

Section 1 Engines

7. The ratio of the number of teeth on the camshaft gear to the number of teeth on the crankshaft gear is _____ to _____.

8. If a new camshaft becomes defective in a short time, the problem was probably caused by _____.

9. A rough or grooved cam lobe also means the engine has a matching, worn _____.

UNIT 6 VALVES AND VALVE TRAINS

RELATED AUTOMOTIVE TERMS

Exhaust Valve: Valve which, upon opening, allows the burned gases to leave the combustion chamber during the exhaust stroke.

Hydraulic Lifter: Valve lifter located between the camshaft and pushrod. Internal oil pressure causes the lifter to expand lengthwise.

Intake Valve: Valve which, upon opening, allows the air-fuel mixture to enter the combustion chamber during the intake stroke. A stratified-charge engine may have a small intake valve in each prechamber and a large intake valve in each main combustion chamber.

Interference Angle: Term describing the grinding of a slight (1- or 2-degree) difference in angle between the valve face and valve seat.

Overhead Valve: Valve located over the piston in the cylinder head (in other words, an I-head arrangement).

Oversize Valve Stem: Term describing a valve that has a stem diameter larger than the stem diameter of the original valve. An oversize valve stem is used to fit a worn valve guide that is reamed oversize.

Pushrod: Solid or hollow rod which serves as a link between the valve lifter and rocker arm.

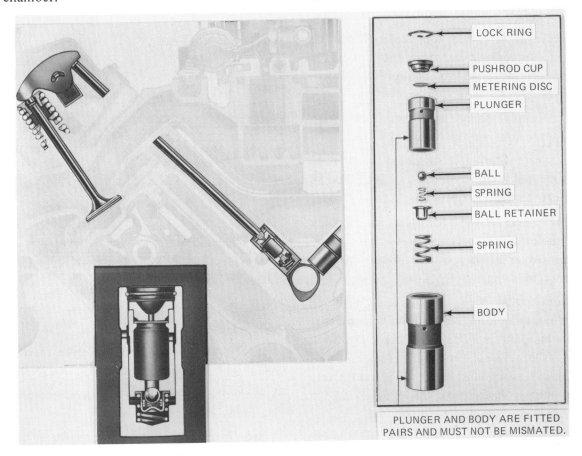

Fig 6-1 Arrangement of Valves and Valve Lifters

Section 1 Engines

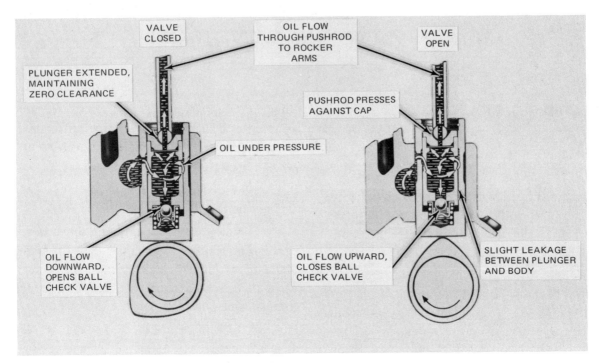

Fig 6-2. Operation of Valve Lifter Mechanism

Rocker Arm: Part that pivots to act as a first-class lever (a lever with the pivot between the applied force and the resistant force) for changing upward pushrod motion into downward valve motion.

Rocker-arm Shaft: A hollow shaft on which the rocker arms may be mounted.

Rocker-arm Stud: A threaded or drive-in stud located in the cylinder head and used to support the rocker arm.

Roller Lifter: A valve lifter featuring a roller which contacts the camshaft to reduce friction. Roller lifters are used in certain high-performance engines.

Sodium-cooled Valve: A partially hollow valve containing metallic sodium that melts at a low temperature (208°F). When the sodium is in its liquid state at operating temperatures, it splashes around inside the valve, transferring heat away from the valve head.

Tappet: A mechanical (solid) valve lifter located between the camshaft and valve stem, usually on L-head engines.

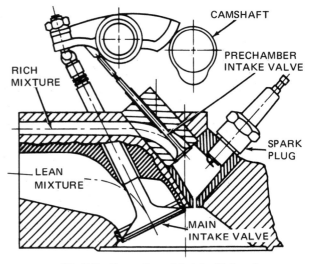

Fig 6-3. Operation of Intake Valves in a Stratified-charge Engine

Valve Clearance: Space between the tip of the valve stem and the solid valve lifter.

Valve Face: The tapered section of the valve head making contact with the valve seat.

Valve Grinding (Refacing): Process of regrinding the valve face.

Valve Guide: The integral or replaceable engine part supporting the valve.

Valve Head: Term designating the enlarged end of the valve.

Valve Keeper (Valve Key or Valve Retainer): Small part that fits into the retainer groove located near the tip of the valve stem to secure the valve and valve spring. Usually, the valve keepers are of the *split-type* design.

Valve Lapping: Process of rotating the valve against its seat after applying a small amount of oil- or water-mixed abrasive to the valve face. This procedure is used to check the grinding accuracy and/or improve the seating, or mating, of the valve face and valve seat.

Valve Lift: Distance that the valve moves from the closed to the open position.

Valve Margin: Width of the edge of the valve head between the top of the valve head and the outer edge of the face. This width is about 1/16 inch (1.59 mm).

Valve Rotator: Part located near the tip of the valve stem that turns the valve slightly during operation on certain applications.

Valve-seat Angle: The angle, measured from the cylinder block or head surface, at which the valve seats are ground.

Valve-seat Grinding: Process of regrinding valve seats.

Valve-seat Insert: A special heat-resistant steel ring inserted as a valve seat.

Valve-seat Width: The actual width of the valve seat contacted by the valve face (about 1/16 inch or 1.59 mm).

Valve-spring Pressure Tester: Testing device calibrated in pounds or kilograms to check valve-spring pressure at a designated length.

Valve Stem: Term designating the long, round section of a valve.

Valve-stem Seal: Oil seal fastened to or located on the valve stem to control oil loss past the valve guides. Usually, this seal consists of neoprene rubber, designed in an O-ring or umbrella style.

Valve Temperature: Operational temperature of a valve. At the exhaust valve head, the temperature may reach 1400°F (760°C) (dull red in color); at the stem, under certain conditions it may be 100°F (37.8°C).

Valve Train: The many parts making up the valve assembly and its operating mechanism.

In the following exercises, indicate the best answer by inserting in the blanks the appropriate number, letter, word(s), or calculation, as required.

PICTORIAL REVIEW

A. Identify the parts of the valve assembly by writing the correct letters from figure 6-4 in the blanks.

1. ____ valve stem
2. ____ retainer grooves
3. ____ valve spring
4. ____ locks (or keys)
5. ____ oil seal
6. ____ valve head
7. ____ damper spring
8. ____ spring retainer

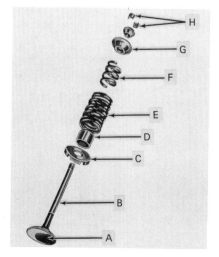

Fig 6-4. Valve and Related Parts

Section 1 Engines

B. Identify the parts of the hydraulic lifter by writing the correct letters from figure 6-5 in the blanks.

1. ____ metering valve
2. ____ retainer ring
3. ____ lifter body
4. ____ check ball
5. ____ pushrod seat
6. ____ plunger spring
7. ____ check ball spring
8. ____ plunger
9. ____ check ball retainer

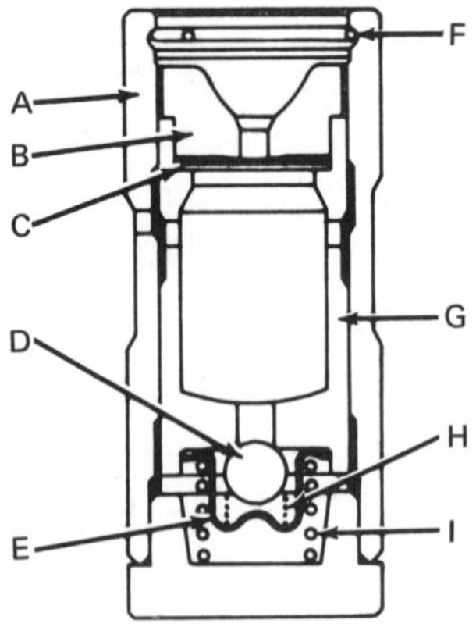

Fig 6-5. Hydraulic Valve Lifter

SUMMARY REVIEW

____ 1. Three valve train parts are the
   a. valve spring, camshaft, and push arm.
   b. pushrod, hydraulic lifter, and rocker arm.
   c. timing chain, camshaft, and valve spring.
   d. valve, valve port, and camshaft.

____ 2. What causes the valve to close after being opened?
   a. camshaft
   b. valve retainer
   c. valve spring
   d. valve lifter

____ 3. The pushrod is located between the
   a. valve and valve spring.
   b. lifter and rocker arm.
   c. valve and rocker arm.
   d. camshaft and lifter.

____ 4. During engine operation, the plunger of a hydraulic lifter moves outward from the lifter body and presses against the pushrod because of
   a. oil pressure.
   b. camshaft force.
   c. centifugal force.
   d. valve-spring pressure.

____ 5. Valve lapping may be suggested
   a. in place of seat grinding.
   b. during a major tune-up.
   c. in place of valve-face grinding.
   d. to check the valve seating after grinding.

6. A valve-spring pressure tester may be calibrated in _____ or _____ .

7. The operational temperature at the head of an exhaust valve may be as high as _____ degrees Fahrenheit.

8. Describe the purpose of a valve rotator. _____
_____

9. How do sodium-cooled valves function to cool the valve head during operation? _____
_____

10. Insert the correct numbers of the matching terms or definitions in the blanks.

    a. ____ valve stem
    b. ____ valve face
    c. ____ valve lift
    d. ____ valve clearance
    e. ____ valve head
    f. ____ valve margin
    g. ____ valve-stem seal

    1. part of valve contacting valve seat
    2. enlarged end of valve
    3. surface width between the valve face and the top of the valve head
    4. space between the tip of the valve stem and the lifter
    5. long, round section of the valve
    6. prevents oil loss past the valve guides
    7. distance that the valve moves

REFERENCE REVIEW

____ 1. The lower part of the lifter contacting the camshaft has its surface ground
   a. convex.
   b. concave.
   c. flat.
   d. oval.

____ 2. Valve springs should be replaced if they
   a. have been overheated.
   b. are crooked.
   c. are weak.
   d. all of these.

____ 3. Rocker arms on small V-8 engines usually receive their oil supply through the
   a. valves.
   b. oil line.
   c. camshaft.
   d. pushrods.

____ 4. Rocker arms are mounted on shafts or
   a. pushrods.
   b. studs.
   c. valve lifters.
   d. valves.

____ 5. Most automotive exhaust valves contain
   a. steel.
   b. sodium.
   c. cast iron.
   d. all of these.

Section 1 Engines

6. Are most valve guides *replaceable* or *integral*? _____

7. Name four ways to service a worn valve guide.

   a. _____ c. _____

   b. _____ d. _____

8. The two most popular valve seat angles are _____ and _____ degrees.

9. Valve-stem seals may be made from or contain what three materials?

   a. _____ c. _____

   b. _____

10. A positive interference angle means the valve face is ground at an angle slightly *less* or *more* than the seat. _____

UNIT 7 ROTARY (WANKEL) ENGINE

RELATED AUTOMOTIVE TERMS

Balance Weight: Part(s) attached to output (main) shaft to maintain dynamic balance.

Center Bearing: Bearing between rotors on multiple-rotor engines.

Combustion Recess: Indented area on the rotor face where part of the burning of the air-fuel mixture occurs.

Eccentric: Engine part(s) integral with main shaft used in the power output process.

End Housing: The enclosure at either end of an RC engine.

Engine Displacement: Number of rotors multiplied by the *swept volume* of one combustion chamber, measured in cubic inches or cubic centimeters. For example, a two-rotor engine

1. Alternator
2. Spark Plug Wire
3. Twin Distributors
4. Fan
5. Engine Mount
6. Air Pump
7. Air Hose
8. Thermal Reactor
9. Rotor Housing
10. Transmission
11. Carburetor
12. Oil Filter
13. Starter
14. Oil Filler Cap

Fig 7-1. Rotary Engine with Emission Controls

Section 1 Engines

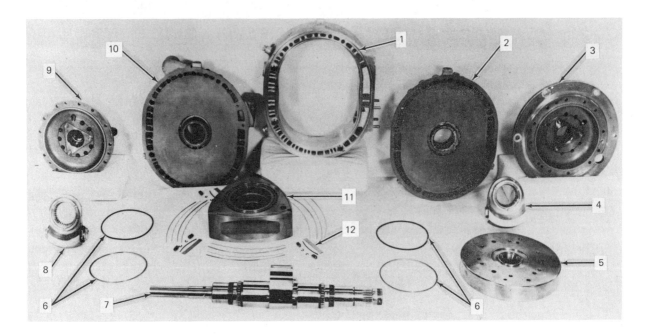

1. Rotor Housing
2. Drive-end Housing
3. Drive-end Cover
4. Drive-end Balance Weight
5. Flywheel
6. Oil Seals
7. Main Shaft
8. Antidrive-end Balance Weight
9. Antidrive-end Cover
10. Antidrive-end Side Housing
11. Rotor
12. Apex Seal

Fig 7-2. Basic Rotary Engine Components

with a rotor housing swept volume of 300 cm^3 (cubic centimeters) has a displacement of 600 cm^3.

Exhaust Port: Peripheral (outer) opening in the rotor housing that allows the burned gases to leave the engine.

Flame Travel: Distance across the combustion chamber which the flame of the ignited mixture travels. This distance is greater in rotary engines than in reciprocating engines.

Gas Transfer Velocity: Speed at which the air-fuel mixture travels (spreads out) in the combustion chamber during the power phase. The gas transfer velocity is considered fast in RC engines.

Intake Port: Peripheral (outer) opening in the rotor housing and/or the opening in the side housing where the air-fuel mixture enters the combustion chamber.

The three moving parts of the rotary engine — the two rotors and the eccentric shaft — perform all the functions of the pistons, rods, valves, cams, lifters, and other parts in reciprocating engines (there are 166 moving parts in the average 6-cylinder piston engine). Aside from having fewer parts, the rotary engine is smaller and lighter in weight.

Fig 7-3. Internal Moving Parts

Main Shaft (Output Shaft): Part that delivers power and contains eccentric(s) that receive power thrusts from the revolving rotor.

Main-shaft Bearings: Bearings, located in the end housings, which support the shaft.

Phases: Term referring to various cycles going on simultaneously in an RC engine.

Unit 7 Rotary (Wankel) Engine

 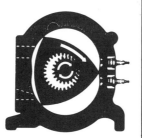 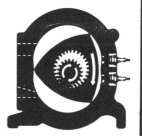 

1. Intake. Fuel/air mixture is drawn into combustion chamber by revolving rotor through intake port (upper left). No valves or valve-operating mechanism needed.

2. Compression. As rotor continues revolving, it reduces space in chamber containing fuel and air. This compresses mixture.

3. Ignition. Fuel/air mixture now fully compressed. Leading sparkplug fires. A split-second later, following plug fires to assure complete combustion.

4. Exhaust. Exploding mixture drives rotor, providing power. Rotor then expels gases through exhaust port.

Fig 7-4. Phases of the Rotary Engine

RC Engine (Rotary Combustion Engine): Four-cycle engine having a revolving triangular-shaped rotor to transfer power thrust via eccentric(s) to the output shaft.

RC 2-60: Engine having two rotors with a 60 in^3 (cubic inch) displacement for each trochoidal chamber.

Rotary Diesel: RC engine operating on diesel principles in which the fuel injected into the combustion chamber at the end of the compression phase is ignited by the heat produced during compression, rather than by the spark from a plug.

Rotor: Revolving triangular metal part that performs the four phases (cycles) of an RC engine; it revolves at one-third of the speed of the output shaft.

Rotor Apex Seals: Metal alloy pressure-sealing strips along the three corners of the rotor.

Rotor Cooling: Process of pumping oil through the rotor to reduce its temperature.

Rotor Side Grooves: Slots cut in the rotor to hold the side (end) seals.

Rotor Face: Outside circumference of the rotor between the apex seals.

Rotor Housing: Engine part having an internal trochoidal shape in which the rotor revolves.

Rotor Radius: Distance from the rotor center to a triangular corner.

Rotor Side (End): Rotor surface perpendicular to the rotor face.

Rotor Side Seals: Oil seals inserted in the sides of the rotor to seal cylinder pressure.

Rotor Width: Distance across a rotor, measured parallel to the main shaft.

Stationary Gear: Small gear attached to an end housing plate.

Stratified-charge Engine: Special system developed to inject fuel into the combustion chamber of rotary or reciprocating engines.

Timing Gears: Rotor internal gear and stationary gear.

Trochoid: The flat-sided oval (figure eight) shape of an RC engine cross section.

Wankel, Dr. Felix: German inventor of the Wankel rotary engine.

Section 1 Engines

In the following exercises, indicate the best answer by inserting in the blanks the appropriate number, letter, word(s), or calculation, as required.

PICTORIAL REVIEW

A. Identify the RC engine parts in figure 7-5 by writing the correct letter in each blank.

Fig 7-5. Rotary Engine

1. _____ fan
2. _____ starter
3. _____ main shaft
4. _____ oil-pump gears
5. _____ rotor
6. _____ disc-brake assembly
7. _____ water pump
8. _____ rotor housing
9. _____ cooling passage
10. _____ spark plug
11. _____ torque converter
12. _____ distributor cap
13. _____ oil dipstick
14. _____ oil filter

B. Identify the RC engine phases by writing the correct letter from figure 7-6 in each blank.

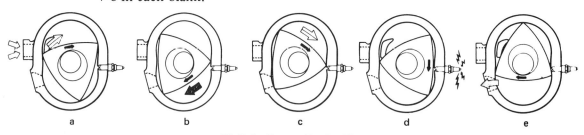

Fig 7-6. Rotary Engine Phases

1. _____ exhaust
2. _____ ignition
3. _____ intake
4. _____ expansion
5. _____ compression

Unit 7 Rotary (Wankel) Engine

SUMMARY REVIEW

___ 1. The RC engine is a _____ engine.

    a. two-cycle   c. reciprocating
    b. four-cycle   d. turbine

___ 2. A trochoidal design resembles a

    a. triangle.   c. figure 0.
    b. rectangle.   d. flat-sided (figure eight)

___ 3. Two different positions where the intake port(s) may be located are in the outer rotor housing or

    a. near the spark plug.   c. rotor side housing.
    b. on the rotor center support.   d. adjacent to the eccentrics.

___ 4. In an RC engine designated as RC 4-50, the 4 refers to the number of

    a. rotors.   c. spark plugs.
    b. carburetors.   d. output shafts.

___ 5. Rotor seals are located on each rotor side and

    a. apex.   c. gear.
    b. face.   d. eccentric.

___ 6. An RC engine has exhaust ports located in the

    a. end housing.   c. outer rotor housing.
    b. side housing.   d. hollow rotor shaft.

___ 7. The eccentric is mounted on or is part of the

    a. fixed gear.   c. output shaft.
    b. end housing.   d. rotor housing.

8. Name two variations in the fuel supply system, other than the conventional carburetor system, that may be adapted for use with the RC engine.

    a. _____   b. _____

9. The number of apex seals on a rotor is _____ .

10. An RC 4-40 engine has a displacement of _____ cubic inches.

Section 1 Engines

11. Insert the correct numbers of the matching terms or definitions in the blanks.

    a. ____ rotor face
    b. ____ trochoid
    c. ____ flame travel
    d. ____ gas transfer velocity
    e. ____ rotor width
    f. ____ apex seals
    g. ____ side seals

    1. internal shape of rotor housing
    2. distance traversed by the ignited mixture
    3. distance measured between the rotor sides
    4. speed at which air-fuel mixture spreads out
    5. seals inserted in the sides of the rotor
    6. seals at the three rotor corners
    7. outside section of rotor between the apexes

REFERENCE REVIEW

____ 1. A single-rotor RC engine has _____ power phase(s) per mainshaft revolution.

    a. one   c. three
    b. two   d. four

____ 2. The part(s) of an RC engine that has (have) much the same function as piston rings in a reciprocating engine is (are) the

    a. rotor.   c. oil seals.
    b. eccentrics.   d. apex seals.

____ 3. Compared to a reciprocating engine, uncontrolled hydrocarbon (HC) emissions from an RC engine are

    a. lower.   c. the same.
    b. higher.   d. less at high speed.

____ 4. Uncontrolled nitrogen oxide (NOx) emissions from an RC engine as compared to a reciprocating engine are

    a. lower.   c. the same.
    b. higher.   d. more at high speed.

____ 5. The rotor is cooled by circulating _____ through it.

    a. water   c. air
    b. antifreeze   d. oil

____ 6. The number of spark plug(s) in a single-rotor RC engine is

    a. one.   c. one or two.
    b. two.   d. three.

Unit 7 Rotary (Wankel) Engine

____ 7. The type of engine oil used in most RC engines compared to that used in reciprocating engines is

    a. much thinner.   c. about the same.
    b. much thicker.   d. higher priced.

8. RC engine displacement is measured in _____ or _____ .

9. Name four RC engine applications.

    a. _____   c. _____
    b. _____   d. _____

10. Indicate how the RC engine is rated as compared to the reciprocating engine by writing *more* or *less* in the blanks provided.

    a. vibrations ____ f. total combustion chambers ____
    b. octane requirement ____
    c. oil consumption ____ g. gas-transfer velocity ____
    d. moving parts ____ h. size per horsepower ____
    e. top rpm ____ i. high-speed torque ____
                              j. weight per horsepower ____

SECTION 2 Fuel Systems

UNIT 8 CARBURETORS

RELATED AUTOMOTIVE TERMS

Accelerator Pump (Plunger or Diaphragm Type): Small pump, located in the carburetor, that supplies extra fuel for rapid acceleration.

Accelerator Pump Nozzle: Fuel discharge opening for accelerator pump.

Air Bleed: Holes or tubes in carburetor to allow air to premix with gas flow.

Air-fuel Ratio: Mixing proportion of air to fuel, generally 17 or 18 parts of air to 1 part of gasoline by weight for warm-engine operation at high speeds, or about 10,000 gallons of air for each gallon of gasoline by volume.

Air Valve (Secondary Auxiliary Throttle): Pivoting plate, located above the secondary throttle valve; assists in controlling secondary fuel flow (four-barrel carburetors).

Altitude-compensating Carburetor: A carburetor that is capable of supplying a desirable and/or a constant air-fuel ratio regardless of altitude and atmospheric pressure.

Antistall Dashpot (Slow-closing Throttle Device): Part on many cars with automatic transmissions to help prevent engine stalling when the throttle is released quickly.

Automatic-choke Housing: Part containing the thermostatic choke spring.

Carburetor: Device used to properly mix air and fuel under various speeds, temperatures, and operating conditions.

Choke Piston: A vacuum-controlled piston used to partially open the choke when the engine starts.

Choke Plate (Valve): Pivoting part also known as a butterfly valve in the air horn that reduces air flow when the engine is cold.

Curb-idle Screw: Adjustable screw that controls the engine hot-idle speed.

Downdraft Carburetor: Carburetor having a downward airflow.

Fast Idle: Term referring to high engine rpm when the choke is closed or partially closed during warm-up.

Fast-idle Cam: A device, having steps of graduated heights, that is controlled by the choke; causes fast idle when the engine is cold.

Fast-idle Screw: Adjustable screw, that contacts the fast idle cam to control the engine speed during warm-up on many carburetors.

Float: Part that floats in the fuel bowl to assist in controlling the gasoline level in the carburetor by operating a float needle valve.

Float Bowl: Section of carburetor main body that acts as a fuel reservoir.

Four-barrel Carburetor (Quad): A carburetor having four venturis, main nozzles, and openings to the intake manifold.

Idle-mixture Screw (Needle): A pointed screw used to control the amount of air-fuel mixture flowing through the carburetor during engine idle.

Unit 8 Carburetors

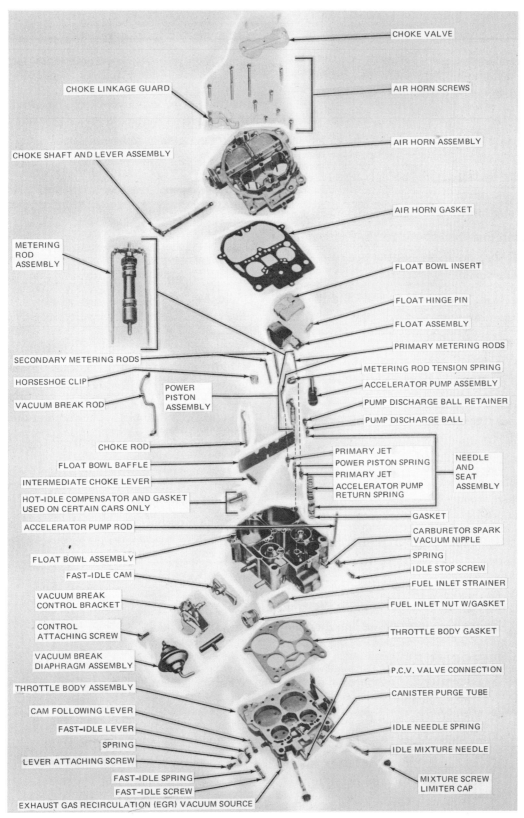

Fig 8-1. Four-barrel Carburetor, Exploded View

Section 2 Fuel Systems

Internal Vent: Vent tube between the float bowl and air horn.

Limiter Cap: A plastic cap fastened over the head of an idle-mixture screw to prevent excessive turning that would enrich the air-fuel mixture.

Linkage: Rod or lever connecting two operating parts.

Main Gas Nozzle (High-speed Nozzle): Discharge tube through which fuel is dispensed during medium- and high-speed operation.

Main Metering Jet(s): Part through which most of the gas flows during medium and high engine speeds.

Metering Rod: Part(s) that raises and lowers during operation to control the fuel-flow quantity on some carburetors.

Needle Valve and Seat: Parts that shut off the gasoline supply when the carburetor float rises.

Pump-discharge Check Valve: Ball or needle that seals the pump system discharge when the system is not in use.

Single-barrel Carburetor: A carburetor having one venturi, main nozzle, and opening to the intake manifold.

Thermostatic Choke Spring: Bimetallic spring that tensions the choke valve toward closed position when cold.

Throttle Body: Lower carburetor section containing the throttle valve(s).

Throttle Plate Valve(s), Primary: Pivoting plate(s), located near the bottom of the throttle body, which control the amount of air-fuel mixture entering the engine and, therefore, the engine speed (rpm).

Throttle Plate(s), Secondary: Second set of throttle plates on four-barrel carburetors; these plates open for full-power operation during high engine speeds.

Unloader: Part that causes a closed choke valve to open partially when the throttle is opened wide, thereby allowing more air into the cylinders to reduce flooding.

Upper Body (Bowlcover or Air Horn): Part that covers the top of the carburetor and provides an attachment for the air cleaner.

Vacuum Break (Kick): The vacuum-operated device that pulls the choke plate partially open when the engine starts.

Venturi: The narrow portion of the air passageway between the choke and throttle plates in a carburetor. As air flows past this constriction, its velocity increases and a partial vacuum is produced, thereby promoting a flow of gas from the main gas nozzle.

In the following exercises, indicate the best answer by inserting in the blanks the appropriate number, letter, word(s), or calculation, as required.

PICTORIAL REVIEW

A. Identify the carburetor parts in figure 8-2 by writing the correct letters in the blanks.

Note: Items 1-10 are parts located on the left side of the carburetor; items 11-18 are parts located on the right side of the carburetor.

1. ____ fuel inlet nut
2. ____ vacuum-break unit
3. ____ choke valve
4. ____ fast-idle cam
5. ____ vacuum-break rod
6. ____ choke rod
7. ____ choke linkage guard
8. ____ PCV connection

Unit 8 Carburetors

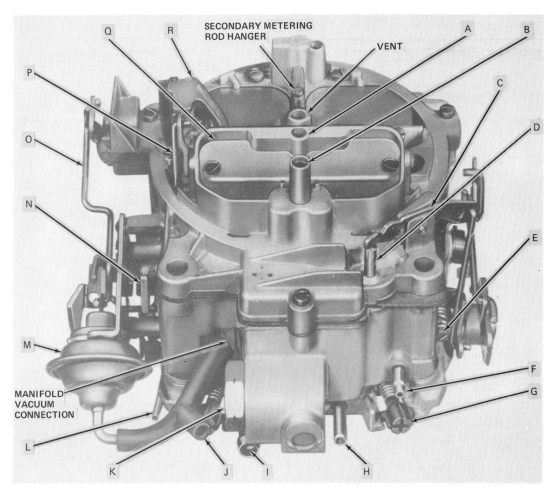

Fig 8-2. Four-barrel Carburetor (Assembled)

9. ____ EGR vacuum signal port
10. ____ idle-limiter cap
11. ____ evaporative emission port
12. ____ vent
13. ____ curb-idle adjusting screw
14. ____ accelerator pump
15. ____ air-cleaner stud hole
16. ____ accelerator-pump lever
17. ____ distributor vacuum port
18. ____ idle-limiter cap

SUMMARY REVIEW

____ 1. The carburetor provides the proper air-fuel ratio during
   a. all conditions.
   b. acceleration.
   c. high-speed operation.
   d. idle- and low-speed operation.

____ 2. Another name for the air horn is the
   a. venturi.
   b. center housing.
   c. upper body.
   d. air valve.

47

Section 2 Fuel Systems

____ 3. The float bowl is usually located in the
   a. air horn.
   b. main body.
   c. venturi.
   d. upper body.

____ 4. The purpose of the vacuum break is to
   a. stop the vacuum.
   b. control the float.
   c. partially open the choke.
   d. partially close the choke.

____ 5. The carburetor venturi causes the
   a. airflow to slow down.
   b. gas flow to slow down.
   c. airflow to speed up.
   d. power valve to open.

____ 6. Most automatic chokes are operated by a thermostatic spring and a(n)
   a. air valve.
   b. vacuum.
   c. air bleed.
   d. pressure.

7. Another name for the dashpot is _____.

8. The purpose of having limiter caps on idle-mixture screws is to _____.

9. The air-fuel ratio at high speed is approximately _____.

10. Insert the correct numbers of the matching terms or definitions in the blanks.
   a. ____ air bleed
   b. ____ unloader
   c. ____ metering rod
   d. ____ fast-idle screw
   e. ____ curb-idle screw
   f. ____ main metering jets
   g. ____ main nozzle

   1. adjusts idle speed on cold engines
   2. allows high-speed gas flow
   3. controls fuel flow quantity
   4. adjusts idle speed on hot engines
   5. discharge opening for high-speed gas flow
   6. air passage holes
   7. partially opens choke valve when throttle is open

REFERENCE REVIEW

____ 1. The choke is usually closed when the engine is
   a. idling.
   b. operating at high speed.
   c. hot.
   d. cold.

____ 2. Engine idle speed is usually set with the automatic transmission selector lever in
   a. neutral
   b. reverse.
   c. drive
   d. park.

Unit 8 Carburetors

___ 3. The high step of the fast-idle cam is contacted by the fast-idle screw when the
   a. engine is cold.
   b. engine is partially warm.
   c. engine is hot.
   d. all of these.

___ 4. In a downdraft carburetor, the choke plate is located
   a. behind the throttle plate.
   b. in front of the throttle plate.
   c. above the throttle plate.
   d. below the throttle plate.

___ 5. The choke unloader is controlled by
   a. the driver.
   b. heat.
   c. vacuum.
   d. an air valve.

___ 6. An idle-mixture limiter cap that has been removed should be replaced by a new
   a. metal cap.
   b. mixture screw assembly.
   c. rubber cap.
   d. plastic cap.

___ 7. The accelerator pump may be a plunger type or a
   a. vacuum type.
   b. diaphragm type.
   c. metering type.
   d. spring type.

___ 8. Most new engines have an idle speed between
   a. 200 and 300 rpm.
   b. 400 and 500 rpm.
   c. 600 and 700 rpm.
   d. 1000 and 1,100 rpm.

___ 9. The tip of the carburetor float needle valve is often manufactured from special
   a. rubber.
   b. aluminum.
   c. copper.
   d. cast iron.

10. Underline the word *closed* or *open* to identify the position of the following carburetor parts during high-speed, heavy-load operation.
   a. power valve   closed   open
   b. choke valve   closed   open
   c. throttle valve   closed   open
   d. float needle and seat closed   open
   e. air valve   closed   open

11. From the following list, underline the parts contained in the most popular carburetor kits for minor rebuilding.

   float   venturi
   main jet(s)   choke spring
   needle and seat   gas filter
   accelerator pump   throttle valve
   metering rod(s)   idle adjusting screw
   gaskets   air valve

49

UNIT 9 CARBURETOR SYSTEMS

RELATED AUTOMOTIVE TERMS

Accelerator Pump Circuit: See unit 8, page 44.

Atomization: A carburetor function of breaking fuel into fine droplets.

Booster Venturi: Ring-shaped venturi(s), located at or above the main venturi, near the high-speed discharge nozzle. Provides added fuel-metering control, especially at low speed.

Carburetor Circuits (Systems): The separate circuits, passages, and related parts designed to perform an operating function or supply the air-fuel mixture under a certain condition.

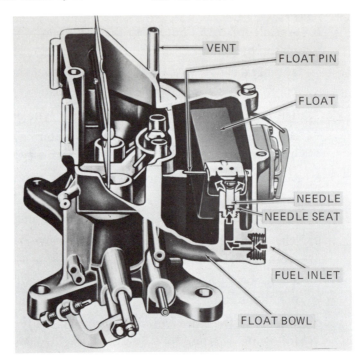

Fig 9-1. Float System

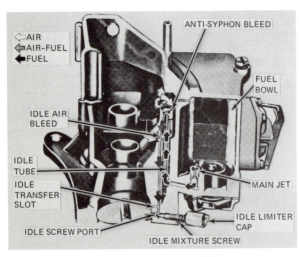

Fig. 9-2. Idle- and Low-speed System

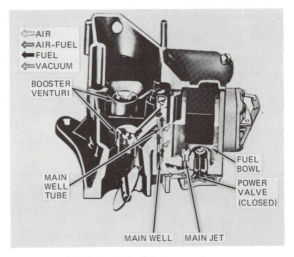

Fig 9-3. Main (High-speed) System

Unit 9 Carburetor Systems

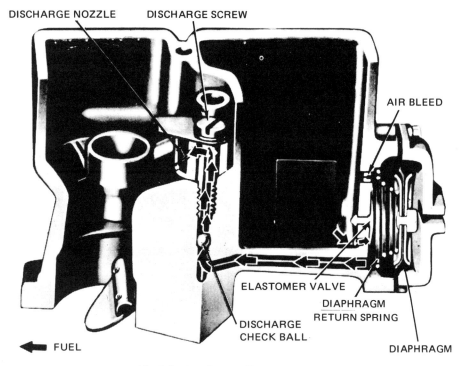

Fig 9-4. Accelerator Pump System

Curb-idle Discharge Port: Hole below the throttle plate for discharge of the idle mixture.

Curb-idle Metering Restriction: Metering jet in the idle passage, used to restrict the amount of fuel that may flow in the idle circuit.

Float Circuit: Circuit maintains the correct fuel level in the carburetor float bowl.

Float Hinge Pin: Pivot for the float.

High-speed (Main) Circuit: Circuit supplies the air-fuel mixture for high-speed cruising.

Hot-idle Compensator: Thermostatically controlled (bimetallic) device on certain carburetors that allows extra air to enter the intake manifold when the engine is hot.

Idle Air Bleed(s): Calibrated hole(s) located along the idle passageway for introducing air into the gas flow to improve atomization.

Idle- and Low-speed (Off-idle) Circuit: Circuit supplies the air-fuel mixture for curb idle and low-speed operation; each circuit has its own discharge port near the throttle plate.

Idle-mixture Needle: Valve used to adjust the air-fuel mixture flow at idle speed.

Low-speed (Off-idle) Discharge Port: Vertical slot or small hole at or slightly above the throttle plate where the mixture discharges during low-speed operation.

Manifold Vacuum: Vacuum supplied by the downward motion of the pistons (or the revolving rotor) on the intake stroke.

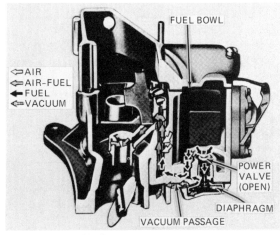

Fig 9-5. Power System

51

Section 2 Fuel Systems

Mechanically Operated Secondary: Secondary throttle valves opened by direct linkage from the primary throttle lever on certain four-barrel carburetors.

Metering Rod: A tapered, movable pin that controls the fuel flow through a carburetor jet. It is designed to be operated by a power piston on some carburetors.

Percolation: The process whereby hot gasoline boils, expands, and discharges from the high-speed nozzle after the engine is turned off, possibly flooding the engine.

Power Circuit: Circuit enriches the air-fuel mixture during high-power operation; this circuit usually is vacuum controlled.

Power Piston: Controlling device in certain power systems; usually it is vacuum operated.

Power Valve: Vacuum-operated controlling device in certain power systems.

Pressure Relief Valve: Fuel bowl vent operated by vapor pressure from evaporated fuel.

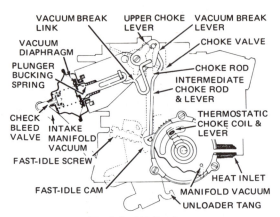

Fig 9-6. Choke System

Primary Idle-transfer Circuit (Low-speed): Circuit supplies air-fuel mixture at speeds above curb idle until high-speed circuit cuts in.

Vacuum-operated Secondary: Secondary throttle valves opened by a vacuum-operated diaphragm on certain four-barrel carburetors.

Vaporization: Process of turning gasoline into a vapor, which is often accomplished after the atomized fuel leaves the carburetor.

In the following exercises, indicate the best answer by inserting in the blanks the appropriate number, letter, word(s), or calculation, as required.

PICTORIAL REVIEW

A. Identify the parts of the float system in figure 9-7.

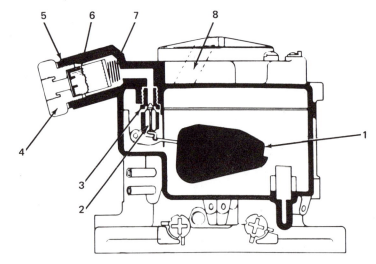

Fig 9-7. Float System

1. _____ 4. _____ 7. _____
2. _____ 5. _____ 8. _____
3. _____ 6. _____

Unit 9 Carburetor Systems

B. Identify the parts of the idle- and low-speed system in figure 9-8 by inserting the correct letters in the blanks.

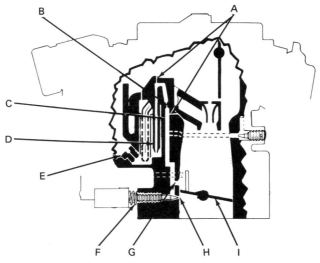

Fig. 9-8. Idle- and Low-speed System

1. _____ main metering jet
2. _____ throttle valve
3. _____ idle passage
4. _____ idle-passage restriction
5. _____ idle-mixture screw
6. _____ idle tube
7. _____ idle air bleeds
8. _____ off-idle discharge (transfer) port
9. _____ idle discharge hole

C. Identify the parts of the accelerator pump system in figure 9-9 by inserting the correct letters in the blanks.

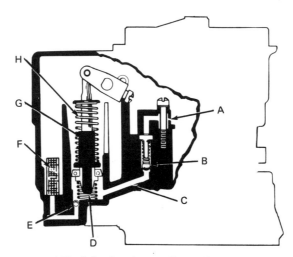

Fig 9-9. Accelerator Pump System

1. _____ pump plunger
2. _____ pump jet
3. _____ duration spring
4. _____ pump return spring
5. _____ pump-inlet screen
6. _____ pump-discharge passage
7. _____ discharge check ball
8. _____ pump-inlet check ball

Section 2 Fuel Systems

D. Identify the parts of the choke circuit in figure 9-10 by writing their correct names in the blanks.

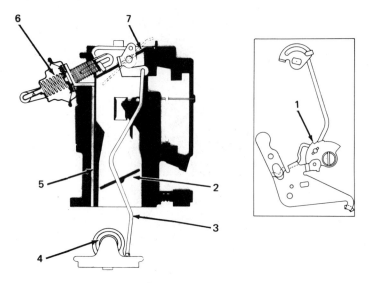

Fig 9-10. Choke System

1. _____
2. _____
3. _____
4. _____
5. _____
6. _____
7. _____

SUMMARY REVIEW

____ 1. The number of circuits contained in most carburetors is

    a. two.   c. six.
    b. four.   d. eight.

____ 2. The float system is designed to

    a. meter the fuel in the carburetor.
    b. store fuel vapors.
    c. supply air and fuel for burning.
    d. maintain the proper fuel level in the float bowl.

____ 3. Low-speed discharge ports are located _____ the idle-discharge port.

    a. beside   c. below
    b. above   d. outside

____ 4. Most of the fuel vaporization should begin to take place in the

    a. gas tank.   c. exhaust manifold.
    b. carburetor.   d. intake manifold.

_____ 5. Booster venturi(s) are usually located _____ the main venturi.
   a. above
   b. below
   c. off the side of
   d. outside

_____ 6. The hot-idle compensator allows extra
   a. air to enter a hot intake manifold.
   b. air to enter a cold intake manifold.
   c. fuel to enter a hot intake manifold.
   d. fuel to enter a cold intake manifold.

_____ 7. The hot-idle compensator is held closed by vacuum and
   a. a coil spring.
   b. venturi air pressure.
   c. a bimetallic spring.
   d. warm air.

8. A booster venturi is used to _____ .

9. Another name for the low-speed circuit is _____ .

10. Insert the correct numbers of the matching terms or definitions in the blanks.
   a. _____ accelerator pump circuit
   b. _____ power circuit
   c. _____ main circuit
   d. _____ idle compensator
   e. _____ vaporize
   f. _____ atomize

   1. admits extra air on hot engines
   2. break into fine droplets
   3. supplies extra fuel for quick engine speedup
   4. supplies fuel for high-speed operation
   5. supplies extra fuel during high engine loads
   6. change from liquid to vapor

REFERENCE REVIEW

_____ 1. During idle-mixture adjustments, the hot-idle compensator, if the carburetor is so equipped, should be
   a. partially open.
   b. open.
   c. closed.
   d. partially closed.

_____ 2. The intake manifold vacuum is usually highest when the engine is operating at
   a. idle speed.
   b. low speed.
   c. cruising speed.
   d. high speed.

_____ 3. The venturi effect in the carburetor causes fuel to discharge from the high-speed nozzle by
   a. lowering the air pressure.
   b. lowering the fuel pressure.
   c. raising the fuel pressure.
   d. raising the air pressure.

Section 2 Fuel Systems

____ 4. The effect of the venturi principle is needed most during operation of the _____ circuit.
   a. idle
   b. low-speed
   c. accelerator pump
   d. high-speed

____ 5. The carburetor circuit delivering the *leanest* mixture is the _____ circuit.
   a. idle
   b. accelerator pump
   c. power
   d. high speed

____ 6. The power circuit usually operates during
   a. engine idling.
   b. engine choking.
   c. low vacuum.
   d. high vacuum.

____ 7. Linkage-operated secondary throttle valves start opening
   a. as soon as the primary throttle valves do.
   b. when the primary valves are about one-half open.
   c. when the primary valves are wide open.
   d. as soon as the engine starts.

____ 8. The length of time in which fuel flows from the accelerator pump nozzle is partially controlled by
   a. air pressure.
   b. venturi pressure.
   c. a duration spring.
   d. a return spring.

____ 9. All fuel used by the engine must pass through the
   a. float circuit.
   b. high-speed (main) circuit.
   c. venturi.
   d. economizer circuit.

____ 10. The float needle is often attached to the float by a
   a. metal screw.
   b. clip.
   c. bolt.
   d. pin.

____ 11. A metering rod, if the carburetor is so equipped, is held down into the metering jet by
   a. spring pressure.
   b. the throttle linkage.
   c. vacuum.
   d. venturi pressure.

____ 12. Secondary throttle valves are operated by vacuum or _____ , if so equipped.

UNIT 10 FUEL SUPPLY SYSTEMS

RELATED AUTOMOTIVE TERMS

Camshaft Eccentric: Cam on camshaft used to operate the fuel-pump rocker arm or pushrod.

Clogged Filter: Term referring to a restricted filter containing excessive amounts of water or sediment (dirt).

Diaphragm: Flexible, multilayered, neoprene rubber sheet that is reinforced with fabric. Movement of the diaphragm creates the pumping action in a fuel pump.

Diaphragm Spring: Spring that maintains tension against the diaphragm, causing the fuel to be expelled through the pump outlet valve.

Electric Fuel Pump: A device having either a reciprocating diaphragm or a revolving impeller operated by electricity to draw fuel from the tank to the carburetor.

Flexible Fuel Line: Neoprene rubber hose, generally located between the metal fuel line and the fuel pump and/or at the gas tank outlet.

Fuel Filter: Replaceable part designed to remove solid particles of foreign matter from the fuel before it enters the carburetor.

Fuel Filter Spring: Spring located behind an in-carburetor filter to hold the filter in position; if the filter is clogged, the spring will compress to allow some fuel to pass.

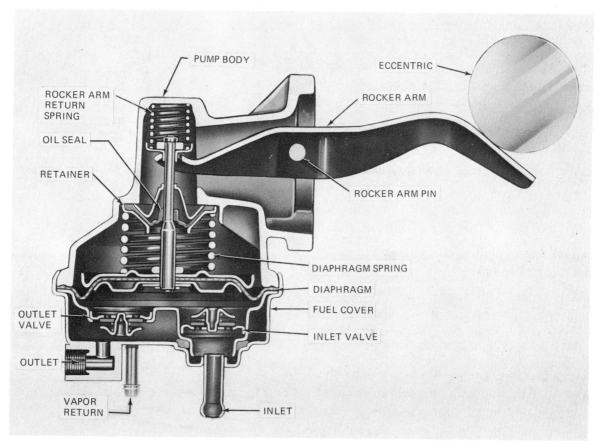

Fig 10-1. Mechanical Fuel Pump

Section 2 Fuel Systems

Fuel Injection: A method of precisely metering fuel to the cylinders using, instead of a carburetor, a high- or low-pressure injection pump and injection nozzles.

Fuel Line: Metal, plastic, or rubber hose used to carry fuel from the gas tank to the carburetor.

Fuel Pump Pressure: Pump outlet pressure, often between 4 and 7 psi (pounds per square inch).

Fuel Pump Vacuum: Suction created at the pump inlet by the motion of the diaphragm at the inlet; 10 inches of vacuum is minimum.

Fuel Pump Vapor Lock: The formation of gasoline vapor in the fuel pump, caused by fuel boiling and resulting in ineffective pumping.

Fuel Pump Volume: Pump outlet capacity, or flow rate, measured in terms of how much fuel can be pumped in a certain period of time (for example, 1 pint in 30 seconds).

Filter Material: Material from which filters are constructed, usually pleated paper, sintered bronze, woven plastic, or ceramic.

In-carburetor Filter: Filter located inside the carburetor at the fuel inlet.

In-pump Filter: Filter located inside the fuel pump.

In-line Filter: Filter located along the fuel line between the fuel pump and carburetor.

In-tank Filter: Filter located over the end of the fuel pickup tube.

Liquid-vapor Separator: An evaporative-control component that allows vaporized fuel to return to the fuel tank, where it condenses to a liquid for reuse.

Mechanical Fuel Pump: A device which draws fuel from the gas tank and delivers it to the carburetor by use of a mechanically operated diaphragm. This is the most popular automotive fuel pump.

Pickup Tube: Tube entering the gas tank to draw off fuel.

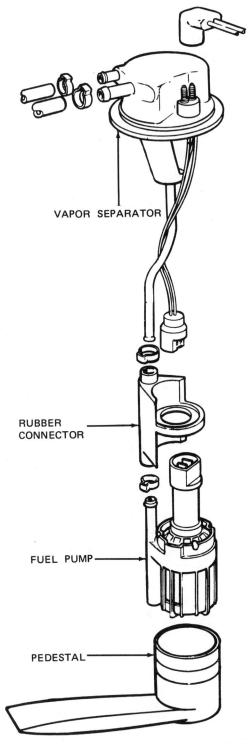

Fig 10-2 Electric Fuel Pump (In-tank Model)

Pump Air Bleed: Small vent holes in the pump body that allow air to enter and leave the pump as the diaphragm moves back and forth.

Pump Link: Short, connecting part between the pump rocker arm and the diaphragm on certain models.

Pump Valves: Check valves that permit fuel to pass through the pump in one direction only.

Pushrod: Metal rod used to transfer motion from the camshaft eccentric to the pump rocker arm on certain V-8 engines, thereby allowing a more remote pump location.

Rocker Arm: A pivoting part in a mechanical fuel pump, one end of which rides on a camshaft eccentric or pushrod, and the other end of which pulls on the diaphragm via a mechanical linkage, causing the diaphragm spring to be compressed.

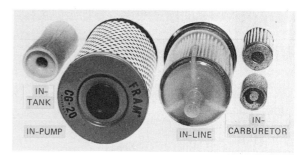

Fig 10-3. Fuel Filters

Rocker-arm Return Spring: Spring that keeps the rocker arm in constant contact with the camshaft eccentric or the pushrod.

Sealed Fuel Pump: A permanently sealed, nonserviceable pump that has its body and cover crimped together.

Vacuum Booster Pump: A combination fuel pump having a vacuum-assist section for operating vacuum-type wipers plus a fuel pump section.

Vapor Return Line: A hose used to carry fuel vapor from the fuel pump or the liquid-vapor separator back to the fuel tank.

In the following exercises, indicate the best answer by inserting in the blanks the appropriate number, letter, word(s), or calculation, as required.

PICTORIAL REVIEW

A. Identify the fuel pump parts in figure 10-4 by writing their correct names in the blanks.

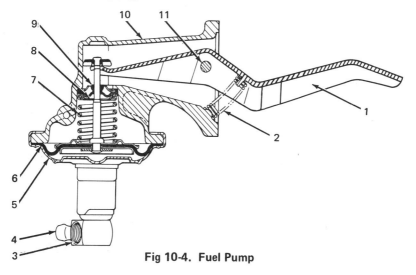

Fig 10-4. Fuel Pump

Section 2 Fuel Systems

1. _____
2. _____
3. _____
4. _____
5. _____
6. _____

7. _____
8. _____
9. _____
10. _____
11. _____

SUMMARY REVIEW

____ 1. Most automotive fuel pumps are operated by
   a. electricity.
   b. a camshaft eccentric.
   c. fuel pressure.
   d. oil pressure.

____ 2. Fuel pump valves are located in the pump
   a. body.
   b. cover.
   c. diaphragm.
   d. pulsation dome.

____ 3. The purpose of the small holes in the fuel pump body is to provide a vent for
   a. air.
   b. water.
   c. fuel.
   d. oil.

____ 4. The part tensioned against the diaphragm, causing the diaphragm to push fuel from the pump, is the
   a. rocker arm.
   b. diaphragm spring.
   c. rocker arm spring.
   d. pushrod.

____ 5. Fuel pump pressure should be approximately
   a. 4 to 7 psi.
   b. 10 inches of vacuum.
   c. 1 pint in 30 seconds.
   d. 1 quart in 1 minute.

____ 6. A fuel pump employing a pushrod is most likely found on an engine having _____ cylinder(s).
   a. one
   b. four
   c. six
   d. eight

____ 7. The material used in constructing a fuel filter often is made from
   a. pleated paper.
   b. porous cast iron.
   c. aluminum.
   d. any of these.

____ 8. A short, flexible neoprene hose is usually located at the
   a. gas tank inlet.
   b. carburetor outlet.
   c. fuel pump inlet.
   d. fuel pump outlet.

9. The two valves found inside a fuel pump are called _____ and _____ valves.

10. Insert the correct numbers of the matching terms or definitions in the blanks.

   a. ____ fuel injection
   b. ____ vapor lock
   c. ____ in-line filter
   d. ____ pump vacuum
   e. ____ pump pressure
   f. ____ pump volume

   1. outlet capacity
   2. provides precise metering of fuel
   3. inlet suction
   4. outlet psi
   5. caused by boiling gasoline
   6. located between fuel pump and carburetor

REFERENCE REVIEW

____ 1. Most defective fuel pumps should be
   a. disassembled.
   b. rebuilt.
   c. replaced.
   d. repaired.

____ 2. A fuel filter located under the hood should be
   a. cleaned when dirty.
   b. replaced at specified intervals.
   c. removed and tested for being clogged.
   d. none of these.

____ 3. The total number of fuel filters on most automobiles is
   a. one.
   b. two.
   c. four.
   d. six.

____ 4. Actual fuel discharge on a mechanical fuel pump occurs when the
   a. high part of the cam lobe (nose) is against the rocker arm.
   b. low part of the cam lobe (heel) is against the rocker arm.
   c. inlet valve opens.
   d. none of the above.

____ 5. Factory-installed, tank-mounted electric fuel pumps are often wired to the ignition switch and
   a. emission controls.
   b. alternator regulator.
   c. temperature sender unit.
   d. oil pressure sender unit.

____ 6. A fuel pump leaking gasoline from its breather holes has a
   a. defective diaphragm.
   b. loose inlet hose.
   c. loose outlet line.
   d. defective oil seal.

____ 7. A pump having a broken rocker arm return spring will usually
   a. stop operating.
   b. become noisy.
   c. leak oil.
   d. leak gasoline.

____ 8. The most frequently performed fuel pump test is for
   a. leaks.
   b. capacity.
   c. pressure.
   d. vacuum.

Section 2 Fuel Systems

____ 9. Fuel pumps should be tested
    a. when disassembled.
    b. off the engine.
    c. before rebuilding.
    d. on the engine.

____ 10. The fuel pump pressure tester is usually connected closest to the
    a. vapor separator.
    b. fuel pump.
    c. carburetor.
    d. gas tank.

____ 11. Fuel pump pressure tests are usually obtained with the engine operating at
    a. idle speed.
    b. 1000 rpm.
    c. cranking speed.
    d. high speed.

12. Hexagonal fuel pump line fittings should be removed with a special tool called a(n) _____ .

UNIT 11 ELECTRONIC FUEL INJECTION

RELATED AUTOMOTIVE TERMS

Absolute Pressure: The actual total pressure, or vacuum measured, including atmospheric pressure (14.7 psi at sea level) as well as the standard gauge pressure reading. For example, a reading of 20 psig (gauge pressure) is equal to 34.7 psia (absolute pressure). The absolute pressure is often detected by a pressure sensor in an EFI system.

Closed-loop EFI System: Cylinder fuel distribution controlled by electronic devices, having a special sensor in the exhaust pipe capable of monitoring oxygen content in the exhaust gases; the sensor sends an input signal to the electronic control unit, which varies certain engine controls to obtain the desired exhaust-gas characteristics.

Cold-start Valve: Component that sends extra fuel to the intake manifold when starting a cold engine.

EFI (Electronic Fuel Injection): Cylinder fuel distribution system controlled by electronic devices. An electronic control unit receives input from several sensing devices and then computes the amount of fuel to be injected (sprayed) at each engine intake valve port. Precision fuel distribution effectively controls exhaust emissions, allowing air-fuel ratios as lean as 19 to 1.

Electronic Control Unit: Central component of an EFI system that receives from sensors input messages relating to engine rpm, engine temperature, air temperature, intake manifold vacuum, and throttle position. After computing fuel requirements, electrical impulses are relayed to a control trigger that opens the injectors as needed.

Exhaust-gas Oxygen Sensor: Component in certain EFI systems capable of sensing the oxygen content in the exhaust gas and then

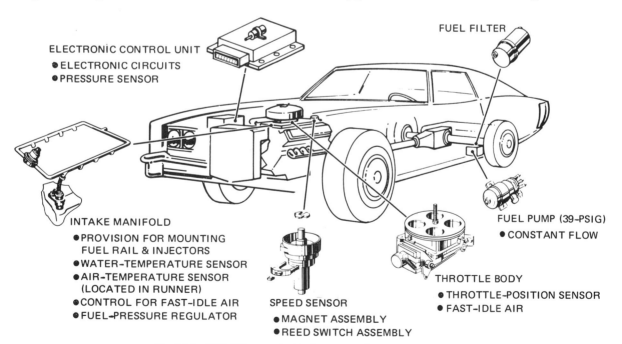

Fig 11-1. EFI (Electronic Fuel Injection) Vehicle Installation

Section 2 Fuel Systems

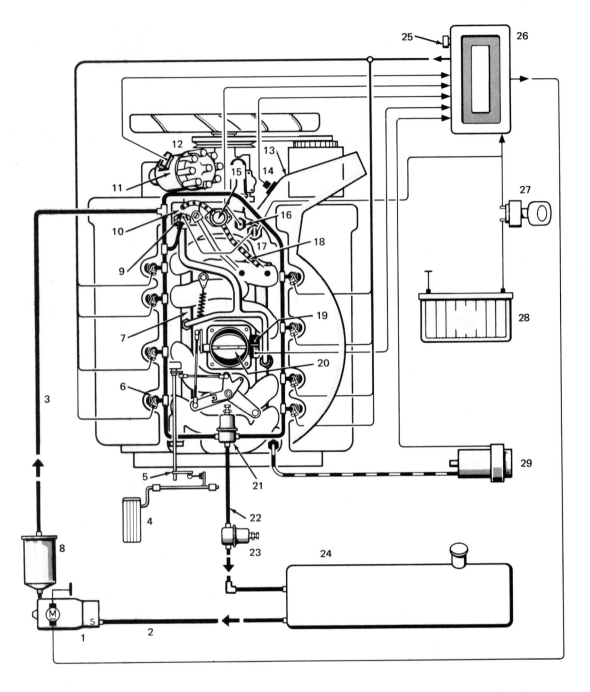

1. Fuel Pump	11. Impulse Trigger	21. Fuel Pressure Regulator
2. Fuel Supply Line	12. Ignition Distributor	22. Fuel Return Line
3. Fuel Pressure Line	13. Air Cleaner	23. Diaphragm Damper
4. Accelerator Pedal	14. Air-temperature Sensor	24. Fuel Tank
5. Regulating Linkage	15. Supplementary Air Valve	25. Idle Speed Screw
6. Injection Valves	16. Cooling Water Temperature Sensor	26. Electronic Control Unit
7. Idling-speed Air Duct	17. Thermal Time Switch	27. Ignition Starter Switch
8. Fuel Filter	18. Supplementary Air Line	28. Battery
9. Starting Valve	19. Throttle Valve Switch	29. Pressure Sensor
10. Idling-air Distributor	20. Throttle Valve	

Fig 11-2. EFI System: Electrical and Pressure Controls

Unit 11 Electronic Fuel Injection

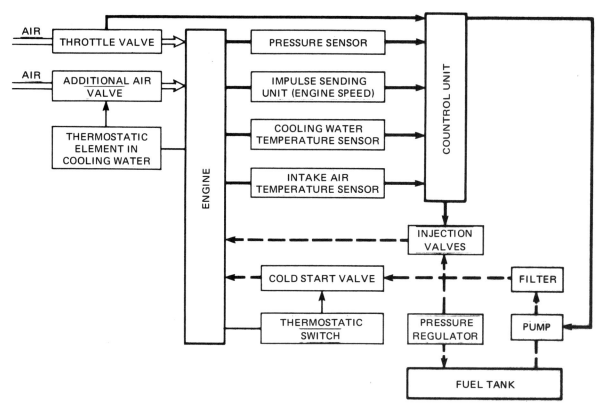

Fig 11-3. Electronically Controlled Gasoline Injection Operational Schematic

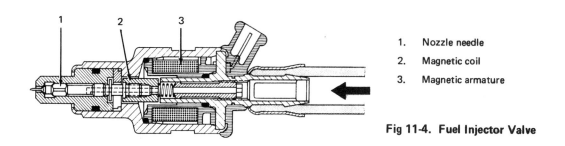

1. Nozzle needle
2. Magnetic coil
3. Magnetic armature

Fig 11-4. Fuel Injector Valve

Fig 11-5. EFI Injector Location and Gasoline Spray Pattern

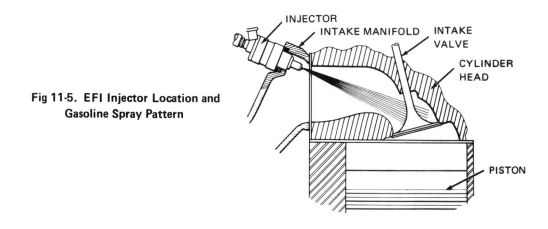

65

Section 2 Fuel Systems

transmitting a voltage to the electronic control unit to adjust the air-fuel ratio accordingly.

Fuel-line Manifold: Tubing system that carries pressurized fuel from the pump to each injector.

Fuel-pressure Regulator (Overflow Valve): Adjustable or nonadjustable component that returns excess fuel from the fuel manifold to the tank.

Group Injection: Method of injecting fuel into the manifold areas of several cylinders at one time, instead of injecting the cylinders individually; the injected fuel actually enters each cylinder as its intake valve is opened.

Impulse Trigger: A device, often located in the distributor, that may be used to time the injector openings, singly or in groups, according to the crankshaft position.

Injector Nozzle: Solenoid-operated valve that opens slightly to allow fuel to spray into the intake manifold near the intake valve ports; the opening-time period is precisely governed by an electronic control unit.

Port Injection: Gasoline injection system having fuel-injector nozzles located in the intake manifold near each intake-valve port. Timed-port injection refers to a system that sprays fuel toward the intake port when the intake valve is open.

Pressure Sensor: Device that relays intake-manifold pressure information, which indicates engine load, to the electronic unit, causing the injection of extra fuel when the vacuum drops.

Speed Sensor: Device that relays engine-speed information to the electronic control unit. The speed sensor may be located in the distributor.

Temperature Sensors: Temperature-sensitive devices that monitor intake air and coolant temperature and then relay this information to the electronic control unit.

Throttle Body: Component bolted to the intake manifold, that contains throttle valves actuated by the accelerator pedal, to control airflow into the engine.

Throttle-position Sensor: Device that senses the position and/or the rate of change in the position of the throttle valves and then relays this information to the electronic control unit. This sensor is mounted on the throttle body.

In the following exercises, indicate the best answer by inserting in the blanks the appropriate number, letter, word(s), or calculation, as required.

PICTORIAL REVIEW

A. Identify the EFI components in figure 11-6 by writing the correct letters in the blanks.

A

B

Unit 11 *Electronic Fuel Injection*

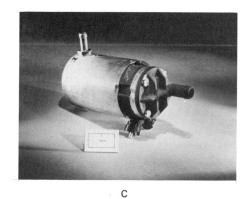

C

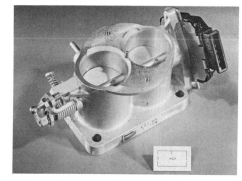

D

E

F

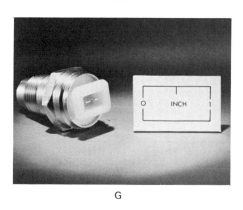

G

H

Fig 11-6. EFI Components

1. ____ oxygen sensor
2. ____ fuel pressure regulator
3. ____ electronic control unit
4. ____ electric fuel pump
5. ____ airflow throttle body
6. ____ injector
7. ____ throttle-position sensor
8. ____ temperature sensor

SUMMARY REVIEW

____ 1. Accurate fuel distribution can result in air-fuel ratios as lean as

    a. 5 to 1.
    b. 9 to 1.
    c. 14.7 to 1.
    d. 19 to 1.

Section 2 Fuel Systems

___ 2. An absolute pressure reading of 20 psia at sea level is equal to a standard pressure gauge reading of
   a. 5.3 psig.
   b. 14.7 psig.
   c. 20 psig.
   d. 34.7 psig.

___ 3. An electronic control unit controls delivery of the correct amount of fuel after
   a. reaching operating temperature.
   b. receiving input from sensors.
   c. the engine misfires.
   d. the correct speed is reached.

___ 4. The tubing system that delivers fuel to the injectors is often called a
   a. solenoid-operated system.
   b. fuel-delivery line.
   c. fuel-line manifold.
   d. injector line.

___ 5. The injectors in an EFI system contain a
   a. variable resistor.
   b. fuel-pressure regulator.
   c. solenoid coil.
   d. all of these.

___ 6. The speed sensor is usually located on the
   a. distributor.
   b. camshaft.
   c. speedometer.
   d. governor.

7. Briefly describe a closed-loop EFI system. _____
_____

8. Define group injection. _____

9. Name the two main functions of a throttle-position sensor.
   a. _____
   b. _____

10. Insert the correct numbers of the matching terms or definitions in the blanks.
   a. ___ fuel-pressure regulator
   b. ___ throttle body
   c. ___ exhaust-gas sensor
   d. ___ impulse trigger
   e. ___ pressure sensor
   f. ___ vacuum operated
   g. ___ injector

   1. overflow valve
   2. monitors oxygen content
   3. located in the intake manifold
   4. full-power switch
   5. located near the intake-valve port
   6. controls airflow into the engine
   7. located in the distributor

Unit 11 Electronic Fuel Injection

REFERENCE REVIEW

____ 1. Most defective EFI components should be
   a. removed for further testing.
   b. replace with a new part.
   c. removed for repair.
   d. replaced with a rebuilt part.

____ 2. The amount of fuel delivered through the injector is determined by the
   a. amount of fuel pressure.
   b. distance the injector opens.
   c. amount of time that the injector is open.
   d. applied voltage intensity.

____ 3. The distance an injector nozzle valve opens
   a. varies with engine speed.
   b. varies with vehicle speed.
   c. varies with air temperature.
   d. is considered very small.

____ 4. The amount of time that an injector nozzle valve is open is in the range of
   a. 3 to 9 ms (milliseconds).
   b. 25 to 50 ms (milliseconds).
   c. 1/4 to 1/2 s (second).
   d. 3/4 to 1 s (second).

____ 5. Pressure in the fuel-line manifold
   a. varies with engine speed.
   b. remains constant.
   c. varies with vehicle speed.
   d. requires frequent adjustment.

____ 6. An EFI component that may be adjustable on certain models is the
   a. electronic control unit.
   b. injector-valve opening distance.
   c. fuel-pressure regulator.
   d. fuel-pump speed.

____ 7. Most EFI fuel pumps are operated by
   a. a camshaft lobe.
   b. a camshaft eccentric.
   c. electricity.
   d. fuel pressure.

____ 8. The fuel-pressure regulator is located near the
   a. fuel pump.
   b. fuel-manifold inlet.
   c. injector nozzles.
   d. fuel-manifold outlet.

9. Are dirt particles entering an EFI fuel system *more* or *less* of a problem than dirt entering a carburetor-equipped system? _____

10. Name four advantages of using an EFI system.
   a. _____ c. _____
   b. _____ d. _____

11. List six monitoring devices, or sensors, that may send inputs to the electronic control unit in an EFI system.
   a. _____ d. _____
   b. _____ e. _____
   c. _____ f. _____

SECTION 3 Electrical Systems

UNIT 12 ELECTRICAL CIRCUITS AND SYMBOLS

RELATED AUTOMOTIVE TERMS

Ampere: A unit of measurement representing the rate of current flow in a circuit.

Circuit: Term describing the path of current flow, including an energy source, a load (component(s) having resistance), and conductors connecting all the parts.

Circuit Breaker: A protective device containing contact points that open the circuit when the current draw is excessive, after which, in some models, the breaker resets automatically.

Closed Circuit: Term describing an operating electric circuit.

Coil: A wire wound in a circular or spiral fashion, often around an iron core. As part of the ignition system, the (ignition) coil is a component used to transform, or step up, the battery voltage to the voltage required to fire the spark plug(s).

Common Point: A connection point for several conductors.

Conductor: Material through which electricity can flow.

Connections: The places where circuit components are joined together.

Continuity: Term indicating a complete (continuous) path through which current can flow.

Current: The progressive movement of free electrons in a complete circuit when voltage is applied. Measured in amperes.

Fuse: A replaceable, one-time protective device that burns out when the current draw is excessive, thereby causing an open circuit.

Ground Circuit: Term referring to the path current follows to the battery after flowing through the circuit load.

Insulator: A poor conductor, placed between one electric source, wire, or component and another, or ground.

Magnetic Field: The lines of force formed around a magnet, or a conductor when current flows through it.

Negative Terminal: The post or terminal on an electric device identified by a minus sign (–).

Nonconductor: Material which does not conduct electricity.

Ohm: A unit of measurement representing resistance (opposition to current flow) in a circuit.

Ohm's Law: I = E/R. Formula expressing the relationship of current (I) to voltage (E) and resistance (R).

Open Circuit: An incomplete circuit that may be caused by a broken or disconnected wire, or an open switch.

Unit 12 Electrical Circuits and Symbols

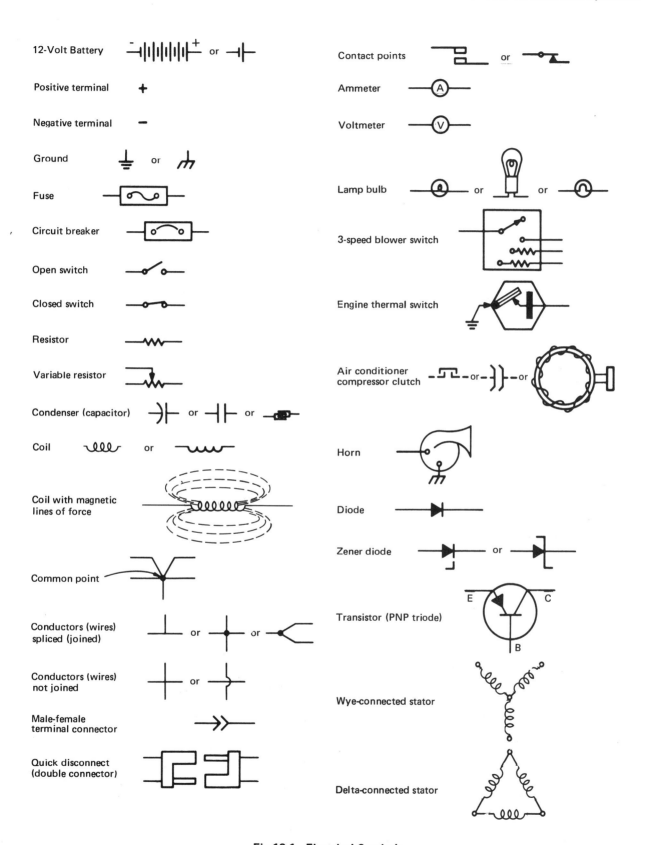

Fig 12-1. Electrical Symbols

Section 3 Electrical Systems

Parallel Circuit: An electric circuit having two or more paths that the current flows through at the same time. The current is divided with more of it flowing through the path of least resistance. An example is shown below.

Polarity: Indication of a positive or negative terminal on a battery or other electrical device.

Positive Terminal: The post or terminal on an electrical device identified by a plus (+) sign.

Primary Coil Winding: A few hundred turns of relatively heavy wire that carries the low input voltage of the coil.

Quick Disconnect: A wiring connection that is designed to snap together or pull apart easily.

Resistance: An opposition to the movement of free electrons (current) in a circuit when voltage is applied. Measured in ohms.

Resistor: An electric device having a resistance to current flow.

Secondary Coil Winding: Several thousand turns of relatively fine wire that carries the high output voltage of the coil.

Series Circuit: An electric circuit having only one path through which the current flows. The current must pass through one component before going on to another. An example is shown below.

Series-Parallel Circuit: A circuit containing both a series and a parallel circuit and, therefore, having a minimum of three loads or electrical devices. An example is shown below.

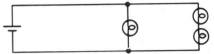

Short Circuit: A circuit defect that has been caused by some abnormal condition such as a "hot" wire losing its insulation and becoming grounded, possibly blowing a fuse. A short circuit in a coil occurs when two adjacent wires lose their insulation and touch, making electrical contact. As a result, the current is permitted to follow a shorter path.

Switch: Manual or automatic device to open and close a circuit.

Test Lamp: Device used to check for the presence of electricity along a circuit or at a connection. The test lamp consists of a light bulb connected to two wires.

Variable Resistor: An adjustable electrical device that controls (varies) the current flow, such as the fuel tank sender unit or the brightness control of the instrument-panel lights.

Volt: A unit of measurement representing electrical pressure (force) in a circuit.

Voltage: Measurement of electrical pressure or potential difference in a circuit.

In the following exercises, indicate the best answer by inserting in the blanks the appropriate number, letter, word(s), or calculation, as required.

PICTORIAL REVIEW

A. In the spaces provided, sketch each electrical symbol or circuit listed below.

1. Ground

2. Lamp Bulb

Unit 12 Electrical Circuits and Symbols

3. Variable resistor   11. Parallel circuit

4. Condenser (capacitor)   12. Transistor

5. Contact points   13. Negative terminal marking

6. Wires not joined   14. Fuse

7. Open switch   15. Series circuit

8. Coil   16. Diode

9. Positive terminal marking 17. Closed switch

10. Wires spliced   18. Twelve-volt battery

SUMMARY REVIEW

___ 1. A complete electric circuit must contain an electric source, a load, and

    a. a switch.   c. a common point.
    b. a capacitor.   d. conductors.

73

Section 3 Electrical Systems

2. The secondary winding of the ignition coil has
   a. many turns of heavy wire.   c. many turns of fine wire.
   b. few turns of heavy wire.   d. few turns of fine wire.

3. A series circuit has _____ path(s) through which the current can flow.
   a. one   c. one or two
   b. two   d. two or more

4. The unit of measurement of electrical resistance is the
   a. ampere.   c. ohm.
   b. volt.   d. resistor.

5. Magnetic lines of force are formed when current flows through a(n)
   a. coil.   c. condenser.
   b. nonconductor. d. open circuit.

6. A ground circuit may also be known as a
   a. parallel circuit.   c. return path through which current flows.
   b. hot circuit.   d. none of these.

7. Disregarding the negligible resistance in the connecting wires, a closed circuit having a 12-volt battery and a lamp with a resistance of 4 ohms, has _____ amperes of current passing through it.
   a. 2   c. 4
   b. 3   d. 6

8. A connection where several wires meet may be called a(n) _____.

9. A poorly conductive material placed between a source of electricity and a ground is known as a(n) _____.

10. Insert the correct numbers of the matching terms or definitions in the blanks.
    a. ___ volt
    b. ___ parallel circuit
    c. ___ shorted coil winding
    d. ___ ampere
    e. ___ resistor
    f. ___ ground circuit
    g. ___ open

    1. measurement of the rate of current flow
    2. contact between adjacent coil wires
    3. device having a resistance to current flow
    4. return path for current flow
    5. measurement of electric pressure
    6. more than one path of current flow
    7. incomplete circuit

Unit 12 Electrical Circuits and Symbols

REFERENCE REVIEW

____ 1. The distributor points function as a
   a. condenser.   c. fuse.
   b. switch.   d. coil.

____ 2. As resistors are added in a series circuit, the amount of current
   a. increases.   c. remains the same.
   b. decreases.   d. increases or decreases depending on the amount of resistance

____ 3. In an ignition primary circuit having a total resistance of 6 ohms at 12 volts, a maximum of _____ amperes may flow.
   a. 2   c. 4
   b. 3   d. 12

____ 4. The approximate amount of resistance in the secondary winding of an ignition coil is _____ ohms.
   a. 10   c. 1,000
   b. 100   d. over 2,000

____ 5. The basic ignition primary circuit is known as a _____ _____ circuit.
   a. series   c. series-parallel
   b. parallel   d. short

____ 6. Compared to high engine speeds, _____ current flows in the ignition coil primary at low engine speeds.
   a. more   c. the same amount of
   b. less   d. no

____ 7. Most lighting circuits from the dimmer switch to the headlights found on automobiles having four headlights are known as _____ circuits.
   a. variable-resistance   c. parallel
   b. series   d. series-parallel

____ 8. If one bulb in a series circuit burns out, the other bulb(s) will
   a. burn out.   c. go out.
   b. dim.   d. not be affected.

____ 9. If one bulb in a parallel circuit burns out, the other bulb(s) will
   a. burn out.   c. go out.
   b. dim.   d. not be affected.

____ 10. The coil primary terminal on the distributor side of most ignition coils has a _____ polarity marking.
   a. reversed   c. positive
   b. magnetic   d. negative

____ 11. The resistance of a single spark plug wire is usually in the range of _____ ohms.
   a. 1 to 500   c. 4,000 to 40,000
   b. 600 to 3,000   d. 50,000 to 80,000

UNIT 13 CONVENTIONAL IGNITION SYSTEM

RELATED AUTOMOTIVE TERMS

Available Voltage: Maximum voltage that can be produced in the secondary ignition circuit.

Battery: Device that stores chemicals capable of producing electricity.

Breaker Cam: Rotating part, located near the top of the distributor driveshaft, that has lobes which cause the points to open.

Breaker (Contact) Points: Switch that opens to interrupt the current flow in the primary circuit.

Buildup Time: The fraction of a second needed to form a magnetic field around the primary coil winding when current is allowed to flow through the winding.

Coil: A transformer containing a primary and secondary winding that acts to boost the battery voltage of 12 volts to as much as 30,000 volts. Usually 4,000 to 10,000 volts are required to fire the spark plugs.

Coil Polarity: Term referring to the positive (+) or negative (−) designation on the coil terminals. The coil is grounded according to

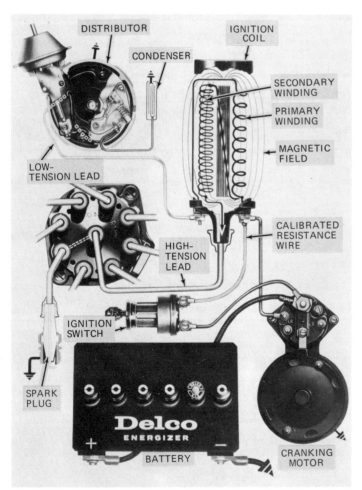

Fig 13-1. Typical Ignition System

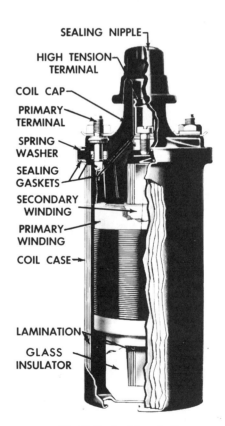

Fig 13-2. Ignition Coil

which battery terminal is grounded. For example, if the negative battery terminal is grounded, the negative terminal of the coil must be grounded (to the distributor side).

Coil Tower: The high-voltage, center terminal of the coil.

Condenser (Capacitor): Electrical device used to reduce arcing at the points by providing a place where the current can momentarily flow as the points begin to open. The condenser discharges as the points close and the process is repeated.

Distributor: Part of the ignition system, consisting basically of a housing, a breaker cam, breaker points, spark advance mechanisms, a capacitor (condenser), a rotor, and a cap.

Distributor Cap: A cover for the distributor, having a central terminal and peripheral terminals (outer terminals — one for each cylinder). The central terminal receives the secondary voltage from the coil, after which it is delivered to each of the peripheral terminals in turn by means of a rotor.

Dwell Angle or Time (Cam Angle): Number of degrees the distributor breaker cam rotates from the time the points close until they open again.

Ignition Switch: On-off switch that connects and disconnects the battery from the ignition system.

Ignition System: The group of components operating together to produce a spark that ignites the combustible mixture in each cylinder at the proper time. At high engine speeds, 12,000 or more sparks per minute can be produced.

Magnetic Field Collapse: Term that refers to the rapid collapse of the primary magnetic field across the secondary coil winding, occurring each time the current flow in the primary coil winding is interrupted as the points open.

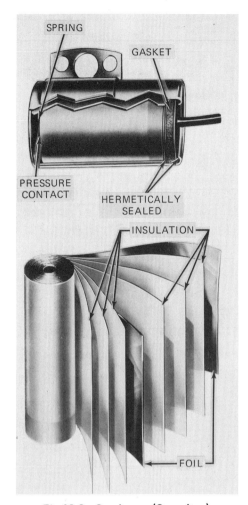

Fig 13-3. Condenser (Capacitor)

Microfarad (μF): Unit of electric capacitance used in rating the electrical size of the condenser.

Oscilloscope: Device used for many tests, such as checking the primary and/or secondary ignition circuit electronically. A visible waveform, representing variations in voltage with respect to time, is displayed on a screen and compared with a normal wave pattern.

Primary Resistance: A calibrated resistance wire or ballast resistor inserted between the ignition switch and coil to reduce the primary voltage at low engine speeds. During cranking (starting), the resistor is bypassed, permitting the full battery voltage to reach the coil primary winding.

Section 3 Electrical Systems

Primary Circuit: Low-voltage side of the ignition system.

Primary Resistance Bypass: Wire that bypasses the primary resistance and supplies full battery voltage to the coil when the engine starting circuit is energized.

Required Voltage: Amount of voltage necessary for the spark to jump across the spark plug gap. The voltage needed, usually 4,000 to 10,000 volts, or 4 to 10 kV (kilovolts), is affected by compression, air-fuel mixture, electrode gap and wear, and engine speed and load.

Rotor: Part that transfers the secondary voltage from the central terminal to the outer terminals of the distributor cap as it rotates inside the cap.

Secondary Circuit: High-voltage side of the ignition system.

Secondary Flashover: Term referring to insulation breakdown on the coil tower, distributor cap, or rotor, allowing high-voltage electricity to reach ground.

Secondary Wire Crossfiring: Term referring to a spark jumping from one spark-plug wire to another, possibly occurring when the wires from adjacent firing cylinders are too close to each other.

Spark-plug Wires: Insulated conductors that carry high voltage from the distributor cap to the spark plugs. Usually, these wires have an internal resistance to promote a more desirable spark at the plug and to suppress radio noise caused by the ignition system.

Spark Plug: Ignition part having two electrodes across which the high-tension spark jumps to ignite the air-fuel mixture in the combustion chamber.

In the following exercises, indicate the best answer by inserting in the blanks the appropriate number, letter, word(s), or calculation as required.

PICTORIAL REVIEW

A. Identify the components of the ignition system in figure 13-4 by writing their correct names in the banks.

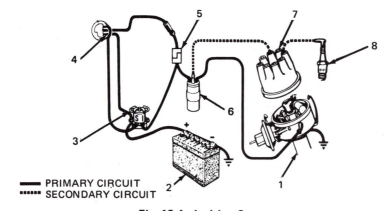

Fig. 13-4. Ignition System

1. _____
2. _____
3. _____
4. _____
5. _____
6. _____
7. _____
8. _____

Unit 13 Conventional Ignition System

SUMMARY REVIEW

____ 1. Three primary ignition circuit components include

    a. the points, condenser, and rotor.
    b. the distributor cap, points, and rotor.
    c. the ignition switch, coil, and spark plugs.
    d. the ignition switch, points, and condenser.

____ 2. The primary-circuit resistor is located between the coil and the

    a. ignition switch.   c. distributor.
    b. spark plugs.   d. points.

____ 3. The term *required voltage* refers to the voltage necessary to

    a. jump the spark-plug gap.   c. overcome the coil winding
    b. supply the primary system.   resistance.
                                 d. start the engine.

____ 4. The rotor carries electricity from the central terminal of the distributor cap to the

    a. spark plugs.   c. spark plug wires.
    b. peripheral cap terminal   d. secondary coil winding.
        inserts.

____ 5. Condenser capacitance is rated in

    a. microamperes.   c. amperes.
    b. microfarads.   d. farads.

____ 6. One condenser function is to

    a. increase the starting voltage.
    b. discharge when the points open.
    c. increase point arcing.
    d. decrease point arcing.

____ 7. Secondary ignition system parts include the rotor, distributor cap, coil secondary winding, and

    a. spark plugs.   c. distributor.
    b. primary spark-plug wires.   d. primary coil windings.

____ 8. A complete ignition coil operates much the same as a(n)

    a. condenser.   c. transformer.
    b. capacitor.   d. inverter.

9. Is the ignition primary circuit considered the *low*- or *high*-voltage side? _____.

10. Another name for dwell time or angle is _____.

11. Define the meaning of the word *dwell* as used in the automotive ignition system. _____

_____

79

Section 3 Electrical Systems

12. Insert the correct numbers of the matching terms or definitions in the blanks.

    a. ____ available voltage
    b. ____ required voltage
    c. ____ secondary flashover
    d. ____ magnetic-field collapse
    e. ____ ballast resistor
    f. ____ spark-plug wires
    g. ____ condenser discharged

    1. occurs when points open
    2. maximum voltage to fire spark plug
    3. secondary resistance
    4. occurs when points close
    5. primary resistor
    6. maximum voltage that can be produced
    7. insulation breakdown

REFERENCE REVIEW

____ 1. The coil primary winding consists of relatively

   a. few turns of fine wire.
   b. many turns of fine wire.
   c. few turns of heavy wire.
   d. many turns of heavy wire.

____ 2. On new automobiles, the side of the coil primary that connects to the ignition switch wire may be marked *battery* or

   a. ground.
   b. positive.
   c. negative.
   d. primary.

____ 3. Typical ignition condensers have a rated capacitance of between _____ µF.

   a. 0.17 and 0.28
   b. 0.31 and 0.62
   c. 6 and 12
   d. 40 and 60

____ 4. A negatively grounded condenser having too low a capacitance will cause the contact-point metal to

   a. last longer.
   b. remain the same.
   c. transfer to the movable contact side.
   d. transfer to the grounded contact side.

____ 5. The spark plug fires at the instant the

   a. coil primary magnetic field starts building up.
   b. coil secondary magnetic field starts building up.
   c. points open.
   d. points close.

____ 6. One purpose of spark-plug resistance wires is to

   a. increase contact-point life.
   b. allow higher engine revolutions.
   c. decrease required voltage.
   d. reduce communications interference.

Unit 13 Conventional Ignition System

___ 7. As the engine speed increases, the primary circuit voltage
   a. remains the same.   c. fluctuates.
   b. increases.   d. decreases.

___ 8. Ignition breaker points are opened by the breaker cam and closed by
   a. the breaker cam.   c. centrifugal force.
   b. spring tension.   d. the magnetic field.

___ 9. The point-dwell period on an eight-cylinder engine compared to a four cylinder is
   a. about the same.   c. less.
   b. more.   d. sometimes lower and sometimes higher.

___ 10. The highest voltage is produced by an operating ignition system when
   a. the spark-plug gaps are too large.   c. rotor flashover occurs.
   b. a spark-plug wire is removed.   d. a spark-plug wire is grounded.

___ 11. The easiest way to check the available secondary voltage is by using a(n)
   a. voltmeter.   c. ohmmeter.
   b. oscilloscope.   d. dynamometer.

___ 12. On most conventional ignition systems, the secondary voltage must jump _____ gaps to reach ground.
   a. one   c. three
   b. two   d. four

81

UNIT 14 CONVENTIONAL DISTRIBUTORS

RELATED AUTOMOTIVE TERMS

Basic Ignition Timing: Operation of adjusting the position of the distributor housing (by rotating it) to cause the sparks to occur and ignite the compressed air-fuel mixture at the precise time recommended by the engine manufacturer.

Breaker Cam: See Unit 13, page 76.

Breaker Plate: Distributor part upon which the breaker points are mounted.

Breaker-plate Ground Wire: Short wire used to ground the movable breaker plate to the distributor housing.

Breaker-point Alignment: Condition referring to the positioning of the breaker point contacts in relation to each other when installed.

Breaker-point Gap (Opening): Space between the fully opened breaker points (when the rubbing block is on the highest tip of one of the cam lobes). This gap may be set or checked with a feeler gauge only when the points are new.

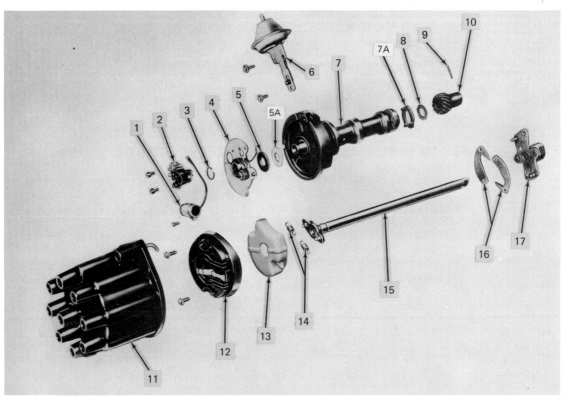

1. Condenser
2. Contact Point
3. Assembly
3. Retaining Ring
4. Breaker Plate
5. Felt Washer
5a. Plastic Seal
6. Vacuum Advance Unit
7. Housing
7a. Tanged Washer
8. Shim Washer
9. Drive Gear Pin
10. Drive Gear
11. Cap
12. Rotor
13. Radio-Frequency Interference (RFI) Shield
14. Weight Springs
15. Main Shaft
16. Advance Weights
17. Cam Weight

Fig 14-1. Conventional Distributor

Unit 14 Conventional Distributors

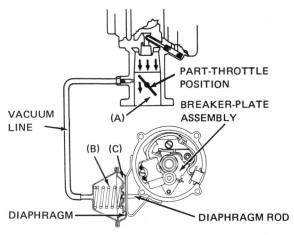

In the part-throttle position, a high vacuum is created at (A), causing air from (B) to be drawn through the vacuum line toward (A). The atmospheric pressure at (C), being greater than the partial vacuum at (B), pushes the diaphragm and the rod to which it is attached to the left, thereby rotating the breaker plate assembly and causing an advance of the spark.

Fig 14-2. Vacuum Advance Mechanism

Breaker (Contact) Points: See Unit 13, p. 76.

Breaker-point Spring Tension: Spring pressure tending to hold the points together; this spring is often adjustable.

Centrifugal Advance (Mechanical): Device used to improve engine performance by advancing the spark as the engine speed increases.

Centrifugal-Advance Weights: Two weights that pivot against spring tension in a centrifugal advance unit as the engine speed increases, thereby advancing the spark timing.

Condenser (Capacitor): See Unit 13, p. 77.

Defective Vacuum Advance: Term referring to a vacuum advance unit that has a defective (ruptured) diaphragm or will not calibrate to specifications.

Distributor: See Unit 13, p. 77.

Distributor Holddown: Bolt (and clamp) retaining distributor in position in engine. It must be loosened to adjust basic timing or removed to pull out the distributor.

Distributor Housing: Metal part which contains or provides a mounting for distributor components.

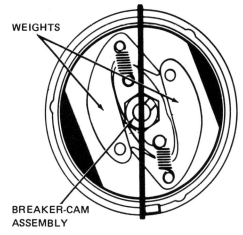

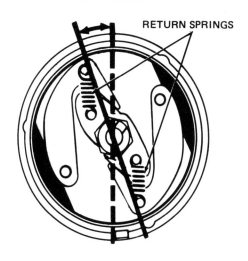

Fig 14-3. Centrifugal Advance

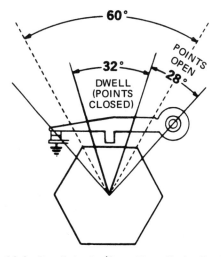

Fig 14-4. Dwell Angle (for a Six-cylinder Engine)

83

Section 3 Electrical Systems

Distributor Shaft: Cylindrical part used to transfer rotary motion from one end having a special drive mechanism or a gear meshed with another gear on the camshaft, to the other (upper) end which is connected to the centrifugal advance mechanism and the breaker cam.

Dwell Meter: Electrical tester used to determine the dwell angle of an operating distributor.

Dwell Variation: Number of degrees the dwell changes as the engine speed is increased. The variation should be less than 3 degrees, except on certain distributors having pivoted breaker plates.

Flex Stone: Special abrasive stick that, in some cases, may be used to true breaker-point surfaces.

Lubricating Felt: Felt material attached to the breaker plate and impregnated with a lubricant that is rubbed on the breaker cam.

Point Metal Transfer: Condition describing the transfer of some metal from one contact to the other, often caused by the condenser having the incorrect capacitance. A condenser capacitance which is too low causes the transfer of metal from the negative to the positive breaker point on a negative-ground system, while too high a condenser capacitance has the reverse effect.

Rotor: See Unit 13, p. 78.

Rubbing Block: Insulated section of the movable breaker-point arm that contacts the breaker cam.

Spark Advance: Distributor operation in which the ignition timing (the breaker-point opening and, therefore, the spark) is set earlier in relation to the crankshaft position. This is necessary to complete the combustion process in time to obtain the maximum downward force on the piston(s) at high engine speeds.

Timing Light: Special stroboscopic tool used to check precisely the timing of the ignition, which is adjusted by loosening the holddown bolt and turning the distributor.

Vacuum-advance Line: Hose connecting the vacuum above the throttle plate in the carburetor directly or indirectly to the vacuum advance.

Vacuum-advance Unit: Device for advancing the spark by rotating or pivoting the breaker plate according to the engine load, thereby providing for more economical operation.

Vacuum-retard Unit: Device used on dual-diaphragm units to retard the spark timing at idle and low engine speeds and, thereby, lower exhaust emissions.

In the following exercises, indicate the best answer by inserting in the blanks the appropriate number, letter, word(s) or calculation, as required.

PICTORIAL REVIEW

A. Identify the distributor parts in figure 14-5 by writing the correct letters in the blanks.

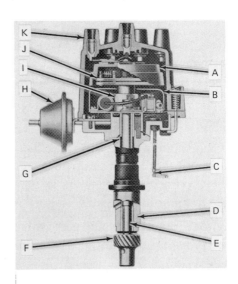

Fig 14-5. Conventional Distributor

Unit 14 Conventional Distributors

1. ____ shaft
2. ____ cam
3. ____ primary wire
4. ____ cap
5. ____ rotor
6. ____ centrifugal weights
7. ____ RFI shield
8. ____ vacuum advance
9. ____ gear
10. ____ shaft bushing
11. ____ housing

B. Plot and draw a line representing the centrifugal advance curve for a distributor having the characteristics listed below.

Degrees of Advance	Rpm
0	300
3	600
6	900
9	1500
12	2100

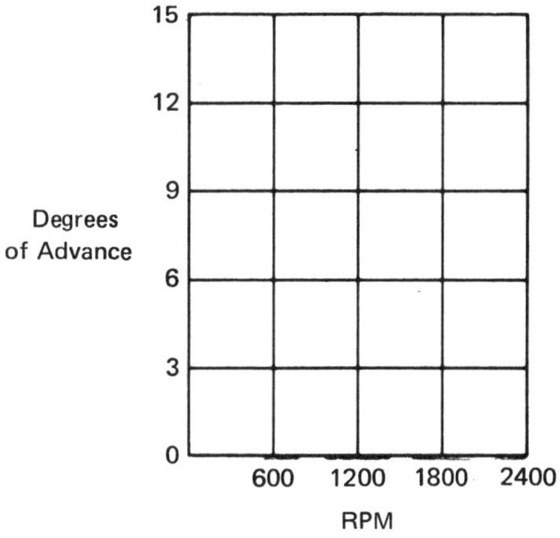

Fig 14-6. Centrifugal Advance Curve

SUMMARY REVIEW

____ 1. One distributor function is to

a. distribute primary sparks.
b. act as a source of primary current.
c. interrupt primary current flow.
d. increase primary voltage.

____ 2. The dwell or cam angle refers to the number of degrees the breaker cam rotates while the

a. engine is starting.
b. engine is operating.
c. points are open.
d. points are closed.

____ 3. The breaker-point gap on an operating distributor is best set with a

a. tachometer.
b. steel scale.
c. feeler gauge.
d. dwell meter.

____ 4. The breaker-point gap may be set accurately using a feeler gauge when the points are

a. operating.
b. removed.
c. new.
d. worn.

____ 5. When the engine is idling, the centrifugal advance weights return to their *at-rest* position due to

a. centrifugal force.
b. oil pressure.
c. tension applied by bimetallic springs.
d. tension applied by coil springs.

85

Section 3 Electrical Systems

___ 6. A vacuum-retard unit may be attached to a distributor to
   a. achieve smoother operation at idle speeds.
   b. decrease emission.
   c. increase fuel economy.
   d. lower engine temperature.

___ 7. The rubbing block is part of the breaker
   a. points.
   b. plate.
   c. cam.
   d. housing.

8. It is necessary to loosen the _____ when adjusting ignition timing.

9. Insert the correct numbers of the matching terms or definitions in the blanks.
   a. ___ breaker cam   1. operates at medium speed
   b. ___ breaker arm spring   2. capacitor
   c. ___ vacuum retard   3. closes points
   d. ___ vacuum advance   4. adjust new points
   e. ___ condenser   5. open points
   f. ___ feeler gauge   6. operates at idle speed
   g. ___ dwell meter   7. adjust new or used points

REFERENCE REVIEW

___ 1. The vacuum advance on certain cars does not start operating until the
   a. engine is overheating.
   b. hot air duct to the air cleaner is open.
   c. choke is closed.
   d. automatic transmission shifts into high.

___ 2. A distributor vacuum advance having a ruptured diaphragm affects mainly
   a. engine performance.
   b. engine life.
   c. idling operation.
   d. fuel economy.

___ 3. Maximum distributor vacuum advance most frequently occurs when the engine is operating at
   a. heavy load.
   b. idle speed.
   c. cruising speed.
   d. high speed.

___ 4. On some cars, the vacuum retard units operate primarily when the engine speed is between
   a. 500 to 1500 rpm.
   b. 1600 and 2000 rpm.
   c. 2100 and 2500 rpm.
   d. 2600 and 3600 rpm.

___ 5. Maximum distributor centrifugal advance most frequently occurs when the engine is operating at
   a. cruising speed.
   b. idle speed.
   c. high speed.
   d. low speed.

Unit 14 Conventional Distributors

___ 6. The metal comprising the breaker points is often made from
   a. carbide steel.   c. aluminum.
   b. tungsten.   d. copper.

___ 7. The spring tension for most breaker points ranges between
   a. 5 and 16 ounces.   c. 24 and 30 ounces.
   b. 17 and 23 ounces.   d. 31 and 36 ounces.

___ 8. The proper breaker-point alignment should be provided when necessary by bending the
   a. breaker plate.   c. movable contact.
   b. distributor plate. d. stationary contact.

___ 9. The breaker points are mounted on the distributor breaker
   a. plate.   c. lever.
   b. housing. d. none of these

___ 10. The distributor shaft speed is _____ that of the crankshaft.
   a. the same as   c. one-half
   b. one-fourth   d. twice

___ 11. During medium engine speeds, the distributor causes the spark at the plug to occur on the four-cycle stroke called
   a. intake.   c. power.
   b. compression. d. exhaust.

___ 12. During ignition timing, it is important to disconnect the
   a. distributor vacuum line(s). c. coil secondary wire(s).
   b. ignition primary lead(s).   d. air cleaner control(s).

UNIT 15 SPARK PLUGS

RELATED AUTOMOTIVE TERMS

Center Electrode: Insulated part that conducts electricity through the spark plug toward the electrode gap.

Ceramic Insulator: Plug section insulating the center electrode from ground.

Electrode Gap: Distance between the center and ground electrode, usually 0.025 to 0.080 inch (0.6 to 2.0 mm).

Firing Order: See Unit 1, p. 1.

Gap Bridging: Term indicating the accumulation of deposits which eventually bridge the electrode gap.

Gasket: Metal ring used on certain spark plugs to seal pressure between the lower section of the spark plug shell and the cylinder head.

Ground (Side) Electrode: Part welded to the lower end of the spark plug shell to provide a path for the electricity to flow after jumping the electrode gap.

Heat Range: The temperature limits within which a spark plug is designed to operate. The heat rate of a spark plug, rated as hot, normal, or cold, is controlled during plug manufacture by varying the length of the exposed lower section of the plug ceramic insulator. For example, a hot plug has a longer insulator and may reach temperatures over 1000°F under load.

Insulator Ribs: Unevenly spaced, circular ridges on the upper section of the insulator, used to reduce or prevent flashover of high-voltage electricity from the terminal to the lower shell.

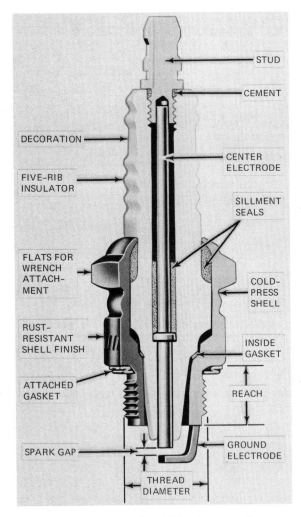

Fig 15-1. Typical Spark Plug Construction

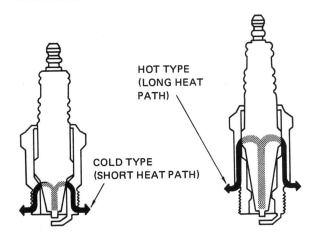

Fig 15-2. Heat Range of Spark Plugs

Unit 15 Spark Plugs

NORMAL OPERATION

Normal plugs have brown to greyish tan deposits and slight electrode wear, indicating correct spark plug heat range and mixed periods of high and low speed driving. Spark plugs having this appearance may be cleaned, regapped and reinstalled.

CARBON FOULED (FUEL FOULED)

Carbon fouled plugs show dry fluffy black deposits which may result from over-rich carburetion, over-choking, a stocking manifold heat valve or clogged air cleaner. Faulty breaker points, weak coil or condenser, worn ignition cables can reduce voltage and cause misfiring. Excessive idling, slow speeds under light load also can keep plug temperatures so low that normal combustion deposits are not burned off. In such a case a hotter type spark plug will better resist carbon deposits.

SCAVENGER DEPOSITS

Fuel scavenger deposits may be white or yellow in color. They may appear to be bad, but this is a normal appearance with certain branded fuels. Such materials are designed to change the chemical nature of deposits to lessen misfire tendencies. Notice that accumulation on the ground electrodes and shell areas may be unusually heavy, but the material is easily flaked off. Such plugs can be considered normal in condition and can be cleaned with standard procedures.

OIL FOULED

Wet oily deposits maybe caused by oil leaking past worn piston rings. "Break-in" of a new or overhauled engine before rings are fully seated may also produce this condition. A porous vacuum booster pump diaphragm or excessive valve stem guide clearances can also cause oil fouling. Usually these plugs can be degreased, cleaned and reinstalled. While hotter type spark plugs will reduce oil-fouling, an engine overhaul may be necessary to correct this condition.

OVERHEATING

Burned or blistered insulator nose and badly eroded electrodes are indications of spark plug overheating. Improper spark timing or low octane fuel can cause detonation and overheating. Lean air fuel mixtures, cooling system stoppage or sticking valves may also result in this condition. Sustained high-speed, heavy-load service can produce high temperatures which require use of colder spark plugs.

WORN OUT

Worn-Out, eroded electrodes and a pitted insulator are indications of 10,000 miles or more of service. Spark plugs should be replaced when these conditions are observed for better gas mileage, quicker starting and smoother engine performance.

Fig 15-3. Operating Conditions of Spark Plugs

Preignition: Term referring to the ignition of air-fuel mixture before the arrival of the spark, possibly caused by too hot a spark-plug heat range, or other problem.

Projected Core-nose Plug: Spark plug having electrodes and an insulator that extend farther outward into the combustion chamber.

Required Voltage: See Unit 13, p. 78.

Resistor Spark Plug: Spark plug having a resistor of 5,000 to 10,000 ohms inside the upper part of the insulator to increase electrode life and suppress radio interference.

Scavenger Deposits: White or yellow carbon deposits that normally occur when certain fuels are burned.

Shell: Outer spark plug casing having flats (forming a hexagonal surface) for a wrench attachment and also a threaded lower end.

Spark Plug: An ignition component, threaded into the cylinder head, that contains two electrodes across which high-voltage electricity jumps to ignite the compressed air-fuel mixture.

Spark-plug Fouling: An accumulation of deposits on the lower, exposed end of the spark plug that act as an electrical conductor, thereby creating a path for electricity to leak to ground rather than jump across the electrode gap.

Spark-plug Gauge: Flat, tapered, or wire gauge tool used for checking the electrode gap spacing.

Tapered Seat: Term referring to the design of the shell sealing surface on certain spark plugs, machined to a 45-degree angle and requiring no separate gasket.

Thread Reach: Length of the threaded plug section ranging from 3/8 to 3/4 inch.

Thread Size (Major Diameter): Distance from the top (crest) of the thread on one side to the top of the thread directly opposite, usually 14 or 18 millimeters.

In the following exercises, indicate the best answer by inserting in the blanks the appropriate number, letter, word(s), or calculation as required.

PICTORIAL REVIEW

A. Identify the spark plug operating conditions shown in figure 15-4 by placing the correct letter in the blank that best describes each condition.

Fig 15-4. Plug Operating Condition and Problems

1. ____ preignition damage
2. ____ chipped insulator
3. ____ bridged gap
4. ____ scavenger deposits
5. ____ overheated
6. ____ carbon fouled (fuel fouled)

Unit 15 Spark Plugs

B. For each plug cross section shown in figure 15-5, label the spark plug heat range (normal, cold, or hot).

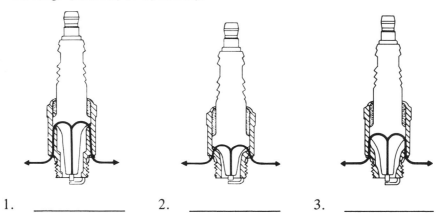

1. _____   2. _____   3. _____

Fig 15-5. Spark Plug Heat Ranges

SUMMARY REVIEW

____ 1. The spark plug is threaded to fit into the

    a. cylinder block.   c. intake manifold.
    b. cylinder head.   d. exhaust manifold.

____ 2. A spark plug with no sealing gasket has a sealing surface that is

    a. flat.   c. curved.
    b. convex.   d. tapered.

____ 3. A spark plug may become fouled because of deposits caused by

    a. lead.   c. gasoline.
    b. oil.   d. all of these.

____ 4. Proper spark-plug servicing tools should always include

    a. a feeler gauge.   c. an electric wire brush.
    b. gasoline for cleaning off grease.   d. all of these.

____ 5. The resistance of a popular resistor spark plug may be

    a. 600 ohms.   c. 10,000 ohms.
    b. 1,000 ohms.   d. 12,000 ohms.

6. From the following list, underline the item(s) that will cause a high required voltage.

    narrow spark plug gap   high output coil
    rich gasoline mixture   low engine speed
    high compression   light engine load

Section 3 Electrical Systems

7. The approximate metric size equivalent to 0.040 inch is _____ millimeter(s).

8. The formation of a carbon deposit across the electrode gap is known as _____.

9. Should the spark-plug gap be adjusted *before* or *after* the abrasive cleaning of a used spark plug? _____

10. Insert the proper numbers of the matching terms or definitions in the blanks.

    a. ____ thread reach   1. has hexagonal surface
    b. ____ insulator   2. thread length
    c. ____ thread size   3. plug temperature
    d. ____ shell   4. welded to shell
    e. ____ heat range   5. thread diameter
    f. ____ ground electrode   6. ceramic material
    g. ____ required-voltage   7. kilovolts
            measurement

REFERENCE REVIEW

____ 1. Spark plugs should be removed and installed using

   a. any deep socket that fits.   c. a 6-point spark plug socket.
   b. a 12-point deep socket.   d. a 12-point spark plug socket.

____ 2. The required voltage of a spark plug is lowest when the electrodes are

   a. flat.   c. used.
   b. convex.   d. opened wide.

____ 3. The electrode gap of a spark plug is adjusted by

   a. lengthening the center electrode.   c. bending the center electrode.
   b. lengthening the ground electrode.   d. bending the ground electrode.

____ 4. Resistor spark plugs reduce electrode erosion (wear) by reducing the

   a. electrode gap.   c. spark portion that erodes electrodes.
   b. electrode length.   d. required voltage.

____ 5. Most spark plug fouling is caused by

   a. defective spark plugs.   c. too high a heat range.
   b. using the wrong gasoline.   d. an engine condition.

6. Many new automobile engines use spark plugs having a small shell to allow

   a. a more desirable placement in the engine.
   b. more space for the pistons.
   c. a higher torque during tightening.
   d. a relatively inexpensive construction.

7. Does a slightly *cold* or *hot* spark plug operate satisfactorily for a longer period of time under a plug fouling condition? _____

8. Name three things the automotive technician may do to reduce radio interference caused by the ignition system.

   a. _____
   b. _____
   c. _____

9. Why should used spark plugs be kept in order when they are removed from the engine? _____

10. Provide the correct procedure for servicing used spark plugs by numbering the steps below in their proper sequence.

    ____ loosen spark plug
    ____ carefully remove wire
    ____ remove spark plug and analyze condition
    ____ file electrode gap
    ____ direct an air blast around spark plug
    ____ adjust electrode gap
    ____ clean spark plug
    ____ test spark plug
    ____ install spark plug and wire

UNIT 16 ELECTRONIC IGNITION SYSTEM

RELATED AUTOMOTIVE TERMS

Air Gap (Between the Pickup Coil and Reluctor Tooth): In a magnetically controlled ignition system, the space between the core of the pickup coil and the point of a reluctor tooth. The gap may be adjustable, using a nonmagnetic feeler gauge.

Amplifier: Electronic unit used to increase electric power, voltage, or current.

Ballast Resistor: Device for limiting voltage or current flow. A *dual ballast resistor* regulates current flow in the primary circuit and electronic circuit.

Capacitor-discharge Ignition System: A system that uses the electrical discharge of a capacitor along with the action of other related parts to speed up the operation of the ignition system and achieve a high peak voltage output.

Contact-controlled Ignition System: A system using breaker points as a method of triggering current flow in the primary circuit. This may be a conventional system or one that employs electronic components.

Control Unit (Electronic Module): A component containing electronic devices such as diodes, transistors, resistors, and capacitors used to control the operation of the primary ignition system.

Diode (Semiconductor): A solid-state device, containing two areas of semiconductor material, that conducts current easily in one direction and blocks current flow in the opposite direction.

Electronic Ignition System (High-energy Ignition or Solid-state Ignition): An ignition system that employs electronic components, such as diodes, transistors, resistors, and capacitors, along with other related parts.

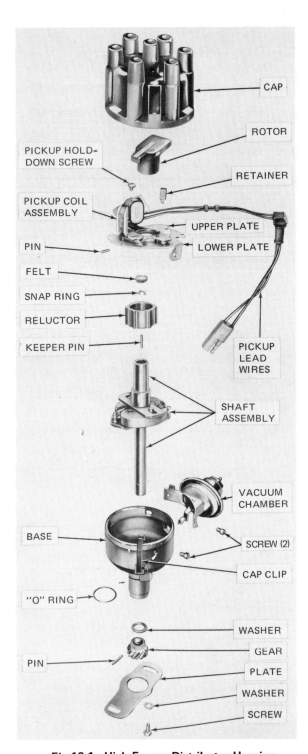

Fig 16-1. High Energy Distributor Housing

Unit 16 Electronic Ignition System

Electronic Ignition System (Light Beam Type): An ignition system that uses a light-emitting diode to produce an infrared light beam which triggers the interruption of the primary current flow. A rotating part with slots (or windows) interrupts the light beam. This system is popular with after-market (add-on) units.

Electronic Ignition System Coil: A special coil having a low resistance in the primary windings, thereby allowing a higher current to flow than in a conventional coil.

Heat Sink: Finned aluminum housing that dissipates heat and serves as a base on which electrical components (principally semiconductor devices) are mounted.

Magnetically Controlled Ignition System: A system using an electronic device such as an inpulse generator or magnetic pickup in the distributor to magnetically trigger (operate) transistors in the electronic control unit.

Magnetic Pickup Coil: A relatively small coil wound on an iron core that is magnetically affected as the reluctor teeth pass by.

Reluctor: A gearlike part, having as many teeth as there are cylinders, attached near the top of the distributor shaft in the same position as the cam in a conventional ignition system. When a reluctor tooth passes the pickup coil core, the resistance to magnetic flux is reduced and, therefore, the magnetic field is strengthened which, in turn, triggers the electronic control unit.

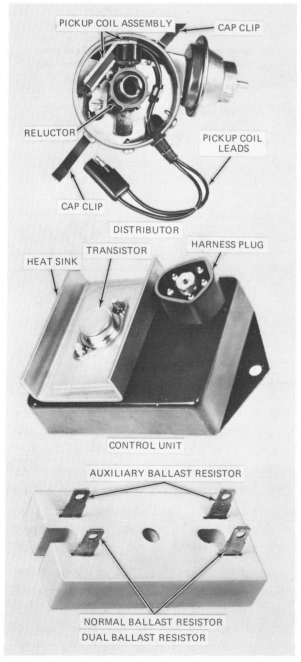

Fig 16-2. Components of an Electronic Ignition System

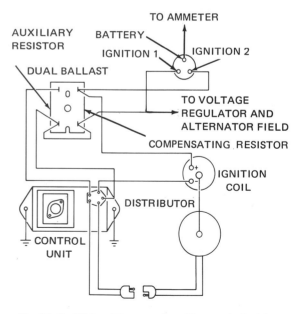

Fig 16-3. Wiring Diagram of an Electronic Ignition System

Section 3 Electrical Systems

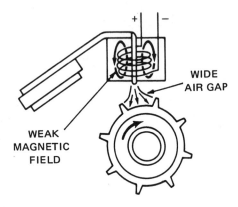

Wide air gap offers resistance and, therefore, weakens magnetic field in pickup coil

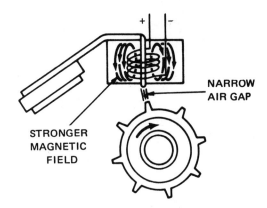

Narrow air gap strengthens magnetic field in pickup coil, inducing a positive voltage at one coil terminal

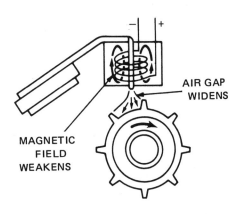

As air gap increases, the magnetic field in pickup coil weakens, inducing a negative voltage at the same coil terminal that triggers the electronic control unit.

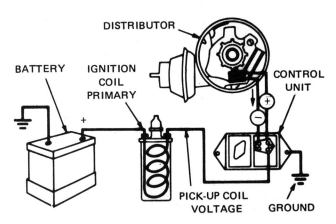

Current flows through the ignition primary circuit until the control unit receives negative voltage from the magnetic pickup coil, interrupting the ignition primary and inducing a high secondary voltage

Fig. 16-4 Operation of an Electronic Ignition

Semiconductor Material: A solid material, usually silicon or germanium, having a relatively high resistance in its pure state. The ability of this material to conduct current is greatly altered by special processing, which determines whether and how conduction may occur.

Solid-state Device: An electronic component, such as a diode or transistor, that performs a specific function in a circuit. Solid-state devices are manufactured from semiconductor material and have no moving parts.

Transistor: A solid-state device that functions as a switch in the electronic ignition system. This device contains three regions (areas) of semiconductor material and features three terminals known as the emitter, the base, and the collector. The term is derived from two words, transfer and resistor.

Unitized Distributor: A special magnetic-pulse distributor that combines the distributor, electronic module, pickup coil, distributor cap, and coil into one compact assembly.

Zener Diode: An electronic component that allows current to flow in one direction at all times and in the opposite direction only after a predetermined voltage has been reached. This property enables it to act as a voltage regulator or limiter.

Unit 16 Electronic Ignition System

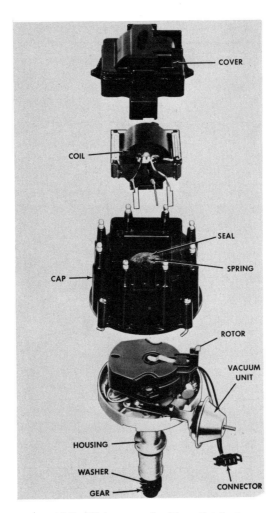

Fig 16-5. High energy ignition distributor

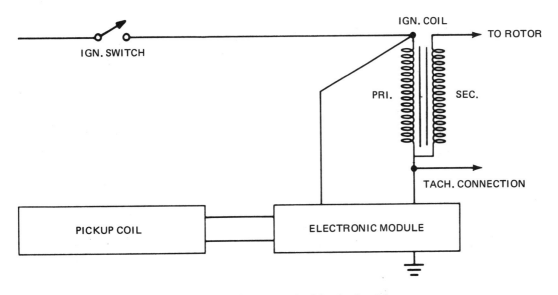

Fig 16-6. High energy ignition basic wiring

Section 3 Electrical Systems

In the following exercises, indicate the best answer by inserting in the blanks the appropriate number, letter, word(s), or calculation, as required.

PICTORIAL REVIEW

A. Identify the parts of the electronic distributor in figure 16-7 by writing their correct names in the blanks.

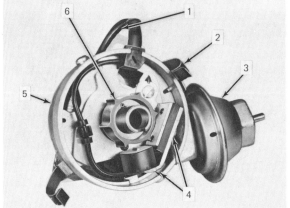

Fig 16-7. Electronic Distributor for a Six-cylinder Engine

1. _____   4. _____
2. _____   5. _____
3. _____   6. _____

B. Identify the parts of the high energy distributor in figure 16-8 by writing the correct letters in the blanks.

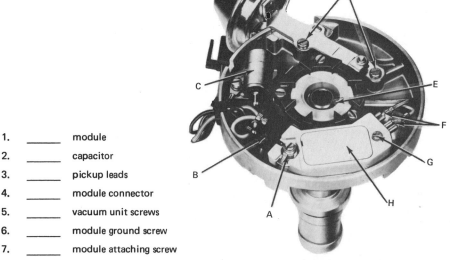

1. _____ module
2. _____ capacitor
3. _____ pickup leads
4. _____ module connector
5. _____ vacuum unit screws
6. _____ module ground screw
7. _____ module attaching screw
8. _____ center "C" washer

Fig 16-8. High-energy Distributor Housing

Unit 16 Electronic Ignition System

SUMMARY REVIEW

____ 1. An amplifier, as used in an electronic circuit, is designed to
   a. resist voltage.　　　c. increase resistance.
   b. limit amperage flow.　d. magnify current or voltage.

____ 2. In a high energy ignition system, the coil is mounted on the
   a. intake manifold.　　c. engine block.
   b. distributor cap.　　d. electronic control unit.

____ 3. A dual ballast resistor regulates current flow to the coil primary winding and the
   a. electronic control unit.　c. spark plug wires.
   b. secondary coil winding.　d. distributor condenser.

____ 4. Compared to a conventional ignition system, the primary coil resistance in an electronic ignition system is
   a. greater.　　c. the same.
   b. less.　　　d. greater in some systems and less in others.

____ 5. The component of an electronic ignition system that is somewhat similar in appearance and location, but not in function, to the distributor cam in a conventional system is called a(n)
   a. capacitor.　　c. impulse coil.
   b. reluctor.　　d. rotor.

6. What electrical properties does a zener diode have that would cause it to be selected and used for a particular electronic circuit.
   _____
   _____

7. Explain what a solid-state device is. _____
   _____

8. Define the term semiconductor. _____
   _____

9. Name the three terminals found on a transistor.
   a. _____　b. _____　c. _____

10. Insert the correct numbers of the matching terms or definitions in the blanks.
   a. ____ solid-state device　1. diode
   b. ____ transistor　　　　　2. condenser
   c. ____ heat sink　　　　　3. electronic module
   d. ____ capacitor　　　　　4. electronic switching device
   e. ____ base circuit　　　　5. gearlike part
   f. ____ control unit　　　　6. grounded to operate transistor
   g. ____ reluctor　　　　　　7. finned aluminum housing

99

Section 3 Electrical Systems

REFERENCE REVIEW

____ 1. Which of the following electronic components allows current to flow through it in either direction?

   a. diode
   b. transistor
   c. resistor
   d. capacitor

____ 2. If the base circuit of certain types of transistors is grounded, current may flow from the

   a. primary to the secondary coil winding.
   b. emitter to the collector.
   c. secondary to the primary coil winding.
   d. collector to the emitter.

____ 3. The advantage(s) of an ignition system using electronic components as compared to a conventional ignition system include which of the following?

   a. less dwell change during operation
   b. less timing change during operation
   c. may fire spark plugs over a longer time
   d. all of the above

____ 4. When making a compression check on a car having a high-energy ignition system, the _____ should be disconnected.

   a. distributor battery wire connector
   b. secondary coil winding
   c. distributor cap wire
   d. vacuum advance line

____ 5. The reluctor triggers the electronic control unit by affecting the magnetic field of the distributor

   a. secondary circuit.
   b. pickup unit.
   c. condenser windings.
   d. ballast resistor.

____ 6. What should be done if tests indicate that the electronic control unit has a defective resistor?

   a. Replace the resistor with one of the same type.
   b. Replace the resistor with one designed for heavy-duty operation.
   c. Replace the entire control unit.
   d. Disconnect the defective resistor and recheck the unit operation.

____ 7. The section of an oscilloscope pattern that is changed most when connected to an electronic ignition system, compared to a conventional system, is the

   a. spark-plug section.
   b. contact-point section.
   c. firing section.
   d. spark section.

Unit 16 Electronic Ignition System

____ 8. The ballast resistor used on certain electronic ignition systems to limit current in the primary coil winding has a resistance of between

a. 0 and 2 ohms.   c. 10 and 20 ohms.
b. 4 and 8 ohms.   d. 25 and 50 ohms.

____ 9. A diode allows current to flow when

a. the current polarity is correct.
b. the base circuit is grounded.
c. it reaches a predetermined temperature.
d. all of the above.

____ 10. Spark plugs may be used for a longer period of time in most electronic ignition systems as compared to conventional systems because they

a. receive less wear.   c. automatically repel deposit
b. may fire under more ad-   buildup
   verse conditions.   d. have steel-plated electrodes.

11. What tool should be used to check the air gap between the reluctor tooth and pickup coil core? _____

12. Underline the components that have no moving parts.

transistor   printed circuit
capacitor   distributor
ignition points   diode

101

UNIT 17 WIRING DIAGRAMS

RELATED AUTOMOTIVE TERMS

Ambient Sensor: A switch having contacts that open and close and, therefore, stop or allow current flow at a predetermined ambient (surrounding) temperature.

Bulkhead Connector: A connector for wires (usually multiple) located where the wires must pass through a partition or lead to another area.

Color-code Chart: Chart listing the colors of wire insulation and, sometimes, the wire sizes for a particular automobile.

Connector: Device used to facilitate the attachment of a wire to a terminal or another wire.

Direct Battery Power: Power available to a circuit in the automobile directly from the battery, without an intermediate switch.

Fuse Panel (Block): An assembly that provides mountings and connections for several fuses which are used to protect individual electric circuits.

Fusible Link: Part of an electric wire or circuit that burns out (melts or opens) when the electric load becomes too great for safe operation.

Grommet: Rubber or plastic eyelet (ring) inserted in a hole to protect wires that pass through it.

Ground Wire: Wire that completes a circuit from an electric load back to the battery.

Harness Clip: Clip used to secure wiring to the car frame or body at various points, thereby providing safe and neat routing.

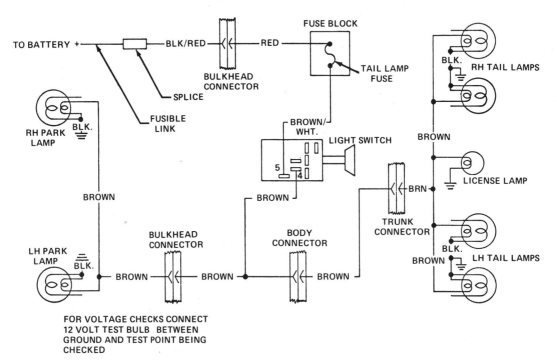

Fig 17-1. Wiring Schematic of a Tail, Park, and License Lamp Circuit

Unit 17 Wiring Diagrams

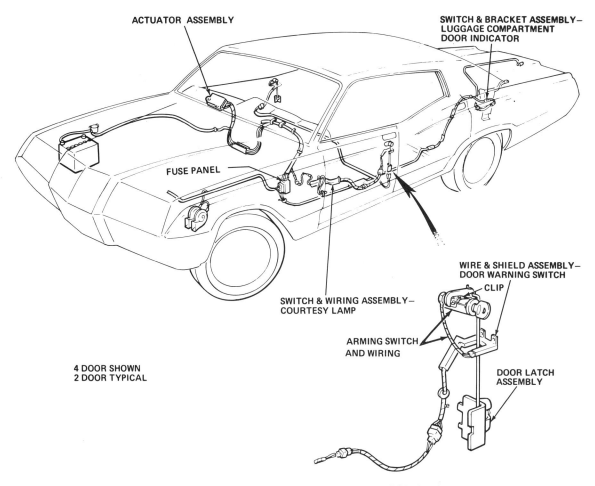

Fig 17-2. Wiring Pictorial of an Antitheft Circuit and Mechanism

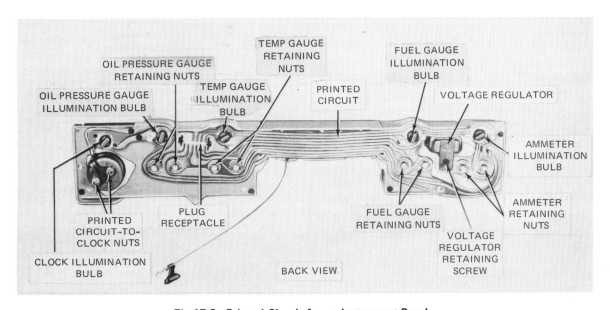

Fig 17-3. Printed Circuit for an Instrument Panel

103

Section 3 Electrical Systems

Hot Wire: Wire that carries current from the ungrounded terminal of the battery to an electric load.

Ignition Switch Power: Power available to a circuit in the automobile only when the ignition switch is closed (on).

Insulation: Material, usually plastic or rubber, wrapped around wire to provide insulating properties.

Junction Box: A box for joining two or more cables or harnesses, and in which groups of individual wires are connected to form junctions.

Pictorial Diagram: A drawing, (often three-dimensional) of the actual layout of electrical parts, wires, and related items, each recognizable by size and shape. Items are shown in their actual relationships to one another.

Printed Circuit: An electric circuit in which the conductors consist of copper strips laid out on a flat, insulating board, thereby reducing the amount of hand wiring required. Advantages are reliability and economy.

Relay: An electromagnetic switch that controls current flow in one circuit and whose operation is controlled by another circuit.

Schematic Diagram: A drawing showing electric components and connecting wires, which are represented by graphic symbols, in one or several circuits. The drawing shows their electrical (but not necessarily their physical) relationships. Sometimes combined with a wiring diagram.

Single-Wire Circuit: A circuit using a single wire and employing metal structures on the automobile, such as the frame or body, as a ground wire.

Solenoid: A cylindrical, hollow-center wire coil energized by a remote current source and having a movable iron core which is placed partially inside the coil. When current is allowed to flow through the coil, a magnetic field is created, causing the core to be pulled farther inside the coil. The mechanical motion of the core may be used in several applications, such as closing contacts or shifting a starter drive gear.

Solid Wire: A conductor consisting of a single wire, usually soft copper.

Splice: The point in a wire circuit where two or more wires in related circuits are connected together.

Stranded Wire: A conductor consisting of several small wires twisted together. It is more flexible than solid wire.

Switch: See Unit 12, p. 72.

Terminal: The point in an electric circuit where a wire is connected to a component.

Test Lamp: See Unit 12, p. 72.

Thermal Switch: A switch that opens or closes a circuit, depending on the temperature surrounding the switch. An example is the sender in the cooling system that completes a circuit to turn on a warning light on the instrument panel if the coolant temperature becomes too high.

Wire Color Code: Solid or striped color identification on the insulation of electric wires.

Wire Gage: The diameter of a wire, identified by a number, such as 6 or 18; the larger the wire number, the smaller the diameter of the wire.

Wiring (Circuit) Diagram: A drawing showing electric components and their interconnecting wiring. The component outlines are often drawn in their true shapes, terminal connections may be shown, and the parts and wires are shown in their physical relationships, using actual wire runs, and showing color codes. Sometimes combined with a schematic diagram.

Wiring Harness: Term denoting several electric wires that are wrapped or lashed together, sometimes with protective tape.

Unit 17 Wiring Diagrams

Wire Placement: Position and routing of wires on an automobile, determined by factory engineers to provide a safe, practical, and economical route.

With Tracer: Term indicating a solid or dashed line of a contrasting color on wire insulation, used for identification purposes where many wires are involved.

In the following exercises, indicate the best answer by inserting in the blanks the appropriate number, letter, word(s), or calculation, as required.

PICTORIAL REVIEW

A. On the wiring schematic in figure 17-4, indicate the four circuits listed below by drawing the designated line codes over the appropriate wiring paths in the schematic:

1. Use the line code — — — — — — to show the ground-wire circuit for the horn button from the relay to ground.

2. Use the line code −o−o−o−o− to show the wires from the relay to the horns.

3. Use the line code ∧∧∧∧∧∧∧ to show all the wires concerned with the ignition-key warning system.

4. Use the line code ∼∼∼∼∼ to show the wire from the power (voltage) source to the relay.

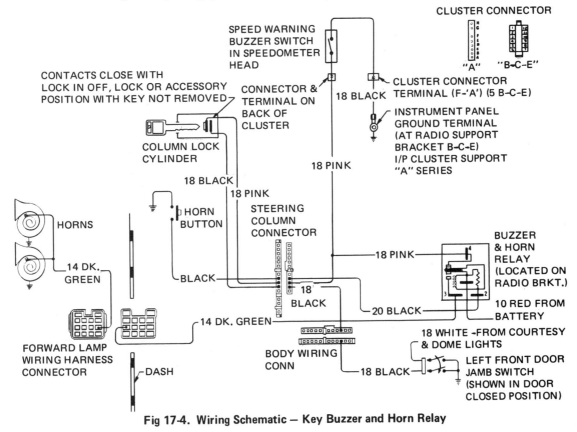

Fig 17-4. Wiring Schematic — Key Buzzer and Horn Relay

Section 3 Electrical Systems

SUMMARY REVIEW

____ 1. A diagram that depicts size and shape is called a _____ diagram.

    a. wiring   c. printed
    b. schematic   d. pictorial

____ 2. Wire insulation is often seen in many different colors for improved

    a. appearance.   c. identification.
    b. current flow.   d. insulation.

____ 3. A color-code chart identifies the

    a. wire length.   c. wire color.
    b. stranded and solid wires. d. insulation color.

____ 4. The main purpose of a printed circuit is to

    a. provide cheaper construction.
    b. eliminate wire congestion.
    c. eliminate most circuit difficulties.
    d. reduce voltage variation due to temperature.

____ 5. On a printed circuit, current is carried by

    a. flat copper strips.   c. stranded wires.
    b. small solid wires.   d. an insulating board.

____ 6. An ambient sensor is sensitive to surrounding

    a. current flow.   c. water pressure.
    b. oil pressure.   d. temperature.

7. Is *solid* or *stranded* copper wire more flexible? _____

8. Does a number 20 wire have a diameter that is *larger* or *smaller* than a number 18 wire? _____

9. Wire insulation is usually made from a material called _____.

10. Insert the correct numbers of the matching terms or definitions in the blanks.

    a. ____ thermal switch   1. completes a circuit from a load to the battery
    b. ____ ground wire   2. circuit protector
    c. ____ single-wire circuit   3. opens or closes a circuit
    d. ____ fusible link   4. multiple disconnect
    e. ____ test lamp   5. car body used as a ground wire
    f. ____ bulkhead connector   6. electromagnetic switch
    g. ____ relay   7. troubleshooting device

Unit 17 Wiring Diagrams

REFERENCE REVIEW

1. Fuse blocks are used to protect _____ automotive circuit(s).

   a. all
   b. one
   c. more than one
   d. a fusible link in

2. The proper solder to use when connecting electric wires together is called

   a. solid core.
   b. acid core.
   c. wire core.
   d. rosin core.

3. A corroded or loose wire in a wiring circuit will increase

   a. resistance.
   b. voltage.
   c. amperage.
   d. all of these.

4. Most automotive grommets are made from

   a. brass.
   b. rubber.
   c. plastic.
   d. steel.

5. Three electrical components that have direct battery power available at their terminals are the starter, horn, and

   a. alternator.
   b. generator.
   c. coil.
   d. dome light.

6. The diameter of a solid number 24 wire is approximately

   a. 0.010 inch.
   b. 0.020 inch.
   c. 0.024 inch.
   d. 0.030 inch.

7. The negative battery cable attaches to the battery and the

   a. engine.
   b. body.
   c. frame.
   d. any of these.

8. The diameter of a solid copper wire may be measured precisely by using a wire gage or a _____.

9. Write the full meaning of the abbreviated wire color code, DK GN/Y Tr _____

10. Name one automotive wire that features stranded construction and one that features solid construction.

    a. stranded: _____
    b. solid: _____

UNIT 18 BATTERIES

RELATED AUTOMOTIVE TERMS

Active Plate Material: The sponge lead spread over the negative plate grid or the lead peroxide spread over the positive plate grid.

Battery Capacity Test (High-discharge or Load Test): A test to determine if the battery voltage will remain above 9.6 under a specified load (usually three times the battery 20-hour rating). A 60-ampere-hour battery should have a 180-ampere load applied for 5 to 15 seconds during this test.

Battery Cell: A section of the battery containing plates, separators, and electrolyte. Each cell in a lead-acid battery produces about two volts.

Battery Charger: Electrical device used for restoring a battery to its original state of charge by passing a current through the battery in a direction opposite to the discharge current flow.

Battery Maintenance: Procedures such as a visual inspection, adding water, cleaning battery top and terminals, tightening hold down, and testing battery.

Battery Rating Methods:

Twenty-Hour Rating: The amount of current a battery can deliver for 20 hours at 80°F without the cell voltage dropping below 1.75 volts. The amount of current in amperes x 20 hours = the number of ampere hours. For example, a battery capable

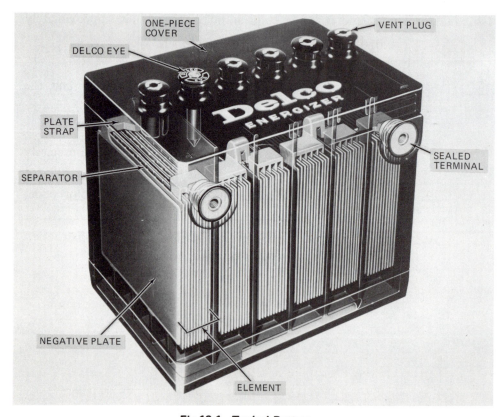

Fig 18-1. Typical Battery

of delivering 3 amperes for 20 hours would be rated at 60 ampere-hours (3 x 20 = 60).

Cold Cranking-power Rating: The number of amperes that a fully charged battery will deliver for 30 seconds at 0°F without the terminal voltage dropping below the minimum needed to start a car (7.2 for a 12-volt battery). This rating method matches battery size to engine size. For example, the minimum battery rating for a 400 CID engine is 400 amperes.

Reserve Capacity Rating: The number of minutes a fully charged battery at 80°F can supply power at 25 amperes to run the ignition, lights, and accessories after a charging system failure or when the engine is not running. A battery with a reserve capacity of 120 would allow a motorist to drive about two hours after charging system failure.

Battery Water: Water used to refill battery cells periodically when the electrolyte has dropped below the recommended level due to evaporation. Distilled water (water containing no minerals) is preferred, but city tap water is usually acceptable.

Booster Battery (Auxiliary Battery, Slave Battery): Battery connected in parallel with a discharged battery in order to start the engine.

Case: Container that holds the battery components.

Cell Connectors: Interconnections between the cells of a battery.

Corrosion: Foreign material that accumulates on or near a battery due to the chemical action of any electrolyte coming in contact with metal such as the battery posts and terminals. This can be removed by scraping, brushing, or applying a solution of baking soda and water.

Direct Current (DC): Electric current that flows in one direction only, such as that pro-

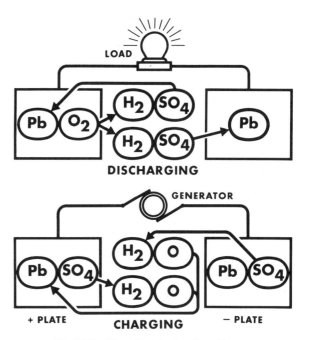

Fig 18-2. Chemical Action in a Battery

duced by a battery. Must also be used to charge a battery.

Dry-charged Battery: Battery having electrolyte added by the dealer at time of sale. It is precharged during manufacture.

Electrolyte: Battery liquid containing sulfuric acid (H_2SO_4) and distilled water (H_2O).

Element: Interwoven assembly of positive and negative plate groups with separators.

Fast Charge: Charging method of supplying a high current flow (40-50 amperes) to a battery for a relatively short period of time.

Hydrogen Gas: Highly explosive gas produced by chemical action inside the battery during charging.

Hydrometer: Tester used to indicate the specific gravity or state-of-charge of a battery.

Lead-acid Storage Battery: Electrochemical device that stores chemicals capable of producing electricity to operate the starter and ignition system until the engien starts. Current is also supplied by the battery when the accessory load is greater than the alternator output, or when the engine is not running.

Lead Sulfate (PbSO$_4$): Chemical formed on the battery plates during discharge, acting to reduce efficiency and power.

Negative Plate: Battery plate containing porous lead (Pb) as the active material. Automotive batteries have one more negative plate per cell than the number of positive plates.

Negative Terminal (Post): Smaller of the two battery connections, marked by a minus symbol (–) or painted black. Usually, this is the ground post.

Plate Grid: Framework of the plates, made of lead alloy, upon which the active plate material is retained.

Positive Plate: Battery plate containing lead peroxide (PbO$_2$) as the active material.

Positive Terminal (Post): Larger of the two battery connections, marked by a plus symbol (+) or painted red. Usually, this is the *hot* post.

Sealed Battery (Maintenance-free Battery): Battery employing construction techniques that make periodic maintenance unnecessary.

Self Discharge: Tendency of most batteries to discharge gradually when not in constant use.

Separators: Insulating material, usually consisting of rubber, plastic, or wood, placed between each two battery plates.

Side-terminal Battery: Battery having its terminal connections on the side rather than the top.

Slow Charge: Charging method of supplying a low current flow (4 amperes or less) to a battery, for a long period of time. This is the preferred method of charging a battery.

Specific Gravity: Term referring to the relative weight of a given volume of a substance (in this case, electrolyte) as compared to the weight of an equal volume of water. In other words, it is the density of the electrolyte as compared to the density of water. The specific gravity of the electrolyte in a fully charged battery should be between 1.260 and 1.280.

Temperature Correction: Numerical adjustment to the specific gravity reading, calculated by adding 0.004 for each 10°F increment above 80°F and by subtracting 0.004 for each 10°F increment below 80°F.

Trickle Charger: A battery charger with a very low output, used by dealers to keep batteries charged before they are sold.

Wet-charged Battery: Battery having electrolyte added by the factory at time of manufacture.

In the following exercises, indicate the best answer by inserting in the blanks the appropriate number, letter, word(s), or calculation, as required.

PICTORIAL REVIEW

A. Identify each part of the battery shown in figure 18-3 by writing the corresponding letter in the blanks.

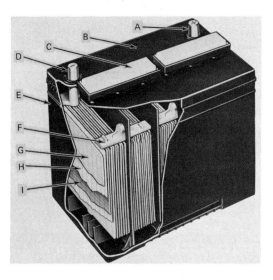

Fig 18-3. Parts of a Battery

1. ____ negative plate
2. ____ cover
3. ____ positive plate
4. ____ vent plug
5. ____ separator
6. ____ positive post
7. ____ plate strap
8. ____ case
9. ____ negative post

B. Indicate, by writing in the numbered blanks, the chemical substances that are decreasing and increasing in the plates and electrolyte.

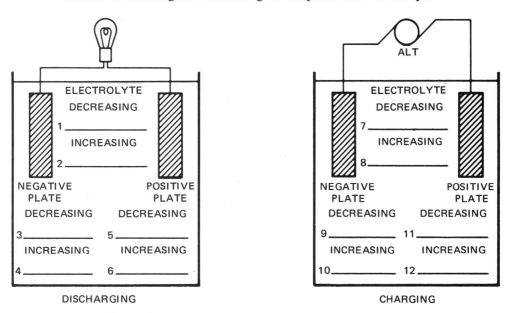

Fig 18-4. Battery Discharge and Charge

SUMMARY REVIEW

____ 1. A battery element contains positive plates, negative plates, and

    a. separators.   c. sulfuric acid.
    b. electrolyte.   d. a container.

____ 2. The negative post of a battery may be identified by which of the following physical characteristics?

    a. smallest post   c. post marked (+)
    b. post painted red   d. all of these

____ 3. A battery capacity test involves placing a load across the terminal posts in an amount that is _____ its ampere-hour rating and then checking the voltage.

    a. equal to   c. three times
    b. twice   d. four times

____ 4. The temperature corrections for a specific gravity reading taken at 120°F. is obtained by

    a. adding 0.020.   c. adding 0.016.
    b. subtracting 0.012.   d. subtracting 0.016.

Section 3 Electrical Systems

___ 5. The preferred battery charging method is known as a _____ charge.

    a. fast   c. trickle
    b. slow   d. quick

___ 6. During battery discharge, part of the surface material on the positive plate changes into

    a. Pb.   c. PbO_4.
    b. PbO_2.   d. $PbSO_4$.

___ 7. During battery charge, the electrolyte becomes

    a. cold.   c. lighter.
    b. depleted.   d. heavier.

8. Give the names and (symbols) for each of the four chemicals inside an automotive battery.

    a. _____ (____)   c. _____ (____)
    b. _____ (____)   d. _____ (____)

9. Name four battery maintenance procedures that will increase the effective life of a battery.

    a. _____   c. _____
    b. _____   d. _____

10. Insert the correct numbers of the matching terms or definitions in the blanks.

    a. ___ fast charger   1. painted black
    b. ___ trickle charger   2. used for batteries in dealers' stock
    c. ___ negative post
    d. ___ positive post   3. active material on positive plate
    e. ___ sponge lead   4. plate framework
    f. ___ lead peroxide   5. painted red
    g. ___ grid   6. high-rate charger
                                         7. active material on negative plate

REFERENCE REVIEW

___ 1. An automotive battery stores

    a. magnetism.   c. heat energy.
    b. chemicals.   d. electricity.

___ 2. The open-circuit voltage of a six-cell automotive storage battery is

    a. slightly more than 12 volts.   c. exactly 12 volts.
    b. slightly less than 12 volts.   d. close to 14 volts.

3. The most popular battery capacity rating in past years has been the
   a. cold rate.
   b. watts rating.
   c. cold discharge rate.
   d. 20-hour rate.

4. An automotive battery at 32°F. has about what percent of its rated power?
   a. 100%
   b. 90%
   c. 75%
   d. 65%

5. Battery plate sulfation occurs primarily because of
   a. a charging rate that is too high.
   b. hot weather.
   c. continuous low-charge operation.
   d. cycling.

6. The number of positive plates in an automotive storage battery is
   a. the same as the number of negative plates.
   b. more than the number of negative plates.
   c. less than the number of negative plates.
   d. varies according to the manufacturer.

7. A battery having a specific gravity reading of 1.170 (25% charged) will freeze near
   a. 32°F.
   b. 20°F.
   c. 0°F
   d. −10°F.

8. If all battery cells continually use an excessive amount of water, the problem usually involves
   a. the charging rate.
   b. a cracked case.
   c. the type of water used.
   d. the battery size or capacity.

9. To activate a dry-charged battery, the automotive technician should add
   a. water.
   b. acid.
   c. premixed electrolyte.
   d. electrolyte mixed on the job.

10. Battery cells are connected in
    a. parallel-series.
    b. series-parallel.
    c. series.
    d. parallel.

11. If electrolyte comes in contact with your skin (or gets in your eyes), *immediately* flush the area with _____ and call a physician.

12. A recently charged automotive storage battery may explode if a spark or flame occurs nearby because inside the battery a gas called _____ is formed.

13. What is the temperature-corrected reading for a specific gravity of 1.260 if taken at 50°F? _____

113

UNIT 19 ALTERNATORS

RELATED AUTOMOTIVE TERMS

Alternating Current (ac): Current that changes direction (alternates) periodically as it flows in an electric circuit.

Alternator: Generator that produces alternating current (ac) and changes it to direct current (dc) for use in the electrical system of an automobile.

Bearings: Components located in the end frames of an alternator to provide a low-friction support for the revolving rotor.

Brush: Carbon part that contacts the rotor slip ring to deliver battery current to the rotating winding.

Capacitor (Condenser): Electrical device designed to dampen peak voltages, protect diodes, and reduce radio interference caused by the alternator and ignition system. A capacitor is capable of accepting and storing an electrical charge. See also Unit 13, p. 77.

Current Regulation: Output control provided for in the design of alternators. External current control is unnecessary.

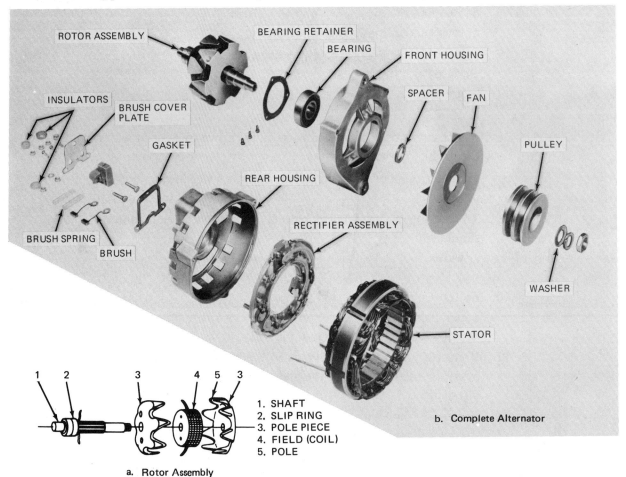

a. Rotor Assembly

1. SHAFT
2. SLIP RING
3. POLE PIECE
4. FIELD (COIL)
5. POLE

b. Complete Alternator

Fig 19-1. Exploded View of an Alternator

Unit 19 Alternators

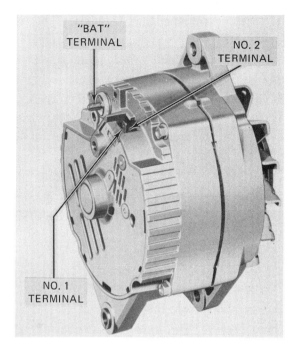

Fig 19-2. Alternator with Integral Transistorized Regulator

Delta-connected Stator: Term describing a stator connection consisting of three sets of windings connected together to resemble a triangle, or the Greek letter delta (△) when represented on a schematic. Each of the three junctions of the separate stator windings connects to wires leading to diodes.

Diode: Component having polarity selectivity which allows current to flow easily in one direction but resists current flow in the opposite direction, thereby acting as an electronic check valve. One application is rectifying (converting) ac to dc.

Diode Testing: Method of checking a diode for proper operation, open, or short. May be checked with an ohmmeter, test lamp, or special diode tester.

Electromagnetic Induction: The process of creating current in a wire by moving the wire through a magnetic field.

Electronic Voltage Regulator (Transistorized Regulator): Voltage regulator containing solid-state components. This device is mount-

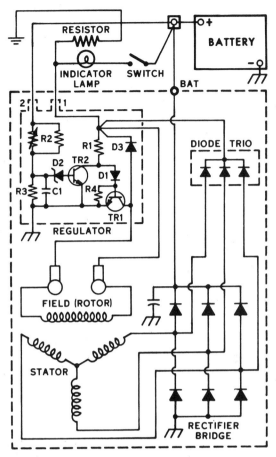

Fig 19-3. Schematic Diagram of an Integral Charging System

ed either in the alternator or in a remote location.

End Frame: Front or rear housing of an alternator which supports or contains various components.

Fan (Alternator): A disc having fins or blades that force air through the alternator for cooling purposes as the disc revolves with the rotor.

Field Current: Current flow through a rotor, usually 2 or 3 amperes, used to produce a magnetic field that induces current in the stator windings. Field current is varied to regulate alternator output.

Heat Sink: Heat dissipating section that holds the insulated diodes or all the diodes, and carries heat away from the devices.

115

Section 3 Electrical Systems

Integral Charging System: Alternator having a built-in, solid-state voltage regulator.

Output Current: Current induced in the stator winding by the rotor magnetic field, changed from ac to dc by rectifying diodes.

Polarity (Magnetic): Property describing the orientation of the North (N) and South (S) poles of a magnet or magnetic field.

Polarizing: Process of permitting a momentary surge of current to pass through a *dc generator*, thereby insuring correct polarity in the pole shoes. DO NOT POLARIZE AN ALTERNATOR unless permitted by special instructions. In an alternator, polarization occurs automatically as current is sent through the rotor windings when the ignition switch is turned on. The output polarity is controlled by the diodes.

Poles: The projecting fingers interspersed along the circumference of each of the pole pieces that comprise the rotor assembly. All the fingers (usually six) on one pole piece are N poles, while those on the other are S poles. When the pole pieces are assembled, the fingers form alternate N and S poles.

Pulley: A wheel attached to the rotor shaft and used to transmit power by means of a drive belt passing over a V-groove on its outer edge.

Rectifier: A diode that changes ac to dc.

Rotor: Rotating part consisting of (in most alternators) the field winding and the alternate N and S poles.

Semiconductor: Name given to a class of electronic parts that conduct electricity under certain conditions. For example, diodes and transistors.

Slip Rings: Smooth copper rings located on the rotor shaft or rotor side. Brushes rubbing against these rings connect the battery current to the rotor field winding.

Stator: The stationary output winding assembly of an alternator, consisting of a laminated steel core and usually three separate windings that fit into slots in the core.

Three Phase: Term referring to a stator winding that consists of three separate sets of coils.

Voltage Regulator: Electrical device used to control the maximum alternator voltage output by regulating the flow of electricity in the field circuit.

Wye-connected Stator: Term describing a stator connection consisting of three sets of windings which resemble the letter Y when represented on a schematic. One end of each of the separate stator windings is connected together, while the other ends connect to wires leading to diodes. (See, for example, figure 19-3.)

In the following exercises, indicate the best answer by inserting in the blanks the appropriate number, letter, word(s), or calculation, as required.

PICTORIAL REVIEW

A. Identify the alternator parts in figure 19-4 by writing their correct names in the blanks.

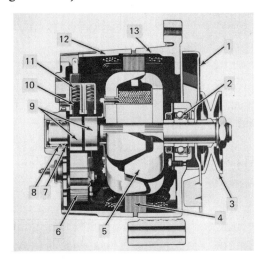

Fig 19-4. Alternator

Unit 19 Alternators

1. _____   8. _____
2. _____   9. _____
3. _____   10. _____
4. _____   11. _____
5. _____   12. _____
6. _____   13. _____
7. _____

SUMMARY REVIEW

____ 1. The alternator output is varied by controlling the

    a. stator current.   c. stator voltage.
    b. diode polarity.   d. field current.

____ 2. The external alternator output control regulates

    a. resistance.   c. voltage.
    b. current.   d. temperature.

____ 3. Both alternator brushes make electrical contact with the

    a. stator.   c. commutator.
    b. rotor N and S poles.   d. slip rings.

____ 4. The brushes of a 40-ampere alternator usually have _____ amperes flowing through them.

    a. 2 to 4   c. 11 to 35
    b. 6 to 10   d. 40 or more

____ 5. During normal operation, diodes may

    a. change polarity.   c. regulate maximum voltage.
    b. become warm.   d. regulate maximum amperage.

____ 6. Diodes may be mounted in the alternator

    a. end frame.   c. rectifying bridge.
    b. heat sink.   d. any of these.

____ 7. Diode testing should include checking for proper operation, shorts, and

    a. grounds.   c. voltage.
    b. opens.   d. all of these.

    8. List two functions of the alternator capacitor.

    a. _____
    b. _____

Section 3 Electrical Systems

9. Name two ways in which stators are connected into the circuit.
   a. _____   b. _____

10. Under what condition, if any, would an automotve technician polarize an alternator? _____

11. Insert the correct numbers of the matching terms or definitions in the blanks.

   a. ____ rectifier   1. capacitor
   b. ____ condenser   2. cools diode
   c. ____ slip ring   3. diode tester
   d. ____ rotor   4. field winding
   e. ____ heat sink   5. diode
   f. ____ transistor   6. semiconductor
   g. ____ ohmmeter   7. brush contact

REFERENCE REVIEW

____ 1. The alternator part that electrically takes the place of the generator field is called the

   a. rotor.   c. heat sink.
   b. diodes.   d. stator.

____ 2. High-output alternators usually have more windings in the

   a. field.   c. stator.
   b. rotor.   d. armature.

____ 3. Rotor slip rings with slight grooves should be

   a. replaced.   c. sanded with emery cloth.
   b. turned in a lathe and   d. filed smooth.
      sanded.

____ 4. Stator wires are connected to the diode leads by a threaded nut or

   a. magnetic induction.   c. plastic connectors.
   b. proper polarity.   d. solder.

____ 5. The voltage at the external output terminal of an automotive alternator with the engine stopped is

   a. 12 volts.   c. 0 volts.
   b. 14 volts.   d. variable depending on the manufacturer.

____ 6. The output of an alternator having a defective diode will be

   a. reduced.   c. stopped entirely.
   b. unchanged.   d. increased.

7. List two reasons explaining why an alternator may produce more current at low engine speed than a generator.

   a. _____

   b. _____

8. Name three things that can cause diode damage.

   a. _____

   b. _____

   c. _____

9. Name three devices that may be used to test diodes.

   a. _____

   b. _____

   c. _____

10. The total number of N and S poles in an alternator is usually
    _____

11. Will an ohmmeter test of a rotor in good condition indicate (a) *high* or *low* resistance across the slip rings and (b) *high* or *low* resistance from a slip ring to the rotor shaft?

    a. _____   b. _____

UNIT 20 STARTING SYSTEMS

RELATED AUTOMOTIVE TERMS

Armature: Rotating motor part containing many loops of heavy wire wound around an iron core and connected to the commutator segments.

Armature Servicing: Procedure that involves turning the commutator in a lathe until smooth, undercutting the mica (insulation between commutator bars) 1/32 inch if required, sanding with a nonconducting abrasive such as a flint-paper strip, checking for alignment, shorts, or grounds, and inspecting the shaft bearing surfaces.

Bendix Folo-Thru Drive: Starter drive engaged by initial rotation of the armature that causes drive pinion to be twisted outward on a threaded sleeve until meshed with the flywheel gear. Folo-Thru mechanism maintains engagement of gears until a predetermined speed (about 400 rpm) is reached. Then it disengages automatically.

Brushes: Parts that make electrical contact with the commutator of the rotating armature. Two brushes are insulated from ground (hot) and two are grounded. Brushes are made primarily of copper with some graphite added.

Brush Holder: Insulated or grounded metal support holding brushes in an alignment to contact commutator properly.

Bushing: Support for rotating armature, one located in each end frame. Usually made from bronze.

Commutator: An assembly of insulated copper segments attached to armature windings, that make electrical contact with the brushes.

Current-draw Test: Test that determines amperes consumed by starter motor during operation.

Field Coils: Heavy copper windings around pole shoes; usually four in a starter. The windings may be connected in series, parallel, or series-parallel.

Field Housing: Starter-motor shell containing field windings and pole shoes.

Gear Reduction: Gear ratio between starter-motor pinion gear and flywheel gear. Armature speed and crankshaft speed total ratio varies

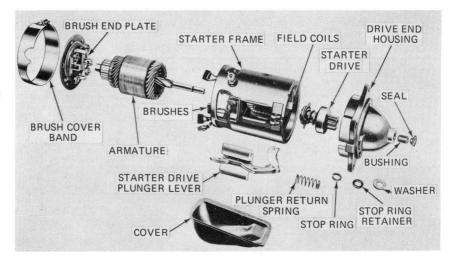

Fig 20-1. Exploded View of a Typical Starter Motor

120

Unit 20 Starting Systems

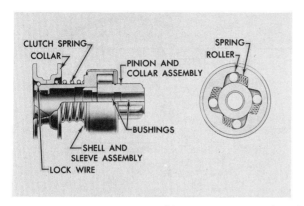

Fig. 20-2. Starter Drive Unit (Overrunning-clutch Type)

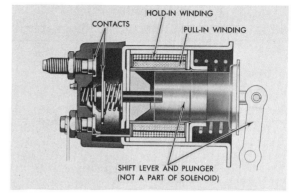

Fig 20-3. Starter Solenoid

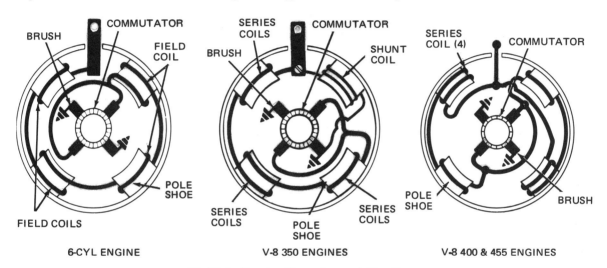

Fig 20-4. Starting Motor Internal Circuits

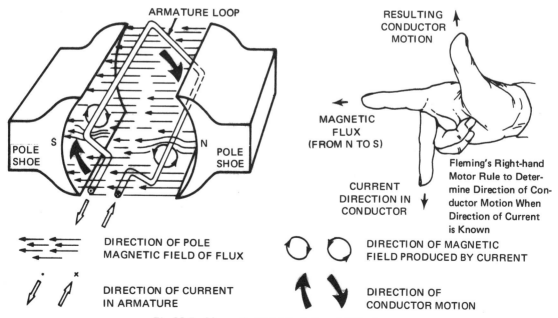

Fig 20-5. Magnetic Field Rotational Effect

Section 3 Electrical Systems

from about 15 to 1 on direct-drive starters to 45 to 1 on those having an internal gear reduction.

Ignition Resistor Bypass: Circuit (on certain models) leading from starter magnetic switch to ignition-coil primary input terminal for bypassing resistance in primary circuit during cranking.

Left-hand Rule for Coils: Rule used with the electron theory of current flow to determine the pole shoe (or core) polarity when the current-flow direction is known. Place the fingers of the left hand around the wire coil so that they point in the direction of current flow. The thumb now points toward the North pole.

Left-hand Rule for Current-carrying Conductor: Rule used to determine the direction of the magnetic field around a current-carrying conductor when the current-flow direction in a coil is known. Place the fingers of the left hand around the conductor so that the thumb points in the direction of current flow. The fingers then point in the direction of the magnetic field around the conductor.

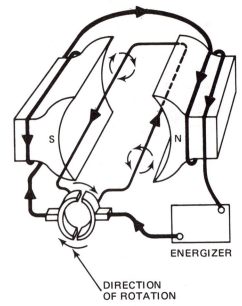

Fig 20-6. Basic Starter Motor Internal Electrical Circuits

No-load Test: Test that determines rpm of removed starter by using a mechanical tachometer having a rubber-tipped shaft placed on drive end of armature shaft.

Overrunning Clutch Drive: Starter drive engaged by mechanical linkage having spring-loaded balls or rollers that wedge on a ramp,

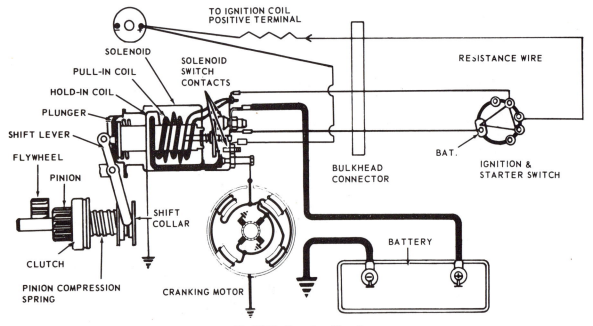

Fig 20-7. Starting Circuit

122

Unit 20 Starting Systems

providing a positive drive engagement until flywheel spins pinion gear faster than starter does, causing it to free-wheel.

Pole Shoes: Soft iron cores around which the field windings are wound. Each pole shoe becomes a strong magnet when current flows through its winding. Each has a North and a South pole.

Right-hand Rule for Motors (Fleming's Right-hand Rule): Rule used to determine the direction of armature rotation. Position the forefinger of the right hand to point in the direction of the field flux (considered to be N to S). The middle finger points in the direction of current flow in the conductor. The thumb then indicates the direction of conductor motion, figure 20-5.

Shunt Field Winding: Single parallel winding usually connected across two or three series windings; a common way of increasing starting torque and limiting maximum armature speed.

Stall-torque Test: Test that determines pound-feet of torque developed by armature when restrained from rotating by a special measuring instrument attached to the drive pinion gear. Stall amperage draw may also be checked during this test.

Starting Circuit: Electric components used in cranking the engine during starting, such as battery, starter motor, control switches, wiring, and relay or solenoid.

Starter (Cranking Motor): Special electric motor designed for the purpose of cranking engine for starting.

Starter Neutral Switch: Safety switch that keeps the starting circuit open between the ignition switch and starter magnetic switch unless the transmission gear selector is in park or neutral on an automatic transmission, or the clutch pedal is fully depressed on a manual transmission.

Starter Relay: Magnetic switch that closes the electric circuit to the starter. It is operated by the ignition switch.

Starter Solenoid: Magnetic switch that shifts the starter drive pinion gear into the flywheel ring gear, then closes the electric circuit to the starter. It is operated by the ignition switch.

Voltage-drop Test: A test that determines the voltage drop in circuit components such as cables and switches.

In the following exercises, indicate the best answer by inserting in the blanks the appropriate number, letter, word(s), or calculation, as required.

PICTORIAL REVIEW

A. Identify each part of the starter in figure 20-8 by writing the correct letters in the blanks.

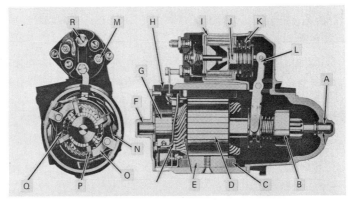

Fig 20-8. Starter

123

Section 3 Electrical Systems

1. ____ overrunning clutch
2. ____ solenoid plunger
3. ____ rubber grommet
4. ____ brush spring
5. ____ ignition-switch terminal
6. ____ battery terminal
7. ____ brush
8. ____ insulated brush holder
9. ____ commutator
10. ____ armature
11. ____ front bushing
12. ____ field coil
13. ____ pole shoe
14. ____ shift lever
15. ____ solenoid
16. ____ grounded brush holder
17. ____ rear bushing
18. ____ plunger return spring

B. Indicate the correct series-parallel circuitry by completing the following exercise (refer to figure 20-4).

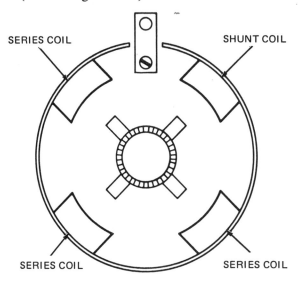

Fig 20-9. Starter Motor Internal Circuit

1. Trace in the internal wiring to show the three series field windings with a solid pencil line (———) and the one shunt field winding with a dashed pencil line (– – – –). Connect wires to hot brushes.

2. Draw the ground symbol on two brushes.

3. Indicate by four arrows the direction of field-current flow around all pole shoes.

4. Mark *N* or *S* to indicate the polarity on the inside and outside of each pole shoe. Use the *left-hand rule*.

SUMMARY REVIEW

____ 1. A starter armature rotates because of magnetic

    a. brushes.   c. attraction.
    b. opposition.   d. switches.

Unit 20 Starting Systems

____ 2. Gear reduction between the drive pinion gear and flywheel ring gear is near

   a. 2 to 1. c. 15 to 1.
   b. 10 to 1. d. 45 to 1.

____ 3. A shunt field winding in a starter has the purpose of aiding starting torque and

   a. limiting armature rpm.   c. increasing circuit resistance.
   b. reducing current   d. protecting the magnetic switch.
      consumption.

____ 4. Starter field windings are wound around a soft iron core called the

   a. armature.   c. laminations.
   b. commutator. d. pole shoes.

____ 5. On most automatic transmission-equipped cars, starting circuit current flows directly from the ignition switch to the

   a. starter neutral switch. c. solenoid.
   b. relay.   d. starter.

____ 6. Tests that may easily be conducted on an installed starter include

   a. current draw. c. no-load rpm.
   b. stall.   d. all of these.

____ 7. During armature servicing, the commutator should be sanded with

   a. wet or dry paper. c. aluminum oxide paper.
   b. flint paper.   d. emery cloth.

8. The gear ratio between the armature and crankshaft on starters having an internal gear reduction is about _____ to _____.

9. The starter magnetic switch is remotely operated by the _____.

10. Insert the proper numbers of the matching terms or definitions in the blanks.

   a. ____ field coil   1. heavy copper wire
   b. ____ pole shoe   2. circuit-resistance check
   c. ____ commutator   3. rpm of removed starter
   d. ____ voltage-drop test   4. copper segments attached to
   e. ____ no-load test   armature windings
   f. ____ undercutting   5. armature service operation
           mica   6. starter torque check
   g. ____ stall test   7. soft iron

125

Section 3 Electrical Systems

REFERENCE REVIEW

____ 1. The ignition resistor bypass circuit operates when the ignition switch is in what position?

   a. on or run
   b. accessory
   c. start
   d. off

____ 2. The most popular starter drive in use today is the

   a. Bendix.
   b. Folo-Thru.
   c. shunt.
   d. overrunning clutch.

____ 3. Starter solenoids usually have two windings called *hold-in* and

   a. primary.
   b. secondary.
   c. pull-in.
   d. field.

____ 4. If a starter drive is defective, it should be

   a. repaired.
   b. replaced.
   c. removed for further testing.
   d. cleaned in solvent and rechecked.

____ 5. Starter bearings should be lubricated

   a. during chassis lubrication.
   b. when disassembled.
   c. once a year.
   d. every 12,000 miles.

____ 6. The device most often used to test for armature winding shorts is a

   a. test lamp.
   b. voltmeter.
   c. ammeter.
   d. growler.

____ 7. A high-amperage reading during a current-draw test could be caused by

   a. grounded field windings.
   b. excessive copper brush deposits along insulated brush holder.
   c. a tight engine.
   d. all of the above.

____ 8. Starter magnetic switches with two small terminals have one wire going to the ignition switch and the other going to a transmission switch or

   a. lighting circuit.
   b. alternator.
   c. coil primary circuit.
   d. battery.

____ 9. A starter that begins to crank the engine but does not continue cranking until the engine starts probably has a defective

   a. drive.
   b. magnetic switch.
   c. brush.
   d. armature.

____ 10. A starter that requires turning the ignition key to "start" several times before operating probably has a defective

   a. drive.   c. brush.
   b. magnetic switch.   d. armature.

____ 11. Armatures that test shorted should be checked for copper deposits between commutator riser bars or be

   a. turned in a lathe.   c. replaced
   b. resoldered.   d. revarnished.

____ 12. The purpose of the visible spring on the overrunning clutch-type starter drive is to

   a. assist gear meshing if necessary.
   b. allow drive to overrun.
   c. retract drive gear when engine starts.
   d. demesh gears when ignition key is released.

SECTION 4 Emission Controls

UNIT 21 POSITIVE CRANKCASE VENTILATION

RELATED AUTOMOTIVE TERMS

Automobile Emissions: Certain impurities that may enter the atmosphere during vehicle operation, usually considered to be:

HC (hydrocarbons): Unburned fuel emitted to the atmosphere. Sources are the crankcase breathing system, exhaust system, and evaporative losses from the fuel tank and carburetor. Hydrocarbons aid in the formation of photochemical smog.

CO (carbon monoxide): Colorless, odorless, invisible gas that is a byproduct of combustion. It is emitted from the exhaust system and dissipates rapidly into the atmosphere, but is dangerous to health in large concentrations.

NO_x (oxides of nitrogen): Byproducts of combustion, created when oxygen and nitrogen unite from combustion chamber heat and pressure. May combine with unburned hydrocarbons, forming photochemical smog.

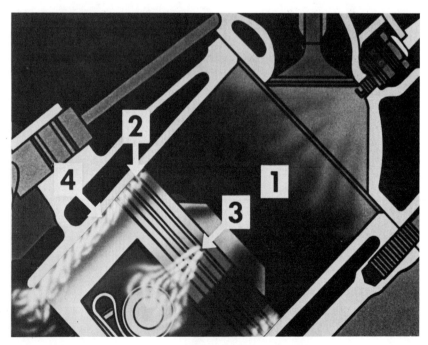

1. High Combustion-chamber Pressure
2. Piston-ring Groove Clearance
3. Piston-ring End Gap
4. Reduced Ring-contact Area as Piston Changes Direction

Fig 21-1. Engine Blow-by Causes

Unit 21 Positive Crankcase Ventilation

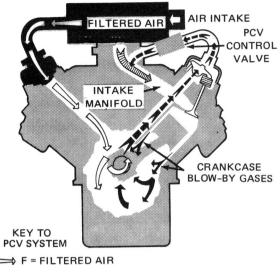

Fig 21-2. PCV System Schematic

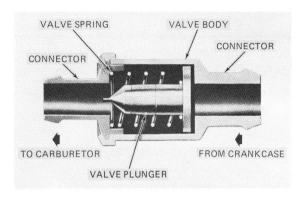

Fig 21-3. PCV Valve

PCV VALVE, IDLING OR LOW-SPEED OPERATION

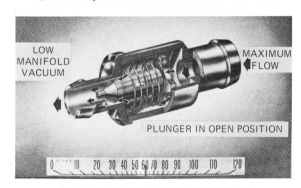

PCV VALVE, HIGH-SPEED OPERATION

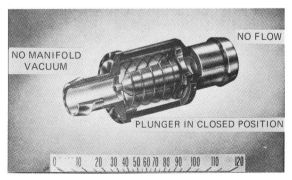

PCV VALVE, ENGINE OFF OR BACKFIRE

Fig 21-4

Backflow: The flow of fumes back out through the crankcase air-inlet system that the PCV valve cannot handle. Direction of flow is opposite from normal operation and may occur in badly worn engines, during high-speed acceleration that causes increased blow-by and low engine vacuum, or when the PCV valve or hose becomes clogged.

Blow-by: High-pressure gases that escape from the combustion chamber past the piston and piston rings into the crankcase during the compression and power strokes.

Closed PCV System: System that requires the fresh air coming into the crankcase to enter by way of the air cleaner instead of through the breather cap, filler tube, and dipstick tube, which are sealed shut. Any backflow enters the air cleaner for recycling, rather than escaping to the atmosphere. Installed on 1968 and newer cars.

Crankcase: The lower section of the engine, inside which the crankshaft rotates. Area confined by the lower block casting and the oil pan.

Crankcase Emissions: Fumes that leave the crankcase by way of a ventilation system.

Section 4 Emission Controls

Crankcase Fumes: Vapors inside the crankcase that could contaminate the air. They include unburned fuel vapors, water vapor, or blow-by gases. Vapors that are not removed by ventilation may condense and form crankcase sludge or dilute the oil.

Crankcase Ventilation: Process of engine vacuum drawing off crankcase fumes (impure air) while fresh air simultaneously enters through a filter. The fumes and vapors are recycled into the intake manifold for burning in the cylinders with the fresh incoming air-fuel mixture.

Crankcase Ventilation Filter: Small filter through which the intake air and backflow air pass. It is located inside or near the air cleaner.

Hydrocarbon Emissions: Discharges from the operation of an automobile engine consisting of vaporized unburned gasoline.

Intake Air: Fresh air drawn into the crankcase by the ventilation system.

Open PCV System: System that has the incoming air entering the crankcase by way of the breather cap on the oil filler tube. Backflow enters the atmosphere after filtering out through the breather cap. Used on most 1963 to 1967 cars.

PCV Hoses: Neoprene rubber hoses connected to one or both ends of a PCV valve. May need periodic internal cleaning.

PCV (Positive Crankcase Ventilation) System: Entire positive crankcase ventilation system including the PCV valve, connecting hoses, fittings, and attachments. Crankcase fumes are removed in a positive manner because the system is powered by engine vacuum.

PCV Valve: Vacuum influenced metering valve that controls the flow of crankcase fumes in the PCV system. The valve allows more flow at high speed than at low speed, and acts as a system shutoff in case of engine backfire to prevent an explosion in the crankcase. PCV valve needs periodic cleaning and/or replacement.

Pollution: The contamination of the environment by automobile emissions and other sources. The maximum vehicle emission limits, in grams per mile, are set by the U.S. EPA (Environmental Protection Agency).

Smog: Term derived from the words "smoke" and "fog." Automobile caused smog occurs when vehicle emissions unite chemically with various atmospheric elements during certain atmospheric conditions.

In the following exercises, indicate the best answer by inserting in the blanks the appropriate number, letter, word(s), or calculation, as required.

PICTORIAL REVIEW

A. Identify the PCV valve components or flow directions in figure 21-5 by writing their names or letters in the blanks.

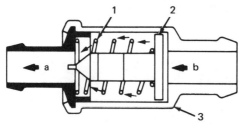

Fig 21-5. PCV Valve

Unit 21 Positive Crankcase Ventilation

1. _____   4. _____ from crankcase
2. _____   5. _____ to carburetor
3. _____

B. Identify which Figure (6A or 6B) shows the PCV system during *normal idling* and *cruising-speed operation* and which shows it during *heavy acceleration* or *high-speed operation*; then, label each appropriately in the blanks.

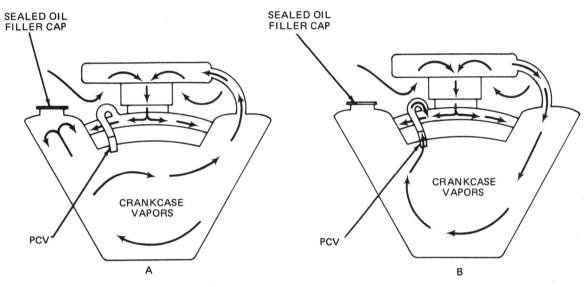

Fig 21-6. PCV System Operation

1. _____   2. _____
   _____   _____

SUMMARY REVIEW

_____ 1. Fumes inside the crankcase may consist of

    a. fuel vapor.   c. water vapor.
    b. blow-by gases.   d. all of these.

_____ 2. The closed PCV system is installed on

    a. all used cars.   c. all new cars.
    b. most 1963 to 1967 cars.   d. none of these.

_____ 3. The PCV valve is located between the

    a. intake manifold and carburetor.
    b. carburetor and air cleaner.
    c. crankcase and intake manifold.
    d. intake manifold and air cleaner.

Section 4 Emission Controls

____ 4. Operation of the PCV system is controlled by

    a. engine vacuum.
    b. system temperature.
    c. a solenoid.
    d. crankcase pressure.

____ 5. A reduced amount of fresh air is drawn into the ventilation system

    a. if the PCV valve is clogged.
    b. during acceleration.
    c. if the engine is badly worn, lowering vacuum.
    d. all of the above.

____ 6. Blow-by enters the engine crankcase past the

    a. valve guides.
    b. pistons and rings.
    c. PCV valve.
    d. breather cap.

____ 7. Backflow in the ventilation system is most likely to occur during

    a. high-speed acceleration.
    b. engine idling.
    c. normal operation.
    d. high-speed deceleration.

____ 8. In case of an engine backfire in the intake manifold, the PCV valve

    a. disintegrates.
    b. closes.
    c. opens wide.
    d. plunger moves to the center position.

9. List three different emissions that result from automobile operation which, if uncontrolled, may pollute the atmosphere.

    a. _____
    b. _____
    c. _____

10. Name two problems that occur in the crankcase if the fumes are not removed.

    a. _____
    b. _____

11. Insert the correct numbers of the matching terms or definitions in the blanks.

    a. ____ crankcase fumes
    b. ____ smoke and fog
    c. ____ PCV
    d. ____ crankcase
    e. ____ backflow
    f. ____ low vacuum occurs
    g. ____ high vacuum occurs

    1. smog
    2. at high speeds
    3. reverse flow of inlet air
    4. positive crankcase ventilation
    5. impure air
    6. lower engine section
    7. at lower speeds

REFERENCE REVIEW

___ 1. The pollution limits that may be emitted from most new automobiles are usually set by the

    a. car manufacturers.   c. state governments.
    b. EPA.   d. city governments.

___ 2. Manufacturers recommend that most PCV valves be replaced under ideal operating conditions

    a. once a month.   c. every two years.
    b. every 1000 miles.   d. every 6000 miles.

___ 3. What is the position of the PCV valve plunger at high speed?

    a. toward the valve outlet side   c. near the valve center
    b. toward the valve inlet side   d. shut off

___ 4. What is the position of the PCV valve plunger at idle speed?

    a. near the valve center   c. toward the valve inlet side
    b. toward the crankcase   d. toward the valve outlet side

___ 5. The PCV valve inlet side is connected to the

    a. crankcase.   c. air cleaner.
    b. intake manifold.   d. carburetor float bowl.

___ 6. In a closed PCV system, the backflow fumes enter the _____ immediately after leaving the crankcase.

    a. carburetor   c. air cleaner
    b. intake manifold   d. atmosphere

___ 7. In an open PCV system, the backflow fumes enter the _____ immediately after leaving the crankcase.

    a. intake manifold   c. air cleaner
    b. atmosphere   d. carburetor

___ 8. The outer body sections of most PCV valves are _____ together.

    a. threaded   c. welded
    b. crimped   d. cemented

___ 9. A new, original equipment PCV valve usually sells for about

    a. fifty cents.   c. two dollars and fifty cents
    b. one dollar.   d. five dollars.

Section 4 Emission Controls

10. Underline the eight terms that best describe the action during idle and high speeds.

	Throttle Position	Engine Compression	Engine Vacuum	Engine Blow-by
Idle Speed:	open closed	higher lower	higher lower	higher lower
High Speed:	open closed	higher lower	higher lower	higher lower

UNIT 22 CARBURETOR EMISSION CONTROLS

RELATED AUTOMOTIVE TERMS

Air Cleaner Thermostat: Temperature-sensitive device that directly or indirectly determines the position of the hot-cold air supply damper valve. The thermostat may be a bulb-type or vacuum-motor type, (having a bimetallic sensor).

Altitude-compensating Carburetor: Carburetor that has the capability of supplying a certain air-fuel mixture regardless of atmospheric pressure at various heights above sea level.

Carburetor Deceleration (Decel) Valve: Special device installed on certain models that allows a small amount of air-fuel mixture to flow to the intake manifold for a few seconds during deceleration (engine slowdown). The decel valve is powered by high vacuum. Operation of this valve allows more complete combustion.

Carburetor Emission Devices: Items attached on or adjacent to the carburetor for the purpose of establishing operating conditions that will lower exhaust emissions.

Dieseling (Run-on) (After-run): Term referring to a situation where the engine continues to run after the ignition switch has been turned off. Two causes of dieseling are high idle speeds and high operating temperatures.

Electrically Assisted Choke: Choke assembly that has an electric heating element that warms the choke bimetallic coiled thermostat spring, thus opening the choke valve more quickly than normal under certain temperature conditions, such as above 60°F.

Fresh Air Inlet Tube: Duct system that allows cooler ambient (surrounding) air to be drawn into the air cleaner from outside the engine compartment after engine warm-up, used on certain models.

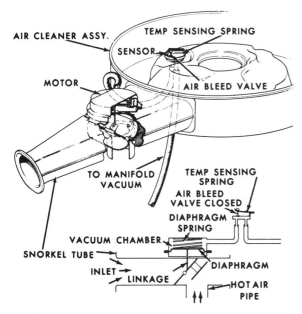

Fig 22-1A. Thermostatically Controlled Air Cleaner — Vacuum-motor Type, Cold-engine Operational Mode

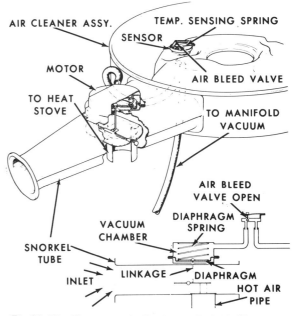

Fig 22-1B. Thermostatically Controlled Air Cleaner — Vacuum-motor Type, Hot-engine Operational Mode

Section 4 Emission Controls

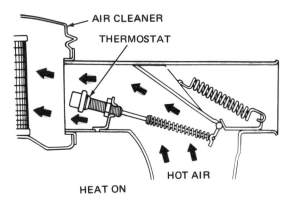

Fig 22-2A. Thermostatically Controlled Air Cleaner — Thermostatic-bulb Type, Cold-engine Operational Mode

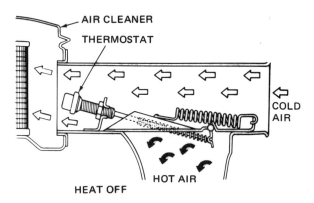

Fig 22-2B. Thermostatically Controlled Air Cleaner — Thermostatic-bulb Type, Hot-engine Operational

Heat Stove (Heat Exchanger) (Heat Shield): Sheet metal surrounding an exhaust manifold which acts as a collector for the hot air that flows to the air cleaner through a hot-air duct.

Hot-air Duct (Shroud): Sheet-metal tubing that carries hot air from the exhaust manifold heat stove to the air cleaner.

Idle-mixture Screw Limiter Caps: Plastic caps snapped on the idle-mixture screw heads. The caps feature projecting tangs (tabs) to limit turning that could cause an over-rich mixture.

Idle-passage Restriction: Small tube or needle inserted in idle passageway to meter (limit) idle air-fuel mixture flow, regardless of external adjusting-screw position, on certain models.

Idle-stop Solenoid (Throttle Solenoid): An electric solenoid that has a plunger which extends when the ignition switch is on, causing the throttle lever to hold the throttle valve partially open and allow a relatively high idle speed. The plunger retracts when the ignition switch is "off," closing the throttle valve to ensure that the engine will stop running.

Lean Mixture: Air-fuel mixture containing a minimum amount of fuel. The mixture may be as lean as 18 to 1 (18 parts of air to 1 part of fuel, by weight) at certain speeds. Lean mixtures burn hotter and cleaner.

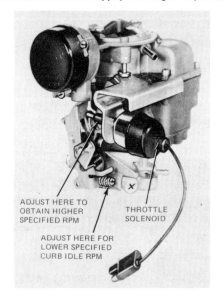

Fig 22-3. Throttle Idle-stop Solenoid

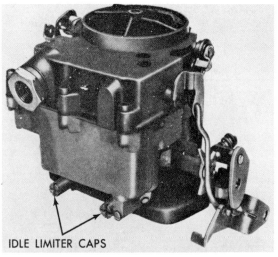

Fig 22-4. Idle Limiter Caps

Unit 22 Carburetor Emission Controls

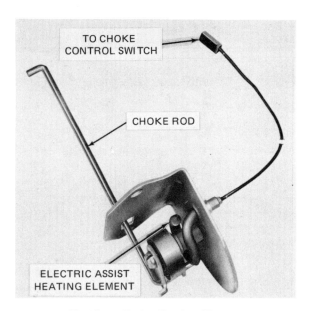

Fig 22-5. Choke Heating Element

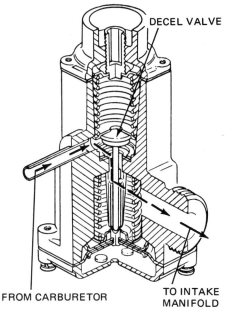

SECTIONAL VIEW
(VALVE SHOWN IN OPEN POSITION)

Fig 22-6. Deceleration Valve

Lean Roll: Term referring to turning adjustable idle-mixture screws inward enough to effect a slight rpm drop, causing a leaner mixture.

Thermostatically Controlled Air Cleaner (Heated-air System): Air cleaner featuring thermostatic devices and controls that can blend the hot and cold air supply, keeping the carburetor incoming-air temperature near or above 100°F. This allows a leaner mixture during warm-up, reduces carburetor icing, promoting better fuel vaporization, and improves driveability.

Vacuum Motor: Vacuum-actuated device that controls the hot-air duct damper valve on certain models. An internal diaphragm attaches to the damper-valve linkage.

In the following exercises, indicate the best answer by inserting in the blanks the appropriate number, letter, word(s), or calculation, as required.

PICTORIAL REVIEW

A. Identify the termostatically controlled air cleaner assembly components in figure 22-7 by writing their correct letters in the blanks.

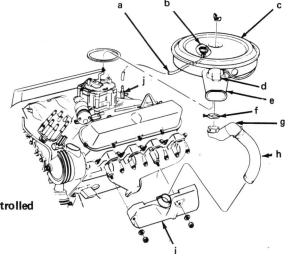

Fig 22-7. Thermostatically Controlled Air Cleaner Assembly

137

Section 4 Emission Controls

1. ____ heat tube
2. ____ vacuum motor
3. ____ intake manifold tee
4. ____ air cleaner assembly
5. ____ duct adapter
6. ____ snorkel tube
7. ____ vacuum source hose
8. ____ heat shield
9. ____ temperature sensor
10. ____ clamp

SUMMARY REVIEW

____ 1. The thermostatically controlled air cleaner functions to blend heated and cooler air, keeping carburetor air temperature above

    a. 100°F.
    b. 140°F.
    c. 160°F.
    d. 180°F.

____ 2. The plunger of an idle-stop solenoid is retracted when the

    a. ignition switch is on.
    b. ignition switch is off.
    c. engine is running.
    d. car is in motion.

____ 3. The purpose of idle-mixture screw limiter caps is to

    a. prevent lean mixtures.
    b. increase hydrocarbon emissions.
    c. prevent rich mixtures.
    d. prevent idle-speed adjustments.

____ 4. The heat from an electrically assisted type choke affects the

    a. choke bimetallic spring.
    b. vacuum motor.
    c. damper valve.
    d. choke vacuum piston.

____ 5. The decel valve, on models so equipped, operates during

    a. periods of low vacuum.
    b. engine acceleration.
    c. certain underload temperatures.
    d. engine slowdown.

____ 6. Lean roll refers to the carburetor _____ adjustment.

    a. choke
    b. hot-idle speed
    c. curb-idle speed
    d. idle mixture

7. Does the number 15 in a 15 to 1 ratio, by weight, refer to the amount of *fuel* or the *air*? _____

8. List two conditions that cause "dieseling."

    a. _____
    b. _____

Unit 22 Carburetor Emission Controls

9. Name four engine-operating benefits obtained from the thermostatically controlled air cleaner.

   a. _____
   b. _____
   c. _____
   d. _____

10. Insert the correct numbers of the matching terms or definitions in the blanks.

    a. ____ idle-stop solenoid   1. heat exhanger
    b. ____ dieseling   2. throttle solenoid
    c. ____ heat stove   3. carburetor deceleration
    d. ____ to meter   device
    e. ____ decel valve   4. leaner mixture
    f. ____ 15 to 1   5. limit flow
    g. ____ 8 to 1   6. run-on
                                    7. richer mixture

REFERENCE REVIEW

____ 1. If the underhood air temperature reaches 150°F, the air-cleaner damper valve, on an operating engine is in the _____ position.

   a. midway open   c. down
   b. up   d. left side

____ 2. During acceleration of a cold engine having a thermostatically controlled air cleaner with a vacuum motor and air bleed valve,

   a. the damper valve remains stationary.
   b. the vacuum-motor spring shortens.
   c. more cooler air will enter carburetor.
   d. more heated air will enter carburetor.

____ 3. Vacuum supplied to the vacuum motor when the air-bleed valve on the temperature sensor opens

   a. is increased slightly.   c. remains the same.
   b. is reduced.   d. is increased a large amount.

____ 4. The curb-idle speed (slower idle position) on a carburetor having an idle-stop solenoid must be adjusted with the

   a. electric wire disconnected.   c. engine turned off.
   b. choke closed.   d. vacuum hose disconnected.

139

Section 4 Emission Controls

____ 5. Electrically assisted choke operation is designed to warm the choke bimetallic spring if the temperature is
   a. below 0°F.
   b. below freezing.
   c. between 20°F and 40°F.
   d. over 60°F.

____ 6. The idle-stop solenoid plunger contacts the _____ during operation.
   a. fast-idle cam
   b. fast-idle adjusting screw
   c. automatic choke
   d. throttle lever

____ 7. Operation time of a decel valve should be between
   a. 1 and 5 seconds.
   b. 8 and 20 seconds.
   c. 30 and 50 seconds.
   d. over one minute.

8. Name three ways engine "dieseling" can be reduced or prevented.
   a. _____
   b. _____
   c. _____

9. What is the name of a tool that helps the technician see whether the damper door on an installed snorkel tube is functioning properly when the direct view is obstructed?
   _____

10. Describe how the temperature-sensing device, in an air cleaner that features a vacuum motor, operates to allow only colder air to enter the carburetor.
    _____
    _____
    _____

11. Idle-screw limiter caps are usually made from a _____ material.

UNIT 23 DISTRIBUTOR CONTROL SYSTEMS

RELATED AUTOMOTIVE TERMS

Ambient Temperature Switch: Switching device that relates outside ambient (surrounding air) temperature to the vacuum control solenoid valve or electronic amplifier. This switch closes an electric circuit above 65°F. It is often located in the front door pillar (post).

Carburetor Vacuum: Ported vacuum obtained from a carburetor source above the throttle plate. It is present after the throttle is partially open. The vacuum raises as the throttle opening increases.

Dual-action Vacuum Advance-retard Unit: A distributor vacuum advance having separate chambers on each side of the diaphragm(s) for spark retard and spark advance. Manifold vacuum allows spark retard at idle and low speed thereby reducing exhaust emissions. Carburetor vacuum allows spark advance above low speed, improving economy.

Electronic Spark Control System: Special system having an electronic control module (amplifier) that receives input from a temperature switch and speed sensor, then reacts to electrically operate a spark vacuum-control solenoid. The spark advance receives vacuum under conditions that reduce hydrocarbon and carbon monoxide exhaust emissions.

Electronic Speed Sensor: Device that permits an electronic-control module to be sensitive to vehicle speed. It may be operated by the speedometer cable.

Intake-manifold Vacuum: Direct vacuum obtained from a source below the throttle plate. Highest vacuum is available during closed-throttle (idle) operation.

Spark Advance: Refers to timing the ignition sparks earlier in relationship to crankshaft rotation.

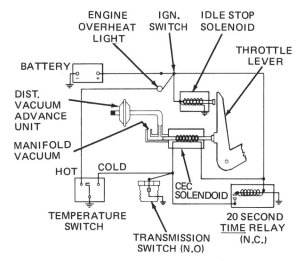

Fig 23-1. Transmission Controlled Spark System

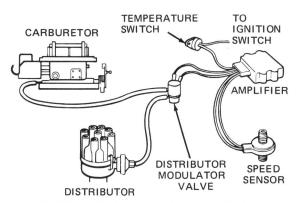

Fig 23-2. Electronic Spark Control System

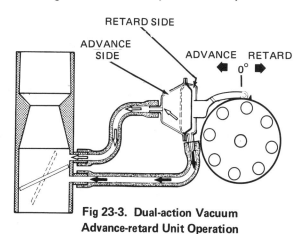

Fig 23-3. Dual-action Vacuum Advance-retard Unit Operation

Section 4 Emission Controls

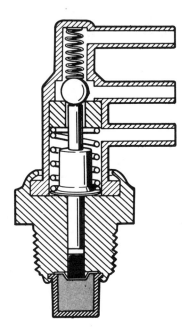

Fig 23-4. Distributor Thermal Vacuum Control Valve

Fig 23-5. Combined Emission Control Solenoid

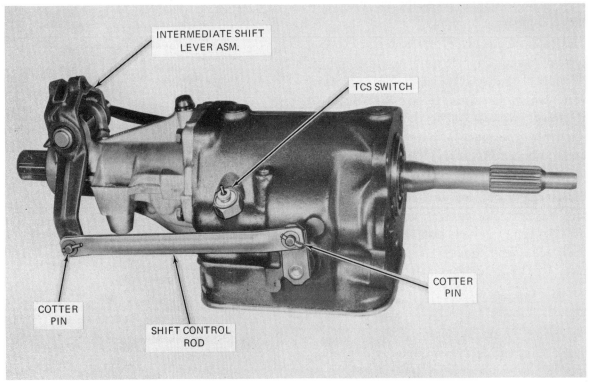

Fig 23-6. Installed Transmission Controlled Spark Switch

Unit 23 Distributor Control Systems

Spark-delay Valve: Special valve that delays spark advance by slowing (restricting) the airflow in the distributor vacuum advance hose. It provides closer control of emissions and improves cold driveability.

Spark Retard: Refers to timing the ignition sparks later in relationship to crankshaft rotation.

Thermal Vacuum Control Valve: Special valve operated by coolant temperature that determines whether carburetor or intake manifold vacuum is supplied to the vacuum advance. The higher intake-manifold vacuum is supplied only during engine-overheat conditions.

Transmission-controlled (Regulated) Spark Advance: System composed of various devices, including a transmission switch, that allow vacuum spark advance to occur only in the highest transmission gear. This reduces hydrocarbon and carbon monoxide exhaust emissions.

Transmission Controlled Spark Solenoid: Electric solenoid that opens or closes the vacuum circuit to the vacuum advance. Input is received from the temperature sensor and transmission switch to determine mode (operational phase).

Vacuum Advance: Vacuum operated device that matches the amount of spark advance or retard with throttle opening and/or operating conditions. Operation causes the distributor breaker plate to rotate or pivot. Mounted on the side of the distributor.

Vacuum Operated Sensing Valve: Special valve that connects the lower carburetor vacuum to distributor advance during normal operation, then switches to higher intake-manifold vacuum during deceleration; used only on certain applications.

In the following exercises, indicate the best answer by inserting in the blanks the appropriate number, letter, word(s), or calculation, as required.

PICTORIAL REVIEW

A. Identify the various distribution control-system components in figure 23-7 by writing the correct figure number and letter of each in the blanks.

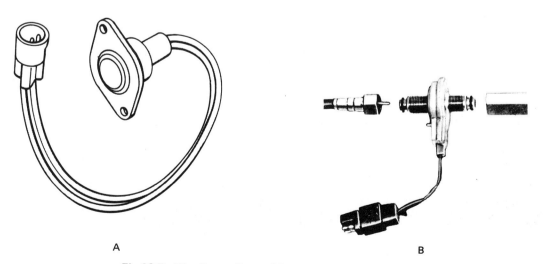

Fig 23-7. Distributor Control System Components

Section 4 Emission Controls

C

D

E

F

FIG 23-7. Continued

____ 1. transmission switch, TCS (CEC) system
____ 2. ambient-temperature switch
____ 3. thermal vacuum control valve
____ 4. vacuum-advance solenoid, TCS system
____ 5. dual-action vacuum advance-retard units
____ 6. speed sensor

SUMMARY REVIEW

____ 1. Intake manifold vacuum is highest when the

    a. engine is idling.   c. deceleration occurs.
    b. throttle is partially open.   d. throttle is fully open.

____ 2. Carburetor vacuum is obtainable when

    a. deceleration occurs.   c. the engine is idling.
    b. the throttle is closed.   d. the throttle is partially open.

____ 3. The location of the vacuum retard port on a dual-action advance is

    a. away from the distributor.   c. pointing downward.
    b. toward the distributor.   d. the same as the advance port.

Unit 23 Distributor Control Systems

___ 4. A thermal vacuum control valve is operated by
   a. ambient temperature.
   b. engine coolant temperature.
   c. a solenoid.
   d. the ignition switch.

___ 5. A thermal vacuum control valve allows full intake-manifold vacuum to the spark advance during
   a. engine starting.   c. engine-overheat conditions.
   b. freeway driving.   d. low-temperature operation.

___ 6. A transmission spark-control switch allows advance
   a. in the highest gear.   c. during low-speed operation.
   b. during acceleration from   d. when the engine is warm.
      a stop.

___ 7. The ambient temperature switch is often located in the
   a. engine cooling system.   c. carburetor.
   b. distributor.   d. vehicle door post.

8. Dual-diaphragm distributor retard vacuum is obtained from the
_____

9. An ambient temperature switch closes the electric circuit if the surrounding air is above _____ degrees Fahrenheit.

10. Insert the correct numbers of the matching terms or definitions in the blanks.
   a. ___ carburetor vacuum   1. operational phase
   b. ___ ambient   2. has one connecting wire
   c. ___ CEC solenoid   3. has more than one connect-
   d. ___ intake-manifold   ing wire
          vacuum   4. direct vacuum
   e. ___ regulated   5. controlled
   f. ___ idle-stop solenoid   6. ported vacuum
   g. ___ mode   7. surrounding

REFERENCE REVIEW

___ 1. Air polluting exhaust emissions are highest during
   a. cruising speed.   c. high speed
   b. idle speed and deceleration. d. idle speed only.

___ 2. Vacuum advance operation on late-model distributors as compared with earlier models is
   a. about the same.   c. delayed.
   b. increased at idle.   d. increased in total amount.

Section 4 Emission Controls

___ 3. If a vacuum retard is featured, maximum spark retard occurs with the engine operating at

   a. cruising speed.
   b. idle and low speed.
   c. highest speed.
   d. all of these

___ 4. The maximum number of vacuum spark retard degrees on distributors so equipped is between

   a. 0 and 4.
   b. 5 and 15.
   c. 16 and 19.
   d. 20 and 25.

___ 5. On systems featuring a spark retard, the retard becomes entirely ineffective at about _____ rpm.

   a. 600
   b. 800
   c. 1,000
   d. 1,400

___ 6. The distributor-advance port of a thermal vacuum control valve is the connection located at the valve

   a. inner end.
   b. center section.
   c. outer end.
   d. any of these

___ 7. Override operation of the thermal vacuum control valve occurs when engine temperature nears

   a. 180°F.
   b. 195°F.
   c. 212°F.
   d. 220°F.

___ 8. An ambient-temperature switch receives electricity from the

   a. electronic amplifier.
   b. solenoid valve.
   c. ignition switch.
   d. transmission switch.

___ 9. The vehicle-speed sensor, on cars so equipped, is usually installed on the

   a. speedometer cable.
   b. transmission.
   c. engine.
   d. distributor.

___ 10. The total number of distributor centrifugal advance degrees in recent years has

   a. remained about the same.
   b. caused vacuum retard on most distributors.
   c. reduced greatly.
   d. increased greatly.

___ 11. The engine will start easier if a way is provided during cranking for

   a. PCV operation.
   b. spark retard.
   c. spark advance.
   d. choke release.

UNIT 24 AIR INJECTION SYSTEM

RELATED AUTOMOTIVE TERMS

Air Injector Pump: Rotary vane pump that supplies pressurized air for injection at each exhaust valve port. Most pumps have two or three vanes.

Air Injector System: Engine emission control system that injects fresh air at each exhaust port. The injected air mixes with the hot exhaust gases, prolonging combustion which reduces hydrocarbon and carbon monoxide exhaust emissions.

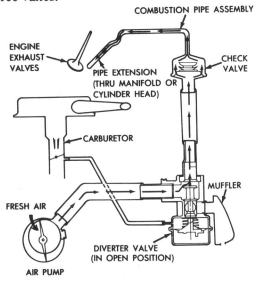

Fig 24-1A. Air Injection System Operational Schematic During Normal Driving and Acceleration

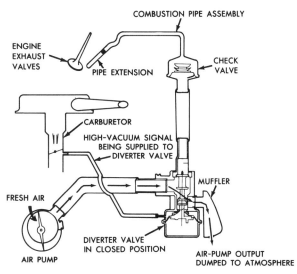

Fig 24-1B. Air Injection System Operational Schematic During Deceleration

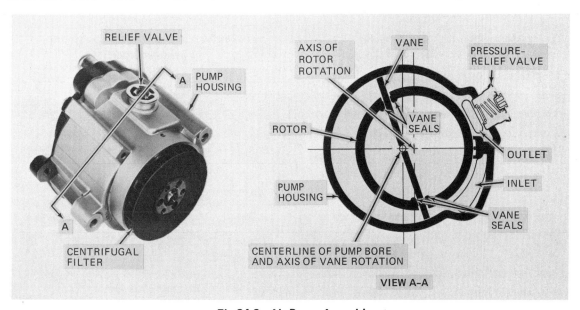

Fig 24-2. Air Pump Assembly

Section 4 Emission Controls

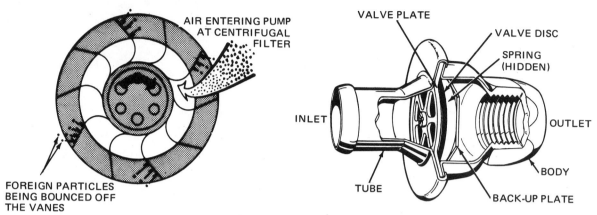

Fig 24-3. Centrifugal Filter Operation

Fig 24-4. Check Valve Assembly

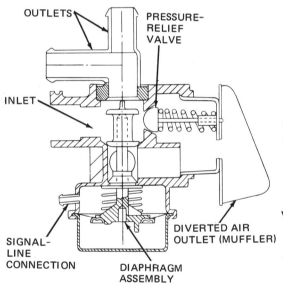

Fig 24-5A. Diverter Valve Assembly, External-muffler Type

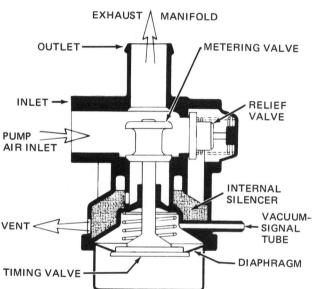

Fig 24-5B. Diverter Valve Assembly, Internal-muffler Type

Air Manifold: System that distributes low-pressure air to each exhaust port. Distribution passages may be externally visible or may be inside cylinder head.

Centrifugal Filter: Revolving air filter that causes dirt particles to bounce off curved vanes, allowing centrifugal force to propel dirt out of the pump. The filter is located behind drive pulley.

Check Valve: One-way valve in air distribution system preventing backflow of exhaust gases into the air pump in case of pump failure, drive belt failure, or engine backfire.

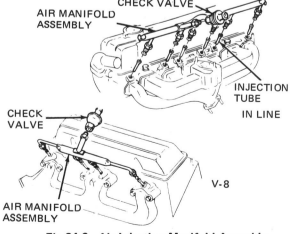

Fig 24-6. Air Injection Manifold Assembly

Unit 24 Air Injection System

Diverter (Bypass) Valve: Normally closed valve that opens during initial engine deceleration and diverts pumped air from the injection system to the atmosphere. A diverter valve eliminates backfire in exhaust system that would occur if the temporary overrich mixture in the manifold is ignited when decelerating. This valve is operated by high intake manifold vacuum.

Injector Nozzle: System component containing the orifice (hole) that meters (controls) pressurized airflow into each engine exhaust port. The nozzles are located in cylinder head or exhaust manifold.

Pressure Relief Valve: Valve that functions to relieve pump output pressure that exceeds a predetermined amount. It usually operates at speeds over 45 mph and is located in pump or on diverter valve.

Silencer (Muffler): Component that muffles (quiets) the sound of air emitted from the diverted valve during deceleration, or pressure relief valve during high speed operation, on certain models.

In the following exercises, indicate the best answer by inserting in the blanks the appropriate number, letter, word(s), or calculation, as required.

PICTORIAL REVIEW

A. Identify the air injection system components in figure 24-7 by writing their correct names in the blanks.

Fig 24-7. Air Injection System

1. _____
2. _____
3. _____
4. _____
5. _____
6. _____

Section 4 Emission Controls

B. Identify the diverter-valve components or areas in figure 24-8 by writing the correct letter in the blanks.

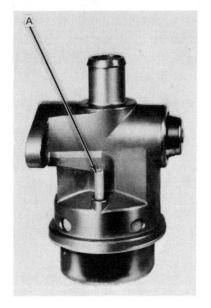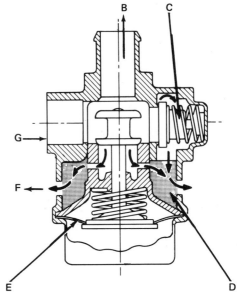

Fig 24-8. Diverter Valve Assembly

1. ____ internal silencer
2. ____ bypass air vent
3. ____ outlet to exhaust manifold
4. ____ intake manifold hose port
5. ____ diaphragm
6. ____ inlet from air pump
7. ____ pressure relief valve

SUMMARY REVIEW

____ 1. The air-pump internal mechanisms causing air to move are called

    a. gears.
    b. eccentrics.
    c. inner and outer rotors.
    d. vanes.

____ 2. The centrifugal filter is located near the pump

    a. center section.
    b. front.
    c. rear.
    d. top.

____ 3. The main purpose of the diverter valve is to

    a. lean out the mixture.
    b. prevent exhaust system backfire.
    c. close the check valve.
    d. prevent intake system backfire.

____ 4. Diverter valves operate to expel air from the injection system during

    a. low speed.
    b. high speed.
    c. acceleration.
    d. deceleration.

Unit 24 Air Injection System

____ 5. The air distribution system to each engine exhaust port may be located
   a. internally only.
   b. externally only.
   c. either internally or externally.
   d. in the intake manifold.

____ 6. The check valve is located closest to the
   a. air manifold.
   b. air pump.
   c. diverter valve.
   d. pressure-release valve.

____ 7. The pressure relief valve reduces pressure from the
   a. air pump.
   b. intake manifold.
   c. diverter outlet.
   d. exhaust manifold.

8. What two air pollutants are reduced by the operation of an air-injection system?
   a. _____   b. _____

9. Name three possible conditions that make a system check valve necessary.
   a. _____   c. _____
   b. _____

10. List two components on which the pressure relief valve may be located.
    a. _____   b. _____

11. Insert the correct numbers of the matching terms or definitions in the blanks.
    a. ____ check valve
    b. ____ vanes
    c. ____ diverter valve
    d. ____ nozzle location
    e. ____ muffler
    f. ____ airflow during deceleration
    g. ____ airflow during acceleration

    1. located on diverter valve
    2. bypass valve
    3. directly into atmosphere
    4. in cylinder head or exhaust manifold
    5. one-way valve
    6. located inside air pump
    7. directed into exhaust ports

REFERENCE REVIEW

____ 1. Air injection into the engine exhaust ports causes the
   a. exhaust manifold to operate cooler.
   b. exhaust manifold to function as an after-burner.
   c. gas mileage to increase.
   d. PCV system to work better.

Section 4 Emission Controls

_____ 2. An air pump operates

    a. when the magnetic clutch is on.
    b. during acceleration.
    c. whenever the engine is running.
    d. during deceleration.

_____ 3. An air pump having defective shaft bearings should be

    a. replaced with a new one.
    b. removed and repaired.
    c. replaced with a rebuilt one.
    d. lubricated more often.

_____ 4. The pump centrifugal filter

    a. must be replaced periodically.
    b. must be cleaned periodically.
    c. is located inside the pump.
    d. is self-cleaning.

_____ 5. A diverter valve is operated by

    a. intake manifold vacuum.   c. the air pump.
    b. exhaust manifold pressure.   d. exhaust manifold vacuum.

_____ 6. The vanes of a centrifugal filter are

    a. curved.   c. round.
    b. flat.   d. S-shaped.

_____ 7. The belt driven air pump

    a. is thermostatically controlled.
    b. emits high air pressure.
    c. operates on demand.
    d. emits low air pressure.

8. Air is emitted through the silencer during what two engine operational phases?

    a. _____   b. _____

9. What condition causes backfire in the exhaust system if the diverter valve becomes inoperative?

_____

_____

10. Pressure relief valves may open at speeds above _____ mph.

11. Does the air-pump shaft usually revolve *faster* or *slower* than the engine crankshaft? _____

UNIT 25   EVAPORATIVE CONTROLS

RELATED AUTOMOTIVE TERMS

Aluminum Heat Dissipator: Flat aluminum heat shield that extends outward from just below the carburetor base on certain models. This keeps some of the engine heat from reaching the carburetor, thus reducing gasoline vaporization inside float bowl.

Canister Filter: Part that cleans air drawn through the charcoal bed by engine vacuum to remove (purge) collected fuel vapors. It is usually located at top or bottom of canister; replaceable on certain models.

Canister Purge Line: Tubing connected between the charcoal canister and carburetor, air cleaner housing, or crankcase ventilation hose. Carries stored vapors into the engine intake system.

Carburetor Internal Vent(s): Vent system used to remove fuel vapors from the float bowl for mixing with the incoming air-fuel mixture. Carburetors no longer have external vents such as idle vents or float-bowl vents open to the atmosphere.

Charcoal Canister: Container filled with activated charcoal granules (porous form of carbon). The charcoal absorbs fuel (hydrocarbon) vapors, primarily when engine is turned off. Granules can absorb several times their

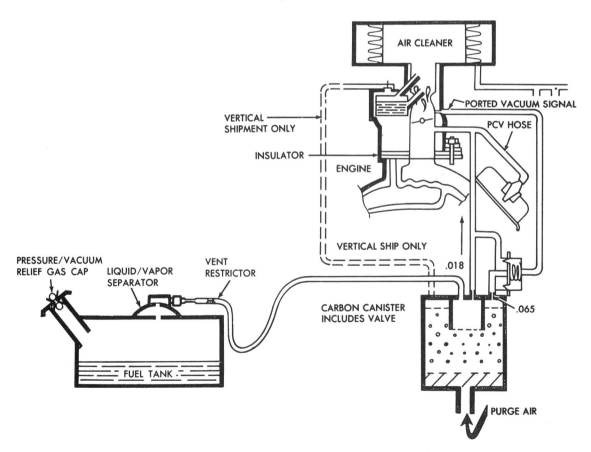

Fig 25-1. Evaporative Control System, Staged-purge Type

153

Section 4 Emission Controls

own weight in vapors. Connecting hoses may attach to a liquid-vapor separator, carburetor, and/or engine intake system. The canister is usually located in engine compartment.

Check Valve: Device preventing liquid gasoline from flowing out of liquid-vapor separator into carbon canister, regardless of vehicle position, on certain models.

Constant Purge Line: Tubing connected between the charcoal canister and the carburetor intake manifold or PCV hose, on certain models. An internal flow restrictor allows fuel vapors to travel into engine at a constant rate.

Evaporative Controls: System designed to eliminate fuel evaporative losses into the atmosphere from the gas tank and carburetor.

Fill Control System: Components designed to limit maximum tank fuel level during filling to 90% to 98% of total tank space. This system may consist of one or more of the following items — special filler pipe extending farther down into tank, "domed" upper tank section, vent line between upper tank section and filler pipe neck, and/or overfill limiting valve on the liquid-vapor separator.

Liquid-vapor Separator: Contained area above and adjacent to the gas tank where fuel vapors collect. Vapors that condense flow back into the fuel tank. Vapors that do not condense flow through tubing into the charcoal canister. Most designs feature vertical standpipes, a check valve, or contain open-cell foam. Separators are not used on all models.

Purge (Stage) Valve: Vacuum-operated canister valve used on certain models that allows constant canister purging at lower speeds, plus increased (variable) flow purging at higher speeds.

Restrictor, Inline: Device reducing tubing internal size, such as used near liquid-vapor separator vent outlet, to meter (restrict) the

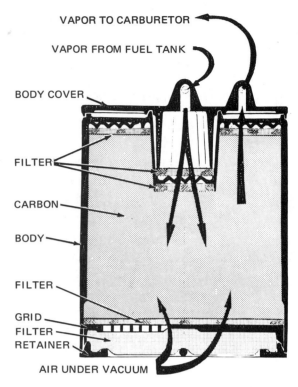

Fig 25-2. Charcoal Canister

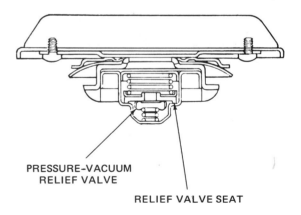

Fig 25-3. Pressure-vacuum Tank Fill Cap

amount of fumes traveling to the charcoal canister.

Tank Pressure and Vacuum Relief System: Consists primarily of tank fill cap specially designed for each vehicle application. It has two normally closed spring-loaded valves. Cap pressure valve may open near 1 psi to relieve tank pressure. Cap vacuum valve may open near 1/4 inch of vacuum to prevent tank collapse as fuel is used. Fill cap may feature a two-step removal procedure.

Tank Vapor Space: Gas-tank area above the allowed fuel level, designed as breathing space for the liquid-vapor separator. Area also compensates for expansion of fuel by heat, and may be 10% or less of total tank volume. Certain models feature a simple domed area.

Variable Purge Line: Tube connected between the charcoal canister and air-cleaner snorkel, on certain models. It allows fuel vapor flow into engine at higher rate as engine speed increases.

In the following exercises, indicate the best answer by inserting in the blanks the appropriate number, letter, word(s), or calculation, as required.

PICTORIAL REVIEW

A. Identify the evaporative system components or areas in figure 25-4 by writing their correct letters in the blanks.

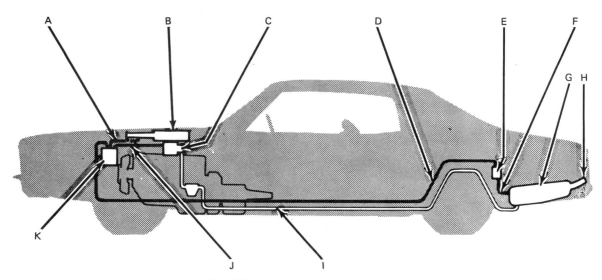

Fig 25-4. Evaporative Control System

1. _____ pressure-vacuum tank fill cap
2. _____ constant purge line
3. _____ variable purge line
4. _____ fuel line to engine
5. _____ fuel tank
6. _____ charcoal canister
7. _____ air cleaner
8. _____ liquid-vapor separator
9. _____ vapor line, separator-to-canister
10. _____ carburetor
11. _____ vent line, tank-to-separator

SUMMARY REVIEW

_____ 1. All new evaporative control systems feature
   a. a purge valve.
   b. a charcoal canister.
   c. a liquid-vapor separator with vertical standpipes.
   d. all of the above.

Section 4. Emission Controls

___ 2. Space allowed for fuel vapors inside the tank amount to a maximum of _____ percent of total tank space.

    a. one   c. ten
    b. five   d. twenty

___ 3. The fill cap pressure valve opens when tank pressure nears

    a. 1/4 psi.   c. 3/4 psi.
    b. 1/2 psi.   d. 1 psi.

___ 4. The purpose of the charcoal granules is to absorb

    a. water vapor.   c. gasoline vapor.
    b. liquid water.   d. liquid gasoline.

___ 5. Vaporized fumes leaving the liquid-vapor separator flow first into the

    a. charcoal canister.   c. carburetor.
    b. fuel tank.   d. air-cleaner snorkel.

___ 6. Standpipe-type liquid-vapor separators may have a tank vapor vent line(s) leading to

    a. the pressure-vacuum fill cap.
    b. more than one upper tank corner.
    c. one lower tank corner.
    d. the purge valve.

___ 7. A liquid-vapor separator design may feature

    a. vertical standpipes.   c. a check valve.
    b. open-cell foam.   d. any of these.

___ 8. The liquid-vapor separator is located near the

    a. fuel tank.   c. purge valve.
    b. charcoal canister.   d. carburetor.

___ 9. The purpose of the purge valve as used on certain models is to control the flow of fuel

    a. liquid from the gas tank.
    b. vapor to the charcoal canister.
    c. liquid from the liquid-vapor separator.
    d. vapor from the charcoal canister.

10. Are charcoal granules *solid* or *porous* carbon? _____

11. What feature does a constant purge line have that allows it to control vapor flow? _____

12. Insert the correct numbers of the matching terms or definitions in the blanks.

    a. ____ charcoal
    b. ____ purge valve
    c. ____ check valve
    d. ____ meter
    e. ____ gasoline
    f. ____ purge line
    g. ____ heat shield

    1. stage valve
    2. restrict
    3. hydrocarbon
    4. rubber tubing
    5. stops liquid flow
    6. porous carbon
    7. flat sheet of aluminum below carburetor

REFERENCE REVIEW

____ 1. Evaporative controls reduce the amount of _____ entering the atmosphere from automotive operation.

   a. carbon monoxide
   b. oxides of nitrogen
   c. hydrocarbons
   d. particulates

____ 2. Fuel vapors from the gas tank reach the charcoal canister

   a. only when the engine is off.
   b. anytime vapor leaves the liquid-vapor separator.
   c. only when the engine is idling.
   d. only when the engine is operating at high speed.

____ 3. The charcoal in the canister

   a. needs occasional replacement.
   b. is self-cleaning.
   c. needs occasional cleaning.
   d. should be tested for flow rate during each tuneup.

____ 4. Charcoal canister filters, if used, should be replaced under normal conditions every

   a. 5,000 miles:
   b. 10,000 miles.
   c. 24,000 miles.
   d. 36,000 miles.

____ 5. The upper end of an internal carburetor vent exits into

   a. a variable purge hose.
   b. the carbon canister.
   c. a constant purge hose.
   d. the carburetor air horn.

____ 6. If a charcoal canister filter is used, it is usually made of

   a. fiberglass.
   b. pleated paper.
   c. sponge rubber.
   d. cotton.

7. List two components of an evaporative control system expected to require servicing.

   a. _____   b. _____

Section 4 Emission Controls

8. What may happen to the gas tank when driving if the fill cap vacuum relief valve sticks shut, or a fill cap with too high a vacuum relief rating is installed? _____
_____

9. Describe the stage tank fill cap removal as used on certain models.
_____
_____

10. Describe how to change a charcoal canister filter on models so equipped. _____
_____

UNIT 26 EXHAUST SYSTEM CONTROLS

RELATED AUTOMOTIVE TERMS

Automobile Exhaust System Controls: Devices incorporated on and/or in the engine exhaust system for reducing air-polluting emissions from the exhaust gases. These include HC, CO, NO_X.

Base Metals: A group of metals that may be combined in various ways to form catalysts. Base metals include chromium, cobalt, copper, iron, nickel, and zinc. These metals work best for controlling NO_X emissions.

Bed-type Converter: A converter having the catalyst material applied over hundreds of porous ceramic or metal pellets (beads) known as substrates. Contents are packed and retained inside a container.

Catalyst: A special material that promotes a chemical reaction between two or more substances without itself being used up or changed in the process.

Catalytic Converter: Device through which exhaust gases may pass. A converter contains one or more chemicals capable of promoting continued burning of exhaust gases, or separates the gases into harmless chemicals.

This may require an air pump, use of lead-free gasoline, and operating temperatures between 900 and 1500°F (482 and 816°C).

Ceramic: A substance made by heating various metal oxides to very high temperatures. It may be used as a catalyst substrate material and is very stable when heated.

Dual-bed Converter: A converter that has two sections containing different catalysts. The first section controls NO_X emissions and the second controls HC and CO emissions.

EGR (Exhaust Gas Recirculation) System: Devices incorporated into the exhaust system on certain engines to allow a variable amount (5 to 13%) of inert gases to recirculate into the engine intake system. The effect is reduced peak combustion temperatures, thus lowering NO_X emissions. Usually operated by carburetor vacuum. A simplified system uses calibrated jets between intake and exhaust passages.

EGR Valve: Control valve that meters a variable amount of exhaust gases back into engine intake system, depending on certain engine operating conditions. It may be

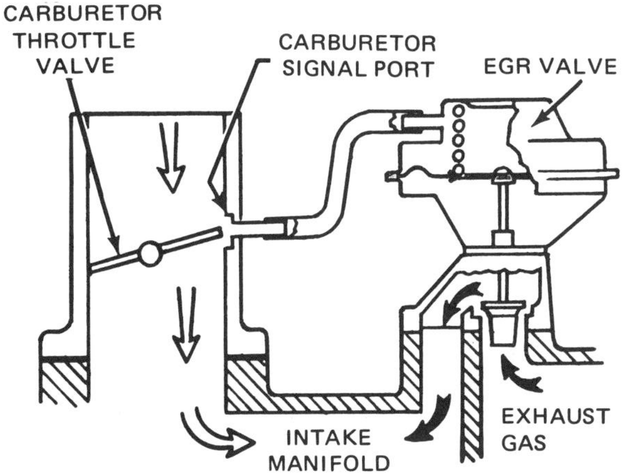

Fig 26-1. Exhaust Gas Recirculation System

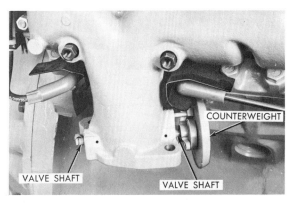

Fig 26-2. Exhaust Manifold Heat Control

Section 4 . Emission Controls

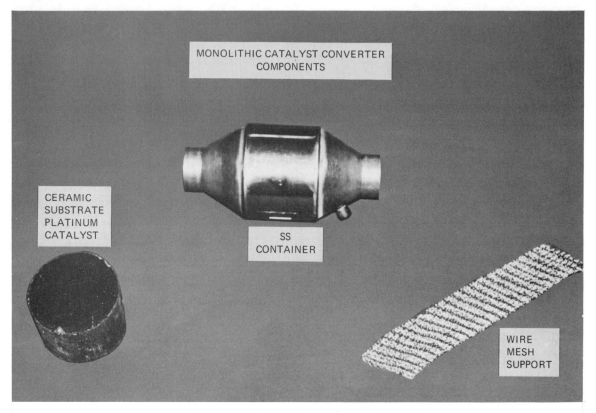

Fig 26-3. Catalytic Converter Monolithic Type

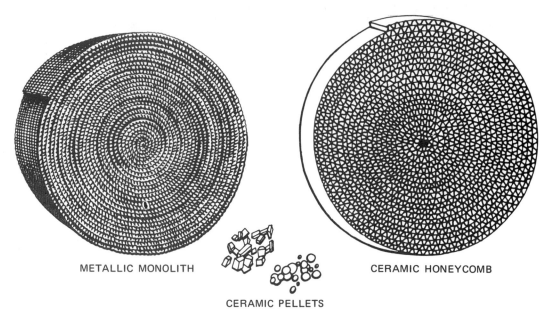

SUPPORT STRUCTURES ON WHICH CATALYSTS ARE DISPERSED MAY BE OF PELLETIZED OR HONEYCOMB DESIGN, USUALLY OF CERAMIC MATERIALS. THE GOULD METALLIC MONOLITH DESIGN (LEFT) IS A COILED STRIP OF OPEN-MESH MATERIAL, WHICH OFFERS SIGNIFICANT ADVANTAGES IN WEIGHT, DENSITY, WARM-UP TIME, AND CATALYTIC ACTIVITY.

Fig 26-4. NO_x Catalyst Construction Techniques

Unit 26 Exhaust System Controls

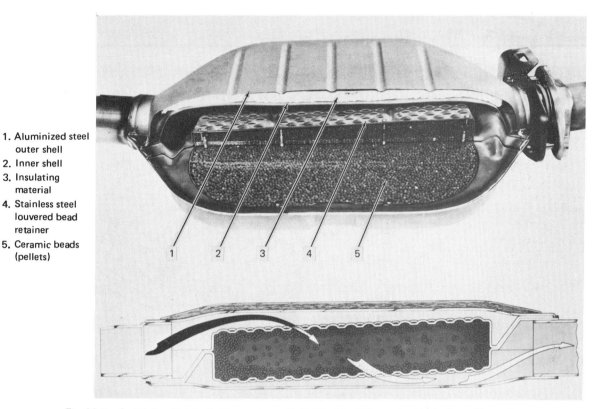

1. Aluminized steel outer shell
2. Inner shell
3. Insulating material
4. Stainless steel louvered bead retainer
5. Ceramic beads (pellets)

Fig 26-5. Oxidizing Catalytic Converter — Pelletized-bed Type, for Underfloor Mounting

interconnected with a vacuum source, automatic transmission vacuum modulator, engine coolant sensor, etc; usually fully open when carburetor port vacuum is over 5 to 8.5 inches.

Exhaust Manifold Heat Control Valve: "Butterfly" valve controlled by a bimetallic spring. Closed when the engine is cold, to direct part of the hot exhaust gases toward intake manifold near carburetor base. Operation aids fuel vaporization to improve cold-engine driveability. It may be operated by a vacuum powered actuator on models that have a catalytic converter.

Honeycomb: One converter internal substrate structure used to support the catalyst material, such as platinum. A honeycomb design allows maximum catalyst surface exposure to exhaust gases. Usually made of ceramic.

Monolithic Converter: A converter that has the catalyst material applied over a

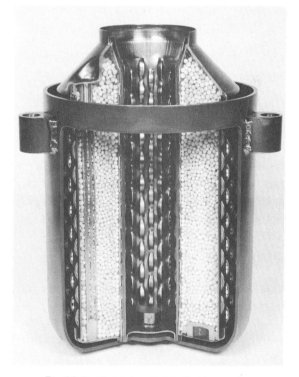

Fig 26-6. Oxidizing Catalytic Converter — Pelletized-bed Type, for Exhaust Manifold Mounting

Section 4 Emission Controls

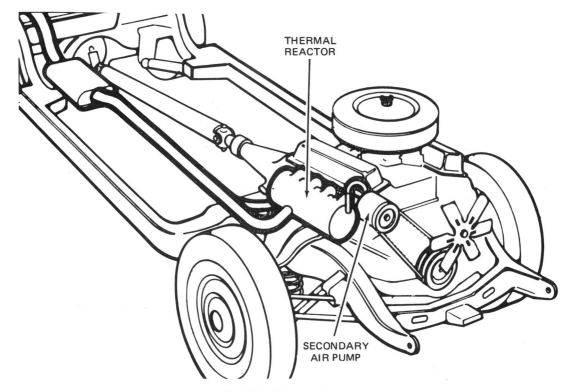

Fig 26-7. Thermal Reactor

spiral wound substrate inside a corrugated wire mesh support. Contents are enclosed in a stainless-steel container.

Noble Metals: A group of metals that resist corrosion and may be used as catalysts. Noble metals include gold, iridium, palladium, platinum, and ruthenium. These metals are rare and expensive.

Oxidation: Chemical reaction in which oxygen is combined with other materials; for example, oxygen combines with HC and CO to form (harmless) H_2O (water) and CO_2 (carbon dioxide). This reaction may occur in a catalytic converter.

Oxidation Catalyst: A catalyst that aids the complete combustion of exhaust gases.

Reduction (Deoxidation): Chemical reaction in which oxygen is removed from a compound to separate the elements into their original states.

Reduction Catalyst: A catalyst that aids in the separation of a compound, for example, NO_X, into its original component parts of nitrogen and oxygen.

Substrate: The material upon or over which the catalyst is placed. Substrate examples are the pellet core substance in a bed-type converter, or spiral-wound framework inside a monolithic converter. It is not affected by converter use because of composition or placement.

Thermal Reactor: Essentially an afterburner (oversize exhaust manifold) which allows the combustion process to continue after the exhaust gases leave the engine. Operating temperature is over 1200°F. The reactor may require an air pump. It reduces emissions of unburned hydrocarbons and carbon monoxide.

Three-way Catalytic Converter: A converter having a catalyst(s) capable of reducing NO_X levels and oxidizing HC and CO at the same time.

Unit 26 Exhaust System Controls

In the following exercises, indicate the best answer by inserting in the blanks the appropriate number, letter, word(s), or calculation as required.

PICTORIAL REVIEW

A. Identify the EGR valve components or areas in figure 26-8 by writing their correct letters in the blanks.

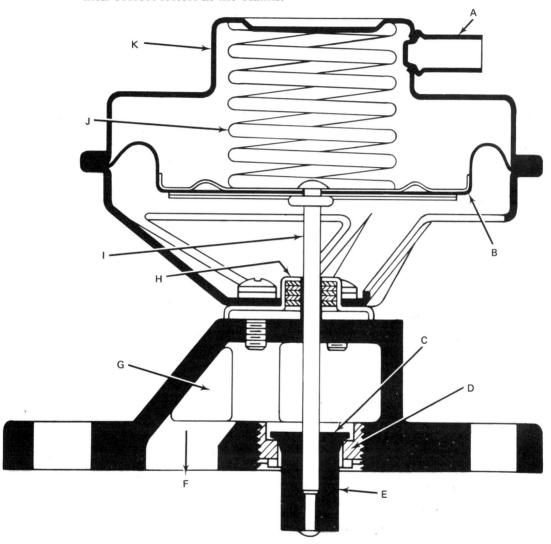

Fig 26-8. EGR Valve

1. _____ closed valve
2. _____ actuating diaphragm
3. _____ valve-stem shaft
4. _____ passage to intake manifold
5. _____ valve seat
6. _____ diaphragm cover
7. _____ exhaust-manifold valve projection
8. _____ spring
9. _____ shaft seal
10. _____ vacuum port to carburetor
11. _____ exhaust passage (valve chamber)

163

Section 4 Emission Controls

B. Identify the exhaust system parts in figure 26-9 by writing their correct names in the blanks.

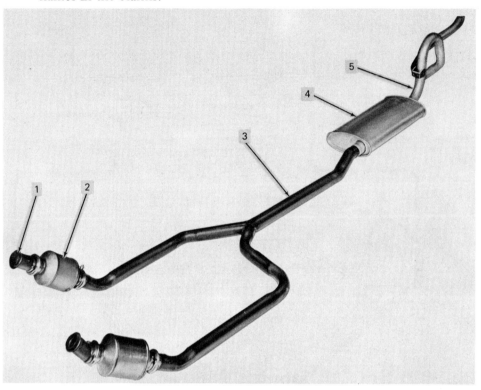

Fig 26-9. Exhaust System

1. _____   4. _____
2. _____   5. _____
3. _____

SUMMARY REVIEW

____ 1. Exhaust-gas recirculation is one method used for lowering emissions of

    a. HC.   c. NO_x.
    b. CO.   d. HC and CO.

____ 2. During a chemical reaction, a catalyst

    a. aids the chemical reaction.   c. may stop the chemical reaction.
    b. is gradually used up.   d. works best when cold.

____ 3. A catalytic converter may require

    a. use of lead-free gasoline.
    b. an air pump.
    c. operating temperatures near 1000°F.
    d. all of the above.

Unit 26 Exhaust System Controls

___ 4. The ceramic material that may be used when manufacturing a catalytic converter is used mainly as
   a. the external container.
   b. a catalyst.
   c. a substrate.
   d. a catalyst substitute.

___ 5. Most monolithic catalytic converters contain
   a. a pelletized bed.
   b. a spiral-wound substrate.
   c. a dual catalytic bed.
   d. all of these.

___ 6. The first section of a dual-bed converter has a catalyst to control emissions of
   a. NO_X.
   b. CO.
   c. HC.
   d. HC and CO.

___ 7. The purpose of a thermal reactor is to
   a. contain the catalytic bed.
   b. cool the exhaust gases.
   c. control NO_X emissions.
   d. continue the combustion process.

___ 8. The purpose of an exhaust-manifold heat control on certain models is to
   a. reduce NO_X emissions.
   b. improve cold driveability.
   c. increase exhaust temperatures.
   d. improve hot operation.

9. Explain what an oxidation catalyst does. _____
   _____
   _____

10. Explain what a reduction catalyst does. _____
    _____
    _____

11. Insert the correct numbers of the matching terms or definitions in the blanks.
    a. ___ noble metal
    b. ___ thermal reactor
    c. ___ substrate
    d. ___ monolithic converter container material
    e. ___ EGR valve
    f. ___ base metal
    g. ___ contains pellets

    1. afterburner
    2. bed-type converter
    3. stainless steel
    4. catalyst core substance
    5. copper
    6. controls recirculation of exhaust gases
    7. platinum

165

Section 4 Emission Controls

REFERENCE REVIEW

____ 1. Leaded gasoline may cause catalysts currently in use to
   a. disintegrate.
   b. become ineffective.
   c. explode.
   d. operate hotter.

____ 2. One catalytic converter may change unburned hydrocarbons and carbon monoxide emissions into harmless water vapor and
   a. sulphur dioxide.
   b. carbon dioxide.
   c. particulates.
   d. nitrous oxides.

____ 3. A catalytic converter may use an auxliary system that pumps _____ into the converter during operation.
   a. air
   b. water
   c. fuel
   d. oil

____ 4. The percentage of exhaust gas recirculated into the intake system during EGR operation varies from
   a. 0 to 4%.
   b. 5 to 13%.
   c. 14 to 23%.
   d. 24 to 30%.

____ 5. The maximum amount of exhaust gas recirculation occurs
   a. at engine idle.
   b. from 5 to 25 mph.
   c. from 30 to 65 mph.
   d. above 65 mph.

____ 6. Most EGR valves receive vacuum from the
   a. intake manifold.
   b. air pump.
   c. PCV system.
   d. carburetor.

____ 7. An EGR valve starts to open at about _____ inches vacuum.
   a. 2 to 3
   b. 7 to 8
   c. 11 to 12
   d. 15 to 16

8. How can the automative technician tell if a catalytic converter is in good working condition? _____

9. Describe any service procedure required if a pelletized catalytic converter has become ineffective. _____

10. Name two main disadvantages that occur from the use of a thermal reactor to control exhaust emissions.
   a. _____
   b. _____

SECTION 5 Brake Systems

UNIT 27 DRUM BRAKES

RELATED AUTOMOTIVE TERMS

Backing Plate: Stamped steel plate upon which the wheel cylinder is mounted and the brake shoes are attached.

Bleeding Brakes: Process of loosening a bleeder screw and expelling air from hydraulic system components. The process sends new brake fluid through the system. It may be accomplished with the use of a special pressurized bleeder tank or by pumping the brake pedal.

Brake Drum: Cylindrical part that rotates with the wheel and surrounds the brake shoes. During stopping, the brake shoes press against

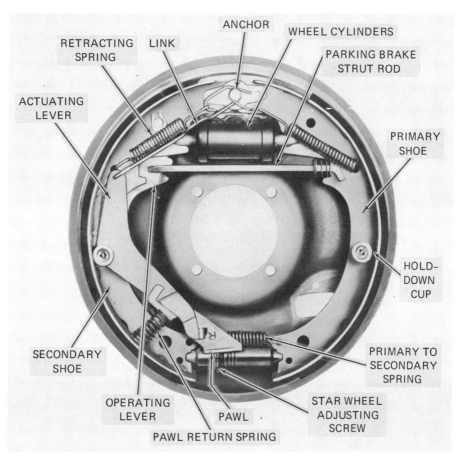

Fig 27-1. Rear Drum Brake Assembly (Lever-actuated Adjuster)

Section 5 Brake Systems

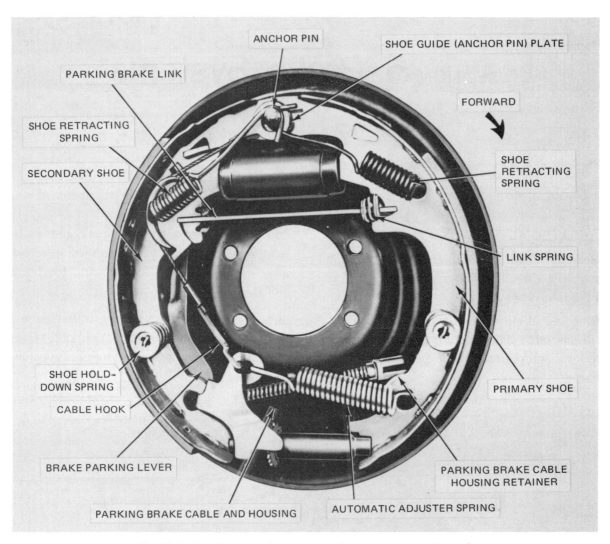

Fig 27-2. Rear Drum Brake Assembly (Cable-actuated Adjuster)

its inside circumference, thus turning mechanical energy of motion (kinetic energy) into heat (thermal) energy.

Brake Fluid: A specially formulated liquid used to transmit brake pedal pressure from the master cylinder to the wheel cylinders.

Brake Lining: Asbestos compound material, usually molded to shape, that is riveted or glued to the brake shoe. It provides the friction necessary to stop the rotating brake drum.

Brake Line Tubing: Plated steel tubing, double flared and double walled, that carries the brake fluid from the master cylinder to the wheel cylinders.

Contour Ground Shoes: Trade practice of *arcing* oversize brake shoes to a slightly smaller installed diameter than the brake drum, promoting smoother and quieter stopping.

Cylinder Bleeder Screw: Hollow valve near top of wheel cylinder used to expel any air that may be in hydraulic system.

Drum Diameter: Distance across the inside of the brake drum. Popular diameters are 7.900, 9, 9.500, 10, 11, 11.030, and 12 inches.

Drum Brake Fade: Term describing loss of braking efficiency due to excessive heat.

Flexible Brake Hose: High-pressure neoprene hose that carries fluid from near the car frame

Unit 27 Drum Brakes

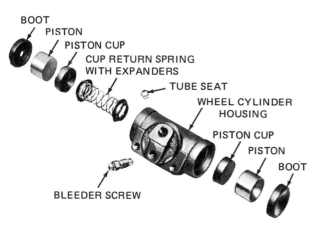

Fig 27-3. Wheel Cylinder

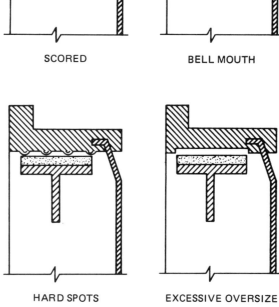

Fig 27-4. Brake Drum Problems

to both front wheels and from the frame area to the rear-axle housing.

Hydraulic Pressure: Pressure developed in the hydraulic system during braking. Pressure is transmitted equally to all parts of the system.

Oversize Drum: Drum that has been turned on a lathe to remove grooves and scratches. Maximum allowable oversize on most automotive drums is 0.060 inch.

Oversize Shoes: Shoe size often installed after the brake drum is turned oversize on a lathe. Each lining is usually 0.030 inch thicker than standard size.

Primary Brake Shoe: Front shoe on self-energizing Bendix-type brakes. The lining may be shorter, thinner, and have different frictional characteristics from the secondary shoe.

Secondary Brake Show: Rear shoe on self-energizing Bendix-type brakes. It usually has a longer and thicker lining, and provides most of the braking force during forward stops.

Self-adjusting Mechanism: Parts and linkages that operate to turn star-wheel shoe adjuster automatically as brake lining wears. It adjusts during backward or forward stops, depending on model.

Self-energizing (Duo-Servo) Action: Term referring to the braking force developed in

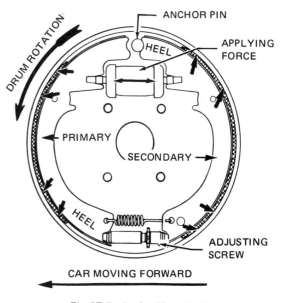

Fig 27-5. Brake Shoe Action

Section 5 Brake System

addition to that produced by the wheel cylinder. During brake application, the leading shoe is dragged downward and away from the shoe anchor pin by the drum. This action applies additional force against the following shoe through the star wheel adjuster when stopping in either direction.

Shoe Hold-down Springs: Coiled compression springs that apply pressure to hold the brake shoes against the backing plate.

Shoe-retracting (Return) Springs: Coiled tension springs that pull the shoes away from the brake drum after the pedal is released. The spring action forces the fluid back into the master cylinder.

Star-wheel Adjusting Screw: Toothed wheel that has left-hand or right-hand threads, depending on which side of the car it is located, and revolves to expand the shoes outward as the lining wears. It is turned manually or by a self-adjusting lever and pawl as needed to maintain desired lining-to-drum clearance.

Wheel Cylinder: Hydraulic cylinder at each wheel that transfers hydraulic pressure developed in the master cylinder to the brake shoes.

Wheel-cylinder Cup: Neoprene-rubber cup that seals the brake fluid in the wheel cylinder.

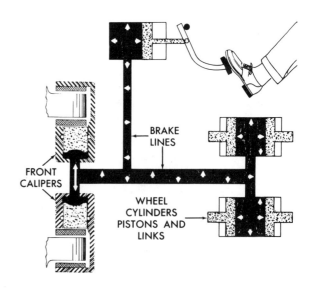

Fig 27-6. Hydraulic System Operation

Wheel-cylinder Honing: Method using a special hone for smoothing and/or removing deposits from the inside of the wheel cylinder during rebuilding.

Wheel-cylinder Piston: Aluminum or sintered-iron component inside a wheel cylinder that supports the cylinder cup.

Wheel-cylinder Spring: Coiled spring inside a wheel cylinder that pushes the cups against the pistons.

In the following exercises, indicate the best answer by inserting in the blanks the appropriate number, letter, word(s), or calculation, as required.

PICTORIAL REVIEW

A. Identify the drum-brake assembly components in figure 27-7 by writing their correct names in the blanks.

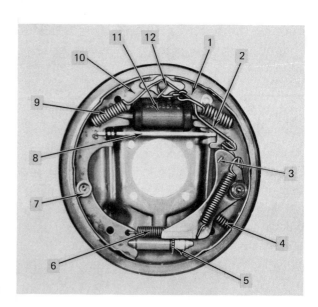

Fig 27-7. Rear Brake Assembly

Unit 27 Drum Brakes

1. _____   7. _____
2. _____   8. _____
3. _____   9. _____
4. _____ 10. _____
5. _____ 11. _____
6. _____ 12. _____

B. Identify the wheel-cylinder assembly components in figure 27-8 by writing their correct names in the blanks.

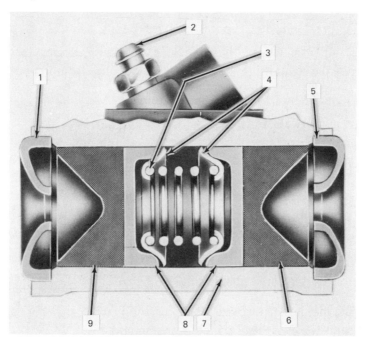

Fig 27-8. Wheel Cylinder

1. _____   6. _____
2. _____   7. _____
3. _____   8. _____
4. _____   9. _____
5. _____

SUMMARY REVIEW

____ 1. Brake lining is composed primarily of

    a. asbestos.   c. copper.
    b. a metallic substance.   d. cast iron.

____ 2. Compared to the secondary shoes illustrated in this unit, the primary shoes may have the

    a. longer lining.   c. thicker lining.
    b. shorter lining.   d. more lining-to-drum contact.

171

Section 5 Brake System

_____ 3. Brake fade is most likely to occur
   a. after several high-speed stops.
   b. when driving in the city.
   c. on a new car.
   d. on a used car.

_____ 4. The wheel-cylinder part that actually seals the brake fluid is called a
   a. piston.
   b. dust boot.
   c. cup.
   d. spring.

_____ 5. The brake-bleeding process removes
   a. air from system.
   b. excess fluid.
   c. excess pressure.
   d. vacuum from system.

_____ 6. Hydraulic-brake tubing is made from
   a. single-wall steel.
   b. double-wall steel.
   c. copper.
   d. aluminum.

_____ 7. The purpose of the wheel-cylinder spring is to
   a. release pressure after braking.
   b. keep pistons upright.
   c. provide shoe support.
   d. hold cups against pistons.

8. What is the name of the brake shoe providing most of the braking force during forward stopping? _____

9. The maximum oversize diameter for many passenger-car brake drums is _____ inch over standard.

10. The smallest brake-drum diameter used on American built cars is _____ and the largest is _____ .

11. The brake-assembly parts are mounted on a component called the _____ .

12. Insert the correct numbers of the matching terms or definitions in the blanks.
   a. ____ retaining-spring metal
   b. ____ usual drum metal
   c. ____ piston metal
   d. ____ backing-plate metal
   e. ____ cylinder-cup material
   f. ____ component holding shoe to anchor pin
   g. ____ component holding shoe to backing plate

   1. cast iron
   2. steel
   3. neoprene rubber
   4. retracting spring
   5. aluminum
   6. spring steel
   7. hold-down spring

Unit 27 Drum Brakes

REFERENCE REVIEW

_____ 1. The self-adjusting brakes shown in this unit operate to tighten the brake shoes
   a. anytime the foot brake is used.
   b. during backward stops.
   c. during forward stops.
   d. when using the parking brake.

_____ 2. Star-wheel adjusters have threads that are
   a. metric.
   b. left-hand.
   c. right hand.
   d. either left- or right-hand.

_____ 3. The highest pressure developed in the hydraulic system during the hardest application of the brake pedal is
   a. under 500 psi.
   b. 600 to 1000 psi.
   c. over 1100 psi.
   d. over 2000 psi.

_____ 4. Brake shoes not in the applied position are
   a. held rigidly in place.
   b. somewhat free to float.
   c. never contact the drum.
   d. attached to anchor bolts at the top and bottom.

_____ 5. The number of flexible brake lines found on most cars is
   a. 1.
   b. 2.
   c. 3.
   d. 4.

6. List four operational characteristics of a high-quality brake lining as compared with a cheap brake lining.
   a. _____   c. _____
   b. _____   d. _____

7. What must be done before loosening the star wheel on self-adjusting brakes after the hole cover is removed?
   _____

8. List two reasons why a wheel cylinder should be serviced during a brake lining replacement.
   a. _____   b. _____

9. Should a properly arced (fitted) "oversize" brake lining have a noticeable lining-to-drum clearance at the lining *center* or *ends*?
   _____

10. During stopping, is the pressure (psi) in the wheel cylinder *more*, or *less*, or *the same* as that in the master cylinder?
    _____

11. The wheel cylinders having the largest inside diameter are on the _____ wheels.

173

UNIT 28 DISC BRAKES

RELATED AUTOMOTIVE TERMS

Applied Hydraulic Pressure: Working pressure developed in the brake hydraulic system as the driver depresses the brake pedal. This pressure must be greater with disc than with drum brakes because discs lack self-energizing (duo-servo) action when applied. Most American disc-brake cars have power assist.

Caliper: One of the major disc-brake components; it contains the piston(s) and attachments for the pads.

Caliper-bore Servicing: A recommended procedure before caliper assembly. The manufacturer may suggest a circular smoothing with crocus cloth or, in some cases, a special hone may be used, followed by cleaning with alcohol or brake fluid.

Disc-brake Fluid: A special fluid having a high boiling point, around 500°F. It must not be left exposed to air as it will attract moisture and be unsafe to use.

Disc-brake Operation: Hydraulic fluid under pressure enters the caliper behind the piston(s), moving the piston(s) outward. This forces the pads against the faces (braking surfaces) of the rotor.

Disc Lathe: Special lathe designed to remove small amounts of metal from the rotor faces to restore a smooth finish. Manufacturers specify minimum rotor thickness.

Disc-pad Adjustment: Provided automatically by the friction of the piston seal against the caliper bore when brakes are applied. No pad-retracting springs are used. Therefore, the pad is always close to the rotor face.

Fastener Tightness: All nuts and bolts, including the wheel lug nuts and those associated with the caliper, must be tightened to manufacturers' specifications with a torque wrench.

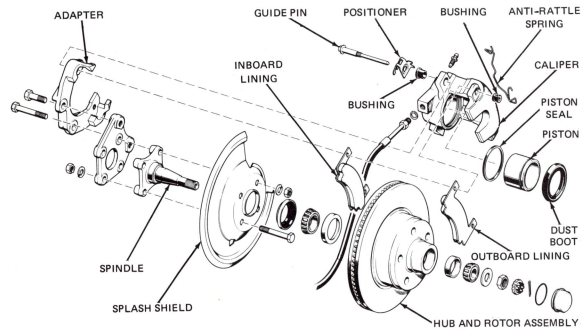

Fig 28-1. Disc-brake Components

Unit 28 Disc Brakes

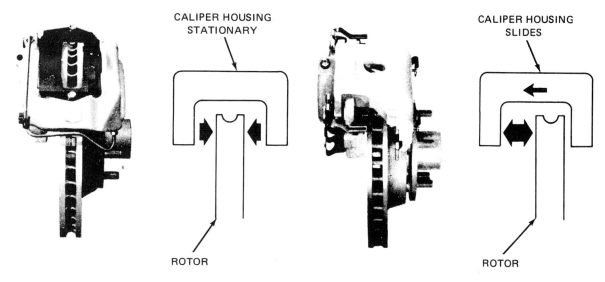

Fig 28-2A. Fixed-caliper Disc-brake Assembly

Fig 28-2B. Floating-caliper Disc-brake Assembly

Fixed Caliper: Two-piece caliper that is bolted directly to the steering knuckle. It usually has four pistons on full-size cars and two pistons on certain smaller cars.

Floating Caliper: One-piece caliper that is free to slide laterally on its mounting bolts. It usually has one piston.

Pad: The asbestos composition lining that is riveted or glued to the flat shoe. Two pads provide stopping friction by rubbing against both sides of the rotor when the brakes are applied.

Piston: Round caliper component that is moved outward by fluid pressure to press the pads against each rotor face.

Piston Removal: Method of pulling piston from caliper. Fluid or air pressure may be applied carefully behind the piston, following instructions, or a special expanding tool may be inserted inside the hollow piston to grip the piston and then twist it out.

Piston Seal: Rubber O-ring, usually of square cross section, placed inside the caliper bore or

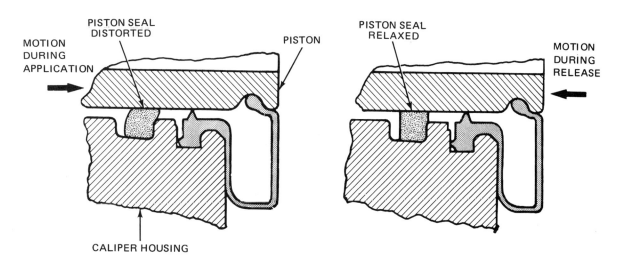

Fig 28-3. Piston and Seal Movement

175

Section 5 Brake System

around the piston. It fits snugly between piston and caliper bore to seal hydraulic fluid. Seal distortion during brake application may also provide slight piston and pad retraction during brake release, to gain running clearance and automatic pad adjustment.

Rotor (Disc): Disc-shaped component that revolves with hub and wheel. The lining pads are forced against the rotor to slow or stop vehicle.

Rotor Face: The flat parallel surface on each side of the rotor contacted by the pads (linings) during stopping.

Rotor-face Parallelism (Thickness Variation): Both sides of the rotor must be parallel within 0.001 inch when measured at several points around the rotor an equal distance (about 1 inch) in from the outside edge.

Rotor Runout: Amount of rotor wobble; it can be checked while installed on the vehicle or in a disc lathe. Specifications often limit maximum runout to 0.001 inch on a lathe or 0.004 inch on the vehicle.

Splash Shield: Stamped sheet-metal plate located behind the rotor to provide component protection from dirt and water.

Unicast Rotor: Type of rotor used on many late-model cars that has the rotor and hub cast as one integral component. It is often made from gray iron rather than cast iron.

Ventilated Rotor: Rotor that has open, ventilated passages between each face for improved heat dissipation.

In the following exercises, indicate the best answer by inserting in the blanks the appropriate number, letter, word(s), or calculation, as required.

PICTORIAL REVIEW

A. Identify the disc brake assembly component in figure 28-4 by writing their correct letters in the blanks.

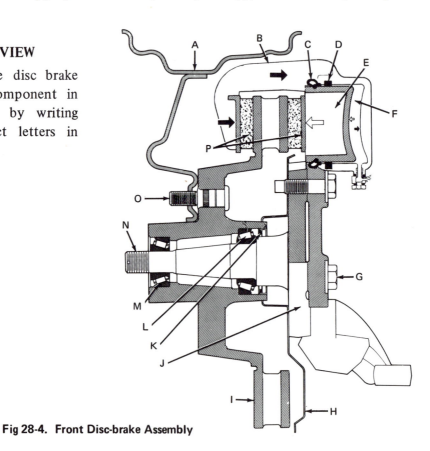

Fig 28-4. Front Disc-brake Assembly

Unit 28 Disc Brakes

1. ____ wheel
2. ____ brake fluid
3. ____ wheel stud
4. ____ outer bearing
5. ____ dust boot
6. ____ grease seal
7. ____ caliper housing
8. ____ spindle
9. ____ mounting bolt
10. ____ inner bearing
11. ____ rotor and hub
12. ____ splash shield
13. ____ piston seal
14. ____ shoe and pad
15. ____ piston
16. ____ steering knuckle

SUMMARY REVIEW

____ 1. The section of the rotor contacted by the lining during stopping is called the
   a. edge.
   b. hub.
   c. face.
   d. caliper.

____ 2. The maximum rotor runout, on a vehicle, allowed by several manufacturers is
   a. 0.001 inch.
   b. 0.004 inch.
   c. 0.010 inch.
   d. 0.060 inch.

____ 3. The maximum rotor thickness variation allowed by manufacturers is
   a. 0.001 inch or less.
   b. 0.003 to 0.005 inch.
   c. 0.006 to 0.010 inch.
   d. 0.012 inch or more.

____ 4. The number of pistons in a fixed-caliper assembly on larger cars is usually
   a. 1.
   b. 2.
   c. 3.
   d. 4.

____ 5. To smooth the caliper bore during servicing, the technician should use
   a. sandpaper.
   b. emery cloth.
   c. crocus cloth.
   d. a drum-brake wheel-cylinder hone.

____ 6. Brake-line pressure in disc-brake calipers during stopping is usually _____ that in drum-brake wheel cylinders.
   a. higher than
   b. lower than
   c. the same as
   d. may be higher or lower than

7. Explain how the pad lining is drawn away from the rotor on certain model disc brakes after the brake pedal is released.

   _____

   _____

8. Define what is meant by a unicast rotor. _____

   _____

Section 5 Disc Brakes

9. The inside face of the rotor is somewhat protected from the weather by the _____ and the outside face by the
   _____

10. Explain how disc-brake pads are adjusted. _____
    _____

11. Insert the correct numbers of the matching terms or definitions in the blanks.

    a. ____ disc runout
    b. ____ fixed caliper
    c. ____ piston removal method
    d. ____ ventilated disc
    e. ____ floating caliper
    f. ____ rotor
    g. ____ parallelism
    h. ____ lining

    1. has one piston
    2. has more than one piston
    3. thickness variation check
    4. hydraulic pressure
    5. pad
    6. wobble
    7. better heat dissipation
    8. disc

REFERENCE REVIEW

____ 1. New disc brake fluid having an original boiling point near 500°F.
   a. must be used for all disc and all drum brake systems.
   b. is unaffected by moisture.
   c. evaporates easily.
   d. must not be left exposed to air.

____ 2. Most new disc brakes on American cars have
   a. a floating caliper.   c. solid rotors.
   b. a fixed caliper.   d. four piston calipers.

____ 3. The part of the disc-brake assembly that provides for pad-to-rotor adjustment is called the
   a. piston seal.   c. floating-caliper positioner.
   b. spring adjuster.   d. bleeder screw.

____ 4. If a caliper-bore hone is used, it should be lubricated with
   a. oil.   c. water.
   b. brake fluid.   d. alcohol.

____ 5. Before changing disc pads, the technician should
   a. test brakes for fade.   c. remove the disc splash shield.
   b. remove some of the brake fluid.
                                   d. adjust the wheel bearings.

Unit 28 Disc Brakes

____ 6. During a disc pad change on a floating-caliper brake, the caliper assembly
    a. need not be disturbed.
    b. should be replaced.
    c. must be disconnected hydraulically.
    d. may be connected hydraulically.

____ 7. To lubricate front wheel bearings on a vehicle having disc brakes, the technician must first remove the
    a. brake fluid.
    b. splash shield.
    c. disc only.
    d. caliper and disc.

8. What important service related to safety must be observed after changing and adjusting the disc pads? _____

9. Does a disc brake operate at a temperature that is *hotter* or *colder* than a drum brake? _____

10. What, if anything, may happen if brake fluid is spilled on an automobile fender? _____

11. Name two tools or ways that may be used to retract pistons before caliper removal.
    a. _____
    b. _____

12. Is a ventilated disc usually *thicker* or *thinner* than a solid disc?
_____

UNIT 29 MASTER CYLINDER AND LINE CONTROLS

RELATED AUTOMOTIVE TERMS

Antiskid Control: Accessory for brake system that operates on rear wheels, or all four wheels, to prevent wheel lockup during braking. Braking pressure is reduced by electronic controls to wheel(s) that are about to lock up and skid.

Bail: Spring-steel wire that holds master-cylinder cover in place on certain models.

Bench Bleeding: The process of filling and bleeding a new master cylinder before installation.

Combination Valve: Nonserviceable integral assembly consisting of brake-pressure differential warning-light switch, proportioning, and metering valves. Used on disc-drum systems.

Compensating Port: Smaller hole between master cylinder reservoir and cylinder that allows fluid to flow into cylinder area(s) ahead of piston before brakes are applied and back into reservoir when released.

Intake (Breathing) Port: Larger hole between master cylinder reservoir and cylinder that allows fluid to flow into cylinder area(s) between cups around the recessed piston section(s), allows pedal to be pumped up.

Line Static Pressure: Hydraulic pressure maintained in drum-brake system by residual check valve when brakes are not applied. This 10 to 15 psi keeps pressure on wheel-cylinder cup lips to seal fluid in as well as air and dirt out.

Master Cylinder: Brake component where pressure is developed when the driver depresses the brake pedal, causing a linkage to move the master cylinder piston(s) forward. It has an integral reservoir filled with brake fluid.

Metering Valve: Line control used on a disc-drum system that delays pressure to front discs until pressure to rear drums is sufficient to overcome shoe return-spring pressure. It may need to be held in the open position during pressure brake bleeding.

Pedal Clearance: Amount of downward brake pedal movement before pushrod contacts piston. It must be near 1/4 inch.

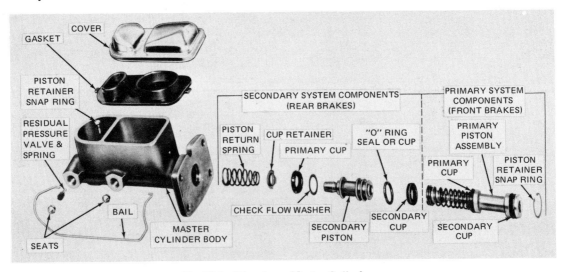

Fig 29-1. Disc-drum Master Cylinder

Unit 29 Master Cylinder and Line Controls

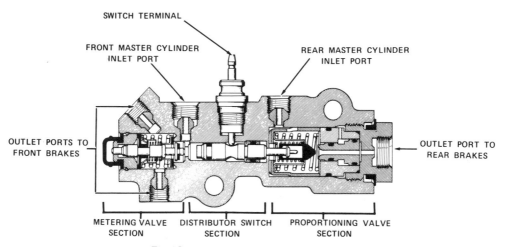

Fig 29-2. Three-function Combination Valve

Piston Cup(s): Neoprene rubber cups that fit on or against piston to seal and contain the fluid.

Piston Return Spring: Spring ahead of piston(s) that help return piston(s) to retracted position after brake pedal is released.

Pressure Differential Warning Switch: Line component that turns on a trouble-indicating light when a pressure difference of 100 psi or more exists between the front and rear hydraulic systems. Its internal piston may or may not be self-centering after operation.

Primary Piston Assembly: Rear master cylinder piston and its related parts. It is usually hydraulically connected to the front brakes.

Proportioning Valve: Line control used on a disc-drum system that reduces pressure to rear drum brakes during a hard stop, preventing rear-wheel skid.

Pumping Brakes: Term referring to driver depressing brake pedal several times in quick succession. During a fast pedal release, additional fluid flows through small holes in front section of piston head and past front cup to be forced into brake system on next pedal application.

Pushrod: Mechanical linkage for transferring force; located between standard brake pedal and master-cylinder piston.

Reservoir Diaphragm Cover Seal: Flexible neoprene rubber covering entire open area at top of master-cylinder reservoir. It keeps air and dirt from coming in contact with fluid.

Secondary Piston Assembly: Front master-cylinder piston and its related parts, operated by hydraulic or mechanical force from the primary piston assembly. It is usually hydraulically connected to the rear brakes.

Secondary Piston Stop Screw: Setscrew designed to keep secondary piston in forward section of master cylinder during assembly and operation. It may be located under or on the side of the master cylinder or inside front reservoir.

Stoplight Switch: Switch operated by hydraulic line pressure, or mechanically by brake-pedal, for turning on rear vehicle stoplights.

Tandem (Dual) Master Cylinder: Master cylinder basically having separate systems and pistons for front and rear brakes or a diagonal combination of same. Failure of one system still allows the other system to operate, but at reduced efficiency.

Tube Seats: Replaceable brass seats that provide a fluid-tight seal against the brake-line flare fitting at the master-cylinder fluid outlet(s).

Section 5 Brake Systems

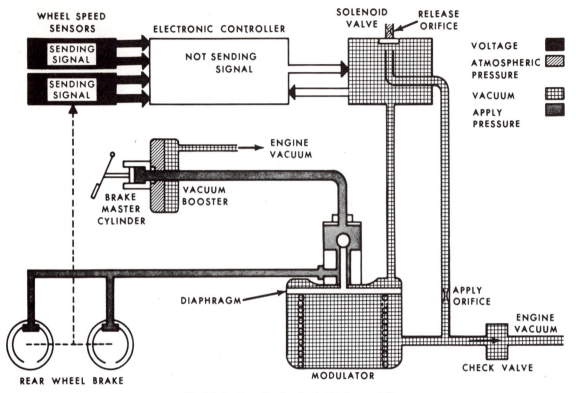

Fig 29-3. Rear Brake Antiskid Control System

In the following exercises, indicate the best answer by inserting in the blanks the appropriate number, letter, word(s), or calculation, as required.

PICTORIAL REVIEW

A. Identify the master cylinder components in figure 29-4 by writing their correct letters in the blanks.

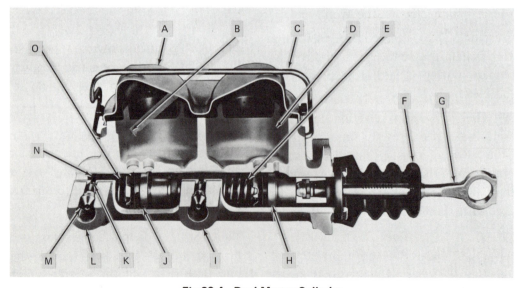

Fig 29-4. Dual Master Cylinder

Unit 29 Master Cylinder and Line Controls

1. ____ tube seat
2. ____ boot
3. ____ secondary piston assembly
4. ____ bail (or retainer)
5. ____ primary return spring
6. ____ residual valve spring
7. ____ secondary outlet port
8. ____ pushrod
9. ____ residual check valve
10. ____ primary piston assembly
11. ____ secondary fluid reservoir
12. ____ primary outlet port
13. ____ cover
14. ____ primary fluid reservoir
15. ____ secondary return spring

SUMMARY REVIEW

____ 1. The master cylinder part contacted by the pushrod during stopping is called the

    a. piston stop.
    b. residual stop.
    c. secondary piston.
    d. primary piston.

____ 2. After the brake pedal is released on a car having drums, the fluid returns to the master cylinder because of the action of the piston-return spring and the

    a. breathing port.
    b. wheel-cylinder spring.
    c. brake-shoe retracting springs.
    d. brake-shoe hold-down springs.

____ 3. On a disc-drum system, the residual check valve is located at or near the

    a. primary outlet port.
    b. secondary outlet port.
    c. primary piston.
    d. secondary piston.

____ 4. The cylinder breathing port allows fluid to flow

    a. in front of the pistons.
    b. in back of the pistons.
    c. around the piston *recessed* section.
    d. into the reservoir from the brake lines.

____ 5. The cylinder compensating ports allow fluid to flow

    a. in back of the primary piston.
    b. for pumping brakes.
    c. into the reservoir from the brake lines.
    d. between reservoirs.

____ 6. Tube seats are located at the cylinder

    a. bleeder valve.
    b. outlet ports.
    c. primary piston.
    d. secondary piston.

Section 5 Brake Systems

____ 7. Before the secondary piston can be removed from the cylinder, it is necessary to remove
   a. the secondary piston stop screw.
   b. the primary piston retaining ring.
   c. the primary piston.
   d. all of the above.

____ 8. The purpose of the proportioning valve on a disc-drum system is to limit pressure to the
   a. front brakes during a hard stop.
   b. rear brakes during a hard stop.
   c. front brakes during an easy stop.
   d. rear brakes during an easy stop.

9. The proper amount of brake-pedal clearance on a car should be near _____ inch.

10. The number of piston return springs on a recent model master cylinder is _____ .

11. Explain what is meant by *bench bleeding*? _____

12. Insert the correct numbers of the matching terms or definitions in the blanks.
   a. ____ proportioning valve
   b. ____ metering valve
   c. ____ pressure differential switch
   d. ____ combination valve
   e. ____ pedal clearance
   f. ____ tandem cylinder
   g. ____ static pressure

   1. three-way valve
   2. delays front-brake application for disc-drum systems
   3. dual cylinder
   4. limits pressure to rear brakes
   5. residual line pressure
   6. turns on warning light under certain conditions
   7. free play

REFERENCE REVIEW

____ 1. The amount of brake pedal clearance on a car with power brakes compared to one without is usually
   a. more.
   b. less.
   c. the same.
   d. may be more or less.

____ 2. The driver may notice the failure of either a front or rear brake system on a recent model car by the warning light and/or
   a. more brake pedal travel.
   b. proportioning valve button position.
   c. stoplights.
   d. pressure-differential valve piston position.

Unit 29 Master Cylinder and Line Controls

_____ 3. The brake system warning-light bulb may be checked easily by turning the ignition switch to the start position or
   a. removing bulb and testing it.
   b. using a test lamp.
   c. apply the parking brake.
   d. using a jumper wire.

_____ 4. Before pressure bleeding the front brakes on a disc-drum system, the technician should
   a. disconnect wire from pressure-differential valve.
   b. recenter pressure-differential valve piston.
   c. add drum-brake fluid to reservoir.
   d. pull or push metering valve stem or button.

_____ 5. On a disc-drum system, residual check valve(s) are located in the
   a. primary outlet port.
   b. secondary outlet port.
   c. both primary and secondary outlet ports.
   d. cylinder reservoir.

_____ 6. A defective proportioning valve should be
   a. removed and cleaned.
   b. removed and tested.
   c. rebuilt.
   d. replaced.

_____ 7. If the proportioning valve is inoperative, the
   a. front brakes will drag.
   b. rear brakes will drag.
   c. front brakes may lock up.
   d. rear brakes may lock up.

_____ 8. Most antiskid brake systems operate on
   a. front brakes.
   b. rear brakes.
   c. both front and rear brakes.
   d. parking brakes.

9. Is the master cylinder disc-fluid reservoir on a disc-drum system *smaller* or *larger* than the drum-fluid reservoir? _____

10. Explain why disc brakes do not have a static line-pressure maintained in their hydraulic system. _____
_____
_____

11. Describe what happens to the secondary piston if a brake line in that section ruptures. _____
_____

185

UNIT 30 POWER BRAKES

RELATED AUTOMOTIVE TERMS

Air Filter: A small mesh filter at the atmospheric air inlet.

Applying Position: Term referring to the relative position of the power cylinder components when the brake pedal is pressed downward.

Atmospheric Pressure: Pressure exerted by air on anything it contacts; 14.7 psi at sea level.

Atmospheric Suspended: Power brake system that has normal atmospheric air pressure applied to both sides of the diaphragm or piston with the pedal in the released position.

Atmospheric Valve: Valve that controls the amount of air applied to the rear of diaphragm or piston on vacuum-suspended types.

Automotive Power Brakes: A brake system having a vacuum- and atmospheric air-operated power booster or hydraulic power boost to multiply braking force.

Brake Feel: Term relating to the driver being able to determine the amount of braking force exerted or required during a stop; provided by the reaction disc, plate, piston, or lever inside the power unit.

Diaphragm- or Piston-return Spring: A heavy coil spring that returns the diaphragm or piston to the rear (at-rest) position when the brake pedal is released.

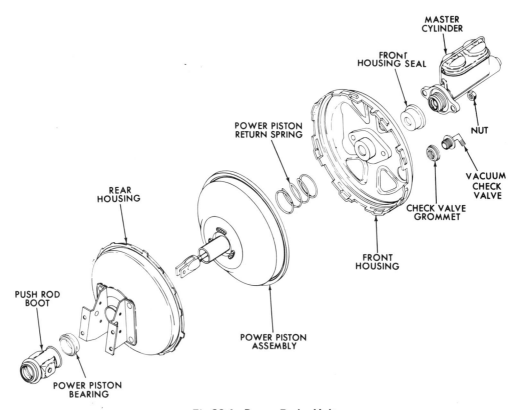

Fig 30-1. Power Brake Unit

Unit 30 Power Brakes

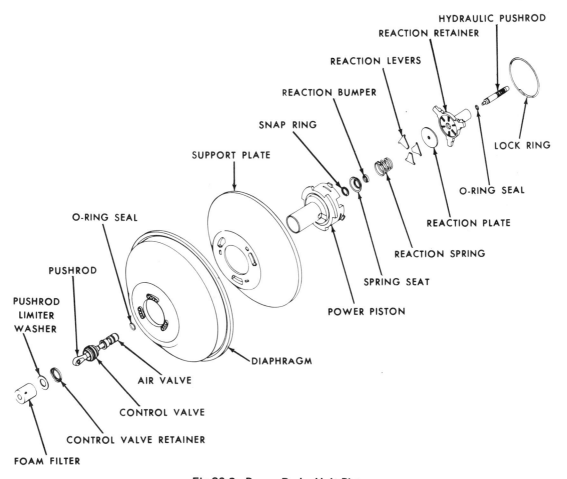

Fig 30-2. Power Brake Unit Piston

Diaphragm Support Plate: Metal disc providing continuous support for the rubber diaphragm inside the power unit.

Diaphragm-type Power Unit: A power unit having a single or double flexible neoprene rubber diaphragm that moves to provide the power braking force.

Holding Position: Term referring to the brake pedal being held in the applied position with a steady pressure.

Piston Rod Adjustment: Factory specified procedure involving gaging and adjusting master-cylinder piston operating rod for proper length.

Piston-type Power Unit: A power unit having a piston that slides to provide the power braking force. It has a lip seal or O-ring seal around its outer circumference.

Power Cylinder: A shell containing the power-brake operating parts.

Power Piston Assembly: Operating parts inside the power cylinder, including the diaphragm or piston, control valve(s), air valve, reaction parts, pushrod(s), plus miscellaneous related parts.

Power Unit Operational Check: Test that can be performed by pumping the brake pedal with the engine off; then applying the pedal firmly while starting the engine, to see if the brake pedal moved downward, indicating the unit is operating.

Power Unit *Runout*: Term referring to the situation occurring when maximum vacuum

187

Section 5 Brake Systems

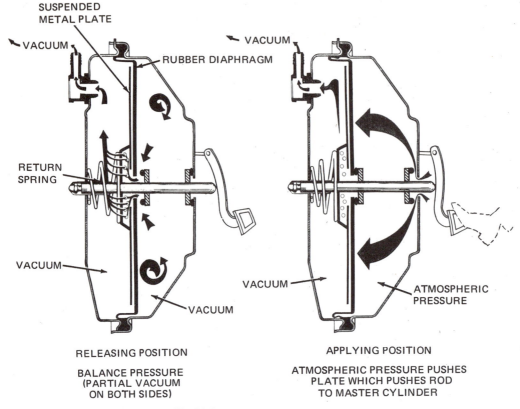

Fig 30-3. Power Brake Unit Operation

is applied in front power unit chamber and maximum atmospheric pressure has entered the rear chamber. Full power application is improved on certain models by using oil pressure developed by the power steering pump rather than air pressure as the booster force.

Releasing Position: Term referring to the relative position of the power cylinder components when the brake pedal pressure is released.

Shell: Outer front and/or rear metal container of the power brake unit.

Tandem (Diaphragm Booster): Double diaphragm power cylinder, providing additional braking force in heavy-duty applications.

Vacuum: An absence of atmospheric air pressure.

Vacuum Check Valve: One-way valve on the power cylinder vacuum supply hose connection. It maintains system vacuum under certain conditions.

Vacuum Suspended: A popular power brake system that has vacuum applied to both sides of the diaphragm or piston with the pedal in released position.

In the following exercises, indicate the best answer by inserting in the blanks the appropriate number, letter, word(s), or calculation, as required.

PICTORIAL REVIEW

A. Identify the power brake assembly parts in figure 30-4 by writing their correct letters in the blanks.

Unit 30 Power Brakes

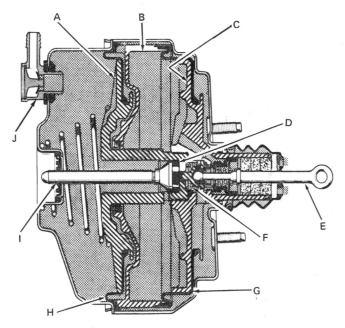

Fig 30-4. Power Brake Assembly

1. ____ reaction disc (or plate)
2. ____ hydraulic pushrod
3. ____ center plate
4. ____ valve-operating pushrod
5. ____ rear diaphragm
6. ____ front diaphragm
7. ____ rear diaphragm plate
8. ____ valve plunger
9. ____ front diaphragm plate
10. ____ vacuum check valve

SUMMARY REVIEW

____ 1. After a brake application, the diaphragm or piston returns to its *at rest* position because of

    a. atmospheric pressure.
    b. vacuum.
    c. a return spring.
    d. the reaction components.

____ 2. On vacuum suspended power systems, the diaphragm or piston has vacuum on both sides during

    a. brake release.
    b. brake application.
    c. brake holding.
    d. all of these.

____ 3. The purpose of a diaphragm support plate is to sustain the diaphragm

    a. at all times.
    b. extreme outer section.
    c. during brake application.
    d. during brake release.

____ 4. The purpose of the power unit reaction components is to

    a. apply additional booster pressure.
    b. stop the car quicker.
    c. help driver sense brake feel.
    d. avoid locking up the wheels during panic stops.

Section 5 Brake Systems

_____ 5. Power unit *runout* refers to
   a. a bent or damaged power cylinder.
   b. maximum applied vacuum.
   c. maximum applied air pressure.
   d. maximum applied vacuum and air pressure.

_____ 6. A brake pedal in the holding position refers to the brake pedal being
   a. pressed downward.
   b. pressed downward and held there steadily.
   c. stuck in downard position.
   d. released and moving upward.

7. Describe the procedure to follow when giving an installed power unit an operational check. _____
_____
_____

8. Explain what is meant by the term *atmospheric suspended* power brake unit. _____
_____

9. Insert the correct numbers of the matching terms or definitions in the blanks.

   a. _____ brake feel
   b. _____ unit runout
   c. _____ vacuum
   d. _____ shell
   e. _____ atmospheric air pressure
   f. _____ diaphragm support
   g. _____ power brake operational theory

   1. reaction parts
   2. power-unit metal container
   3. pressure differential causes motion
   4. disc plate
   5. lack of air pressure in an enclosed container
   6. 14.7 psi at sea level
   7. maximum applied vacuum and air pressure

REFERENCE REVIEW

_____ 1. The most popular type of automotive power brake unit today is the
   a. atmospheric suspended type.
   b. tandem-diaphragm type.
   c. piston type.
   d. single-diaphragm type.

_____ 2. The vacuum available to the power-brake unit during stopping is usually between _____ inches.
   a. 0 and 12
   b. 13 and 25
   c. 26 and 38
   d. 39 and 50

Unit 30 Power Brakes

_____ 3. Most automobiles having power brakes feature
   a. larger front and rear wheel cylinders.
   b. wider brake shoes or pads.
   c. thicker brake shoes or pads.
   d. none of these.

_____ 4. The master cylinder and power unit are fastened together by
   a. lock or retaining rings.
   b. threaded fasteners.
   c. welding.
   d. a circular clamp.

_____ 5. A vacuum check valve is used on the power unit to
   a. increase atmospheric pressure.
   b. close atmospheric port.
   c. maintain some system vacuum.
   d. assist power-unit return spring.

_____ 6. A tandem diaphragm booster is used on
   a. most automotive power-brake systems.
   b. light-duty applications.
   c. heavy-duty applications.
   d. no automobiles.

_____ 7. Atmospheric air enters a power unit through a
   a. hollow pushrod.
   b. diaphragm.
   c. tubing from the engine.
   d. filter.

_____ 8. If the power booster unit fails to provide braking assist, the brakes will
   a. fail to operate.
   b. operate at reduced efficiency.
   c. operate only if the engine is running.
   d. operate as usual.

_____ 9. If the pushrod at the front of the power unit is adjusted too long, the
   a. brakes will not apply.
   b. compensating port will be blocked.
   c. the intake port will be blocked.
   d. power unit will not operate.

_____ 10. The part likely to be defective if brake fluid is drawn through the power unit to the intake manifold by vacuum, is the
   a. one-way valve.
   b. hydraulic check valve.
   c. master cylinder secondary piston seal.
   d. master cylinder primary piston seal.

11. Explain what effect the automobile power-brake unit has on usable engine horsepower. _____
_____

191

SECTION 6 Suspension and Steering

UNIT 31 FRONT SUSPENSION

RELATED AUTOMOTIVE TERMS

Ball (Spherical) Joint: Suspension component that attaches the steering knuckle to either control arm. It features a ball-and-socket joint to allow pivoting in various directions.

Ball Joint Free-play (Slack): Allowable motion between the ball and joint housing, checked with the load removed. Radial free-play is horizontal motion and axial free-play is vertical motion checked with a special gage.

Ball Joint Internal Lubrication: Ball joint assembly may be prelubricated and sealed at the factory or it may have provision for periodic lubrication.

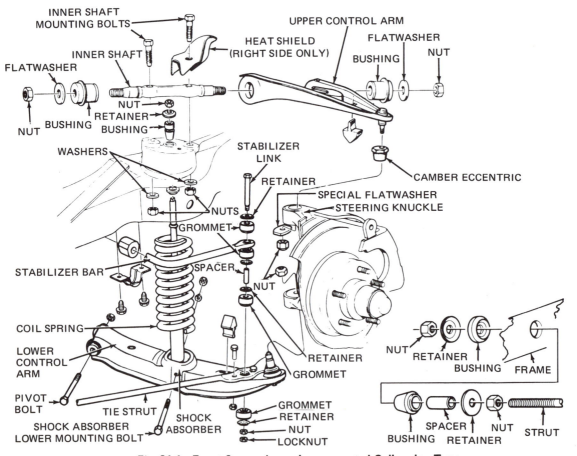

Fig 31-1. Front Suspension — Low-mounted Coil-spring Type

Unit 31 Front Suspension

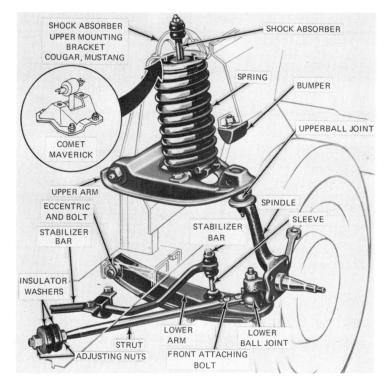

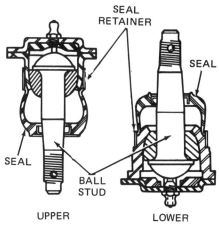

Fig 31-3. Ball Joint Assembly

Fig. 31-2. Front Suspension — High-mounted Coil-spring Type

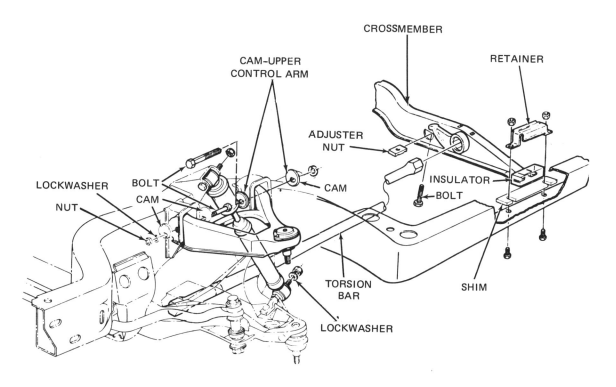

Fig 31-4. Front Suspension — Torsion-bar Type

Section 6 Suspension and Steering

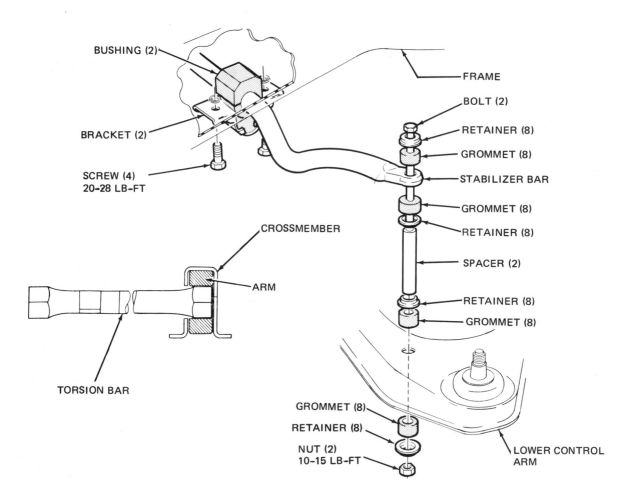

Fig 31-5. Front Stabilizer Bar Mounting

Ball Joint Preload: Term relating to certain joints having constant friction between the ball and joint housing socket. May be spring loaded.

Ball Joint Seal: Neoprene rubber seal fitting over ball joint stud against housing, keeping grease in and dirt out of the joint.

Coil Spring: A spring-steel bar that is wound into a spiral shape to provide the necessary springing effect on most front suspensions.

Coil Spring Suspension: A front suspension featuring a coil spring rather than a torsion bar or leaf spring.

Dampening (Friction) (Following) Ball Joint: The ball joint on a control arm that does not carry the vehicle load, but merely provides a pivot between the control arm and the steering knuckle.

Front Suspension System: Group of related automobile components that has several functions: provides for support of the vehicle front section, allows wheels to move vertically as they travel over the road surface, and provides adjustments for front wheel alignment.

High-mounted Coil Spring Suspension: A type of suspension having a coil spring located

Unit 31 Front Suspension

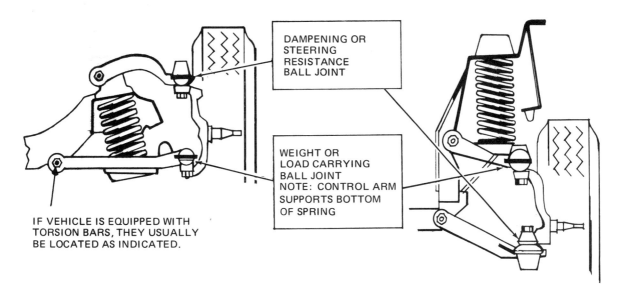

Fig 31-6. Weight carrying and Dampening Ball Joints on High and Low Coil Spring Front Suspensions

above the upper control arm, with the top end of the spring contacting the car body inside a spring tower. This type is found primarily on vehicles with *unitized* bodies.

Inner Shaft: Shaft upon which the inner end of the upper control arm pivots.

Load carrying Ball Joint: The ball joint supporting the vehicle weight. It is the lower ball joint on low-mounted coil spring or torsion bar suspensions and the upper ball joint on high-mounted coil spring suspensions.

Lower Control Arm: A front suspension part connected between the pivoting attachment point on the car frame and the lower ball joint, which is fastened to its outer end.

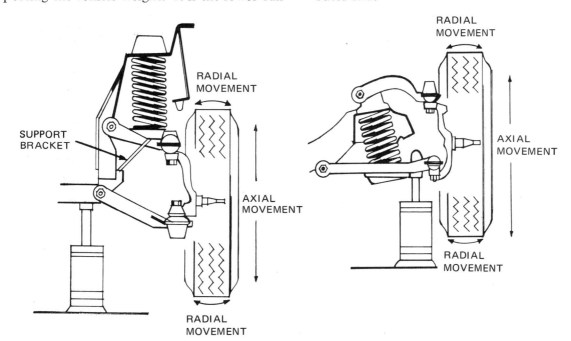

Fig 31-7. Ball joint Checking Procedure on High and Low Coil Spring Front Suspensions

195

Section 6 Suspension and Steering

Low-mounted Coil Spring Suspension: A type of suspension having a coil spring located above the lower control arm, with the top end of the spring contacting the car frame. This type is found primarily on vehicles having a separate frame or stub frame.

Pivot Bushings: Rubber bushings located at the inner end of the control arms where pivoting occurs.

Rubber Bumpers: Rubber stops positioned on or near a control arm to limit the maximum upward or downward travel of the arm.

Sprung Weight: Vehicle weight supported by the springs; includes such parts as the body, engine, and transmission.

Stabilizer Bar: A spring steel bar interconnected between the lower control arms and the vehicle framework. It increases stability by reducing sidesway (lean).

Steering Knuckle (Spindle): Cast or forged suspension part connected between the ball joints. This part contains the wheel hub spindle, supports the brake components, and provides an attachment location for the steering linkage.

Strut Rod: Heavy steel rod attached between car framework and lower control arm outer end on many vehicles; determines fore-and-aft position of outer arm.

Torsion Bar: A long spring steel bar that provides the necessary *springing effect* on certain front suspensions by twisting rather than compressing or bending; adjustable for tension.

Torsion Bar Suspension: A suspension featuring a torsion bar rather than a coil or leaf spring.

Unsprung Weight: Vehicle weight not supported by the springs. This includes such parts as the steering knuckle, brake assembly, tire and wheel. A smoother ride is possible if unsprung weight is kept to a minimum.

Upper Control Arm: A front suspension part connected between the pivoting attachment point (inner shaft) on the car-frame crossmember and the upper ball joint, which is fastened to its outer end.

In the following exercises, indicate the best answer by inserting in the blanks the appropriate number, letter, word(s), or calculation, as required.

PICTORIAL REVIEW

A. Identify the front suspension parts in figure 31-8 by writing their correct names in the blanks.

1. _____
2. _____
3. _____
4. _____
5. _____

6. _____
7. _____
8. _____
9. _____
10. _____

Unit 31 Front Suspension

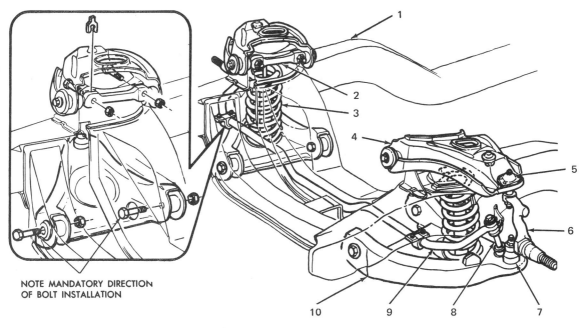

NOTE MANDATORY DIRECTION OF BOLT INSTALLATION

Fig 31-8. Front-suspension Assembly

SUMMARY REVIEW

____ 1. An automobile should produce a smoother ride if

    a. unsprung weight is kept to a minimum.
    b. sprung weight is kept to a minimum.
    c. vehicle weight is kept to a minimum.
    d. all of the above.

____ 2. The automobile suspension system(s) featuring height adjustment is the system(s) having

    a. torsion bars.   c. leaf springs.
    b. coil springs.   d. all of these.

____ 3. Another name for the dampening ball joint is the

    a. load-carrying joint.   c. friction joint.
    b. pivoting joint.   d. all of these.

____ 4. One ball joint likely to have allowable free-play in its unloaded position is located on the

    a. upper control arm on high-coil models.
    b. lower control arm on high-coil models.
    c. upper control arm on low-coil models.
    d. upper control arm on torsion bar models.

____ 5. The inner end of the upper control arm usually pivots on

    a. a threaded shaft.   c. lubricated bushings.
    b. a stabilizer bar.   d. rubber bushings.

Section 6 Suspension and Steering

_____ 6. The stabilizer bar improves vehicle handling by reducing vehicle
   a. nose dive during stops.   c. center of gravity.
   b. lean on turns.   d. riding height.

_____ 7. The strut rod helps determine the position of the
   a. stabilizer bar.   c. lower control arm.
   b. upper control arm.   d. steering knuckle upper end.

8. Are high-mounted coil springs usually found on automobiles having a *unitized body* or a *separate frame*? _____

9. List four parts that attach to or on the steering knuckle.
   a. _____   c. _____
   b. _____   d. _____

10. Name two purposes for the ball joint seal.
    a. _____   b. _____

11. Another name for all ball joints is _____ .

12. Insert the correct numbers of the matching terms or definitions in the blanks.
    a. ____ radial motion   1. limits maximum motion
    b. ____ axial motion   2. twists
    c. ____ spindle   3. steering knuckle
    d. ____ coil spring   4. bends
    e. ____ torsion bar   5. in-and-out free play
    f. ____ leaf spring   6. compresses
    g. ____ rubber bumper   7. up-and-down free play

REFERENCE REVIEW

_____ 1. If control arm rubber pivot bushings show perceptible wear, the _____ must be replaced.
   a. front suspension   c. inner pivot shaft
   b. control arm   d. rubber bushings

_____ 2. A torsion bar usually attaches to the vehicle framework and the
   a. outer end of the upper control arm.
   b. inner end of the upper control arm.
   c. outer end of the lower control arm.
   d. inner end of the lower control arm.

_____ 3. The amount of torque required to twist the stud in a disconnected dampening ball joint should range from _____ pound-feet.
   a. 0 to 1/2   c. 8 to 12
   b. 1 to 6   d. 14 to 20

Unit 31 Front Suspension

_____ 4. With the automobile jacked up in the correct place, ball-joint free play can best be determined by moving the wheel as specified and checking the motion with a
   a. micrometer.
   b. dial indicator.
   c. ball joint checking gage.
   d. steel scale or rule.

_____ 5. To check the load-carrying ball joint for slack on vehicles having low-mounted coil springs or torsion bars, a jack should support the vehicle weight at the
   a. front frame cross member.
   b. framework behind front wheel.
   c. lower control arm outer end.
   d. lower control arm inner end.

_____ 6. To check the load-carrying ball joint for slack on vehicles having high-mounted coil springs, the jack should support the vehicle at the
   a. front cross member.
   b. steering knuckle.
   c. lower control arm outer end.
   d. lower control arm inner end.

_____ 7. Allowable free play in a dampening ball joint is usually
   a. zero.
   b. 0.030 inch.
   c. 0.060 inch.
   d. 0.0300 inch.

_____ 8. Allowable axial free play in one original equipment manufacturer's load-carrying ball joint in the unloaded position is about
   a. 0.060 inch.
   b. 0.280 inch.
   c. 0.300 inch.
   d. 0.500 inch.

9. The lower control arm inner pivot may provide for adjusting the front wheel alignment angle called _____ while the lower strut rod may provide for adjusting the alignment angle called _____ .

10. It is often recommended that a _____ be placed between the upper control arm and the framework member when replacing or checking the load-carrying ball joint free play on automobiles having a high-mounted coil spring.

11. Name four ways ball joints are attached to control arms.
    a. _____   c. _____
    b. _____   d. _____

12. Explain in detail the procedures and precautions for lubricating ball joints having plugs rather than fittings.
    a. procedure _____
    b. precautions _____

13. Explain why a vehicle having a minimum of unsprung weight should ride smoothly. _____

199

UNIT 32 REAR SUSPENSION

RELATED AUTOMOTIVE TERMS

Coil Spring: See Unit 31, page 194.

Coil Spring Seats: Formed mounts that determine the coil spring position on the car frame and rear axle housing. Seats may have sound-insulating pads.

Control Arms (Links): Pivoting rear suspension upper and lower support arms attached between the automobile frame and the differential housing to position the rear axle assembly on models having coil springs. There are usually three or four per car.

Leaf Spring: A suspension spring featuring flat leaves of spring steel having graduated lengths. The spring may be multileaved or single leaf. The number of leaves depends on vehicle application.

Leaf Spring Center Bolt: A bolt passed through a hole in the center of each spring leaf for holding the leaves together. The bolt head locates the spring position on the axle-housing mount.

Leaf Spring Hanger: Car frame attachment bracket for the eye at the front of the rear leaf spring which allows front of spring to pivot.

Leaf Spring Shackle: Swing attachment for rear of leaf spring, located between car frame and spring eye. It provides for spring-length change during flexing.

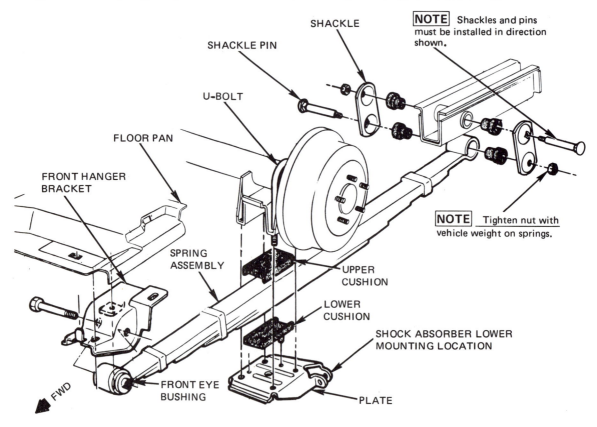

Fig 32-1. Rear Suspension, Leaf Spring Type

Unit 32 Rear Suspension

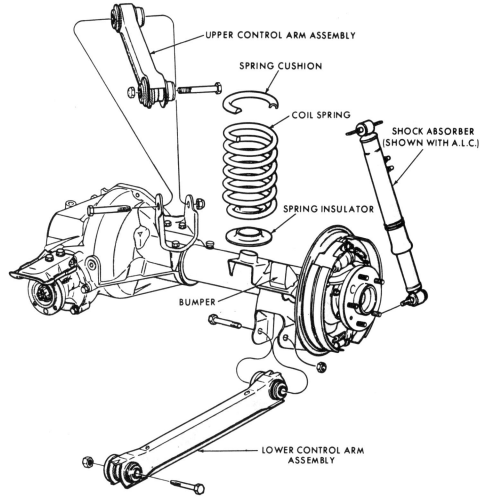

Fig 32-2. Rear Suspension, Coil Spring Type

Leaf Tip Inserts: Small, replaceable pads of plastic, asbestos, or rubber placed between spring leaves near their ends to promote slippage between the leaves during flexing.

Main (Master) Leaf: Spring leaf, usually top, on multiple leaf springs that provides the main vehicle support and contains the spring-mounting "eyes."

Multileaved Spring: A suspension spring having more than one leaf.

Rear-end Torque: Twisting reaction of rear-axle assembly in a direction opposite to that of wheel rotation when power is applied. It is controlled by the control arms in coil-spring models and by the leaf springs in models having leaves.

Rebound Clips: Metal clamps placed at intervals around multileaved springs to prevent the leaves from becoming separated on rebound. Usually three or four clips per spring.

Rubber Bumper: Rubber stop on the car frame that prevents metal-to-metal contact when the rear-axle housing moves to its maximum upward position.

Single-leaf Spring: A spring having one leaf. It may be tapered thinner and wider toward the ends, allowing a variable flexing rate.

Spring Eye: Term designating the main spring-leaf ends that are formed in an O-shape for placement of the rubber spring-mounting bushings.

Section 6 Suspension and Steering

Spring Leaf: A long, flat section of spring steel making up all or part of a leaf spring.

Spring Rate: The relationship of spring deflection to load applied, such as the amount of weight required to deflect the rear spring one inch.

Spring Steel: A special heat-treated alloy steel used in various automotive suspension systems that has elasticity (will return to its original shape after flexing, within design limits).

Spring Windup: Term referring to the slight S-Shape assumed by the leaf spring during extreme acceleration and braking. It may be controlled by traction bars on high-performance models.

Stabilizer Bar: A long spring steel bar attached to the car frame and connected to the rear axle housing on each side of the vehicle to reduce sidesway (lean) on certain models.

Track Bar: Long steel bar attached to the axle housing on one side of the car and the car frame on the other side. This bar maintains sideways alignment between axle housing and frame on certain coil spring equipped models.

U-bolts: Bolts that are U-shaped to fit around rear axle housing for clamping the leaf spring to the housing.

Variable Rate Spring: A spring that increasingly resists deflection as the load is increased. For example, such as a coil spring having its coils closer together at one end, or a single-leaf spring that is thinner near the ends.

Zinc Inner Liner: Thin zinc-metal leaf between the longer steel leaves to control sliding friction between the leaves and prevent corrosion on certain models.

In the following exercises, indicate the best answer by inserting in the blanks the appropriate number, letter, word(s), or calculation, as required.

PICTORIAL REVIEW

A. Identify the rear suspension parts shown in figure 32-2 by writing the correct names in the blanks.

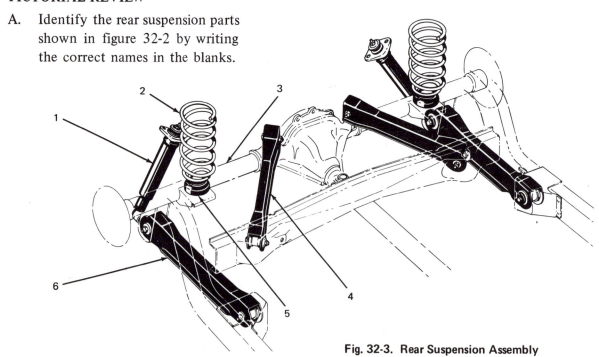

Fig. 32-3. Rear Suspension Assembly

Unit 32 Rear Suspension

1. _____ 4. _____
2. _____ 5. _____
3. _____ 6. _____

B. Identify the rear suspension parts shown in figure 32-4 by writing the correct names in the blanks.

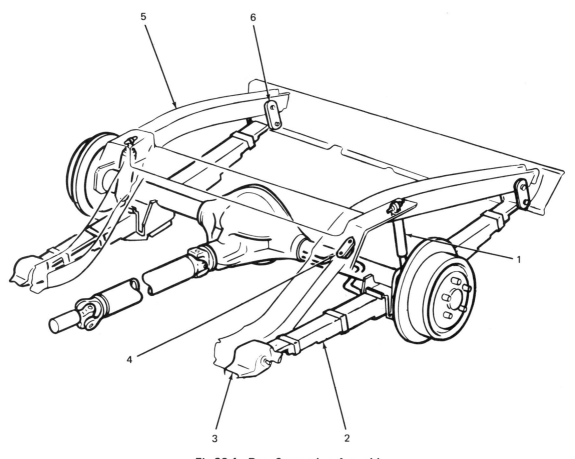

Fig 32-4. Rear Suspension Assembly

1. _____ 4. _____
2. _____ 5. _____
3. _____ 6. _____

SUMMARY REVIEW

____ 1. A rear stabilizer bar is usually attached to the rear axle housing and the

    a. lower control arm.
    b. upper control arm.
    c. car framework.
    d. spring seat.

Section 6 Suspension and Steering

_____ 2. The purpose of a rear track bar is to

    a. reduce spring windup.
    b. control rear-axle torque during acceleration and braking.
    c. reduce sidesway.
    d. maintain sideways rear-axle-to-frame alignment.

_____ 3. The name of the part contacted by a rubber bumper mounted on the frame side rails when the rear axle assembly *bottoms* is called the

    a. coil or leaf spring.   c. upper control arm.
    b. rear-axle assembly.   d. spring hanger.

_____ 4. An example of a variable-rate spring would be a coil spring that

    a. is long.
    b. is heavy duty.
    c. has close coils at one end only.
    d. has separated coils at both ends.

_____ 5. The function of a leaf spring shackle is to

    a. allow for spring length changes.
    b. allow front of spring to pivot.
    c. control sidesway.
    d. control rear torque.

_____ 6. A broken rebound clip may cause the

    a. spring to bottom.   c. shackle to break.
    b. ride to become rougher.   d. leaves to separate.

_____ 7. Spring windup may occur on automobiles having

    a. leaf springs.   c. strong coil springs.
    b. weak coil springs.   d. traction bars.

_____ 8. A zinc inner liner between certain spring leaves may reduce spring corrosion and control

    a. sideways friction between leaves.
    b. lengthwise friction between leaves.
    c. vehicle sidesway.
    d. spring windup.

9. Is the spring hanger usually mounted near the *front* or *rear* of the leaf spring? _____

10. Name two functions of a leaf spring center bolt.

    a. _____

    b. _____

11. Insert the correct numbers of the matching terms or definitions in the blanks.

   a. ____ spring windup
   b. ____ spring eye
   c. ____ spring rate
   d. ____ leaf-tip insert
   e. ____ U-bolts
   f. ____ spring steel
   g. ____ control arms

   1. weight to deflect spring one inch
   2. plastic pad
   3. O-shaped end
   4. retains leaf spring to axle housing
   5. heat-treated alloy metal
   6. mounting links
   7. rear end torque

REFERENCE REVIEW

____ 1. The part that acts as a stop to limit the downward motion of the rear axle assembly is the
   a. track bar.
   b. lower control arm.
   c. shock absorber.
   d. spring.

____ 2. New tip inserts on leaf springs are easiest to replace if the _____ is supported on jackstands.
   a. rear axle assembly
   b. rear springs
   c. car frame
   d. control arms

____ 3. If a broken leaf is replaced on a multileaved spring, also replace the
   a. U-bolts.
   b. spring shackle.
   c. spring hanger.
   d. center bolt.

____ 4. The suspension components that minimize sound transfer to the frame from the leaf springs are
   a. rebound clips.
   b. rubber bushings.
   c. spring hangers.
   d. spring shackles.

____ 5. During leaf spring removal, one set of supporting jackstands must be placed under the
   a. car frame.
   b. rear springs.
   c. lower control arms.
   d. shock absorber mounts.

____ 6. If the rubber bushings located in the leaf spring eyes are worn, it will be necessary to replace the
   a. shackle.
   b. rubber bushings.
   c. spring.
   d. shackle bolts.

____ 7. The number of leave(s) found in most automotive leaf springs is
   a. one.
   b. two.
   c. three.
   d. four or more.

Section 6 Suspension and Steering

8. Are stabilizer bars more often used on the *front* or *rear* suspension system? _____

9. The suspension component(s) that minimize(s) sound transfer from the coil spring to the frame is known as the_____ .

10. What feature may the control arms have to change the pinion drive angle vertically? _____

11. Explain why leaf springs are sometimes called semielliptical springs._____

12. The minimum number of control arms on a rear coil spring suspension is _____ .

UNIT 33 SHOCK ABSORBERS

RELATED AUTOMOTIVE TERMS

Adjustable Shock Absorber: A shock having an external adjustment to calibrate the shock precisely for various operating conditions.

Air Shocks: Shock operating on principles of air pressure; may also have a hydraulic section.

Automatic Level Control: A shock system provided as an accessory on certain automobiles to maintain automatically the correct "riding height" under various loads. Air pressure operated. Primarily used for the rear suspension.

Compression (Base) Valve: Calibrated valve located at the base of the shock providing variable resistance to fluid flow during compression (shock shortening).

Dampening Effect: Term describing the effect shocks have on reducing suspension-spring oscillations.

Defective Shock Absorber: A shock that fails to provide sufficient dampening action. It may be worn out, have been mechanically damaged, or leak excessively.

Double Acting Shock Absorber: A shock that provides a dampening effect on both compression and rebound. Shock action may provide for more dampening on rebound than on compression, depending on the application.

Load-leveler Shock Absorber: A special shock having an external coil spring attached to the shock for carrying a portion of the vehicle

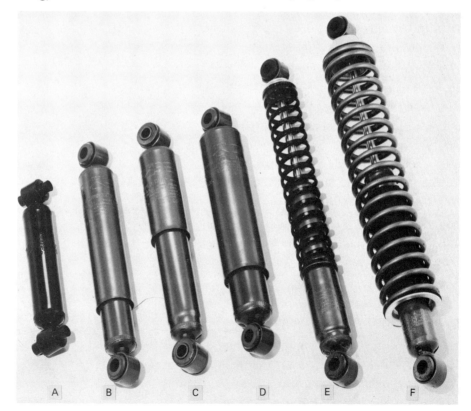

A. Standard Duty
B. Heavy Duty
C. Heavy Duty
D. Extra-heavy Duty
E. Front Load Leveler
F. Rear Load Leveler

Fig 33-1. Shock Absorber Types

Section 6 Suspension and Steering

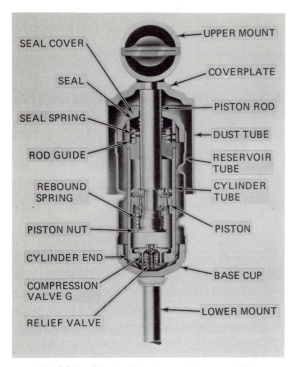

Fig 33-2. Shock Absorber — Cutaway View

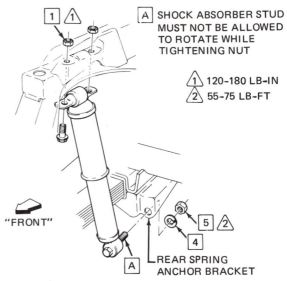

Fig 33-3. Shock Absorber Mounting

load. They may be installed at the rear and/or front of certain automobiles.

Mounting Grommets: Rubber bushings used at both ends of the shocks for mounting. They reduce the transfer of sounds and jarring motions between the shocks and their mounting points on the vehicle, and may be replaceable.

Oil Reservoir: Shock section containing an extra fluid supply to meet operational requirements. Some fluid flows through the base valve alternately to and then from the reservoir during compression and rebound.

Piston Rod: Plated rod attached to the shock piston, usually extending from top of shock to provide attachment to vehicle frame.

Piston Rod Seal: Nonreplaceable oil seal around movable piston rod, located at the upper end of the hydraulic cylinder.

Rear Suspension Rebound Stop: A function of the rear shocks as they limit the distance the rear axle assembly can move downward. This requires supporting the rear axle assembly when replacing shocks.

Rebound (Piston) Valve: Calibrated valve mounted on shock piston that provides variable resistance to fluid flow during rebound (shock lengthening).

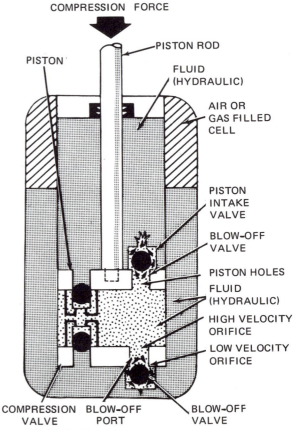

Fig 33-4. Shock Absorber Action: Compression

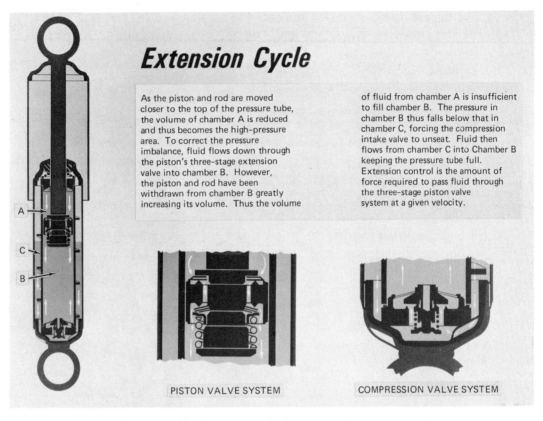

Fig 33-5. Shock Absorber Action: Extension or Rebound

Shock Absorber: An assembly that operates hydraulically to dampen vehicle spring oscillations (reduce bouncing) and to help keep the tires in contact with the road surface.

Shock Compression: Term referring to the shock in a shortened position, which occurs when the wheel moves upward.

Shock Fluid: Specially formulated hydraulic fluid used inside shocks.

Shock Hydraulic Principles: Fluid is forced through orifices and/or valves at a controlled rate to provide the desired dampening effect.

Shock Mounting Position: The direction and/or angle at which a shock is mounted. It may be vertical, horizontal, or slanted inward at the top.

Shock Operational Check: Method used to check shock efficiency. Possible ways include bouncing vehicle bumpers vigorously and observing shock dampening action, or pumping brakes slowly at low speed to see if a vehicle "rocking" motion is set up.

Shock Piston: Component attached to the bottom of the piston rod and containing the rebound valve. It operates back and forth inside the inner cylinder.

Shock Rebound: Term referring to the shock absorber in a lengthened position, which occurs when the suspension or spring moves downward.

Spring Oscillation: Continued up-and-down (compression-and-rebound) motion of the spring after the wheel has encountered a bump or hole on the road surface. It diminishes gradually, depending on the condition of the shock.

Telescoping (Direct-acting) Shock Absorber: A shock having certain working parts that move in-and-out during compression and rebound.

Section 6 Suspension and Steering

In the following exercises, indicate the best answer by inserting in the blanks the appropriate number, letter, word(s), or calculation, as required.

PICTORIAL REVIEW

A. Identify the shock absorber components in figure 33-6 by writing their correct letters in the blanks.

1. ____ relief valve
2. ____ base cup
3. ____ upper mount
4. ____ dust tube
5. ____ seal
6. ____ lower mount
7. ____ cover plate
8. ____ piston rod
9. ____ reservoir tube
10. ____ piston
11. ____ compression valve
12. ____ cylinder tube
13. ____ seal cover

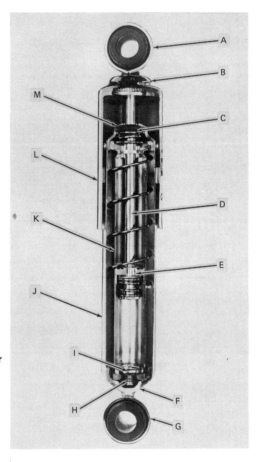

Fig 33-6. Shock Absorber

SUMMARY REVIEW

____ 1. The purpose of a shock absorber is to
   a. raise the suspension slightly.
   b. reduce spring oscillations.
   c. provide an adjustable ride.
   d. increase shock rebound.

____ 2. The word "dampening" as it refers to shock absorbers, means
   a. diminish oscillations.   c. rebound.
   b. telescoping.   d. compression.

____ 3. The shock compression valve is located on or in the
   a. reservoir area.   c. upper mounting stud.
   b. shock lower portion.   d. piston rod.

4. Fluid leaves the shock inner cylinder during
   a. shock rebound.
   b. spring rebound.
   c. spring compression.
   d. shock lengthening.

5. On a late-model car front suspension having high-mounted coil springs, the lower shock mount attaches to the
   a. upper control arm.
   b. lower control arm.
   c. car framework.
   d. steering knuckle.

6. A shock containing a badly leaking piston rod seal should have
   a. fluid added.
   b. the seal replaced.
   c. the shock replaced.
   d. a rebuilding kit installed.

7. The shock oil reservoir is located near the section known as the
   a. inner.
   b. upper.
   c. lower inner.
   d. lower outer.

8. The amount of rear suspension rebound is limited by the
   a. suspension springs.
   b. spring shackles.
   c. rubber bumpers.
   d. shock absorbers.

9. Describe what is meant by a double-acting shock. _____

10. Insert the correct numbers of the matching terms or definitions in the blanks.
    a. ____ dampening
    b. ____ base valve
    c. ____ piston valve
    d. ____ rebound motion
    e. ____ compression
    f. ____ stops rear axle downward travel
    g. ____ stops rear axle upward travel

    1. reduce oscillations
    2. reaction motion in opposite direction
    3. rubber bumper
    4. compression valve
    5. shorten
    6. rebound valve
    7. shock absorber

REFERENCE REVIEW

1. Factory installed shocks on new cars are usually known as
   a. O.E.M.
   b. heavy-duty.
   c. load-levelers.
   d. air-hydraulic.

2. Shock absorber fluid has a viscosity (thickness) closest to another fluid used in
   a. standard transmissions.
   b. automatic transmissions.
   c. engines.
   d. rear axle assemblies.

Section 6 Suspension and Steering

___ 3. Load-leveler shocks should be installed on the rear of
   a. all full-size automobiles.
   b. original equipment heavy-duty suspension.
   c. all compact-size automobiles.
   d. automobiles carrying heavy loads at the rear.

___ 4. Standard shock absorbers must be held upright (vertically) during off-the-car motion checking because of possible
   a. air locks.   c. shock damage.
   b. fluid leakage.   d. excessive motion resistance.

___ 5. Most front shocks are located
   a. on the upper control arm.   c. inside the coil spring.
   b. on the steering knuckle.   d. parallel with the torsion bar.

___ 6. On a front suspension having torsion bars, the lower shock mount attaches to the
   a. upper control arm.   c. car framework.
   b. lower control arm.   d. steering knuckle.

___ 7. The compressor that produces the pressure to operate the shocks having automatic level control is powered by
   a. the fan belt.   c. electricity.
   b. oil pressure.   d. engine vacuum.

8. Explain how the "ride" of an automobile is affected by defective shock absorbers. _____
   _____

9. What is likely to happen if an automobile is raised on a frame-contact hoist and a rear shock is removed without using an additional support stand? _____
   _____

10. Describe three ways to check an installed shock absorber.
    a. _____
    b. _____
    c. _____

11. Make a list of four reasons why an automotive technician may recommend shock replacement during a visual inspection of a used installed shock absorber.
    a. _____   c. _____
    b. _____   d. _____

UNIT 34 WHEEL ALIGNMENT ANGLES

RELATED AUTOMOTIVE TERMS

Alignment Adjustment Method: The way manufacturers provide for changing caster, camber, and toe-in; methods include shims, eccentric washers, elongated slots, or changing the length of a rod.

Ball Joint Centerline: An imaginary line drawn through the centers of the upper and lower ball joints.

Camber Angle: The amount, measured in degrees from the vertical, that the tire top is tilted outward (positive) or inward (negative). Positive camber reduces road shock transferred to the steering system, puts more vehicle weight on the inner front wheel bearing, and reduces steering effort. This angle is adjustable.

Caster Angle: The amount, measured in degrees from the vertical, that the upper ball joint is located behind (positive) or ahead of (negative) the lower ball joints. Positive caster assists in maintaining directional stability and in straightening the front wheels after a turn. This angle is adjustable.

Curb (Trim) Height: Proper height of the automobile as specified by the manufacturer, measured from the frame or a suspension component to the floor on certain automobiles, and between suspension components on others. Adjustable at the front if the car is torsion bar equipped.

Front End Geometry: Term referring to the angular relationships involving the front suspension, steering system, and tires.

Front Wheel (Front End) Alignment: The procedure of using specialized equipment to check certain steering and front suspension angles and making the changes (adjustments) necessary to meet factory specifications.

Included Angle: The sum of the camber angle added to the steering-axis inclination angle.

Preliminary Alignment Checks: An inspection of the suspension and steering components to determine whether certain specifications, defects, or looseness require correction before performing a wheel alignment. Items included are shocks, wheel bearings, ball joints, steering

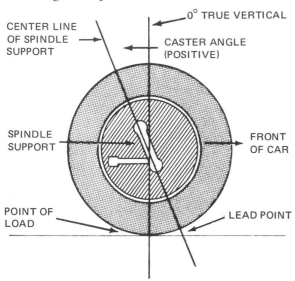

Fig 34-1. Principles of Caster

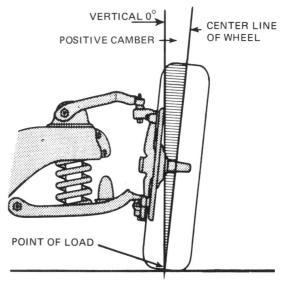

Fig 34-2. Principles of Camber

Section 6 *Suspension and Steering*

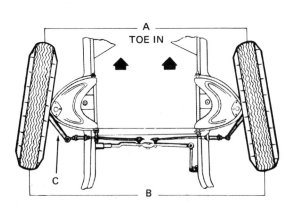

Fig 34-3. **Principles of Toe-in**

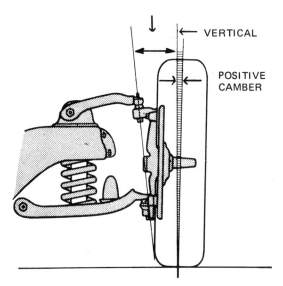

Fig 34-4. **Steering Axis (Ball Joint) Inclination**

joints, curb height, tire pressure, balance, run-out, tire wear patterns, etc.

Slip Angle: The difference in the path the wheels follow during a turn compared to the actual direction they are pointing. Centrifugal force at higher speeds increases the slip angle.

Steering Axis (Ball Joint) Inclination: The amount, measured in degrees from the vertical, that the ball joint centerline is tilted inward at the top to position the ball joint centerline toward the wheel centerline at the point where the two lines intersect the road surface. This angle promotes easier turning (steering), helps keep wheels pointed straight ahead, and reduces road shock transfer to the steering system. It is not adjustable.

Steering Wheel Centering: The procedure of turning both tie rod couplings equally in the proper direction to correctly position the steering-wheel spokes. This procedure also places the steering gears on their high (center) position.

Toe-in: The amount, measured in inches or millimeters, that the front of the front tires are closer together than the back of the front tires, when the car is not moving (running toe-in should be near zero at highway speeds).

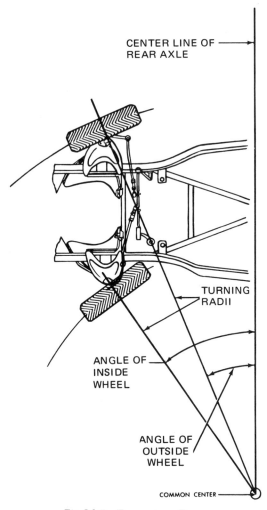

Fig 34-5. **Toe-out on Turns**

Toe-in compensates for the tendency of the front wheels to angle outward at higher speeds because of friction with the road and other alignment angles. This angle is adjustable by changing the length of the tie rods.

Toe-out on Turns: The amount the front of the front tires separate during turns; varies with the sharpness of the turn. This amount is set by angling the short steering arms inward where they attach to the steering knuckle. It is not adjustable.

Wheel Centerline: An imaginary line through the center of the tire. It is a vertical line if the tire is exactly in an upright position.

In the following exercises, indicate the best answer by inserting in the blanks the appropriate number, letter, word(s), or calculation, as required.

PICTORIAL REVIEW

A. Identify the front suspension angles in figure 34-6 by writing their correct letters in the blanks.

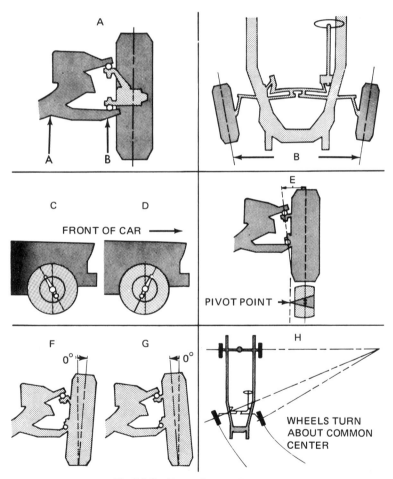

Fig 34-6. Front Suspension Angles

1. ____ toe-in
2. ____ positive camber
3. ____ positive caster
4. ____ toe-out on turns
5. ____ suspension height check
6. ____ negative camber
7. ____ ball joint inclination
8. ____ negative caster

Section 6 Suspension and Steering

SUMMARY REVIEW

1. The phrase "front-end geometry" refers to
   a. alignment checks.
   b. alignment adjusting procedure.
   c. parts angular relationships.
   d. alignment equipment.

2. The angle formed when the top of the wheel slants outward is known as
   a. positive camber.
   b. negative camber.
   c. positive caster.
   d. negative caster.

3. The angle formed when the upper ball joint is positioned ahead of the lower ball joint is known as
   a. negative camber.
   b. negative caster.
   c. positive caster.
   d. positive camber.

4. The included angle is the sum of the steering-axis inclination angle added to the angle called
   a. toe-in.
   b. toe-out.
   c. caster.
   d. camber.

5. During a sharp left turn, the front wheels should have
   a. toe-out.
   b. toe-in.
   c. zero caster.
   d. zero toe-in.

6. At a speed of 50 mph, both front wheels should have
   a. zero steering-axis inclination.
   b. toe-out.
   c. zero toe-in.
   c. toe-in.

7. List four items to observe prior to checking and/or adjusting front-wheel alignment relative to the tires.
   a. _____
   b. _____
   c. _____
   d. _____

8. Name four different ways manufacturers provide for changing the alignment angles.
   a. _____
   b. _____
   c. _____
   d. _____

9. How is toe-in adjusted on most automobiles? _____

10. Describe how to center the steering wheel if the spokes are not in the desired position. _____

11. Insert the correct numbers of the matching terms or definitions in the blanks.

   a. ____ steering axis inclination
   b. ____ toe-in
   c. ____ one alignment preliminary check
   d. ____ tire slip angle
   e. ____ positive caster
   f. ____ negative camber
   g. ____ positive camber

   1. wheels closer together at the front
   2. curb height
   3. ball joint centerline slanted backward at the top
   4. wheel centerline slanted inward at the top
   5. increases at high speed
   6. wheel centerline slanted outward at the top
   7. ball joint inclination angle

REFERENCE REVIEW

____ 1. One reason certain automobiles have positive caster is to
   a. reduce tire wear.
   b. make turning easier.
   c. reduce road shock.
   d. increase directional stability.

____ 2. During a wheel alignment, the front wheels should have
   a. toe-in.
   b. toe-out.
   c. zero toe-in.
   d. a positive slip angle.

____ 3. The alignment angle usually adjusted last is
   a. caster.
   b. camber.
   c. toe-in.
   d. steering axis inclination.

____ 4. If the steering-axis inclination angle is out of specifications, the automotive technician should
   a. replace parts.
   b. adjust toe-out on turns.
   c. adjust ball joint inclination.
   d. adjust steering axis inclination.

5. Underline what happens to caster and camber if an eccentric at the rear of an upper control arm is moved outward.
   Caster: more negative   more positive   unchanged
   Camber: more negative   more positive   unchanged

6. Underline what happens when front and rear upper control arm eccentrics are moved inward equally.
   Caster: more positive   more negative   unchanged
   Camber: more positive   more negative   unchanged

7. Underline the angles usually considered adjustable.
   a. toe-in
   b. toe-out on turns
   c. steering axis inclination
   d. camber
   e. caster
   f. slip

Section 6 Suspension and Steering

8. Should the *left-* or the *right*-side suspension have up to 1/2 degree more positive caster, if there is a difference? _____

9. Does lengthening the tie rods, located behind the suspension, *increase* or *decrease* the toe-in? _____

10. Should the gap on a tie-rod coupling clamp be positioned *in alignment with* or *away from* the coupling gap? _____

11. List four vehicle operational effects of improperly aligned front wheels.

    a. _____ c. _____
    b. _____ d. _____

12. What two alignment angles are most likely to cause improper tire wear if they do not meet factory specifications?

    a. _____ b. _____

UNIT 35 TIRES

RELATED AUTOMOTIVE TERMS

Bead: Steel wires around inner edge of both tire sides. It is wrapped with rubber and controls the "rim diameter."

Bias-ply Belted Tire: A tire that has the ply cords placed diagonally across the tire from bead-to-bead, with alternate ply layers crisscrossing diagonally in opposite directions. In addition, there are belts running around the tire circumference under the tread section only. Belts reduce tread distortion, increase tread life, and minimize rolling friction.

Bias-ply Tire: A tire that has the ply cords placed diagonally across the tire from bead-to-bead, with alternate ply layers criss-crossing diagonally in opposite directions.

Construction: Physical makeup of a tire, including rubber, plies, bead, sidewall, tread, inner liner, ply-cord angle, and belts, if any.

Cord Material: Substance used in tire construction to provide strength and maintain desired shape; may be rayon, nylon, fiberglass, polyester, steel, etc.

Drop Center Rim: Automotive wheel that has a smaller diameter center section, to facilitate tire replacement.

Lateral Runout: The measured amount of sideways wobble on a rotating tire. Allowable maximum ranges from 0.060 inch (1.52 mm) on some cars to 0.100 inch (2.54 mm) on others.

Load Range (Rating): Term designating the maximum weight tires are designed to support, usually related to a specific air pressure. Tires labeled "load range B," for example, are equivalent to a four-ply rating and can carry a maximum of 1150 pounds each at 32 psi inflation.

Manufacturer's Code: Lettered marking code on tire sidewall indicating tire manufacturer, plant, tire size, type of construction, and date of manufacture.

Plies: The layers of rubber-impregnated cord material in the tire casing.

Ply Rating: Term formerly used to designate the load-carrying capacity of a tire, not always the actual number of plues but the rated strength. A four-ply rated tire may have two plies but is considered as strong as a standard four-ply tire.

Radial-ply Belted Tire: A tire having the ply cords placed at right angles (perpendicular) to the beads, plus belts under the tread section. It has the least tread distortion while moving, which minimizes tread wear and rolling friction.

Radial Runout: The measured amount of out-of-roundness on rotating tires. Allowable maximum ranges from 0.050 inch (1.47 mm) on some cars to 0.090 inch (2.29 mm) on others.

Rim Safety Ridge: Small metal ridge just inside tire-bead section to retain the tire position on the rim in case of a "flat" or "blowout." Tends to keep the bead of an uninflated tire out of the rim drop-center area.

Tire Functions: Reduces jolts imparted to the vehicle caused by road irregularities (cushions ride). Supports vehicle weight plus provides friction against the road surface during starting, cruising, stopping, steering, etc.

Tire Inflation: Air pressure inside tire, measured in psi (pounds per square inch). Pressure should be checked when tire is cool or has been driven less than one mile.

Section 6 Suspension and Steering

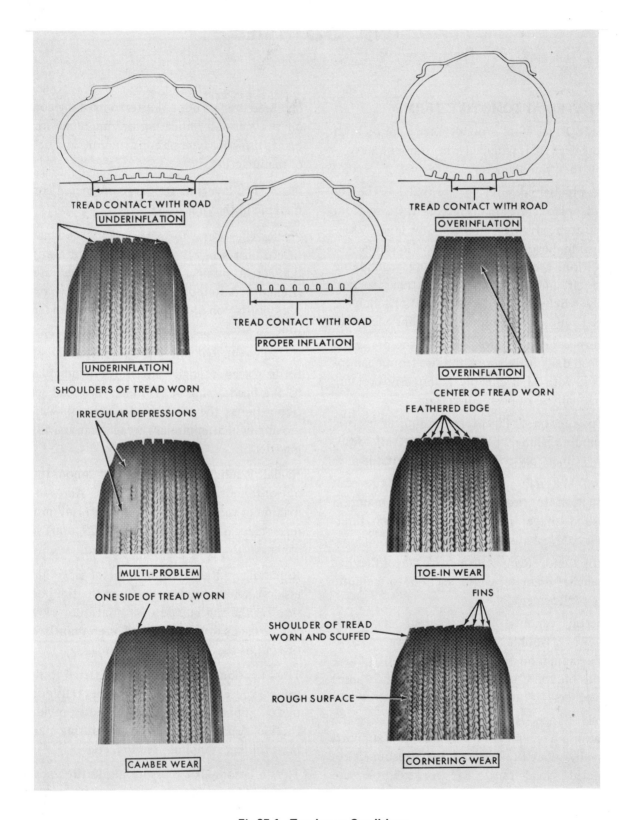

Fig 35-1. Tread-wear Conditions

Unit 35 Tires

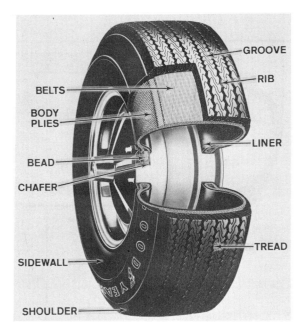

Fig 35-2. Tubeless-tire Construction

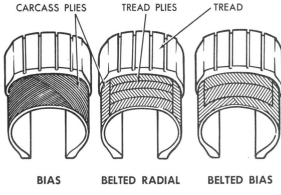

Fig 35-3. Types of Tire Construction

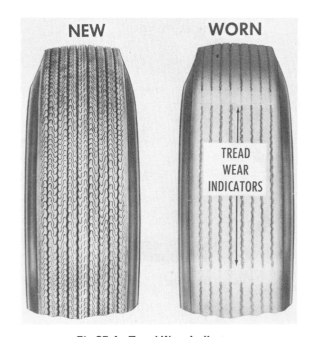

Fig 35-4. Tread Wear Indicators

Tire Rotation: Switching tires around to various positions on vehicles to equalize tire wear. It is not recommended that radial tires and certain bias-belted tires be switched from side-to-side, only from front-to-back on the same side.

Tire Sidewall: That part of the tire between the "bead" and the "tread pattern."

Tire Size: Designated size of a tire. Most new tires are rated by cross-sectional size, such as A, B, C, D, E, F, G, H, J, L, etc.; series (aspect ratio) (height/width), such as 83, 78, 70, 60, etc; and rim diameter, such as 13, 14, 15, 16, etc. An H78-15 tire has a larger cross section than a "G" series tire, is 78% as high as it is wide, and fits a 15-inch diameter wheel.

Tire Trueing: Procedure of "rounding" a tire by removing rubber so the tread face forms a true circle by using special equipment to remove high-tread areas while revolving the tire; should be done while tire is supporting vehicle weight.

Tread Distortion: Tread shape change on certain tires as rotating contact is made with the road surface. It is less on tires having belts.

Tread Wear Indicators: Projections of rubber 1/16-inch high in the bottom of the tread grooves spaced around the tire to identify a tire worn to the recommended safe limit.

Tubeless Tire: A tire having an integral inside rubber liner to retain air. The liner is used in place of an inner tube.

Valve Stem: Assembly mounted in rim (or inner tube) to provide a method of increasing or decreasing air pressure inside tire.

Wear Pattern: Visible tire tread wear. Normal wear pattern evident by an evenly worn tread.

221

Section 6 Suspension and Steering

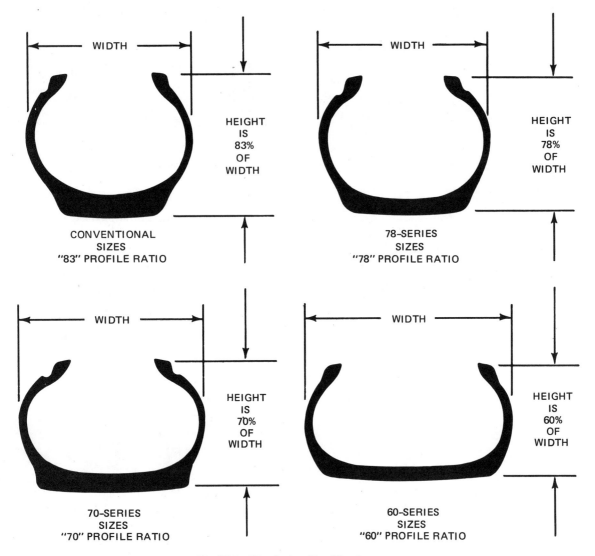

Fig 35-5. Tire Series Classifications

Abnormal wear pattern evident by an unevenly worn tread, such as excessive wear on one side of the tread (camber problem), too much or too little wear at tread center compared to both edges (inflation or cornering problem), saw-toothed wear across tread face (toe-in problem), flat spot (cupped) wear (multiproblem).

Wheel Nuts: Threaded nuts used to retain the wheel to the studs on the hub assembly. They should be tightened with a torque wrench, especially on cars having disc brakes.

In the following exercises, indicate the best answer by inserting in the blanks the appropriate number, letter, word(s), or calculation, as required.

PICTORIAL REVIEW

A. Identify the tire sections in figure 35-6 by writing their letters in the blanks.

Unit 35 Tires

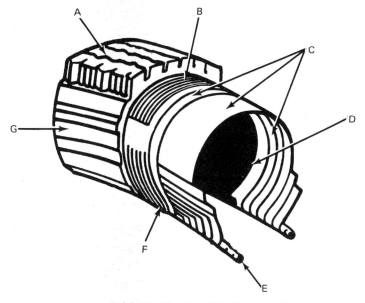

Fig 35-6. Tubeless Tire Construction

1. _____ inner layer (liner)   5. _____ sidewall rubber
2. _____ bead wires   6. _____ rubber chamber
3. _____ tread rubber   7. _____ belts
4. _____ body plies

B. Indicate the tread wear problem by writing the cause in each blank.

Fig 35-7. Tread Wear Problems

1. _____   2. _____   3. _____

C. Indicate the type of tire construction by writing the name in each blank.

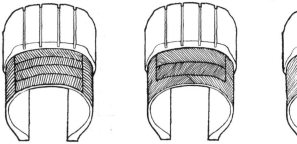

Fig 35-8. Types of Tire Construction

1. _____   2. _____   3. _____

223

Section 6 Suspension and Steering

SUMMARY REVIEW

____ 1. Tires labeled as having a "load range B" are equivalent in load-carrying capacity to a

    a. four-ply tire.   c. one-ply tire.
    b. four-ply rated tire.   d. six-ply tire.

____ 2. The term "ply rating" refers to the

    a. actual number of plies.   c. allowable inflation pressure.
    b. rated strength.   d. aspect ratio.

____ 3. An underinflated tire will wear the tread most near the

    a. edges.   c. outside.
    b. center.   d. inside.

____ 4. Tires worn down just to the tread-wear indicators have _____ of tread left.

    a. 0.030 inch   c. 1/16 inch
    b. 1/32 inch   d. 1/8 inch

____ 5. Tire pressure should be checked when the tire is

    a. driven over ten miles.   c. warm.
    b. worn down to the wear   d. cool.
        indicators.

____ 6. Maximum radial runout specified by certain automobile manufacturers is

    a. 0.010 inch.   c. zero.
    b. one inch.   d. 0.050 inch.

____ 7. The purpose of tire rotation on certain automobiles is to

    a. avoid balancing.   c. allow ply separation.
    b. avoid alignments.   d. equalize wear.

8. What are two main functions of tires?

    a. _____   b. _____

9. List five cord materials used in ply construction.

    a. _____   d. _____
    b. _____   e. _____
    c. _____

10. Is a *78 series* or a *70 series* tire wider? _____

11. Explain the purpose of the rim safety ridge. _____
_____

12. Insert the correct numbers of the matching terms or definitions in the blanks.

    a. ____ radial runout
    b. ____ saw-toothed wear
    c. ____ outside tread wear
    d. ____ lateral runout
    e. ____ excess center tread wear
    f. ____ bias-belted tire
    g. ____ radial-belted tire
    h. ____ aspect ratio

    1. ply cords perpendicular to beads
    2. out-of-roundness
    3. toe-in problem
    4. height/width
    5. camber problem
    6. ply cords at a 30- or 40-degree angle to the beads
    7. sideways wobble
    8. overinflation

REFERENCE REVIEW

____ 1. Tread distortion is least on
   a. radial tires.
   b. bias radial tires.
   c. bias-ply tires.
   d. bias-ply belted tires.

____ 2. A four-ply rated (two-ply) tire usually has ply cords that are _____ than a tire with four full plies.
   a. larger in diameter
   b. smaller in diameter
   c. the same diameter
   d. larger on some and smaller on others

____ 3. A tire having excess radial runout will cause
   a. vibration and shake.
   b. alignment problems.
   c. a tire-pressure increase.
   d. wheel weights to fly off.

____ 4. Tires labeled as having a "load range D" are equivalent in load carrying capacity to a
   a. two-ply tire.
   b. four-ply rated tire.
   c. six-ply tire.
   d. eight-ply rated tire.

____ 5. Front tires having "feather edge" wear on each tread section with the sharp edges pointing outward have
   a. excess toe-in.
   b. caster wear.
   c. excess toe-out.
   d. camber.

____ 6. Tire wear caused by fast cornering appears similar to wear caused by
   a. improper caster.
   b. overinflation.
   c. improper camber.
   d. underinflation.

____ 7. A radial tire wears less than other tires discussed in this unit because it has
   a. less tire pressure.
   b. more tire pressure.
   c. less tread distortion.
   d. more tread distortion.

Section 6 Suspension and Steering

____ 8. A bias-ply belted tire that shows extra wear on the second tread section in from each edge is considered to be

a. underinflated.   c. improperly balanced.
b. overinflated.   d. normal.

____ 9. If tire rotation is suggested by the manufacturer, the mileage interval most often mentioned is

a. 1,000.   c. 5,000.
b. 2,000.   d. 10,000.

____ 10. Rubber valve stems should be replaced

a. yearly.   c. at every second tire replacement.
b. when replacing every tire.   d. before wheel balancing.

11. Give two reasons why it may be advisable to rotate tires.

a. _____
b. _____

12. Give two reasons why it may be inadvisable to rotate tires.

a. _____
b. _____

13. List six causes of tire tread flat spotting (cupping) along the outside edge.

a. _____   d. _____
b. _____   e. _____
c. _____   f. _____

UNIT 36 WHEEL BALANCING

RELATED AUTOMOTIVE TERMS

Balancing Preliminary Steps: Procedures necessary on tire and wheel assembly before balancing to ensure accurate balancing. Includes such steps as checking lateral and radial runout, cleaning wheel, removing stones from tread, checking air pressure, visually inspecting tread, etc.

Bubble Balancer: A balancer using an air bubble visible in a contained liquid to show whether or not the tire and wheel are "in balance" statically. The tire and wheel are considered statically balanced if the bubble is centered in its area.

Centrifugal Force: The outward force away from the center (axis) of rotation acting on a revolving object. Centrifugal force increases as the square of the speed. Centrifugal force at 40 mph is four times that at 20 mph.

Dynamically Balanced: Term referring to a tire that is balanced while spinning (in motion) so that it will rotate without wobbling from

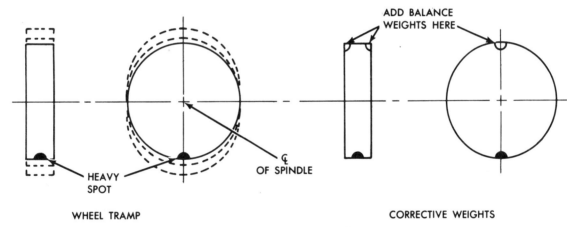

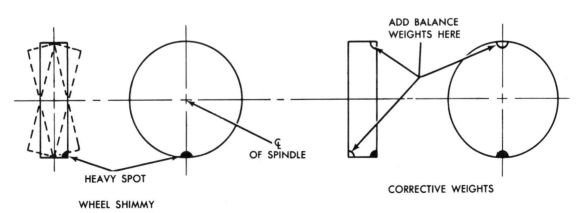

Fig 36-1. Types of Unbalance Conditions

Section 6 Suspension and Steering

unbalance. The weight-mass centerline and tire centerline are in the same plane with equal distribution on each side of the centerline. A spinning balancer normally is used.

Off-the-car Spinning Balancer: A balancer that performs the balancing operation off the car. Static and dynamic balancing may be accomplished.

On-the-car Spinning Balancer: A balancer that spins the tire, wheel, and drum or disc assembly to perform both static and dynamic balancing while on the car. Special procedures are required on rear wheels if car has a limited-slip differential. Rebalancing is required after tire rotation.

Spinning Balancer: A balancer that rotates the tire to determine the amount and location of any unbalanced condition.

Statically Balanced: Term referring to a tire that is balanced at rest (not in motion) so that it will not spin when free to rotate on a spindle. Weight mass is distributed evenly around the circumference of the tire or the axis of rotation. Either a bubble or spinning balancer may be used.

Tire Balancing: The procedure of using special equipment for identifying the lighter portions of a tire and adding lead weights until opposite tire sections weigh the same.

Tire Centerline: A line drawn through the exact physical center of a tire. A vertical line if the tire is in an upright position.

Tire Unbalance: Term meaning that a tire may be out-of-balance statically and/or dynamically. Weight mass is not distributed evenly around and across the tire.

Tire Weight-mass Centerline: A line drawn through the tire sections where the weight mass is concentrated. Dynamic unbalance is indicated if the weight mass line is diagonal to the tire centerline.

Weight Mass: A concentration of weight around the tire; may or may not be equally

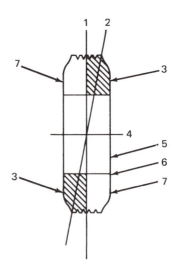

1. TIRE CENTERLINE
2. TIRE WEIGHTMASS CENTERLINE ON DYAMICALLY UNBALANCED WHEEL
3. HEAVIER TIRE SECTION–CONCENTRATION OF WEIGHT MASS
4. AXIS OF ROTATION
5. WHEEL
6. RIM LINE
7. LIGHTER TIRE SECTION

Fig 36-2. Wheel and Tire Nomenclature

distributed. Position of weight mass is identified by the weight-mass centerline.

Wheel Shimmy: Term describing the wobbling motion during rotation of a dynamically unbalanced tire. Shaking motion is back-and-forth sideways, caused by centrifugal force acting on the heavier tire section(s) located toward the side of the tire, and attempting to rotate in the same plane as the tire centerline.

Wheel Tramp: Term describing the hopping motion during rotation of a statically unbalanced tire. Motion may be up-and-down or forward-and-backward; caused by centrifugal force acting on a heavy tire section located near the tread-face center.

Wheel Weights: Lead weights used during the balancing process to equalize the weight mass around and across the tire; may be attached to the rim with clips or special adhesive.

Unit 36 Wheel Balancing

In the following exercises, indicate the best answer by inserting in the blanks the appropriate number, letter, word(s), or calculation, as required.

PICTORIAL REVIEW

A. Identify the tire and wheel nomenclature in figure 36-3 by writing the correct terms in the blanks.

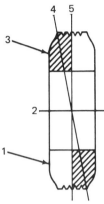

1. _____
2. _____
3. _____
4. _____
5. _____

B. Complete the following static-balance exercises:

1. Blacken two numbered sections to show static unbalance.

2. Mark an "X" two places where weights may be added to correct static unbalance.

3. Draw two arrows near the tire to indicate the erratic motion of a revolving statically unbalanced tire.

C. Complete the following dynamic balance exercises:

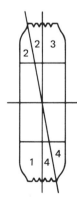

1. Blacken two numbered sections to show dynamic unbalance.

2. Mark an "X" two places where weights may be added to correct dynamic unbalance.

3. Draw two arrows near the tire to indicate the erratic motion of a rotating dynamically unbalanced tire.

229

Section 6 Suspension and Steering

SUMMARY REVIEW

1. The tire centerline always passes through the
   a. center of the tire.
   b. center of the weight mass.
   c. tire lighter section.
   d. tire heavier section.

2. The tire weight mass centerline always passes through the
   a. tire heavier section.
   b. center of the tire.
   c. tire lighter section.
   d. center of the wheel.

3. Centrifugal force does not act on a tire that is
   a. balanced dynamically.
   b. at rest.
   c. balanced statically.
   d. in motion.

4. Static unbalance usually causes wheel
   a. wear.
   b. bending.
   c. shimmy.
   d. tramp.

5. A tire statically out of balance will tend to shake the wheel
   a. sideways and downward.
   b. to the left and right.
   c. from side to side.
   d. vertically and horizontally.

6. Dynamic unbalance usually causes wheel
   a. wear.
   b. tramp.
   c. shimmy.
   d. hop.

7. A spinning balancer is used to balance a tire
   a. statically and dynamically.
   b. statically.
   c. off the car only.
   d. dynamically.

8. A bubble balancer is used to balance a tire
   a. statically.
   b. dynamically.
   c. statically and dynamically.
   d. on the car.

9. List four steps preliminary to wheel balancing.
   a. _____   c. _____
   b. _____   d. _____

10. Balancing weights attach to the wheel by what two methods?
    a. _____   b. _____

11. Insert the correct numbers of the matching terms or definitions in the blanks.
    a. ___ wobble   1. static
    b. ___ weight mass   2. shimmy
    c. ___ spinning balancer   3. wheel weights
    d. ___ bubble balancer   4. dynamic and static
    e. ___ lead metal   5. concentration of weight
    f. ___ centrifugal force   6. outward force on rotating object
    g. ___ tramp   7. wheel hop

Unit 36 Wheel Balancing

REFERENCE REVIEW

1. An out-of-balance tire-and-wheel assembly adversely affects the performance of the
   - a. shock absorbers.
   - b. suspension system.
   - c. steering system.
   - d. all of these

2. Before performing a wheel balance, the technician should
   - a. align the front wheels.
   - b. check rear wheel tracking.
   - c. clean tire and wheel.
   - d. all of these

3. What tires should be balanced?
   - a. both front and rear
   - b. rear only
   - c. front only
   - d. all tires including spare

4. Most balancing should occur when the tire is
   - a. new.
   - b. driven 1,000 miles.
   - c. rotated.
   - d. worn in the tread center.

5. At what automobile speed will an unbalanced tire most likely be noticed?
   - a. 5 to 15 mph
   - b. 20 to 30 mph
   - c. 40 to 60 mph
   - d. 70 plus mph

6. If a tire is out-of-balance dynamically only and is supported on an axis free to roll, the tire
   - a. will rotate.
   - b. heavy section will go down.
   - c. will not rotate.
   - d. light section will go down.

7. The minimum number of weights used during off-the-car dynamic balancing is
   - a. one.
   - b. two.
   - c. three.
   - d. four.

8. If a tire is out-of-balance statically only and is supported on an axis free to roll, the tire
   - a. heavy section will go down.
   - b. will not rotate.
   - c. light section will go down.
   - d. will rotate two or three turns.

9. During static balancing, the weight(s) should be placed
   - a. on outside of wheel.
   - b. on inside of wheel.
   - c. equally on both sides of wheel.
   - d. so they do not show.

10. Should a tire be balanced *statically* or *dynamically* first?

231

Section 6 Suspension and Steering

11. What operation may need to be performed at the caliper on disc-brake vehicles before balancing the tires on the car?
_____
_____

12. Describe how to balance rear wheels on a car having a limited-slip differential with an on-the-car spinning balancer.
_____
_____

UNIT 37 STANDARD STEERING AND LINKAGE

RELATED AUTOMOTIVE TERMS

Energy-absorbing (Collapsible) Steering Column: A column designed to shorten (telescope) if the car front encounters an impact serious enough to force the column into the passenger compartment or cause the driver to be thrown against the steering wheel. This column must be replaced if collapsed.

Idler Arm: Pivoting component that supports the right side of the steering relay rod in about the same manner as the pitman arm supports the left side.

Intermediate Steering Rod (Relay Rod, Center Link, Drag Link): Rod that transfers steering motion from the steering pitman arm to the tie rods.

Knuckle Arm: Arm extending backward from steering knuckle to provide attachment for tie rods.

Pitman Arm: Arm attached to the pitman shaft that moves the relay rod as the steering wheel is turned.

Pitman Shaft (Cross Shaft, Sector Shaft): Steering gearbox component that transfers motion from the internal worm shaft or ball nut to the external pitman arm.

Rack-and-pinion Steering Gear: Gearbox that contains a small pinion gear that meshes with

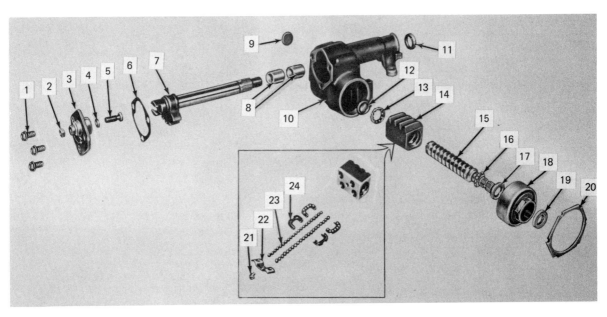

1. Side-Cover Screws
2. Lash-Adjuster Locknut
3. Side Cover and Bushing
4. Lash-Adjuster Shim
5. Lash-Adjuster Screw
6. Side-Cover Gasket
7. Pitman Shaft
8. Pitman-Shaft Bushings
9. Expansion Plug
10. Steering-Gear Housing
11. Pitman-Shaft Seal
12. Worm-Bearing Race—Lower
13. Worm-Bearing—Lower
14. Ball Nut
15. Wormshaft
16. Worm Bearing—Upper
17. Worm-Bearing Race—Upper
18. Adjuster Plug
19. Wormshaft Seal
20. Adjuster-Plug Locknut
21. Clamp Screw
22. Ball-Guide Clamp
23. Balls
24. Ball Guides

Fig 37-1. Standard Steering Gear

Section 6 Suspension and Steering

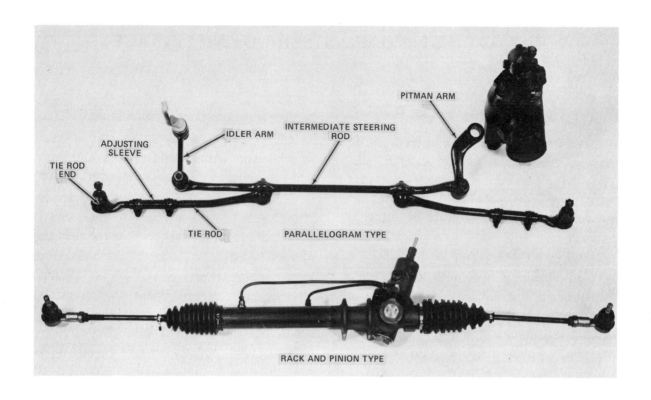

Fig 37-2. Steering Linkage

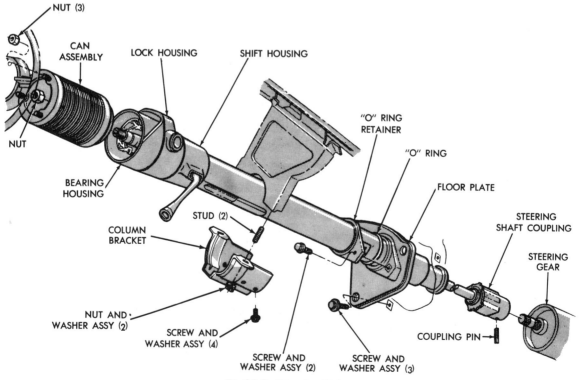

Fig 37-3. Steering Column

Unit 37 Standard Steering and Linkage

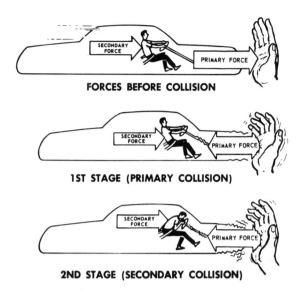

Fig 37-4. Steering Column Reaction Forces During Collison

a gear rack (steel bar, usually square, with gear teeth machined along one side). The rotating pinion gear moves gear rack to the left or right. Tie rods attach to ends of the gear rack.

Recirculating Ball Steering Gear: A low-friction steering gearbox that has a ball nut supported on the worm shaft by a number of (about 40) ball bearings that travel in matching grooves inside the ball nut and outside the worm shaft which acts as a rolling thread. The ball bearings then roll out through guide tubes and back into another ball-nut section (recirculate). Ball-nut rack teeth engage the pitman shaft gear sector.

Steering Column: Tubing through which the steering shaft mounts and rotates. It may provide mounting for transmission selector or shifting mechanism, directional flasher switch, and ignition switch.

Steering Gearbox: Housing containing the parts that change the rotating motion of the steering wheel to reciprocating motion for the steering linkages. This unit provides gear reduction and torque increase.

Steering-gear Ratio: The gear reduction between the worm gear and pitman-shaft gear

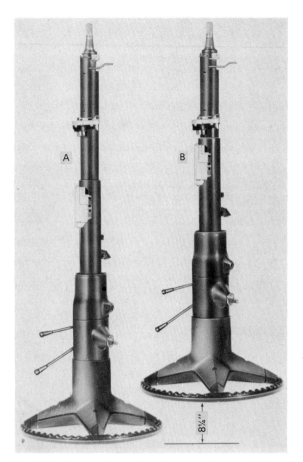

Fig 37-5. Energy Absorbing Steering Column, Before and After Collapse

sector, ranges from between 12 to 1 (fast) and 25 to 1 (slow).

Steering Linkage: The rods, pivoting joints, and supporting parts that transfer steering motion from the pitman arm to both knuckle arms.

Steering Lock: Locking device on steering column that prevents steering wheel rotation and/or selector lever motion unless unlocked using ignition key.

Steering Shaft: Shaft extending from the steering wheel toward the gearbox through the steering column.

Steering Universal Joint: Flexible coupling that provides attachment between steering shaft and worm shaft on certain models. Reduces road shock transfer to the steering wheel,

Section 6 Suspension and Steering

and permits shafts to operate at slightly different angles.

Tie Rod: Rod connecting steering linkage together. Usually located between the knuckle arm and the relay rod. Overall length is approximately that of lower control arm.

Tie Rod Coupling: Threaded coupling (sleeve) between tie rod and tie rod end. Adjustable lengthwise to set front-wheel toe-in. It has LH threads on one end and RH threads on the other.

Tie Rod End: Pivoting joint located near the outer end of the tie rod.

Tilt and Telescoping Steering Column: A column having an upper section that may be moved a controlled amount and locked into place at a higher or lower position and away from or toward the driver.

Worm Shaft: Steering gearbox component that transfers motion from the steering wheel shaft to the pitman shaft. Its working surface has spiral grooves resembling a coiled worm.

In the following exercises, indicate the best answer by inserting in the blanks the appropriate number, letter, word(s), or calculation, as required.

PICTORIAL REVIEW

A. Identify the standard steering gear parts in figure 37-6 by writing their correct names in the blanks.

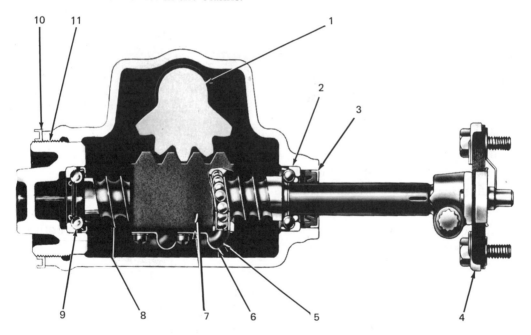

Fig 37-6. Standard Steering Gear

1. _____
2. _____
3. _____
4. _____
5. _____
6. _____
7. _____
8. _____
9. _____
10. _____
11. _____

B. Identify the parallelogram steering linkage components in figure 37-7 by writing their correct names in the blanks.

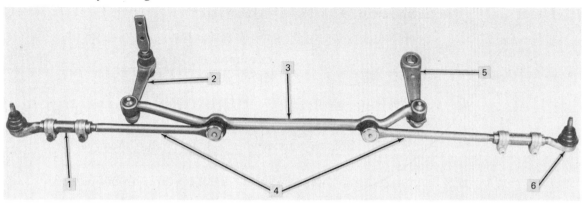

Fig 37-7. Parallelogram Steering Linkage

1. _____   4. _____
2. _____   5. _____
3. _____   6. _____

SUMMARY REVIEW

____   1. An energy absorbing steering column that is partially collapsed should be

      a. straightened.   c. checked for safe operation.
      b. lengthened.   d. replaced.

____   2. One purpose of a recirculating ball type steering gear is to reduce the

      a. manufacturing costs.   c. number of parts.
      b. operating costs.   d. operating friction.

____   3. Recirculating balls travel between the ball nut and the

      a. worm nut.   c. gear rack.
      b. steering-wheel shaft. d. worm shaft.

____   4. On cars having rack-and-pinion steering, the gear rack attaches to the

      a. tie rods.   c. pitman arm.
      b. knuckle arms.   d. relay rod.

____   5. Which component is not considered a part of the steering linkage?

      a. spindle   c. idler arm
      b. tie rod   d. intermediate rod

____   6. The component that transfers motion directly to the intermediate rod when the steering wheel is turned is called the

      a. pitman shaft.   c. worm shaft.
      b. pitman arm.   d. tie rod.

Section 6 Suspension and Steering

____ 7. The outer tie rod end attaches to the

  a. idler arm.   c. knuckle arm.
  b. pitman arm.   d. relay rod.

____ 8. The idler arm is about the same length as the

  a. tie rod.   c. pitman arm.
  b. tie rod end.   d. relay rod.

9. What are two other names for the pitman shaft?

  a. _____   b. _____

10. The steering linkage part having a length adjustment is the _____.

11. Insert the correct numbers of the matching terms or definitions in the blanks.

  a. ____ steering lock   1. 15 to 1
  b. ____ slow steering ratio   2. worm shaft
  c. ____ preloaded   3. 24 to 1
  d. ____ relay rod   4. features both LH and RH
  e. ____ fast steering ratio   threads
  f. ____ universal joint   5. flexible coupling
  g. ____ tie-rod coupling   6. ignition switch
                                  7. center link

REFERENCE REVIEW

____ 1. Most cars have a steering column that under certain conditions will

  a. tilt.   c. swing away.
  b. lengthen.   d. collapse.

____ 2. The number of total steering wheel turns, lock-to-lock, most likely used on a 15 to 1 steering gear ratio is near

  a. one.   c. five.
  b. three.   d. seven.

____ 3. A rack-and-pinion steering gear is most often used on

  a. small-size cars. c. stock cars.
  b. full-size cars.   d. four-wheel drive vehicles.

____ 4. The steering ratio on a heavy car with standard steering is likely to be near

  a. 1 to 1.   c. 15 to 1.
  b. 10 to 1.   d. 25 to 1.

____ 5. The worm shaft is supported in the steering gearbox by

  a. the recirculating balls.   c. one bearing.
  b. two bearings.   d. two bushings.

Unit 37 Standard Steering and Linkage

____ 6. Wormshaft bearing preload should be adjusted to between
  a. 10 and 20 pound-feet.   c. 1 and 5 pound-inches.
  b. 1 and 10 pound-feet.   d. 15 and 25 pound-inches.

____ 7. The first adjustment to perform during standard steering gearbox assembly is on the
  a. pitman shaft bearings. c. ball nut preload.
  b. ball nut clearance.   d. worm shaft bearings.

____ 8. The pitman shaft gear sector-to-ball nut tooth clearance is always performed with the pitman shaft
  a. turned to the left.   c. in center position.
  b. turned to the right.   d. in any position.

____ 9. The steering system part that should be disconnected before performing the pitman shaft gear sector-to-ball nut adjustment on a car is the
  a. steering universal joint coupling.   c. steering shaft.
  b. pitman arm.   d. tie rods.

____ 10. The pitman shaft is usually supported in the steering gearbox by
  a. the recirculating ball. c. one bearing.
  b. two bushings.   d. two bearings.

____ 11. If a tie rod must be removed and then used again, the tapered stud should be removed from the tapered hole with
  a. a forked driver.   c. vise grips.
  b. a special puller.   d. heat.

____ 12. Usually, the first steering system component needing replacement from normal wear on a used car is the
  a. idler arm.   c. knuckle arm.
  b. pitman arm.   d. relay arm.

UNIT 38 POWER STEERING

RELATED AUTOMOTIVE TERMS

Constant Ratio Steering Gear: Steering gear having the same gear ratio when the wheels are near the straight-ahead position as during extreme turns.

Control Valve: Mechanism that controls the amount of power assist relayed to the steering linkage via a power piston; located inside steering gearbox or on steering relay rod.

Fluid Cooler: Small component in hydraulic line near pump containing tubing (sometimes finned) to reduce power steering fluid temperature on certain air-conditioned cars.

Integral-type: Power steering system having the power assist mechanism and related controls inside the steering gearbox.

Linkage-type: Power steering system having the control valve and power cylinder attached to the steering linkage under the car.

Manual Operation: Refers to driver being able to operate steering system in case engine stops or a system failure occurs. Increased turning effort is required.

Power Cylinder: Linkage-type steering component attached between the frame and the steering relay rod. Fluid is directed to either

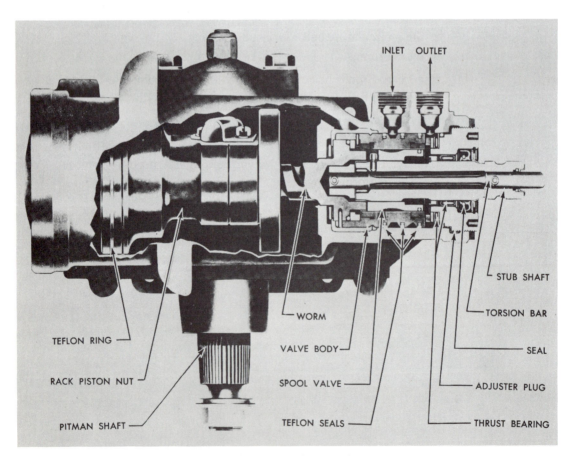

Fig 38-1. Power Steering Gear

Unit 38 Power Steering

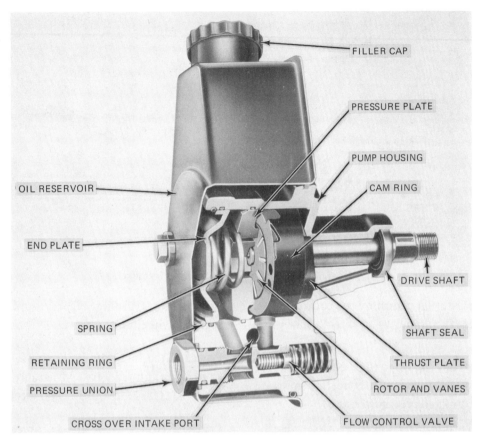

Fig. 38-2. Power Steering Pump

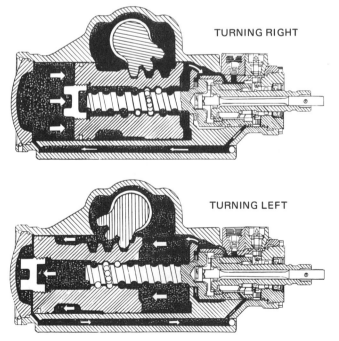

Fig 38-3. Integral-Type Power Steering Gear

241

Section 6 Suspension and Steering

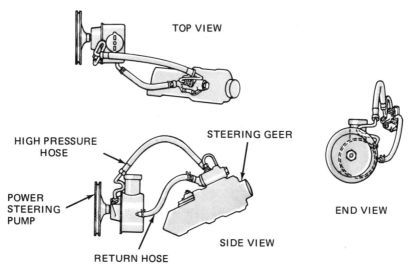

Fig 38-4. Integral-Type Power Steering Installation

side of the internal piston by the control valve, determining the amount and direction of power assist.

Power Piston: Component reacted on by pressurized fluid to assist wheel turning on integral or linkage-type systems.

Power Steering: A power assisted steering system that uses hydraulic pressure to increase the torque (turning effort) applied to the steering wheel by the driver.

Power Steering Fluid: Special hydraulic fluid formulated to withstand extremely high system pressures and temperatures.

Pressure Hose: Special reinforced high-pressure hose through which the pressurized fluid

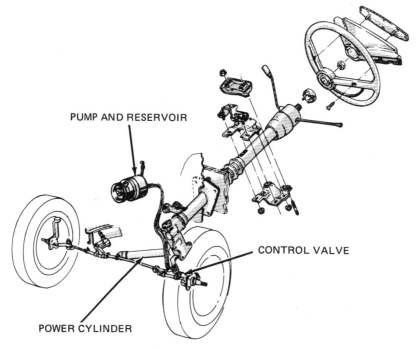

Fig 38-5. Linkage-Type Power Steering Installation

flows from the pump to the steering gear assembly or control valve.

Pump: Hydraulic pump driven by a belt from a crankshaft pulley; it provides the "boost" pressure (up to 1300 psi) necessary to operate the power-steering system.

Pump Reservoir: Container located on or adjacent to pump providing fluid for system operation.

Return Hose: Low-pressure hose through which fluid returns to the pump reservoir after leaving the steering gear assembly or control valve.

Road Feel: Term relating to the driver being able to sense the car directional control from the movement transmitted to him through the steering wheel by the front wheels. It is less on power steering equipped cars.

Variable-ratio Steering Gear: Steering gear having a different gear ratio (typically 16 to 1) when the wheels are in the straight ahead (driving) position than during an extreme turn (typically 13 to 1). This is accomplished by center pitman-shaft sector tooth being longer than the others.

In the following exercises, indicate the best answer by inserting in the blanks the appropriate number, letter, word(s), or calculation, as required.

PICTORIAL REVIEW

A. Identify the integral type power-steering gear components in figure 38-6 by writing their correct letters in the blanks.

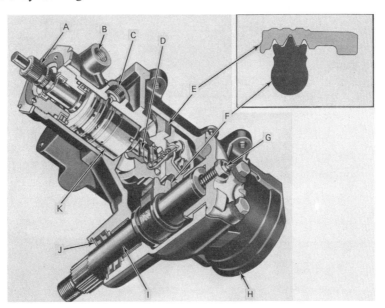

Fig 38-6. Power Steering Gear

1. ____ pitman gear adjuster
2. ____ worm
3. ____ housing
4. ____ valve body
5. ____ fluid inlet
6. ____ fluid outlet
7. ____ pitman shaft
8. ____ rack piston nut
9. ____ stub shaft
10. ____ pitman-shaft seal
11. ____ pitman-shaft gear

Section 6 Suspension and Steering

B. Identify the gear shapes in figure 38-7, then label which gearset is *constant ratio* and which is *variable ratio*.

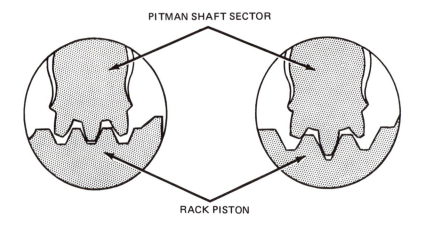

Fig 38-7. Steering Gear Tooth Shapes

1. _____ ratio   2. _____ ratio

SUMMARY REVIEW

____ 1. The "road feel" on cars having power steering, compared with those having standard steering is

    a. adjustable.   c. less.
    b. more.   d. the same.

____ 2. A power steering fluid oil cooler is used on

    a. all cars.   c. certain air conditioned cars.
    b. all air conditioned cars.   d. cars having automatic transmissions.

____ 3. Highest line pressure occurs during

    a. highway driving.   c. right turns.
    b. left turns.   d. parking.

____ 4. Pressure inside the two power steering hoses is

    a. equal.   c. unequal.
    b. about the same.   d. adjustable.

____ 5. When the variable ratio steering gear is positioned to have a 16 to 1 ratio, the car is most likely

    a. on the highway.   c. turning a corner.
    b. parking.   d. all of these.

____ 6. A constant ratio steering gear has sector teeth that are

    a. unequal in height.   c. meshed with the control valve.
    b. equal in height.   d. meshed with the worm gear.

7. A variable ratio steering gear varies the ratio from about 16 to 1 to
   a. 10 to 1.
   b. 13 to 1.
   c. 20 to 1.
   d. 25 to 1.
8. Does the integral-type rack piston move *up* or *down* during a right turn? _____
9. Between what two parts of the automobile does the linkage-type power cylinder attach?
   a. _____   b. _____
10. Most power steering pumps are mounted on the _____.
11. Insert the correct numbers of the matching terms or definitions in the blanks.
    a. ___ worm gear
    b. ___ rack piston
    c. ___ right turn
    d. ___ steering linkage
    e. ___ rotor
    f. ___ left turn

    1. higher pressure above rack piston
    2. higher pressure below rack piston
    3. part inside the rack piston
    4. control valve may attach to
    5. pump vanes attach to
    6. contacts pitman gear sector

REFERENCE REVIEW

1. Power steering system pressure
   a. varies depending on use.
   b. is constant.
   c. is lowest during turns.
   d. is adjustable.
2. If a power steering hose breaks, the steering system operates
   a. manually.
   b. about the same.
   c. with reduced power assist.
   d. hydraulically.
3. If more power assist occurs in one direction than another on a car having the linkage-type system, the _____ should be adjusted.
   a. power-cylinder length
   b. pump pressure
   c. power-cylinder piston
   d. control-valve centering spring
4. Air is bled from the power steering system by
   a. loosening the gearbox.
   b. loosening pump bleeder screw.
   c. turning the wheels back and forth.
   d. loosening the pump belt.
5. The most popular power steering pumps operate to produce pressure by the use of
   a. gears.
   b. rollers.
   c. vanes.
   d. slippers.

Section 6 Suspension and Steering

___ 6. The pitman shaft seal is
   a. the same size as the wormshaft.
   b. replaceable.
   c. nonreplaceable.
   d. secured to the pitman shaft by retaining rings.

___ 7. The steering gear ratio most likely used on a small car with power steering is near
   a. 1 to 1.
   b. 10 to 1.
   c. 15 to 1.
   d. 25 to 1.

___ 8. The number of external adjustments on the outside of most power steering gears is
   a. 0.
   b. 1.
   c. 2.
   d. 3.

___ 9. The choice between having an integral or linkage power steering system on a particular car is made by the
   a. customer.
   b. dealer.
   c. car manufacturer.
   d. any of these

10. How will the power steering pump sound if the fluid level is low? _____

11. What is the likely problem if a squealing noise occurs somewhere in the power steering system during turns? _____

12. The type of power steering system found on most new cars is the _____.

SECTION 7 Lubrication

UNIT 39 ENGINE LUBRICATION SYSTEMS

RELATED AUTOMOTIVE TERMS

Drilled Oil Passage: Hole drilled in various parts of the engine for pressurized oil to flow through.

Filter Bypass: Spring-loaded valve built into or next to most filters. Allows oil to pass around the element of a clogged filter.

Filter Element Material: Substance inside filter used to clean (filter) particles of carbon, metal, sludge, etc. from the oil. Materials used include clay, cotton, paper, special fibers, etc.

Friction: Resistance to motion between any two moving objects. The amount of friction depends on surface finish, speed of motion, pressure, kind of material, applied lubricant, etc.

Full-flow Filter: Oil filter that cleans (filters) all the oil each time it is pumped through the

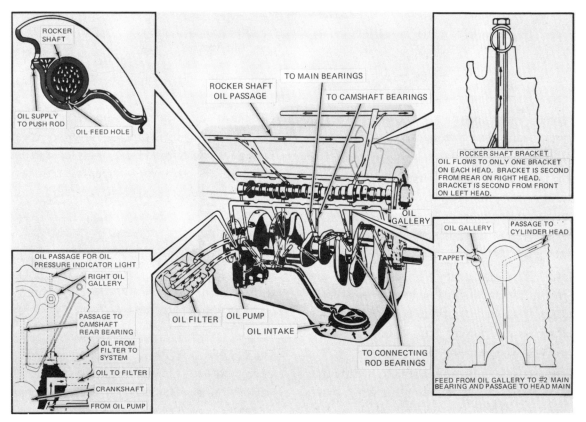

Fig 39-1. Reciprocating Engine Lubrication System

Section 7 Lubrication

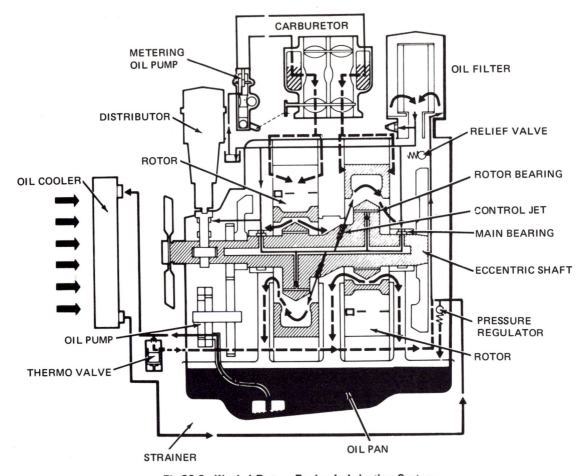

Fig 39-2. Wankel Rotary Engine Lubrication System

engine. It may contain a bypass valve that opens if the filter becomes clogged, allowing unfiltered oil to circulate.

Gear-type Pump: Oil pump that uses two rotating gears to draw in oil. Oil is carried around outer pump body in cavities between gear teeth and then dispensed under pressure as the gear teeth mesh together.

Motor Oil Functions: Various jobs oil performs inside an engine, such as lubricating to reduce wear and friction, cooling, cleaning, sealing compression, and filling clearance spaces between moving parts.

Multiviscosity Oil: An oil able to maintain its viscosity over a wider temperature range than a single-viscosity oil. An example would be SAE 10W-40 (Society of Automotive Engineers).

Oil Additives: Special chemicals added to an oil by the manufacturer to improve its performance. Certain additives may cause the oil to clean the engine (detergents), reduce viscosity change, or resist corrosion and foaming, etc.

Oil Classifications (Service Ratings): Ratings of oil quality for various applications suggested by concerned organizations: SA for light duty, SB for medium duty in 1963 and older cars, SC for 1964-67 cars, SD for 1968-71 cars, SE for 1972-77 cars, etc.

Oil Cooler: A device mounted outside the engine to cool the engine oil, on certain applications. Most often used on air-cooled engines or water-cooled engines in heavy-duty service. A cooler may feature "finned" tubing.

Unit 39 Engine Lubrication Systems

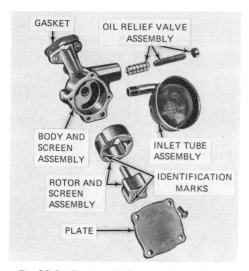

Fig 39-3. Engine Oil Pump, Rotor Type

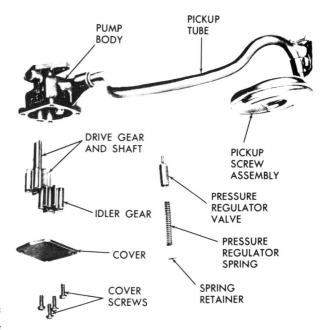

Fig 39-4. Engine Oil Pump, Gear Type

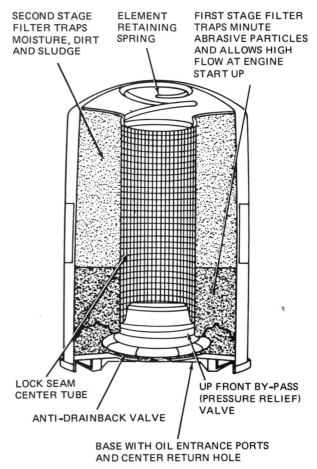

Fig 39-5. Spin-on Oil Filter, Two-stage Type

Oil Filter: Component that removes abrasive particles from the motor oil by a straining process before the oil circulates through the lubrication system. Usually located near oil pump. It should be replaced periodically.

Oil Gallery: Main lengthwise passage drilled or cast into the cylinder block. It receives pressurized oil from the oil pump for distribution throughout the engine.

Oil Intake Screen: Strainer screen at lower end of oil pickup tube in sump; removes any larger oil contaminant particles.

Oil Pour Point: Oil characteristic relating to the ability of an oil to flow at a specified low temperature.

Oil Pressure: Pressure developed by the pump to force oil through the lubrication system; may range from 15 to 75 psi depending on engine rpm, temperature, and oil viscosity.

Oil Pump: Pump that draws oil from the sump (crankcase reservoir), then forces the oil under pressure through the engine lubrication system. It is driven directly or indirectly by the camshaft.

Oil Pressure Sender Unit. A device that sends (relays) a signal concerning the amount of engine oil pressure to the dash gage or warning

Section 7 Lubrication

light. It is usually located near the oil pump, filter, or gallery.

Oil Sludge: An accumulation of thickened oil, water, carbon, and dust particles inside an engine. This condition occurs most often on engines run cold, at slow speed, on short trips, without adequate oil and filter changes, with inadequate crankcase ventilation, or using nondetergent oils.

Oil Viscosity Rating: A numerical rating of oil thickness (resistance to flow), such as SAE 10, 20, or 30, which are known as single-viscosity oils. Viscosity can be determined by a viscometer. See Viscosity Index.

Pressure Lubrication: System providing lubrication to moving parts from oil pressurized by the pump.

Pressure Relief Valve: A special valve having a calibrated spring working against a movable plunger or ball to regulate maximum oil pressure. High pressure causes the spring to compress, allowing excess oil to return to the pump inlet or the sump.

Rotor-type Pump: Oil pump that uses two rotors, one having internal and one having external teeth to draw in and dispense oil in much the same manner as the gear-type pump.

Splash Lubrication: System providing lubrication to moving parts from oil "splashed" around by ear projections, connecting-rod

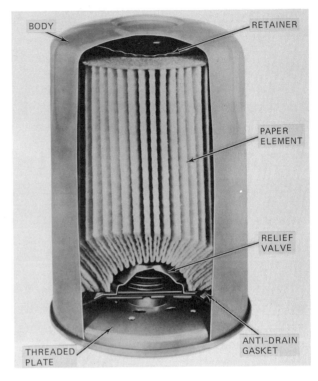

Fig 39-6. Spin-on Oil Filter, Pleated-paper Type

dippers, or from oil thrown off around bearings that receive oil under pressure. This system may be used as the only lubrication method in small, one-cylinder engines.

Viscosity Index: A numerical oil-rating system concerned with how much a certain oil will change viscosity (resistance to flow, thickness) when its temperature changes. Higher numbers denote less viscosity change when temperature changes occur.

In the following exercises, indicate the best answer by inserting in the blank the appropriate number, letter, word(s), or calculation, as required.

PICTORIAL REVIEW

A. Identify the engine lubrication system areas or components in figure 39-7, by writing their correct letters in the blanks.

1. ____ oil pump
2. ____ oil filter
3. ____ oil intake
4. ____ main oil gallery

5. ____ oil to main bearing
6. ____ oil to cam bearing
7. ____ oil to rocker arms
8. ____ oil pressure relief valve

Unit 39 Engine Lubrication Systems

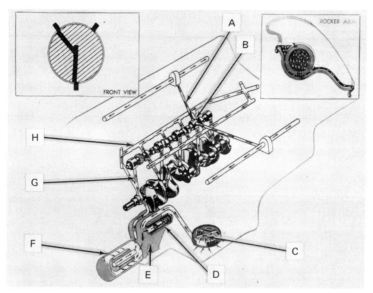

Fig 39-7. Engine Lubrication System

B. Identify the oil pump components in figure 39-8 by writing their correct letters in the blanks.

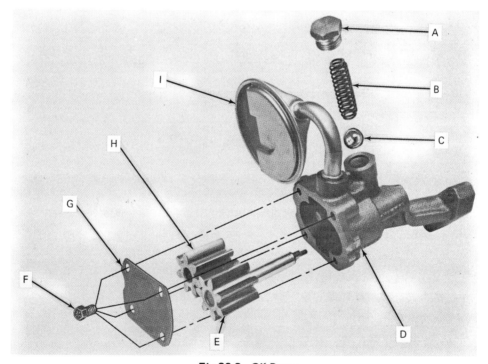

Fig 39-8. Oil Pump

1. ____ pressure relief ball
2. ____ pickup screen
3. ____ drive gear
4. ____ driven gear
5. ____ cover bolt(s)
6. ____ pressure relief spring
7. ____ spring retainer
8. ____ oil pump cover
9. ____ oil pump body

251

Section 7 Lubrication

C. Perform the following exercises on oil pump operation, using figure 39-9.
1. Label *oil inlet* on drawing.
2. Label *oil outlet* on drawing.
3. Draw two long dashed lines from the oil pump inlet to the outlet, tracing the path the oil follows through the pump.
4. Add four arrows along each dashed line to show the direction of oil flow.

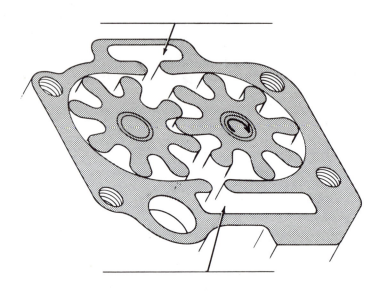

Fig 39-9. Oil Pump Operation

SUMMARY REVIEW

____ 1. Most reciprocating engine moving parts are lubricated with oil supplied by
   a. splash.
   b. pressure.
   c. gravity.
   d. splash and gravity.

____ 2. The lubricating system component that regulates maximum oil pressure is the
   a. oil filter.
   b. pump gear or rotor.
   c. pressure relief valve.
   d. check valve.

____ 3. Connecting-rod bearings receive oil directly from the
   a. main bearing area.
   b. camshaft bearing area.
   c. oil pump.
   d. main oil gallery.

____ 4. All automobile engine lubrication systems now have a
   a. gear-type oil pump.
   b. oil filter.
   c. oil cooler.
   d. all of these

____ 5. An oil passage drilled lengthwise in the block is often called a
   a. line.
   b. dispenser.
   c. storage area.
   d. gallery.

____ 6. After leaving the oil pump, the oil travels directly to the
   a. pickup screen.
   b. filter.
   c. oil gallery.
   d. main bearings.

____ 7. The oil pump is driven from the
   a. camshaft.
   b. crankshaft timing gear.
   c. camshaft timing gears.
   d. oil sump.

8. What is the leading cause of oil-sludge formation inside an engine?
   _____

9. Name six functions of a motor oil.
   a. _____   d. _____
   b. _____   e. _____
   c. _____   f. _____

10. Friction between moving parts in an engine depends upon what five items?
    a. _____   d. _____
    b. _____   e. _____
    c. _____

11. The lower section of the oil pan may be called a _____ .

12. Insert the correct numbers of the matching terms or definitions in the blanks.
    a. ____ oil classification
    b. ____ viscosity
    c. ____ viscosity index
    d. ____ pour point
    e. ____ single viscosity
    f. ____ multiviscosity
    g. ____ oil additivie

    1. ability to flow at low temperature
    2. service rating
    3. thickness determined by viscometer
    4. 10, 20, or 30
    5. indication of thickness change with various temperatures
    6. detergent
    7. 10W-30

REFERENCE REVIEW

____ 1. Valves and rocker arms receive lubrication by oil supplied through the hollow rocker arm shaft(s) or the
   a. valve cover(s).
   b. hollow intake manifold.
   c. external oil line(s).
   d. hollow pushrods.

Section 7 Lubrication

____ 2. Most oil additives should be blended into the oil by the
    a. oil manufacturer.   c. car owner.
    b. service technician.   d. person changing the oil.

____ 3. The best type of filter element material to use in an engine is
    a. paper.   c. clay.
    b. cotton.   d. that recommended by the engine manufacturer.

____ 4. Before installing a new oil pump on an engine, the technician should
    a. test it for output pressure.   c. check gears for "end-play."
    b. fill it with oil or special lubricant.   d. test relief valve pressure.

____ 5. Oil-pump gear "end-play" may be checked using a
    a. inside micrometer.
    b. straightedge and feeler gage.
    c. outside caliper and steel rule.
    d. special gage.

____ 6. During an engine overhaul, the oil pickup screen should be
    a. adjusted for metering quantity.   c. cleaned.
    b. flow tested.   d. replaced.

____ 7. An engine having low oil pressure probably needs
    a. a stronger pump relief valve spring.
    b. a pump relief valve adjustment.
    c. rebuilding.
    d. the pump driveshaft replaced.

____ 8. A defective oil sender unit should be
    a. tested and repaired.   c. replaced with a new one.
    b. tested at various temperatures.   d. replaced with a rebuilt one.

9. Explain how to check actual engine oil pressure on an automobile having an indicating light rather than a pressure gage. _____

10. What would the effect on oil pressure be if the pump relief valve stuck in the open position? _____

11. Is the pump pressure relief valve *open* or *closed* when the engine is not operating? _____

12. List two engine operating conditions that may cause the filter bypass valve to open.
    a. _____
    b. _____

UNIT 40   CHASSIS LUBRICATION

RELATED AUTOMOTIVE TERMS

Antifriction Bearing: A bearing designed to reduce friction through the use of steel balls, rollers, or needles, allowing "rolling" friction rather than "sliding" friction to occur.

Ball Joint Lubrication: Greasing of ball joint as suggested by the manufacturer. This job is easiest to perform if ball joint is in an unloaded position. Most cars that have "low-mounted" coil springs or torsion bars should be jacked up near lower control arm outer end. Most cars that have "high-mounted" coil springs should be jacked up at center of front frame crossmember, in the same manner as when checking ball joints.

Chassis Lubrication: The procedure of applying the correct type and amount of grease at recommended intervals to the chassis lubrication points. Also includes related jobs such as adding or changing fluids, and miscellaneous services including tire pressure and safety checks.

Gear Oil: Liquid lubricant used in such places as a standard transmission or differential. Usually has an SAE number of 80, 90, or above. Number 80 gear oil has about the same viscosity as number 30 motor oil. It may have additives useful for a specific purpose, such as an EP (extreme pressure) additive to avoid being squeezed out from between gear teeth.

Grease: Lubricant consisting of a stable mixture of oil, soap thickeners (usually lithium, sodium, or calcium), and other ingredients for the desired physical or operating characteristics; different greases should not be mixed.

Grease Fitting: The part a grease gun fits on during the greasing process. The fitting may be straight, angled at 45°, or angled at 90°. It may have a 1/16- or 1/8-inch pipe thread or be pressed in. Grease fittings contain a one-way check valve.

Grease Plug: Small plug, usually having a 1/16-inch pipe thread, placed in a lubrication hole by the vehicle manufacturer when danger of overlubrication by high-pressure equipment exists. It should be removed for lubrication and then reinstalled.

Grease Seal: Part designed to contain a lubricant and exclude contaminants from the outside. Working surface may be neoprene rubber, felt, cork, asbestos, or other material not adversely affected by the lubricant involved. It is replaceable.

Hypoid Lubricant: A type of differential gear oil used for the "hypoid" gears normally found on new cars. Such gears have the drive pinion entering the differential case below the ring-gear centerline. This design produces a gear-tooth sliding action when the teeth mesh.

Inside-vehicle Lubrication Services: Work performed inside the vehicle during a chassis lubrication; may include changing the mileage sticker, lubricating the ignition-lock cylinder, glove-compartment hinges and lock, and inspection of safety-related items.

Limited-slip Differential Gear Oil: A specially formulated gear oil required in limited-slip differentials because of the extreme pressures on the clutch cones or clutch plates and discs.

Lubrication Guide Book: Specially prepared book detailing required lubrication services and related information for each make and model of automobile.

Lubrication Gun Adapters: Various adapters allowing lubrication when special conditions exist. An adapter may be flexible, low pressure, have pressure release, right-angled, etc.

Section 7 Lubrication

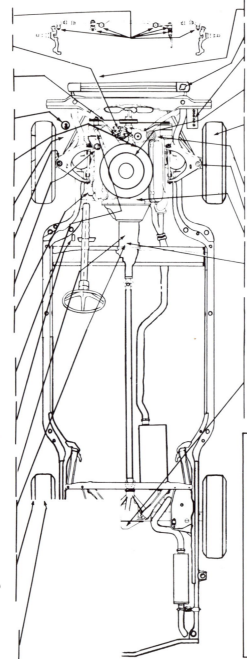

STEERING LINKAGE - LUBE (7)
-CL- 6,000 Mi. or 4 Mos.
Whichever Occurs First

DISTRIBUTOR CAM LUBRICATOR
Replace 12,000

ENGINE BELTS - Check Condition and
Proper Tension 6,000 Mi. or 4 Mos.

EVAPORATION CONTROL CANISTER FILTER
Replace filter on underside of canister every 12
months or 12,000 miles, whichever occurs first.

FUEL FILTER - Replace With Recommended
Element 12,000 or 12 Mos.
Whichever Occurs First

WINDSHIELD WASHER FLUID
Check Level Periodically

LOWER BALL JOINTS (2) - CL - 6,000 Miles
or 4 Mos. Whichever Occurs First

ENGINE OIL - Drain and Refill - EO - 4 Mos.
Never exceed 6,000 miles between changes.

STD. STEERING GEAR - Lubed for Life SG -
Used for refill after repair only

POWER STEERING RESERVOIR - Check
Fluid Level -PSF-
Whichever Occurs First 4 mos. or 6,000

BRAKE MASTER CYLINDER -
Maintain Level 1/4" ± 1/8" Below
Top of Each Reservoir - HBF-
Whichever Occurs First 4 mos. or 6,000

MANUAL TRANSMISSION - Maintain at Filler
Opening - Flushing & Seasonal Changes NOT
Recommended. M.P.G. - S.A.E. - 80 or 90 GL-5
(SAE 80 in Canada)

CHECK CLUTCH LASH – ("A" Series Only)
Adjust if necessary 6,000

BRAKE MECHANISM - Apply at Starwheel
Point of Contact and Lightly to 6 Surfaces
on Which Shoe Rim Rests -BL- 12,000

TIRES – Rotate
Maintain Pressure Periodically
Refer to Group 3 For
Correct Pressure 6,000

AIR CONDITIONER - Functional Check
Once a Year

RADIATOR - Check Coolant level at each oil change.
Replace every 24,000 Miles or 24 Months

ENERGIZER (Battery) - Check Level Periodically

**CRANKCASE VENTILATION ELEMENT AND AIR
CLEANER ELEMENT** - Inspect at each oil change
replace if necessary. Replace at least every 24,000
miles - more often under dusty conditions.

FRONT WHEEL BEARINGS - (Disc Type Brakes)
Inspect and lubricate with a premium high melting
point wheel bearing grease when brakes are serviced.
Part No. 1051344 or equivalent)

OIL FILTER ELEMENT - Replace With First Oil
Change and Then at Alternate Oil Changes.
UPPER BALL JOINTS (2)
-CL- 6,000 Mi. or 4 Mos.
Whichever Occurs First

PCV VALVE - Replace 24,000 miles or 24 months.

TURBO HYDRAMATIC 350-375B
Clean Strainer at - 24,000 Normal
12,000 Heavy Duty
TURBO HYDRAMATIC 400
Replace Filter at - 24,000 Normal
12,000 Heavy Duty

STANDARD DIFFERENTIAL - REAR AXLE -
Maintain at filler opening to 3/8" below - Flushing
& seasonal changes NOT recommended.
MPG - SAE - 80 or 90. (SAE 80 in Canada)

For complete Refill use only factory hypoid gear
lubricant - Unless axle in service 1,000 miles or more.
Then use MPG - SAE - 90 (SAE 80 in Canada)
POSITIVE TRACTION DIFFERENTIAL — Change
lube every 12,000 miles. Maintain at filler opening
to 3/8.. below — Use Part No. 1051022 or
equivalent)

If vehicle is used for trailering, drain and refill every
12,000 miles using lubricants recommended for
standard and positive traction differentials.

LUBRICANTS

CL	Chassis Lubricant - Water Resistant Extreme Pressure EP No. 2 Multi-purpose Grease Which Meets G.M. Spec. 6031M
AT	DEXRON Automatic Transmission Fluid G.M. Part No. 1050568-69-70 or Equivalent
EO	Engine Oil (Current Viscosity) SE*
HBF	Hydraulic Brake Fluid - Delco Super No. 11* or equivalent
BL	Brake Lube, Self-adjusting Per Spec. M.P. 6805
MPG	Multi-Purpose Gear Lubricant GL-5
TL	Lube Conforming to G.M. Specification 1051022
SG	Calcium Soap # 2 Meeting G.M. Spec. 4673M. Do Not Use CL
PSF	Buick Power Steering Gear Fluid or Equivalent Meeting G.M. Part No. 1050017 or equivalent

*Equivalent Acceptable if it Meets Specifications.

Fig 40-1. Chassis Lubrication Chart

Lubrication Interval: Factory recommended mileage and/or time limit after which periodic lubrication services should be performed.

Multipurpose Grease: A grease specially formulated to permit use in a variety of applications.

Outside-vehicle Lubrication Services: Work performed outside the automobile during a chassis lubrication. It may include checking tire pressure, lubricating door and trunk hinges and locks, cleaning windshield, and inspection of safety-related items.

Overlubrication: Term referring to application of lubricant amounts in excess of factory recommendations; may overload or damage grease seals.

Permanently Lubricated Joint: A moving joint consisting of low-friction materials, having improved seals, and lubricated by the manufacturer for the life of the joint. This joint is found on suspension and/or steering systems in certain applications.

Sealed Bearing: A bearing such as those found on many rear axle shafts or at the front of alternator rotor shafts, that is lubricated and permanently sealed by the manufacturer; seal contains the grease while keeping out contaminants; replaceable in most cases.

Under-hood Lubrication Services: Work performed under the hood during a chassis lubrication. It may include lubrication of distributor, manifold heat-control valve, upper suspension, hood hinges, hood latch; also, checking levels of fluids in the engine crankcase, brake master cylinder, radiator, battery, steering; plus checking belts, and inspection of safety-related items.

Under-vehicle Lubrication Services: Work performed under the vehicle during a chassis lubrication. It may include changing oil, filters, checking or changing transmission fluid or gear oil and differential gear oil. Also may include lubricating the suspension and steering system, universal joints, clutch and/or transmission linkage, front-wheel bearings, and inspection of safety-related items.

Chassis Lubrication Abbreviations

DE: door ease

MO: motor oil

AF (AT) (ATF): automatic transmission fluid

BL: brake lubricant

EP: extreme pressure additive (included)

PSF: power steering fluid

GL: gear lubricant

SG: steering gear lubricant

SL: silicone lubricant

MP: multipurpose

FG: flake graphite

LE: lock ease

RB (RR): rubber lubricant

HBF: heavy-duty brake fluid

EC: engine coolant

EO: engine oil

CL: chassis lubricant

WB: wheel bearing lubricant

Section 7 Lubrication

In the following exercises, indicate the best answer by inserting in the blank the appropriate number, letter, word(s), or calculation, as required.

PICTORIAL REVIEW

A. Identify the grease fittings and adapters in figure 40-2 by writing their correct letters in the blanks.

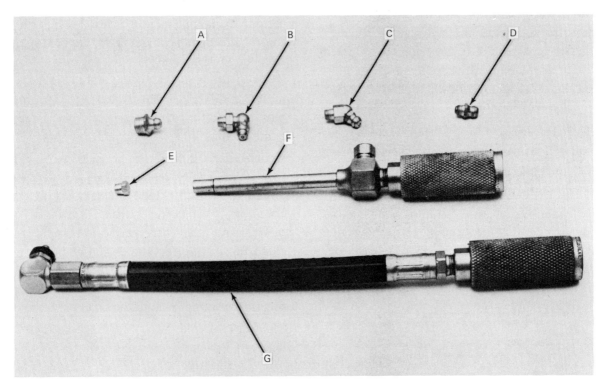

Fig 40-2. Grease Fittings and Adapters

1. ____ 45° fitting
2. ____ 90° fitting
3. ____ grease plug
4. ____ 1/8" straight fitting
5. ____ pressure-release adapter
6. ____ flexible adapter for plug hole
7. ____ 1/16" straight fitting

B. Fill in the periodic lubrication and service chart in figure 40-3 to indicate the following:

1. The periodic interval in miles and/or months, or none; in column I.

2. The lubricant or fluid abbreviation, or none; in column II.

3. The type of service, such as drain and fill, check level, lubricate, replace, clean, or none, in column III.

258

Lubrication or Service	Indicate: -periodic interval in mi and/or mo -or none	Indicate: -lubricant or fluid abbreviation -or none	Indicate type of service: -drain & fill -check level -lubricate -replace -clean -or none
1. Suspension system			
2. Steering system			
3. Power-steering reservoir			
4. Standard steering gear			
5. Engine oil			
6. Engine oil filter			
7. PCV valve			
8. Standard differential			
9. Automatic transmission (normal service)			
10. Automatic transmission (heavy-duty service)			
11. Air and breather filter			
12. Radiator coolant (replacement)			
13. Brake master cylinder			
14. Fuel filter			
15. Front-wheel bearings			
16. Evaporative canister filter			

Fig 40-3. Periodic Lubrication and Service Chart

SUMMARY REVIEW

____ 1. Ball joints on cars having "low-mounted" coil springs are easiest to lubricate if the car weight is supported by a

    a. frame-contact hoist.
    b. jack under the car center.
    c. drive-on hoist.
    d. jack under the lower control arm.

____ 2. Ball-joint plugs should be

    a. replaced with grease fittings.
    b. used only once.
    c. replaced with oversize.
    d. reinstalled after lubrication.

____ 3. Hypoid gear lubrication is required in

    a. standard transmissions.
    b. automatic transmissions.
    c. standard differentials.
    d. all of these

Section 7 Lubrication

___ 4. "Sealed" bearings are often located on the
   a. rear alternator rotor shaft.
   b. differential drive pinion.
   c. standard transmission input shaft.
   d. rear axle shaft.

___ 5. Overlubrication is most likely to cause immediate damage to the ball joint
   a. spherical ball.
   b. seal.
   c. housing.
   d. tension spring.

___ 6. An antifriction bearing is usually located on the
   a. rear axle shaft.
   b. connecting rod.
   c. rear transmission.
   d. all of these

7. List six fluid levels that could be checked under the hood during a chassis lubrication.
   a. _____ c. _____ e. _____
   b. _____ d. _____ f. _____

8. Name three popular soap thickeners used in grease manufacture.
   a. _____ b. _____ c. _____

9. Two popular standard transmission gear-oil viscosity numbers are _____ and _____ .

10. Write the words represented by the following chassis-lubrication abbreviations.
   a. EO _____   e. WB _____
   b. ATF _____ f. LE _____
   c. DE _____   g. PSF _____
   d. HBF _____ h. SL _____

REFERENCE REVIEW

___ 1. The mileage limits that different automobile manufacturers suggest driving before a chassis lubrication is suggested ranges from
   a. 2,000 to 4,000 miles.
   b. 5,000 to 10,000 miles.
   c. 6,000 to 36,000 miles.
   d. 25,000 to 50,000 miles.

___ 2. Lubrication guidebooks distributed by the major oil companies usually contain information on
   a. fluid capacities.
   b. tuneup data.
   c. vehicle lubrication points.
   d. all of these

___ 3. During a chassis lubrication, grease should be pumped into a ball joint having a grease plug, until
   a. grease flows freely from the joint.
   b. the seal just starts to expand.
   c. five ounces of grease is used.
   d. the grease gun is empty.

Unit 40 Chassis Lubrication

_____ 4. Although most car manufacturers recommend a special high pressure power-steering fluid if the system is empty, they usually allow _____ to be added if the reservoir fluid is slightly low.
   a. automatic transmission fluid
   b. standard transmission fluid
   c. motor oil
   d. brake fluid

_____ 5. The first indication of trouble caused by a standard gear oil being put in a limited-slip differential would likely be
   a. worn out gears.
   b. noise on straight roads.
   c. noise during turns.
   d. worn out bearings.

_____ 6. The lubricant used in most differentials is
   a. limited-slip gear oil.
   b. multipurpose gear oil.
   c. automatic fluid.
   d. chassis lubricant.

_____ 7. The best grease gun adapter to use when lubricating universal joints that have fittings, is the
   a. flexible.
   b. high-pressure.
   c. pressure-release.
   d. right angle.

8. The working surface that most front wheel grease seals are made from is _____ .

9. Should the sharp edge of a single-lip neoprene rubber seal be installed *toward the lubricant* or *away from the lubricant*?
   _____

10. Name four reasons why it is a good idea to perform the "miscellaneous" services along with a chassis lubrication.
    a. _____
    b. _____
    c. _____
    d. _____

11. List five safety related items that can be checked under the car when the car is raised on a lube rack.
    a. _____
    b. _____
    c. _____
    d. _____
    e. _____

SECTION 8 Power Train

UNIT 41 CLUTCHES

RELATED AUTOMOTIVE TERMS

Clutch Disc: Circular-shaped component that transfers power from the flywheel and pressure plate to the splined clutch shaft. It has a friction facing (lining) on each side.

Clutch (Bell) Housing: Cast iron or aluminum shell that surrounds clutch assembly, located between the engine and transmission.

Clutch Pedal: Pivoting component inside the vehicle which the driver depresses, using foot pressure, to operate the clutch mechanically or hydraulically.

Clutch Purpose: Device for connecting and disconnecting the power flow between the engine and standard transmissions. The clutch is used during starting, shifting, and stopping.

Clutch Release (Throw Out) Bearing: Component that contacts, then moves the release levers when the clutch pedal is depressed. It is attached to clutch release fork and slides on the transmission front bearing retainer extension.

Clutch Release Fork: Pivoting clutch housing component that transfers motion from the free-play adjusting rod on the clutch linkage to the attached clutch release bearing. This fork reverses direction of applied motion.

Clutch Shaft: Transmission power input shaft upon which the clutch disc is splined and on which it slides.

Coil-spring Clutch: A clutch having the pressure plate tensioned against the disc by several coil springs that are located between the plate

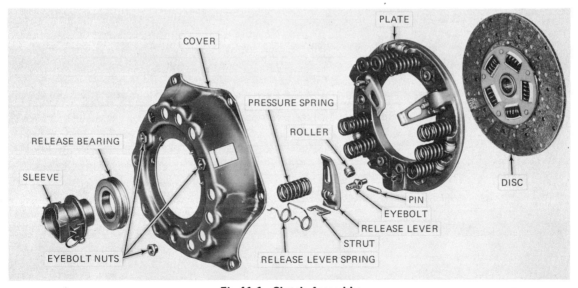

Fig 41-1. Clutch Assembly

Unit 41 Clutches

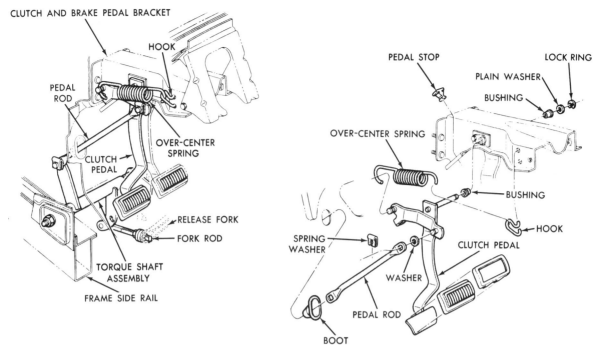

Fig 41-2. Clutch Pedal and Linkage

and the cover. These springs are available in various tensions.

Cushioning Springs: Waved spring steel segments to which the clutch disc lining is attached by brass rivets. They provide a "cushioning" effect, allowing smoother starts as the waved segments flatten during clutch engagement.

Dampening Springs: Coil springs, usually four to six, located between clutch disc hub and outer disc. Dampening springs reduce transfer of torsional vibration from the crankshaft and allow smoother starts as the springs compress during clutch engagement.

Diaphragm-spring Clutch: A clutch having the pressure plate tensioned against the disc facing (lining) by flexible diaphragm springs, often disc-shaped, rather than by coil springs.

Flywheel: Front most part of a clutch assembly that is bolted to the engine crankshaft. Its rear surface provides a smooth friction area for the disc front facing to contact during clutch engagement.

Hydraulically Operated Clutch: Clutch operated by hydraulic pressure transferred from a small master cylinder on the firewall to a slave cylinder on the clutch housing which moves the clutch release fork.

Multiple-disc Clutch: Clutch which has more than one disc, designed for certain heavy-duty applications. It has "drive" (pressure) plates that are smooth on both sides between each pair of discs.

Pedal "Free Play": Amount of downward clutch pedal motion before the clutch release bearing has moved enough to contact the release levers; the distance is specified in service manuals.

Pressure Plate Assembly: Assembly of various parts that operate to "press" clutch disc against the flywheel, engaging power flow to the clutch shaft, or "release" the disc, disengaging power flow.

Pressure Plate Cover: Outer part of pressure plate assembly that bolts to the flywheel and to which various assembly components mount.

263

Section 8 Power Train

Release Levers: Pivoting pressure plate components that retract (move backward) the pressure plate, compressing the springs and releasing the disc during clutch disengagement. The levers are operated by the clutch release bearing.

Semicentrifugal Clutch: Clutch having weighted components in pressure plate, such as rollers or release levers, that apply additional force against pressure plate to hold disc tighter during high engine rpm.

In the following exercises, indicate the best answer by inserting in the blanks the appropriate number, letter, word(s), or calculation, as required.

PICTORIAL REVIEW

A. Identify the clutch assembly components in figure 41-3 by writing their correct names in the blanks.

Fig 41-3. Clutch Assembly

1. _____ 6. _____
2. _____ 7. _____
3. _____ 8. _____
4. _____ 9. _____
5. _____ 10. _____

Unit 41 Clutches

B. Identify the clutch disc components in figure 41-4 by writing their correct letters in the blanks.

Fig 41-4. Clutch Disc

1. ____ stop pin
2. ____ splined hub
3. ____ facings (linings)
4. ____ cushioning spring
5. ____ outer hub flange
6. ____ torsional spring

SUMMARY REVIEW

____ 1. Most automotive clutches are located between the transmission and the
    a. engine.
    b. driveshaft.
    c. rear axle.
    d. differential.

____ 2. The clutch pilot bushing is usually located in the
    a. flywheel.
    b. crankshaft.
    c. disc.
    d. pressure plate assembly.

____ 3. The parts of the pressure plate assembly that hold the plate against the disc are the
    a. eyebolts.
    b. release levers.
    c. release bearings.
    d. springs.

Section 8 Power Train

___ 4. Clutch-disc cushioning springs are used to reduce
    a. dampening vibrations.   c. jerky starts.
    b. torsional vibrations.   d. vehicle speed.

___ 5. The clutch release bearing should contact the release levers when the
    a. vehicle is driven at high speed.
    b. vehicle is driven in high gear.
    c. vehicle is driven at low speed.
    d. clutch pedal is depressed.

___ 6. A clutch release bearing slides back-and-forth during clutch operation on the
    a. clutch shaft.
    b. pressure plate assembly.
    c. transmission bearing retainer.
    d. disc hub splines.

___ 7. Clutch linings are usually secured to the disc by
    a. bonding cement.   c. steel rivets.
    b. brass rivets.   d. metal screws.

8. Name two types of pressure plate assemblies in popular use on today's automobiles.
    a. _____   b. _____

9. Describe two reasons why dampening springs are used in a clutch disc.
    a. _____
    b. _____

10. Describe the special feature of a semicentrifugal clutch.
_____
_____

11. Insert the correct numbers of the matching terms or definitions in the blanks.
    a. ___ clutch lining   1. bell housing
    b. ___ clutch housing   2. throw out bearing
    c. ___ coil springs   3. clutch shaft
    d. ___ flat waved springs   4. pedal clearance
    e. ___ clutch release bearing   5. dampening springs
                           6. disc facing
    f. ___ splined part   7. cushioning springs
    g. ___ free play

Unit 41 Clutches

REFERENCE REVIEW

____ 1. The service life of a clutch is determined mainly by the
   a. brand of clutch.
   b. driver of vehicle.
   c. size of engine.
   d. disc-facing material.

____ 2. The amount of pedal free play on full-size American cars is approximately
   a. one-fourth inch.
   b. one-half inch.
   c. one inch.
   d. one and three-fourths inches.

____ 3. During clutch replacement, it is also a good idea to replace the
   a. clutch release bearing.
   b. transmission fluid.
   c. flywheel.
   d. clutch linkage.

____ 4. Pressure plate retaining bolts should be tightened
   a. to 50 pound feet.
   b. a small amount at a time.
   c. all at once.
   d. to 5 pound inches.

____ 5. In most cases, defective pressure plate assemblies should be repaired or rebuilt by
   a. a dealer technician.
   b. a specialized clutch rebuilder.
   c. the car factory.
   d. a truck mechanic.

____ 6. If the clutch-facing surface of a used flywheel has heat cracks, the flywheel should be replaced or
   a. filed smooth.
   b. reground.
   c. sanded lightly with crocus cloth.
   d. rubbed with crack filler.

____ 7. Clutch release ball bearing lubrication is provided
   a. by the bearing manufacturer.
   b. during chassis lubrication.
   c. when changing the motor oil.
   d. during clutch replacement.

8. List four places where a small amount of grease may be applied during clutch replacement.

   a. _____   c. _____
   b. _____   d. _____

9. List three different situations under which the clutch release bearing may be revolving.

   a. _____
   b. _____
   c. _____

Section 8 Lubrication

10. Name two classes of vehicles where a hydraulic clutch may be used.

    a. _____ b. _____

11. Identify the proper sequence of operation in most clutch systems, after the driver depresses the pedal, by numbering the items.

    a. __1__ pedal   e. _____ clutch release bearing
    b. _____ clutch release fork f. _____ pressure plate
    c. _____ free-play adjusting g. _____ clutch linkage
             rod   h. _____ clutch release levers
    d. _____ disc

UNIT 42 STANDARD TRANSMISSIONS

RELATED AUTOMOTIVE TERMS

Ball Bearing: An antifriction bearing that uses steel balls revolving between an inner and outer "race" to reduce wear, heat, and friction. Ball bearings are mounted in case on input and output shafts.

Case: Hollow casting that serves as a base to hold or mount transmission parts.

Countergear: An integral cluster of three or more various sized gears that revolve on the countershaft to provide the desired gear ratios, usually for second, low and reverse. It is located in lower transmission case.

Detent Ball, Plunger, or Cam: Part that is forced into a notch on the shift rail or mechanism by a coil spring, to hold the transmission in the selected gear position.

Extension Housing: Rear housing containing the output shaft and transmission-to-crossmember mounting.

Four-speed Transmission: A transmission providing four forward gear ratios, one reverse ratio, and neutral. This permits closer matching of engine speed to load requirements than three-speed transmission.

Gear Ratio: The speed relationship between a driving (input) and a driven (output) gear. A driving gear revolving twice for each driven gear revolution is an example of a 2 to 1 speed ratio.

Helical Gear: A gear having teeth cut at an angle across its face or diagonally to the rotational axis. It is stronger and operates more quietly than a spur gear.

Input (Clutch) Shaft: Forward shaft that transfers power from the splined clutch disc hub to the transmission countergear.

Needle Bearing: An antifriction bearing consisting of many small steel rollers that revolve between a gear and shaft to reduce wear, heat, and friction. Often located inside countergear, reverse idler, and input shaft.

Output (Main) Shaft: Rear shaft that transfers power from the involved transmission gear to the driveshaft slip yoke. This shaft is splined at or near both ends.

Rear Seal and Bushing: Oil seal and bushing inside rear of extension housing in which driveshaft slip yoke revolves.

Reverse Idler Gear: Gear transferring power in reverse only, from the countergear to the reverse gear on the main shaft. It rotates on a separate shaft, reversing the direction of countergear motion and consists of one or two gears.

Shift Rail: Steel rod upon which certain shifter forks mount. The rail slides forward or backward in the case during gear shifting.

Shifter Fork: A Y-shaped part that fits on and moves a synchronizer sleeve or gear into mesh with the desired matching component.

Snap Ring: C-shaped spring steel part that snaps into a shaft groove (undercut) to retain parts and/or control "end play."

Speedometer Drive Gear: Spiral gear attached to or machined into the main shaft. The drive gear turns the driven gear that rotates the speedometer cable.

Spur Gear: A gear having teeth cut straight across its face, parallel to the rotational axis.

Standard Transmission: A transmission that must be shifted into the various gears manually.

Synchronizer: Component that operates so that two gears about to be "meshed" together are revolving at or near the same speed.

Section 8 Power Train

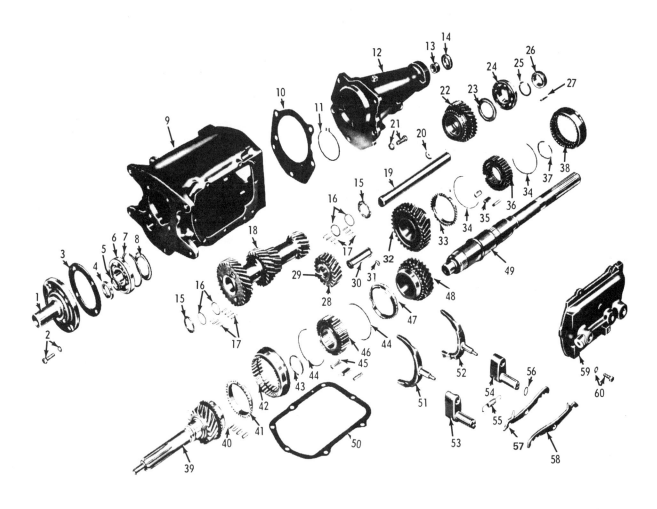

1. Bearing Retainer
2. Bolts and Lock Washers (4)
3. Bearing Retainer Gasket
4. Retainer Oil Seal
5. Bearing-To-Gear Snap Ring
6. Main Drive Gear Bearing
7. Bearing-To-Case Snap Ring
8. Oil Slinger
9. Transmission Case
10. Extension Housing Gasket
11. Bearing-To-Housing Snap Ring
12. Extension Housing
13. Extension Housing Bushing
14. Rear Oil Seal
15. Countergear Thrust Washers (2)
16. Bearing Washers (4)
17. Countershaft Bearing Rollers (116)
18. Countergear
19. Countershaft
20. Woodruff Key
21. Bolts and Lock Washers (5)
22. Reverse Gear
23. Thrust Washer
24. Rear Mainshaft Bearing
25. Bearing-To-Shaft Snap Ring
26. Speedometer Drive Gear
27. Retaining Clip
28. Reverse Idler Gear
29. Reverse Idler Bushing
30. Reverse Idler Shaft
31. Woodruff Key
32. 1st Speed Gear
33. 1st Speed Blocker Ring
34. Synchronizer Key Springs (2)
35. Synchronizer Keys (3)
36. 1st & Rev. Synchronizer Hub
37. Hub-To-Mainshaft Snap Ring
38. 1st & Rev. Synchronizer Sleeve
39. Main Drive Gear
40. Mainshaft Pilot Bearings (16)
41. 3rd Speed Blocker Ring
42. 2nd & 3rd Synchronizer Sleeve
43. Hub-To-Mainshaft Snap Ring
44. Synchronizer Key Springs (2)
45. Synchronizer Keys (3)
46. 2nd & 3rd Synchronizer Hub
47. 2nd Speed Blocker Ring
48. 2nd Speed Gear
49. Mainshaft
50. Side Cover Gasket
51. 2nd & 3rd Shifter Fork
52. 1st & Rev. Shifter Fork
52. 2nd & 3rd Shifter Shaft
54. 1st & Rev. Shifter Shaft
55. Detent Spring
56. "O" Ring Seals (2)
57. 1st & Rev. Detent Cam
58. 2nd & 3rd Detent Cam
59. Side Cover
60. Bolts and Lock Washers (7)

Fig 42-1. Standard Transmission, Three-Speed

Unit 42 Standard Transmission

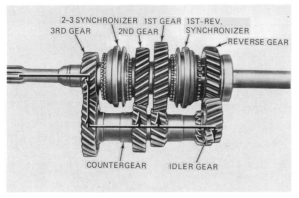

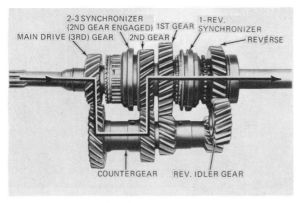
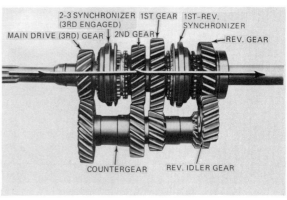
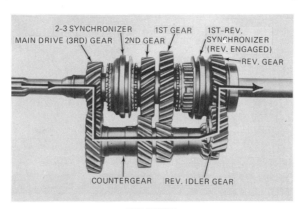

Fig 42-2. Standard Transmission, Power-Flow

Eliminates "grinding" if gears are shifted properly while in motion.

Three-speed Transmission: A transmission providing three forward gear ratios, one reverse ratio and neutral.

Thrust Washer: A flat metal washer placed between a revolving gear and a stationary part such as the case. This controls gear "end play" and case wear.

Torque Multiplication: An increase in turning or twisting effort obtained at a loss of rotational speed, such as acquired through transmission gears. Torque increase is proportional to speed decrease.

Section 8 Power Train

In the following exercises, indicate the best answer by filling in the blanks the appropriate number, letter, word(s), or calculation, as required.

PICTORIAL REVIEW

A. Identify the standard transmission parts in figure 42-3 by writing their names in the blanks.

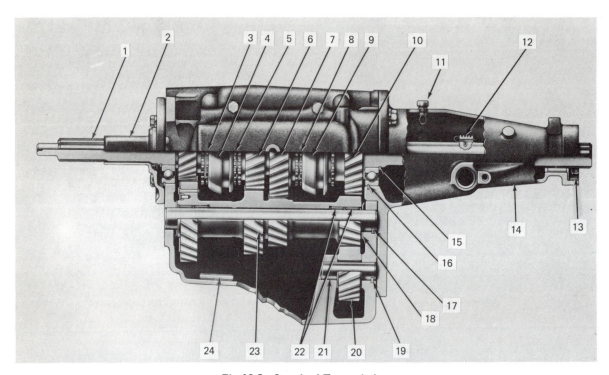

Fig 42-3. **Standard Transmission**

1. _____
2. _____
3. _____
4. _____
5. _____
6. _____
7. _____
8. _____
9. _____
10. _____
11. _____
12. _____
13. _____
14. _____
15. _____
16. _____
17. _____
18. _____
19. _____
20. _____
21. _____
22. _____
23. _____
24. _____

SUMMARY REVIEW

____ 1. A torque increase may be gained at the expense of
   a. losing power.
   b. losing speed.
   c. increasing gas mileage.
   d. all of these

____ 2. A synchronizer sleeve is moved directly by the
   a. selector lever.
   b. synchronizer lever.
   c. shifter rail.
   d. shifter fork.

____ 3. When a synchronizer operates, the two involved adjacent moving parts have their speed
   a. reduced.
   b. increased.
   c. unequalized.
   d. equalized.

____ 4. Two advantages gained by using helical gears rather than spur gears in a transmission are
   a. cost and noise level.
   b. cost and strength.
   c. strength and less end thrust.
   d. noise level and strength.

____ 5. The number of machined gears found on most countergears is
   a. 1 or 2.
   b. 2 or 3.
   c. 3 or 4.
   d. 4 or 5.

____ 6. The outer bearing at the rear of the input shaft contains
   a. bushings.
   b. balls.
   c. rollers.
   d. needles.

____ 7. Needle bearings are most often found inside the _____ gear.
   a. counter
   b. reverse idler
   c. low
   d. second

____ 8. The rear of the output shaft receives support from
   a. a bushing.
   b. a ball bearing.
   c. a roller bearing.
   d. needle bearings.

____ 9. The speedometer drive gear is found on the
   a. clutch shaft.
   b. main shaft.
   c. countershaft.
   d. input shaft.

10. Describe the purpose of a detent device. _____

11. Name two reasons for using thrust washers in a transmission.
   a. _____   b. _____

12. List two purposes of transmission snap rings.
   a. _____   b. _____

13. Insert the correct numbers of the matching terms or definitions in the blanks.

    a. ___ input shaft
    b. ___ helical gear
    c. ___ detent device
    d. ___ output shaft
    e. ___ blocker ring
    f. ___ needles
    g. ___ spur gear

    1. ball or cam
    2. clutch shaft
    3. teeth cut straight
    4. main shaft
    5. rollers
    6. teeth cut diagonally
    7. synchronizing part

REFERENCE REVIEW

___ 1. Before pulling the second- and high-gear synchronizing hub from an output shaft, a _____ must be removed.

   a. roll pin
   b. internal snap ring
   c. locknut
   d. external snap ring

___ 2. When the front synchronizer sleeve is moved forward, _____ gear is obtained.

   a. first
   b. second
   c. high
   d. reverse

___ 3. When the rear synchronizer sleeve is moved forward, _____ gear is obtained.

   a. first
   b. second
   c. high
   d. reverse

___ 4. During rear extension housing-seal replacement, it is often a good idea also to change the

   a. rear bushing.
   b. rear bearing.
   c. gear oil.
   d. housing gasket.

___ 5. The front transmission grease seal is attached to the front

   a. bearing retainer.
   b. input shaft.
   c. transmission case.
   d. oil slinger.

___ 6. What part does the rear extension housing seal lip contact to contain the gear oil?

   a. output shaft
   b. driveshaft
   c. universal-joint slip yoke
   d. countershaft rear surface

___ 7. The reverse idler gear revolves

   a. only in reverse.
   b. only in low and reverse.
   c. any time the input shaft turns.
   d. any time the output shaft turns.

Unit 42 Standard Transmissions

8. The countergear shaft is held in the correct position and prevented from turning on most transmissions by a
   a. lock pin.
   b. woodruff key.
   c. interference fit at the rear.
   d. snap ring.

9. The countergear is located in the _____ section of the case.
   a. lower
   b. upper
   c. side
   d. rear

10. If spur gears are used in a standard transmission, they would most likely transfer power in
    a. first.
    b. neutral.
    c. high.
    d. reverse.

11. Does the reverse idler gear rotate in the *same direction* as or in the *opposite direction* from the input shaft? _____

12. Name four gears, in the proper sequence, that transfer power during reverse.
    a. _____   c. _____
    b. _____   d. _____

13. Describe a special procedure to follow when removing the countershaft that keeps the needle bearings in place.
    _____

14. Underline the "constant mesh" gears found in most new synchronized transmissions.
    a. input gear to countergear
    b. countergear second gear to mainshaft second gear
    c. countergear low gear to mainshaft low gear
    d. reverse idler to countergear reverse gear

UNIT 43 AUTOMATIC TRANSMISSIONS - TORQUE CONVERTER

RELATED AUTOMOTIVE TERMS

Converter Check Valve: Valve that operates to keep the converter filled with fluid at all times.

Converter Cooling: Air and/or liquid cooling system that reduces converter fluid temperature. Excess heat is usually dissipated by pumping hot fluid through a cooler in the radiator.

Converter Drain Plug: A 1/8-inch pipe plug threaded into the converter front outer area on certain applications, allowing converter fluid to be drained.

Coupling Point: Term referring to the turbine speed closely approaching (near 90% of) the impeller speed. This occurs toward higher speeds under lighter loads.

Flex Drive Plate: Disc-shaped steel part transferring power from the crankshaft to the torque converter. This part may flex slightly during operation.

Impeller (Converter Pump): Driving member inside converter that consists of numerous vanes that direct fluid flow toward the turbine. The vanes are welded to the inside of the converter housing at the rear.

Roller Clutch: Clutch containing a number of rollers that operate by wedging on a ramp between an inner and outer race to lock up (drive) when the outer race is turned in one direction and to slip (overrun) when it is turned in the opposite direction.

Rotary Oil Flow: Term referring to the oil flow path around the converter inside as a

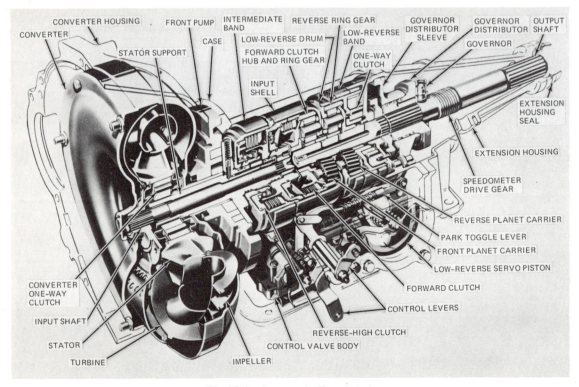

Fig 43-1. Automatic Transmission

result of the torque converter revolving. Flow direction is about parallel to flywheel.

Sealed Torque Converter: Converter that is welded together into a nonserviceable unit after assembly.

Sprag Clutch: Clutch containing numerous sprags (oblong parts) that operate by tilting between an inner and outer race to lock up (drive) when the outer race is turned in one direction and to slip (overrun) when it is turned in the opposite direction.

Starter Ring Gear: A relatively large diameter starter driven gear attached over the torque converter or flywheel flex drive plate.

Stator: Reaction member unit inside the converter having vanes to redirect the fluid flow that discharges from the turbine center back toward the impeller at an angle most advantageous to torque multiplication. Mounted on a one-way roller or sprag clutch.

Torque Converter: Unit that transfers power from the engine to the transmission input shaft by directing and redirecting fluid flow. Capable of increasing torque (twisting effort) if converter turbine speed is less than impeller speed.

Torque Multiplication: Torque increase as a result of converter action that allows the turbine (driven member) to resolve slower than the impeller (driving member) during acceleration and heavy load conditions. The ratio may be as much as 2 to 1.

Turbine: Driven member inside converter consisting of many vanes that receive fluid flow from the impeller. It is welded together as a separate revolving unit inside the front of the converter. The turbine hub is splined to and drives the transmission input shaft.

Turbine (Input) Shaft: Shaft that transfers power from the converter turbine into the transmission, splined at both ends.

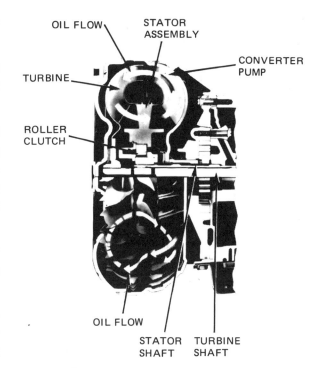

Fig 43-2. Torque Converter Operation

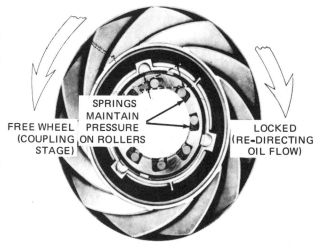

Fig 43-3. Stator Action, Showing One-Way Roller Clutch

Vanes: Scientifically designed and positioned fins that direct or redirect fluid flow inside the converter. Vanes are usually curved.

Vortex Oil Flow: Term referring to the circular oil flow path as it leaves the impeller, travels to the turbine, then through the stator, and back into the impeller. Flow direction is about parallel to the turbine shaft.

Section 8 Power Train

In the following exercises, indicate the best answer by inserting in the blanks the appropriate number, letter, word(s), or calculation, as required.

PICTORIAL REVIEW

A. Identify the torque converter assembly components in figure 43-4 by writing their correct letters in the blanks.

1. ____ input (turbine) shaft
2. ____ turbine
3. ____ impeller (pump)
4. ____ stator
5. ____ housing
6. ____ one-way roller clutch

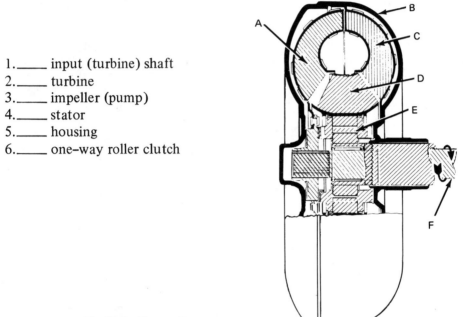

Fig 43-4. Torque Converter

B. Identify the sprag clutch, roller clutch, inner races, outer races, rollers, and sprags in figure 43-5 by writing their correct names in the blanks.

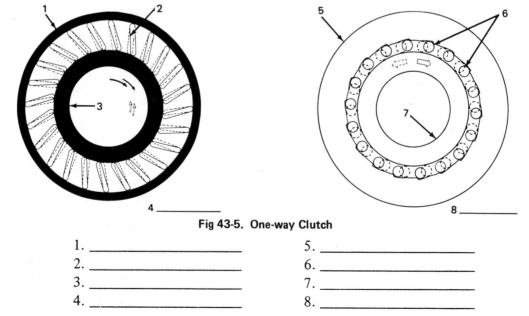

Fig 43-5. One-way Clutch

1. _____
2. _____
3. _____
4. _____

5. _____
6. _____
7. _____
8. _____

278

Unit 43 Automatic Transmissions — Torque Converter

SUMMARY REVIEW

___ 1. The part of the converter that allows torque multiplication is the
   - a. stator.
   - b. turbine.
   - c. pump.
   - d. impeller.

___ 2. Most torque converter outer housing sections are held together by
   - a. fine thread bolts.
   - b. welding.
   - c. coarse thread bolts.
   - d. bonding cement.

___ 3. On cars so equipped, the converter drain plug is located at the converter
   - a. center.
   - b. front.
   - c. outside circumference.
   - d. back.

___ 4. The torque converter member that drives the fluid is the
   - a. impeller.
   - b. stator.
   - c. one-way clutch.
   - d. turbine.

___ 5. A torque converter that is defective should be
   - a. removed for further testing.
   - b. flushed out with fluid.
   - c. replaced.
   - d. repaired by a dealer technician.

___ 6. The flex drive plate is bolted to the
   - a. front pump and stator.
   - b. turbine and input shaft.
   - c. one-way clutch and converter.
   - d. converter and crankshaft.

___ 7. The stator performs the task of
   - a. driving the impeller.
   - b. redirecting fluid flow to impeller.
   - c. driving the turbine.
   - d. redirecting fluid to turbine.

8. Maximum torque increase as a result of converter action is about _____ to _____ .

9. Another name for the input shaft is the _____ shaft.

10. List two different parts to which the starter ring gear may be attached.
    - a. _____
    - b. _____

Section 8 Power Train

11. Insert the correct numbers of the matching terms or definitions in the blanks.

   a. ____ vortex flow
   b. ____ stator
   c. ____ turbine
   d. ____ drive converter
   e. ____ rotary flow
   f. ____ one-way clutch part
   g. ____ impeller

   1. converter pump
   2. oil flow caused by impeller vanes
   3. driven member
   4. oil flow caused by converter revolving
   5. flex plate
   6. reaction member
   7. roller

REFERENCE REVIEW

____ 1. The torque converter performs about the same function as the _____ in cars having standard transmissions.
   a. clutch
   b. flex plate
   c. transmission
   d. pump

____ 2. Maximum torque multiplication occurs within the converter during acceleration from
   a. a stop.
   b. low speed.
   c. medium speed.
   d. high speed.

____ 3. The rear of the torque converter is supported by a
   a. roller bearing.
   b. bushing.
   c. ball bearing.
   d. clutch assembly.

____ 4. Drive hub tangs protruding from the rear of the converter turn the
   a. front clutch.
   b. reverse clutch.
   c. output shaft.
   d. front pump.

____ 5. The rear of the input shaft is usually splined to a
   a. clutch assembly.
   b. output shaft.
   c. planetary sun gear.
   d. front pump.

____ 6. The stator one-way clutch "free wheels" most during
   a. engine idle.
   b. low-speed driving.
   c. medium-speed acceleration.
   d. freeway driving.

____ 7. The stator one-way clutch functions most during
   a. the coupling point.
   b. engine idle.
   c. low-speed acceleration.
   d. high-speed acceleration.

____ 8. After leaving the converter, fluid often travels to the
   a. front pump.
   b. band assembly.
   c. radiator cooler.
   d. clutch assembly.

9. Torque converter fluid capacity on full-size American cars usually ranges from _____ quarts.

   a. 0 to 1 c. 4 to 8
   b. 2 to 3 d. 9 to 13

10. Vanes inside a converter have a shape that is

    a. square. c. curved.
    b. flat.   d. round.

11. Underline the symptoms of a defective torque-converter stator one-way clutch.

    a. poor low-speed acceleration
    b. poor high-speed acceleration
    c. large drop in engine speed when shifting from N to D
    d. no drop in idle speed when shifting from N to D
    e. high stall speed
    f. low stall speed

12. List four places from which engine oil or transmission fluid may leak inside the converter housing area.

    a. _____ c. _____
    b. _____ d. _____

13. Describe how a removed converter can be checked for leaks.
    _____
    _____

UNIT 44 AUTOMATIC TRANSMISSIONS – HYDRAULIC CONTROL SYSTEMS

RELATED AUTOMOTIVE TERMS

Accumulator Piston: A smaller second piston inside certain servos to assist in smooth band application by tightening the band around the drum gently, using low pressure before the larger servo piston takes over with high pressure.

Band: Circular steel C-shaped band internally lined with a bonded friction material. One band end is held by the case or band adjuster and the other end is connected to a hydraulic servo. Servo operation causes the band to contract around a drum, stopping rotation.

Clutch Discs: Flat thin discs inside a clutch assembly that are alternately splined internally and externally. One-half of the discs are steel, which may have a slight cone shape for smoother application, and the rest are either copper or lined with a bonded friction facing material.

Clutch Drum (Cylinder) Assembly: Component usually containing from five to ten clutch discs plus other operating parts, such as the clutch piston, hub, pressure or backing plate(s), spring(s), seals, snap rings, etc.

Front Pump: Fluid pump that produces hydraulic pressures necessary for transmission operation. Most have an internal and external toothed gear, the latter driven by tangs on the torque converter rear hub.

Governor: Speed sensitive assembly, driven by the output shaft, that supplies primary control of when shifts occur. Centrifugal force causes a valve to move against a spring, allowing pressurized fluid to move on toward shifting valves.

Hydraulic Line Pressure: Oil pressure in the different transmission circuits. Pressure varies according to the circuit involved, selector position, engine speed, and engine load.

Hydraulic System: System supplying automatic control of the transmission after the selector lever is moved, by sending fluid to the involved parts at the needed pressure.

Manual Control Valve: Spool valve that determines fluid flow from the valve body to various hydraulic circuits. Located in the valve body. Its position is controlled by vehicle driver through the selector lever.

Modulator (Throttle) Valve: Spool valve located inside the valve body and controlled by the vacuum modulator to increase modulator oil pressure during heavy loads, holding the band(s) and/or clutch(es) tighter. Also decreases oil pressure during light loads, allowing smoother shifts.

Oil Strainer: Component through which oil is filtered before reaching oil pump. Usually located at or near bottom of transmission oil sump, may be replaceable.

Pressure Regulator: Spring loaded valve device that controls main line pressure by limiting maximum pump output pressure.

Servo: Unit having an internal movable piston that is operated by hydraulic pressure to contract (tighten) a band around a drum, stopping rotation.

Shift Valve: Valve body component acted on by oil pressure, allowing fluid flow to the involved band(s) and/or clutch(es) at the appropriate time, causing the transmission to upshift or downshift.

Vacuum Modulator: Vacuum sensitive unit that acts on the modulator (throttle) valve inside the valve body to increase modulator

Unit 44 Automatic Transmissions – Hydraulic Control Systems

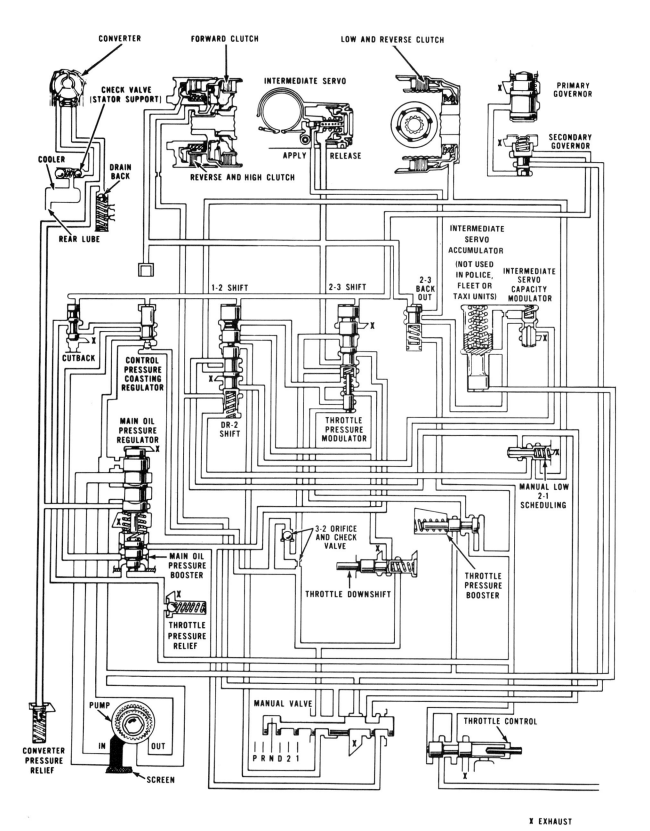

Fig 44-1. Hydraulic Control System

283

Section 8 Power Train

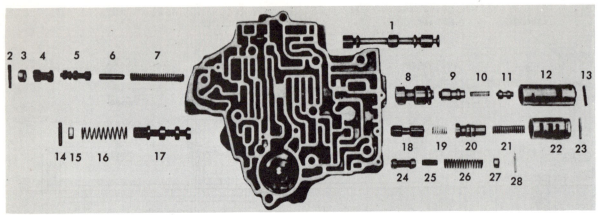

1. Manual Valve	8. 1-2 Valve	15. Bore Plug	22. 2-3 Bushing
2. Retaining Pin	9. 1-2 Detent Valve	16. 1-2 Accumulator Secondary Spring	23. Retaining Pin
3. Bore Plug	10. 1-2 Regulator Spring	17. 1-2 Accumulator Valve	24. 3-2 Valve
4. Detent Valve	11. 1-2 Regulator Valve	18. 2-3 Valve	25. Spacer
5. Detent Regulator	12. 1-2 Bushing	19. 3-2 Intermediate Spring	26. 3-2 Spring
6. Space	13. Retaining Pin	20. 2-3 Modulator Valve	27. Bore Plug
7. Detent Spring	14. Retaining Pin	21. 2-3 Valve Spring	28. Retaining Pin

Fig 44-2. Control Valve Body Assembly

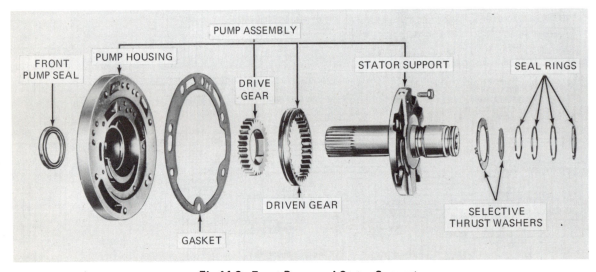

Fig 44-3. Front Pump and Stator Support

Fig 44-4. Pressure Regulator Valve

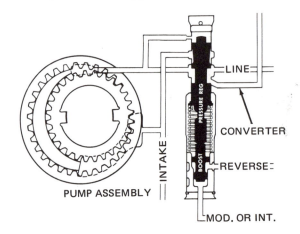

Unit 44 Automatic Transmissions – Hydraulic Control Systems

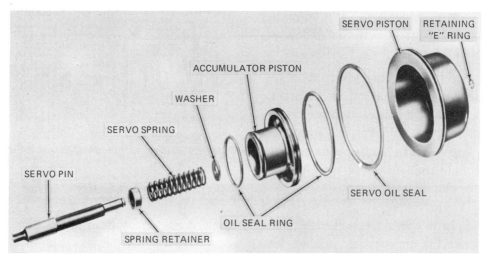

Fig 44-5. Servo and Accumulator Assembly

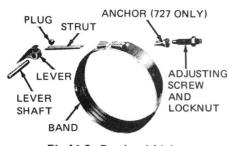

Fig 44-6. Band and Linkage

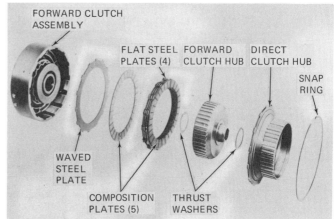

Fig 44-7. Clutch Assembly

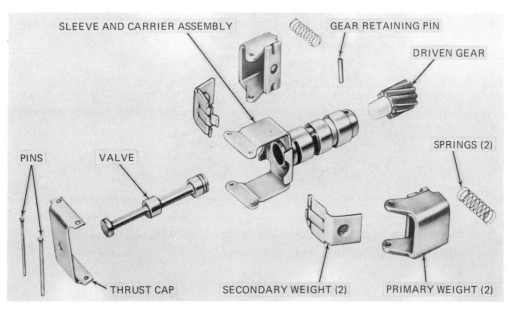

Fig 44-8. Governor Assembly

285

Section 8 Power Train

oil pressure during acceleration. It is connected by tubing to the intake manifold and may be altitude compensated.

Valve Body Assembly: Assembly containing a large number of parts that act as the brain of an automatic transmission. Receives messages on gear selected, vehicle speed, throttle opening and engine load. Then operates, automatically sending fluid to apply appropriate band(s) and/or clutch(es).

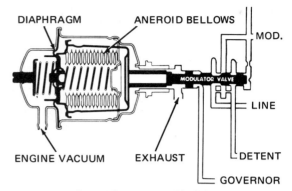

Fig 44-9. Vacuum Modulator

In the following exercises, indicate the best answer by inserting in the blanks the appropriate number, letter, word(s), or calculation, as required.

PICTORIAL REVIEW

A. Identify the servo parts in figure 44-10 by writing their correct names in the blanks.

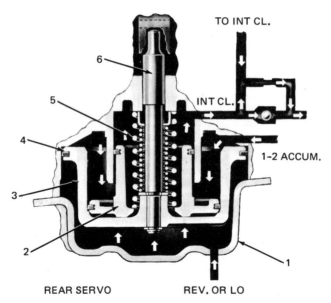

Fig 44-10. Hydraulic Servo

1. _____   4. _____
2. _____   5. _____
3. _____   6. _____

B. Identify the band and linkage assembly components in figure 44-11 by writing their correct letters in the blanks.

1. ___ band   4. ___ strut
2. ___ adjuster   5. ___ lever shaft
3. ___ lever   6. ___ O-ring

Unit 44 *Automatic Transmissions — Hydraulic Control Systems*

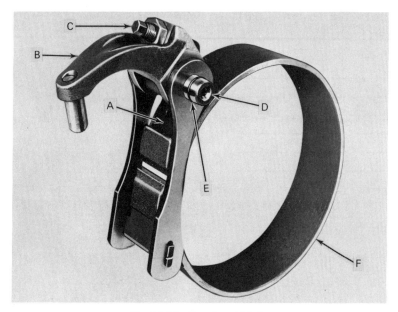

Fig 44-11. Band and Linkage

C. Identify the clutch assembly components in figure 44-12 by writing their correct letters in the blanks.

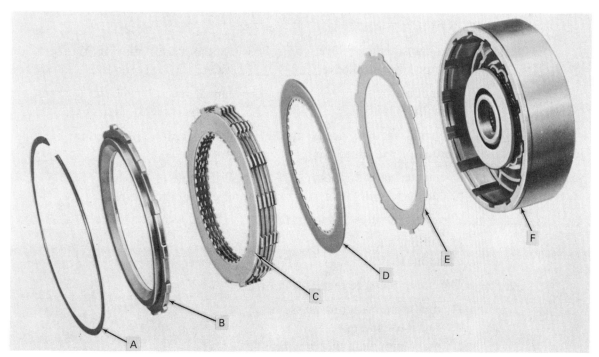

Fig 44-12. Clutch Assembly

1. ____ clutch housing
2. ____ snap ring
3. ____ waved steel plate
4. ____ composition plates
5. ____ backing (pressure) plate
6. ____ flat steel plates

287

Section 8 Power Train

D. Identify the governor parts in figure 44-13 by writing their correct names in the blanks.

1. _____
2. _____
3. _____
4. _____
5. _____
6. _____

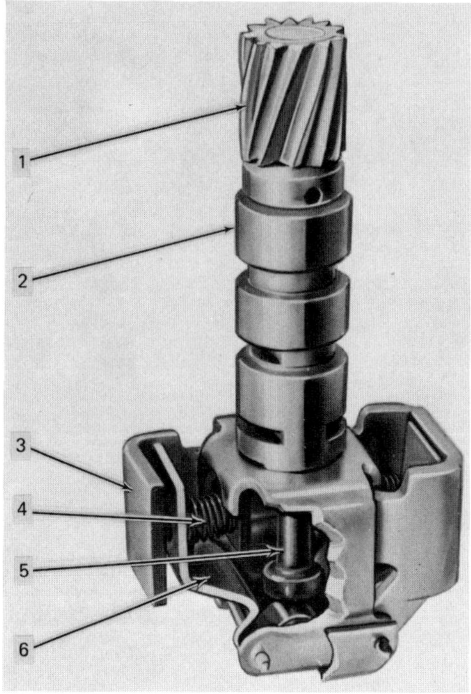

Fig 44-13. Governor

SUMMARY REVIEW

____ 1. The transmission valve controlled by the driver moving the selector lever is called a _____ valve.

    a. modulator   c. manual
    b. shift   d. governor

____ 2. If engine vacuum drops during vehicle operation, the vacuum modulator will cause the

    a. manual valve to move.   c. oil pressure to increase.
    b. pump to spin faster.   d. oil pressure to decrease.

____ 3. The front pump is driven by the

    a. turbine shaft.   c. servo.
    b. input shaft.   d. converter.

____ 4. The pump pressure regulator controls

    a. minimum main line pressure.
    b. regulator spring tension.
    c. maximum main line pressure.
    d. governor output pressure.

____ 5. One end of a band is held in a fixed position while the other end connects to a

    a. governor.   c. clutch disc.
    b. servo.   d. modulator.

Unit 44 Automatic Transmission – Hydraulic Control Systems

____ 6. An accumulator is located inside certain
   a. servos.   c. modulators.
   b. governors.   d. pumps.

____ 7. The primary purpose of the governor is to control the
   a. shift speeds.   c. vacuum modulator.
   b. main line pressure. d. converter pressure.

____ 8. The governor is driven by the transmission
   a. clutch drum.   c. input shaft.
   b. rear pump.   d. output shaft.

9. Clutch discs are alternately splined _____ and _____ .

10. Describe the purpose of an accumulator. _____
_____

11. Explain why steel clutch disc(s) may have a cone or waved shape.
_____

12. Insert the correct numbers of the matching terms or definitions in the blanks.
   a. ____ modulator valve   1. holds clutch assembly
   b. ____ snap ring   together
   c. ____ servo   2. vacuum modulator location
   d. ____ governor   3. has friction lining
   e. ____ inside case   4. speed sensitive device
   f. ____ outside case   5. valve body location
   g. ____ band   6. throttle valve
                              7. band applier

REFERENCE REVIEW

____ 1. A shift speed that is too high could be caused by
   a. a sticking governor valve.   c. a tight band.
   b. lower modulator line   d. a servo stuck open.
      pressure.

____ 2. The valve body assembly contains the
   a. 1-2 shift valve.   c. servo.
   b. governor valve.   d. clutch hub.

____ 3. Most transmission valves are shaped like a
   a. straight rod.   c. coil spring.
   b. spool.   d. gear.

____ 4. Servo parts needing replacement during transmission overhaul usually include the
   a. inner piston.   c. seals.
   b. outer piston.   d. all of these.

Section 8 Power Train

_____ 5. Immediately after tightening a band adjustment the specified amount, the technician should

    a. tighten the locknut with an adjustable wrench
    b. check band for centering.
    c. loosen or tighten adjuster specified amount; then tighten locknut.
    d. operate at stall speed for one minute to check for slippage.

_____ 6. The clutch piston retaining snap ring should be removed

    a. after compressing piston return spring(s).
    b. with a screwdriver.
    c. before the clutch discs.
    d. using air pressure.

_____ 7. Operating damage to a steel clutch disc face is usually caused by

    a. excessive oil pressure.
    b. a manual valve malfunction.
    c. worn bands.
    d. excessive heat.

_____ 8. Before installation, new clutch discs should be

    a. coated with motor oil.
    b. wiped clean with a shop rag.
    c. coated with transmission fluid.
    d. tested for strength.

_____ 9. A defective vacuum modulator may cause

    a. erratic upshifts.
    b. high line pressure.
    c. fluid loss.
    d. all of these.

10. Is the line pressure in reverse *higher* or *lower* than in drive?
_____

11. What transmission component may be altitude compensated?
_____

12. Name two ways to check a vacuum modulator.

    a. _____
    b. _____

UNIT 45 AUTOMATIC TRANSMISSIONS – PLANETARY GEARS

RELATED AUTOMOTIVE TERMS

Compound Planetary Gear Set: Two adjacent sets of planetary gears that may be meshed with an extended common sun gear, increasing their versatility.

Constant Mesh: Term referring to gears that mesh continually, such as planetary gears. This eliminates the clashing or grinding that may occur when other types of gears are shifted together.

High Gear (Direct Drive): Obtained from a planetary gear set when any two members (sun gear and planet gears or planet gears and internal gear) are locked together.

Intermediate Gear: Obtained from a planetary gear set when the sun gear is held and power is applied to the internal gear. Involves a small torque increase.

Internal (Annular) (Ring) Gear: Outer planetary gear set component having internal teeth

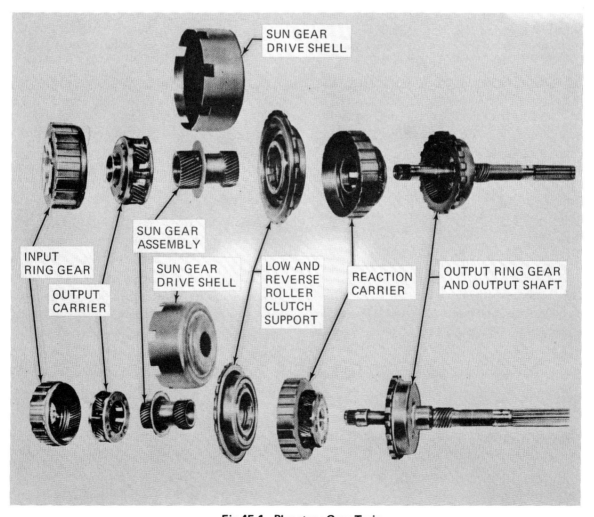

Fig 45-1. Planetary Gear Train

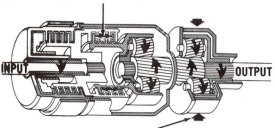

The forward clutch is applied. The front planetary unit ring gear is locked to the input shaft.

The low and reverse clutch (low range) or the one-way clutch (D1 range) is holding the reverse unit planet carrier stationary.

FIRST GEAR

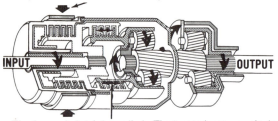

The intermediate band is applied. The reverse and high clutch drum, the input shell and the sun gear are held stationary.

The forward clutch is applied. The front planetary unit ring gear is locked to the input shaft.

SECOND GEAR

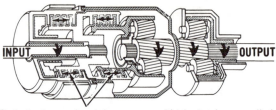

Both the forward and the reverse and high clutch are applied. All planetary gear members are locked to each other and are locked to the output shaft.

HIGH GEAR

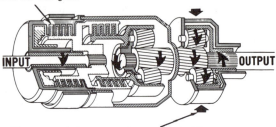

The reverse and high clutch is applied. The input shaft is locked to the reverse and high clutch drum, the input shell and the sun gear.

The low and reverse clutch is applied. The reverse unit planet carrier is held stationary.

REVERSE

Fig 45-2. Power Flow Through Planetary Gears and Clutch Packs

that mesh with the planet gears. Rotation may be started or stopped by the operation of a clutch or band.

Long Planet Pinions: Smaller diameter pinion gears meshing with the sun gear in certain applications. Transfers power in the opposite direction to the adjacent larger diameter pinion gear that, in turn, meshes with an internal gear.

Low Gear: Obtained from a planetary gear set when the internal gear is held and power is applied to the sun gear; involves a torque increase.

Needle Bearings: Small diameter roller bearings upon which the planet gears revolve.

Neutral: Obtained from a planetary gear set when all members (gears and planet carrier) are left free to rotate at will.

Pinion Pin (Shaft): Hardened steel shaft upon which the planetary pinion gears and bearings revolve. It is located in the pinion carrier.

Planet Pinions: Small gears that travel around (orbit) the sun gear, meshing with and rotating between the sun and internal gears.

Planet Pinion Carrier (Cage): Frame providing mounting support for planet gears.

Planetary Gear Set: A group of gears named after the solar system because of their arrangement and action. This unit consists of a center (sun) gear around which pinion (planet) gears revolve. The assembly is placed inside a ring gear having internal teeth. All gears mesh constantly. Planetary gear sets may be used to increase or decrease torque and/or obtain neutral, low, intermediate, high or reverse.

Reverse Gear: Obtained from a planetary gear set when the planet-gear carrier is held and power is applied to the sun gear; involves a torque increase.

Sun Gear: Center gear the planet gears mesh with and revolve around.

Unit 45 Automatic Transmissions – Planetary Gears

In the following exercises, indicate the best answer by inserting in the blanks the appropriate number, letter, word(s), or calculation, as required.

PICTORIAL REVIEW

A. Identify the planetary gear set components in figure 45-3 by writing their correct letters in the blanks.

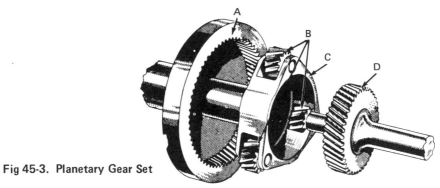

Fig 45-3. Planetary Gear Set

1. _____ planet carrier   3. _____ internal gear
2. _____ planet pinion gears   4. _____ sun gear

B. Identify which planetary gear set in figure 45-4 will best produce the ratio and direction of low, intermediate, high, and reverse by writing the appropriate name in each blank.

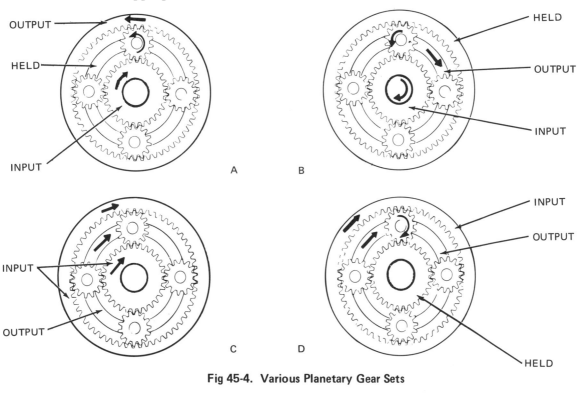

Fig 45-4. Various Planetary Gear Sets

1. _____   2. _____   3. _____   4. _____

293

Section 8 Power Train

SUMMARY REVIEW

____ 1. Compound planetary gear sets may have a common

    a. short planet pinion gear.   c. planet carrier.
    b. sun gear.   d. internal gear.

____ 2. The member driven to obtain a small torque increase in intermediate with a simple planetary gear set is the

    a. sun gear.   c. internal gear.
    b. planetary pinion gears.   d. external gear.

____ 3. The member driven to obtain a torque increase in reverse is the

    a. planetary pinion gears.   c. sun gear.
    b. internal gear.   d. planet carrier.

____ 4. The member that may be held to obtain a large torque increase in low with a simple planetary gear set is the

    a. internal gear.   c. sun gear.
    b. planet carrier.   d. planetary pinion gears.

____ 5. The long planet gears, when used, mesh with the short planet gears and the

    a. sun gear.   c. long pinion gears.
    b. internal gear.   d. annular gear.

____ 6. The center gear of a planetary gear set is called a _____ gear.

    a. sun   c. planet
    b. pinion   d. internal

____ 7. Most planet gears revolve on

    a. copper bushings.   c. brass bushings.
    b. ball bearings.   d. needle bearings.

____ 8. The component usually not used to provide input power for a single planetary gear set is

    a. the sun gear.   c. the planet carrier.
    b. the internal gear.   d. all of these.

9. The internal gear may also be known as a _____ gear or a _____ gear.

10. How is high gear obtained from a planetary gear set?

_____

Unit 45 Automatic Transmissions — Planetary Gears

11. Insert the correct numbers of the matching terms or definitions in the blanks.

 a. ____ carrier
 b. ____ planet gears
 c. ____ planet shaft
 d. ____ constant mesh gears
 e. ____ driving member in reverse
 f. ____ planetary gear set named after
 g. ____ outer gear

1. cage
2. pin
3. no gear shifting
4. solar system
5. pinions
6. internal gear
7. sun gear

REFERENCE REVIEW

____ 1. High is obtained from a planetary gear set by
 a. applying clutches and releasing bands.
 b. releasing clutches.
 c. releasing clutches and applying bands.
 d. applying bands.

____ 2. Neutral is obtained from a planetary gear set by
 a. applying clutches and releasing bands.
 b. applying bands and clutches.
 c. releasing bands and clutches.
 d. applying bands only to stop rotation.

____ 3. The rear internal gear often is attached to the
 a. transmission case.   c. sun gear.
 b. input shaft.   d. output shaft.

____ 4. In reverse, the internal gear revolves in the same direction as the
 a. planet carrier.   c. sun gear.
 b. planetary pinions.   d. input shaft.

____ 5. The rotation of the planet pinions during low gear is
 a. stopped.   c. slower than internal gear.
 b. on their shafts.   d. in the same direction as internal gear.

____ 6. If one planetary pinion gear has worn teeth, the technician should replace the
 a. worn gear only.   c. entire gear set involved.
 b. transmission.   d. clutches.

____ 7. The numerical gear ratio in reverse as compared with low is usually
 a. higher (toward 3 to 1).   c. either higher or lower.
 b. lower (toward 1 to 1).   d. the same.

Section 8 Power Train

_____ 8. The numerical gear ratio in high as compared with reverse is usually

    a. lower (toward 1 to 1).   c. the same.
    b. higher (toward 3 to 1).   d. either lower or higher.

9. Are planetary gear sets located toward the *front* or *rear* of a transmission? _____

10. List two reasons why a planetary gear set usually lasts longer than a sliding gear in a standard transmission.

    a. _____
    b. _____

UNIT 46 DRIVE LINES

RELATED AUTOMOTIVE TERMS

Centering Ball and Seat: Constant velocity joint parts that maintain operating alignment of the double joint. Consists of a ball stud, ball seat, and spring that are located inside the center yoke.

Constant Velocity (Double Cardon) Universal Joint: Special assembly having two universal joints back-to-back. This eliminates transmitted speed fluctuations evident with single joints; reduces vibrations or allows an increased shaft operating angle. Often installed when front and rear shaft operating angles are different.

Coupling Yoke (Link): Integral or separate component to which the universal joint bearing cups attach. The yoke has a Y-shape, allowing joint-operating space. Two required for each joint.

Cross and Roller Joint: Popular type of joint, featuring a center X-shaped cross (spider) that pivots inside bearing cups on roller (needle) bearings during operation. The operating angle causes a slight variation in transmitted speed.

Drive Line: Assembly of various parts including the drive shaft, universal joints, and connecting yokes that transmit torque from the transmission to the differential.

Drive (Propeller) Shaft: Hollow steel shaft that connects the transmission output shaft to the differential drive pinion yoke through universal joints at each shaft end.

Drive Shaft Runout: Amount of sideways wobble in a revolving drive shaft. This may be checked at shaft center and ends with a dial indicator or runout gage. Maximum usually specified as less than 0.025 inch (0.635 mm).

Drive Shaft Speed Fluctuation: Slight speed changes in the drive shaft rotation caused when the shaft operating angle tilts the standard single universal joint cross in various directions. Drive shaft speed increases and decreases twice each revolution. Constant velocity joints eliminate speed fluctuations.

Hotchkiss Drive: Popular type drive line (system) that features an open or visible drive shaft. Drive thrust is transmitted from the axle assembly to the vehicle frame via leaf springs or control arms.

Inertia Weight: Small steel flywheel used to dampen out drive line vibrations on certain applications. It may be located on the slip yoke, drive pinion yoke, or near an end of the drive shaft.

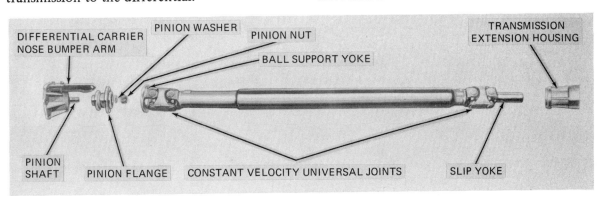

Fig 46-1. Drive Line Assembly

Section 8 Power Train

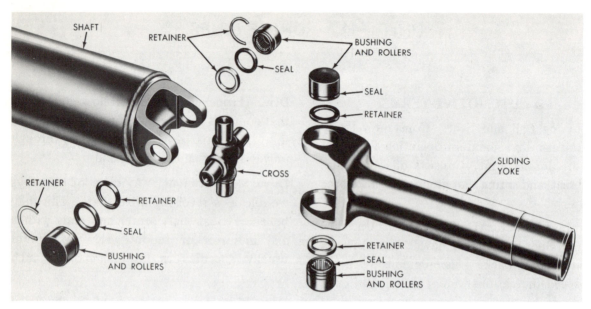

Fig 46-2. Single Universal Joint

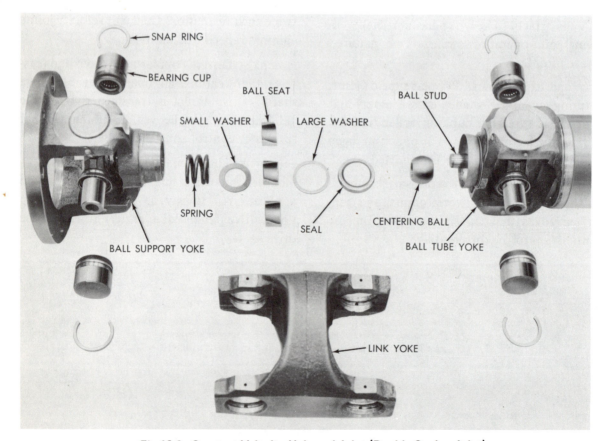

Fig 46-3. Constant Velocity Universal Joint (Double Cardon Joint)

Unit 46 Drive Lines

Slip Yoke: Component that allows the drive line to adjust for variations in length as the rear axle assembly moves. A popular type has the slip yoke internal splines sliding on the transmission output shaft external splines.

Two-piece Drive Shaft: Type having two sections because of length, obstructions, or operating angle. This type requires a center support bearing mounted on the vehicle frame. It has universal joints at both ends and in the center.

Universal Joint: Component that allows drive line power transfer at a slight angle. Necessary as the rear axle assembly moves up and down over the road surface.

Universal Joint Operating Angle: Angle between the drive shaft and the shafts to which it connects. Often ranges from 0 to 3 degrees at the front and 2 to 10 degrees at the rear.

Universal Joint Retainer: Device employed to keep the universal joint bearing cups properly located in their connecting yokes. It may be snap rings located internally or externally, U-bolts, fine-thread bolts and clamps, or a substance such as melted nylon or other plastic injected into grooves in the yoke and bearing cups after assembly.

In the following exercises, indicate the best answer by inserting in the blanks the appropriate number, letter, word(s), or calculation, as required.

PICTORIAL REVIEW

A. Identify the drive-line assembly components in figure 46-4 by writing their letters in the blanks.

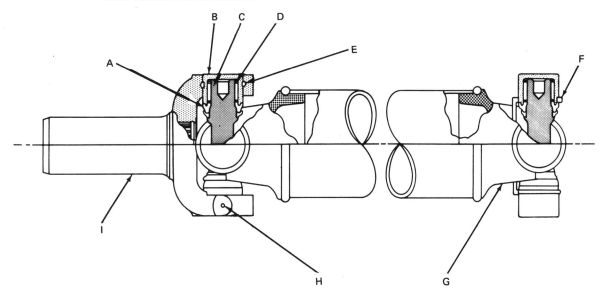

Fig 46-4. Drive Line Assembly

1. ____ needle bearing roller
2. ____ slip yoke
3. ____ retainer snap ring
4. ____ injected plastic bearing retainer
5. ____ plastic injection hole
6. ____ tube yoke
7. ____ bearing seal
8. ____ round bearing cup
9. ____ universal joint cross

299

Section 8 Power Train

SUMMARY REVIEW

___ 1. A universal joint performs the function of allowing the drive shaft to
   a. be removed easily.
   b. change length.
   c. bend sideways.
   d. transfer torque at an angle.

___ 2. The purpose of a slip joint is to allow the drive shaft to
   a. change length.
   b. change angle.
   c. rotate.
   d. bend upward or downward.

___ 3. The use of constant velocity universal joints
   a. reduces speed fluctuations.
   b. reduces vibrations.
   c. allows increased operating angles.
   d. all of these.

___ 4. A universal joint cross usually pivots against
   a. a bushing.
   b. needle bearings.
   c. the slip yoke.
   d. all of these.

___ 5. The drive-shaft center section is constructed from
   a. steel tubing.
   b. a steel shaft.
   c. a solid iron shaft.
   d. stainless steel tubing.

___ 6. Maximum allowable shaft runout is usually
   a. 0.025.
   b. 0.050.
   c. 0.075.
   d. 0.125.

___ 7. Hotchkiss drive is found on vehicles with
   a. an enclosed drive shaft.
   b. a torque tube drive line.
   c. an open drive shaft.
   d. all of these.

8. If the universal joint operating angles are different, does the *front* or *rear* have the sharper angle? _____

9. Rear universal joint operating angles range from _____ to _____ degrees.

10. What keeps a constant velocity joint operating in alignment?
   _____

11. Insert the correct numbers of the matching terms or definitions in the blanks.
   a. ___ drive shaft   1. spider
   b. ___ constant velocity   2. injected nylon
   c. ___ cross   3. sideways wobble
   d. ___ joint retainer   4. propeller shaft
   e. ___ slip yoke   5. small flywheel
   f. ___ runout   6. double cardon
   g. ___ inertia weight   7. frontmost part of drive line

REFERENCE REVIEW

1. The most recently developed universal joint retainer used features
    a. internal snap rings.   c. external snap rings.
    b. injected nylon.   d. clamps.

2. All universal joints on new cars manufactured since 1970
    a. may be lubricated after disassembly.
    b. may not be considered a serviceable item by the car manufacturer.
    c. may be lubricated without disassembly.
    d. are replaceable using a new original equipment joint.

3. Most serviceable universal joints should be disassembled
    a. with a C-clamp.   c. using a vise or press.
    b. on the vehicle.   d. by factory technicians only.

4. The most likely cause of a constant-velocity joint becoming misaligned is a broken
    a. universal joint cross. c. centering spring.
    b. needle bearing cup.   d. yoke.

5. Before disassembling a serviceable constant velocity universal joint,
    a. remove plastic snap rings.   c. remove external retaining rings.
    b. make alignment marks.   d. remove centering spring.

6. If a serviceable slip yoke is replaced because of deep grooves worn in its outer wearing surface, also replace the
    a. universal joint.   c. transmission extension bushing.
    b. drive shaft.   d. drive pinion yoke.

7. Slip yoke splines, on cars with automatic transmissions, should be lubricated during assembly with
    a. automatic transmission fluid.
    b. engine oil.
    c. grease.
    d. standard transmission gear oil.

8. A two-piece drive shaft requires the use of
    a. four or more universal joints.
    b. two constant velocity joints.
    c. a solid steel drive shaft.
    d. a center support bearing.

9. Drive shafts may be corrected for slight unbalance by the technician using
    a. hose clamps.   c. a square piece of steel.
    b. lead wheel weights.   d. a grinder.

Section 8 Power Train

_____ 10. During assembly of a serviceable universal joint, the numerous bearings inside the bearing cup should be retained in place using

    a. grease.   c. a dummy shaft.
    b. a clip.   d. a special tool.

_____ 11. A replacement universal joint that features a grease fitting should be lubricated

    a. every 1,000 miles.   c. using a low-pressure adapter.
    b. every 2,000 miles.   d. using a high-pressure adapter.

12. Describe a method for changing an incorrect rear universal joint operating angle on a car having leaf springs.

_____
_____

UNIT 47 REAR AXLE ASSEMBLY

RELATED AUTOMOTIVE TERMS

Axle Shaft: Alloy steel shaft that transfers torque from the differential side gears to the rear wheels. This shaft also supports vehicle weight on most passenger cars. It is splined at inner end and usually flanged at outer end for wheel mounting.

Carrier Housing: Cast iron rear axle assembly section that contains the working parts of the differential.

Differential: Section of rear axle assembly that provides three functions: allows the wheels to revolve at different speeds during turns, provides the final gear reduction, and changes the angle of drive 90 degrees.

Differential Cover: Steel cover bolted to rear axle housing on integral carrier differentials. Cover removal provides access for servicing differential.

Full-floating Axle: An axle that performs only one function: to transfer torque to drive the vehicle. This type is popular on trucks.

Housing Breather: Venting device that allows air to enter or leave the axle housing.

Integral-carrier Differential: Rear axle assembly that has a nonremovable cast iron differential carrier housing. Differential service work must be performed on vehicle. This type is popular on many small cars and some large cars.

Rear Axle Assembly: Group of parts that operate to transfer driving torque from the drive shaft to the rear wheels. Incorporates mounting pads for the rear springs and shocks.

Rear Axle Housing: Basic framework of the rear axle assembly inside which the individual

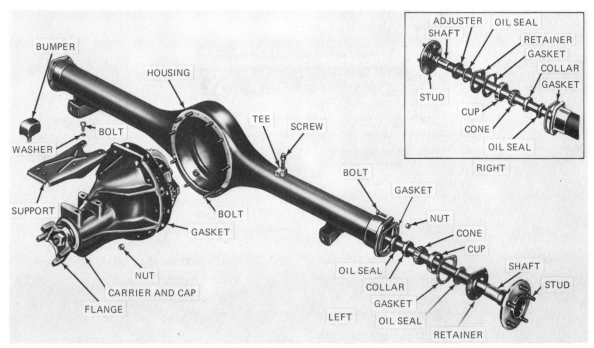

Fig 47-1. Rear Axle Assembly

303

Section 8 Power Train

parts, including the differential and axles, are mounted and/or operate.

Rear Axle Seal: Lubricant seal pressed into axle housing that retains differential gear oil. Working surface (lip) of seal contacts axle adjacent to bearing.

Rear Wheel Bearing: Antifriction bearing located near outer end of axle shaft that supports vehicle weight. It may feature balls, tapered rollers, or straight roller bearings.

Removable Carrier Differential: Rear axle assembly that has a cast iron differential carrier housing that is removable from the rear axle assembly for service work.

Semifloating Axle: Popular automotive system in which the axle shaft provides three functions: transfers torque to drive the vehicle, supports the car weight, and retains the wheel.

Wheel-bearing Retaining Collar: Steel ring installed over the axle shaft against the wheel bearing after bearing is pressed on; tight fit of collar on axle retains bearing.

In the following exercises, indicate the best answer by inserting in the blanks the appropriate number, letter, word(s), or calculation, as required.

PICTORIAL REVIEW

A. Identify the rear axle housing assembly components in figure 47-2 by writing their correct letters in the blanks.

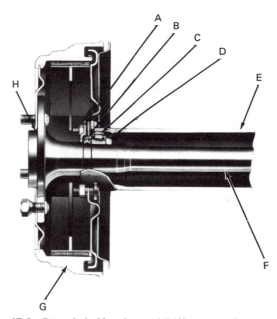

Fig 47-2. Rear Axle Housing and Differential, Cutaway View

1. ____ axle housing
2. ____ axle bearing retainer ring
3. ____ rear axle bearing
4. ____ axle bearing retainer plate
5. ____ rear axle seal
6. ____ brake drum
7. ____ axle shaft
8. ____ axle flange

304

Unit 47 Rear Axle Assembly

B. Identify the rear-axle assembly components in figure 47-3 by writing their correct letters in the blanks.

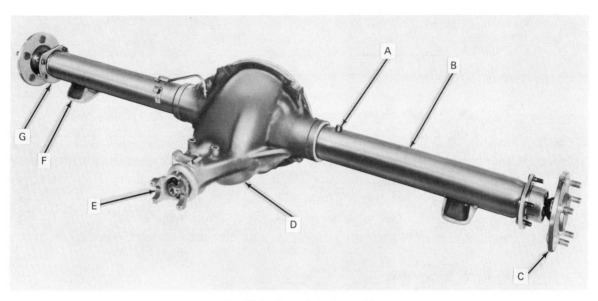

Fig 47-3. Rear Axle Assembly

1. ____ leaf spring mounting pad
2. ____ differential carrier
3. ____ axle shaft flange
4. ____ housing breather
5. ____ tubular axle housing
6. ____ U-joint companion flange
7. ____ brake backing-plate flange

SUMMARY REVIEW

____ 1. The differential operating components actually mount on the

    a. axle tubing.   c. rear axle housing.
    b. carrier housing.   d. differential cover.

____ 2. The inner end of the axle shaft is splined to the

    a. ring gear.   c. differential case.
    b. pinion gear.   d. side gear.

____ 3. An axle grease seal is retained in the housing by

    a. an interference fit.   c. a locknut.
    b. a snap ring.   d. the axle bearing.

____ 4. The outer end of most axle shafts is

    a. splined.   c. flanged.
    b. tapered.   d. grooved.

____ 5. The rear axle bearing is located nearest the

    a. axle inner end.   c. axle center.
    b. axle outer end.   d. differential carrier.

Section 8 Power Train

6. Is the removable carrier type differential more popular on *full-size* or *compact-size* American cars? _____

7. List three functions of a semifloating axle shaft.

   a. _____
   b. _____
   c. _____

8. Insert the correct numbers of the matching terms or definitions in the blanks.

   a. ____ full-floating axle   1. axle type used on most trucks
   b. ____ cast iron   2. housing tubing metal
   c. ____ semifloating axle   3. axle shaft metal
   d. ____ formed steel   4. carrier housing metal
   e. ____ alloy steel   5. axle type used on most cars

REFERENCE REVIEW

____ 1. Differential gear lubricant should always be maintained at a level that is
   a. at the top of the filler plug hole.
   b. at the bottom of the filler plug hole.
   c. as recommended by vehicle manufacturer.
   d. three inches deep.

____ 2. On cars having a removable differential carrier, the rear cover is usually
   a. riveted on.   c. bolted on.
   b. cemented on.   d. welded on.

____ 3. A misaligned rear axle housing should be
   a. replaced.   c. straightened.
   b. reinforced.   d. rebuilt by the factory.

____ 4. The housing breather is usually located on the
   a. carrier housing bottom.   c. axle housing tubing.
   b. differential cover.   d. carrier housing top.

5. List two ways rear axle bearings on new cars are lubricated.

   a. _____
   b. _____

6. List two ways to install the tight fitting axle-bearing retaining collar.

   a. _____   b. _____

306

7. Name three different ways to remove the gear oil from the differential housing.

   a. _____
   b. _____
   c. _____

8. Explain how to remove an axle shaft retained by a C-washer.
   _____
   _____
   _____

9. Describe how the rear wheel hub is mounted when a full-floating axle shaft is used. _____
   _____

UNIT 48 CONVENTIONAL DIFFERENTIALS

RELATED AUTOMOTIVE TERMS

Backlash: Clearance between the faces (contacting surfaces) of two meshing gears. It is the distance the ring gear can be rotated back-and-forth without moving drive pinion. Checked using a dial indicator.

Bearing Preload: Additional tightness applied to a tapered roller bearing after "free play" has just been eliminated.

Bevel Gear: A form of spur gear in which the teeth are cut at an angle to form a cone shape. This allows a gear set to transmit power at a 90° or other angle. Operation is somewhat noisy. Examples are differential pinion gears and side gears. Bevel gear teeth are straight lengthwise.

Collapsible Spacer: Steel tube-like part between drive pinion bearings that shortens (collapses) as the drive pinion flange nut is tightened. Spacer must be replaced during each assembly procedure.

Differential Case: Center unit of the differential that serves as a mounting place for the ring gear. Also contains the side gears, differential pinion gears and pinion shaft.

Drive pinion Flange (Yoke): Differential part that carries the power from the rear universal joint to the splined drive pinion.

Gear Ratio: The speed relationship between a driving and a driven gear. A 3 to 1 differential ratio has a drive pinion that turns three times for each ring gear revolution.

Hypoid Gear Set: Two gears able to transmit power at a 90° or other angle. The driving gear centerline is below driven gear centerline to allow for lowering drive shaft. Gear tooth face

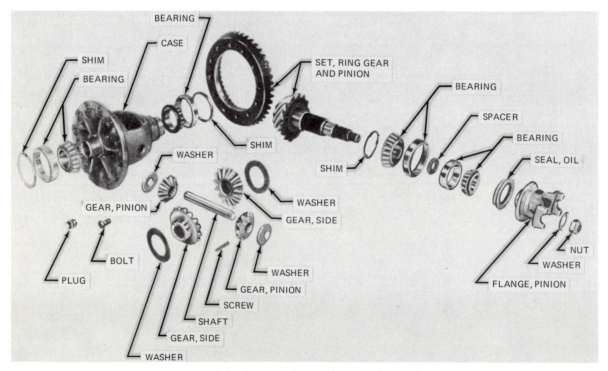

Fig 48-1. Conventional Differential Assembly

Unit 48 Conventional Differentials

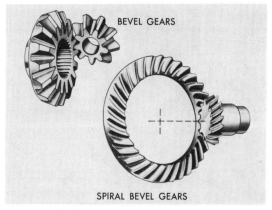

Fig 48-2. Typical Bevel Gears

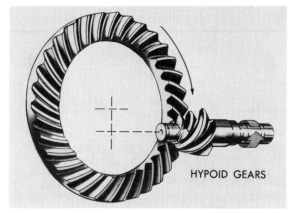

Fig 48-3. Typical Hypoid Gears

is curved lengthwise for strength and quiet operation. Gear teeth meshing involves a sliding action, requiring a special lubricant. This gear set is currently used for the ring gear and drive pinion on American cars.

Pinion Gear Shaft (Pin): Small shaft upon which the differential pinion gears are mounted and on which they spin during turns. Shaft transmits power from the case to the pinion gears.

Pinion Gears: Small bevel gears that, along with the side gears, provide the "differential action" during turns. Pinion gears transfer power from the pinion gear shaft to the side gears.

Pinion Seal: Part that prevents differential gear oil from leaking out past drive pinion flange outer surface. It is replaceable.

Ring Gear and Drive Pinion Set: Main differential gear set that provides a gear reduction (torque increase) and changes the angle of drive 90°. These gears must be used only as a matched set.

Roller Bearings: Antifriction bearings that function as mounts for the differential case and drive pinion. The rollers are usually tapered.

Side Bearing Adjuster: Component having external threads for controlling the position and preload of the differential case side bearings on certain applications. The adjuster is

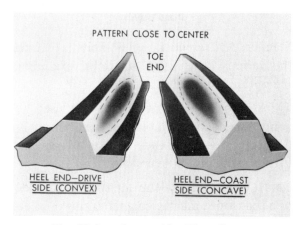

Fig 48-4. Acceptable Ring Gear Tooth Pattern

threaded into the carrier and bearing cap; usually turned with a spanner wrench.

Side Bearing Cap: Component that retains the side bearings against the carrier. It is bolted in place.

Side (Axle) Gears: Bevel gears that transfer power from the differential pinion gears to the splined axle shafts. Also involved with the "differential action" during turns.

Spiral Bevel Gear Set: Two gears able to transmit power at a 90° or other angle; centerlines of both meshing gears are in the same plane. The gear tooth face is curved lengthwise for strength and quiet operation. Formerly used for ring gear and drive pinion on American cars.

309

Section 8 Power Train

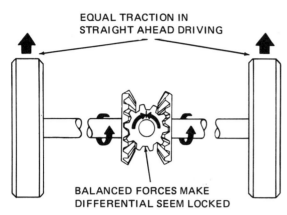

Fig 48-5A. Differential Inactive during straight ahead driving

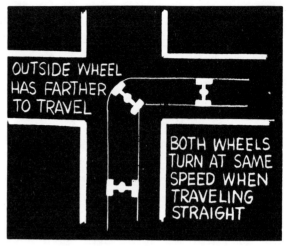

Fig 48-5B. Need for differential action

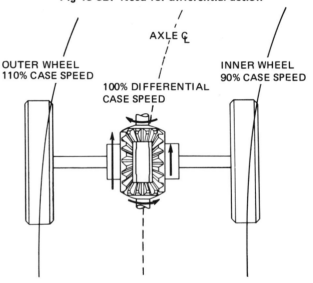

Fig 48-5C. Differential action on turns

Standard Differential: Assembly providing the various differential functions, excluding the optional limited-slip feature.

Thrust Block: Hollow component used to control axle shaft end play on certain models. Contacted by inner ends of rear axle shafts. Fits over the pinion gear shaft.

Tooth Coast Side: Term referring to the side of a gear tooth making contact during deceleration. Concave side of curved ring gear tooth.

Tooth Contact Pattern: Section of gear tooth face making contact during operation (meshing). Pattern should be along center section of ring gear tooth to reduce gear noise and wear. Pattern may be visually checked during servicing by using a "special" substance on several ring gear teeth, then rotating ring gear against the pinion.

Tooth Drive Side: Term referring to the side of a gear tooth making contact during acceleration. Convex side of curved ring gear tooth.

In the following exercises, indicate the best answer by inserting in the blanks the appropriate number, letter, word(s), or calculation, as required.

PICTORIAL REVIEW

A. Identify the conventional differential assembly components in figure 48-6 by writing their letters in the blanks.

1. ____ drive pinion
2. ____ bearing cap
3. ____ ring gear
4. ____ pinion shaft lock bolt
5. ____ drive pinion companion flange

Unit 48 Conventional Differentials

6. ___ differential case
7. ___ side gear
8. ___ front dust deflector
9. ___ differential carrier
10. ___ drive pinion oil seal
11. ___ axle C-lock
12. ___ side bearing shim
13. ___ drive pinion shim
14. ___ cover gasket
15. ___ collapsible bearing spacer
16. ___ cover
17. ___ case side bearing
18. ___ pinion shaft
19. ___ differential pinion gear
20. ___ axle shaft
21. ___ drive pinion front bearing
22. ___ pinion gear thrust washer
23. ___ drive pinion rear bearing

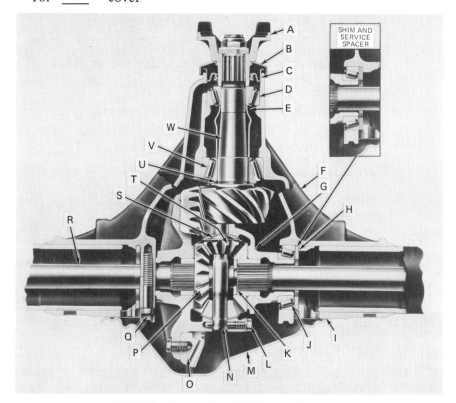

Fig 48-6. Conventional Differential Assembly

SUMMARY REVIEW

___ 1. The largest casting of the assembled differential is called the
   a. carrier.
   b. case.
   c. axle housing.
   d. differential housing.

___ 2. Between what two gears do differentials provide a backlash adjustment?
   a. ring gear and side gear
   b. pinion gear and side gear
   c. pinion gear and ring gear
   d. ring gear and drive pinion

311

Section 8 Power Train

3. The type of gear used for the side gears is the
   a. spiral.
   b. spur.
   c. bevel.
   d. hypoid.

4. Why do hypoid gears require a special lubricant?
   a. tooth metal is too hard
   b. tooth metal is too soft
   c. tooth sliding action
   d. gears revolve faster

5. The ring gear and drive pinion allow
   a. a torque increase.
   b. a gear reduction.
   c. a 90° drive angle change.
   d. all of these.

6. What gear(s) spin on a staionary shaft during turns?
   a. drive pinion gear
   b. axle gears
   c. pinion gears
   d. all of these

7. The smallest gears inside the differential case are called
   a. axle gears.
   b. pinion gears.
   c. drive pinion gears.
   d. side gears.

8. How may the automotive technician check ring-gear-to-drive-pinion tooth contact pattern during assembly? _____

9. Give three reasons why hypoid gears are used in most differentials today.
   a. _____
   b. _____
   c. _____

10. Does the *left* or *right* side gear revolve slower on a left turn?
    _____

11. The ring gear bolts to the differential _____.

12. Insert the correct numbers of the matching terms or definitions in the blanks.

    a. ____ pinion flange   1. pin
    b. ____ pinion gear shaft   2. preload
    c. ____ attaches with bolts   3. concave side
    d. ____ ring gear tooth   4. matched gear set
             drive side   5. convex side
    e. ____ ring gear tooth   6. yoke
             coast side   7. side bearing cap
    f. ____ ring gear and drive
             pinion
    g. ____ opposite of "free
             play"

Unit 48 Conventional Differentials

REFERENCE REVIEW

____ 1. The part that must be removed to change the drive pinion seal is the
   a. drive pinion.
   b. differential carrier.
   c. differential case.
   d. drive pinion yoke.

____ 2. Drive pinion bearing preload on most cars with used bearings should be near
   a. 5 pound inches.
   b. 12 pound inches.
   c. 25 pound inches.
   d. 37 pound inches.

____ 3. Drive pinion bearing preload is increased on most cars by
   a. reducing axle shaft endplay.
   b. tightening a nut.
   c. using an old collapsible spacer.
   d. adjusting case-bearing preload.

____ 4. Specified ring-gear-to-drive-pinion backlash on most cars is nearest
   a. 0.008 inch.
   b. 0.016 inch.
   c. 0.025 inch.
   d. 0.050 inch.

____ 5. What will wear out first if hypoid gear oil is not used in a new differential?
   a. drive pinion bearings
   b. side gears and pinion gears
   c. case bearings
   d. ring gear and drive pinion

 6. Would a differential gear ratio of 2.75 to 1 be considered a *high* or *low* numerical ratio for a passenger car? _____

 7. List the two most popular ways to change the contact pattern on a certain ring gear and drive pinion gear set.
   a. _____
   b. _____

 8. For what reason must the collapsible spacer between the drive pinion bearings be replaced during each assembly procedure?
   _____
   _____

 9. Why should drive pinion yokes on most new cars be removed and installed using special tools? _____
   _____

10. List the eight differential components in the order they transmit power from the yoke to the axle.
   a. drive pinion yoke
   b. _____
   c. _____
   d. _____
   e. _____
   f. _____
   g. _____
   h. rear axle shaft

UNIT 49 LIMITED-SLIP DIFFERENTIALS

RELATED AUTOMOTIVE TERMS

Brake Cone (Cone Clutch): Major component of one limited-slip differential type. It has an external taper that wedges against a matching surface in the case, providing the limited-slip action. Outward wedging force is supplied by the preload springs and the pinion gears pressing against the side gears. Cone is splined to the axle shaft along with the side gear.

Clutch Hub: Special hub used in certain applications such as single-pack types. Located between the splined discs and side gear and splined to both.

Clutch Pack Ear (Tab) Guides: U-shaped metal parts used with certain multiple-disc clutch assemblies. They fit over external locating tabs to align and secure the "fixed" discs inside the case.

Cone Lubrication Grooves: External spiral grooves around the cone clutch retaining lubricant.

Fixed Discs: Multiple-disc clutch components having external splines or tabs (ears) fitting into the differential case.

Limited-slip Differential (Anti-spin, Controlled Differential, Positive Traction, Positraction, Safe-T-Track, Sure-grip, Traction-lok, Twin-grip): Names used by various manufacturers to denote a differential having special friction mechanisms tending to keep both rear-

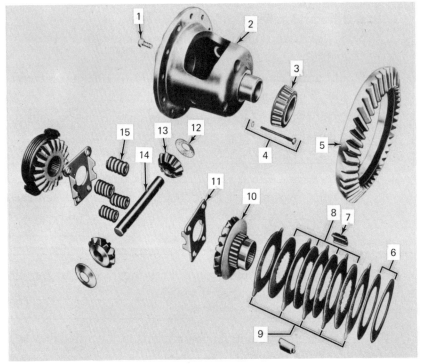

1. Ring Gear-to-Case Bolt
2. Differential Case
3. Side Bearing
4. Pinion Lock Screw and Washer
5. Ring Gear
6. Shim
7. Clutch Pack Guide
8. Clutch Disc
9. Clutch Plates
10. Side Gear
11. Spring Retainer
12. Pinion Thrust Washer
13. Pinion Gear
14. Pinion Shaft
15. Preload Spring

Fig 49-1. Limited-Slip Differential Case Assembly, Multiple-disc Clutch Type

Unit 49 Limited-slip Differentials

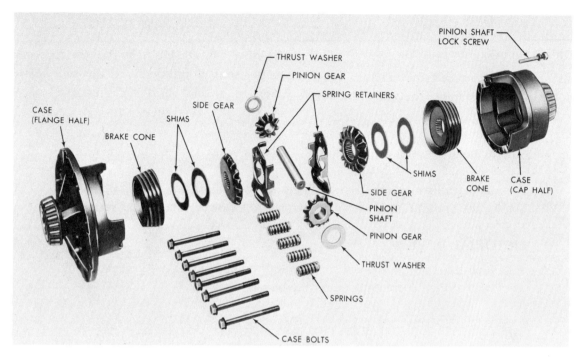

Fig 49-2. Limited-Slip Differential Case Assembly, Cone-clutch Type

axle shafts rotating at the same speed regardless of unequal tire-to-road surface friction.

Limited-slip Gear Oil: Lubricant specified for use in certain limited-slip differentials. Use of a wrong lubricant may cause chattering during turns and/or wear to the parts.

Multiple-disc Clutch: Major section of one limited-slip differential type, consists of several discs alternately splined (or attached) inside to the side gear or outside to the case. Force against the clutch discs from the preload springs (and pinion gears driving the side gears) presses the discs together. This tends to cause the case and side gears to revolve at the same speed, providing the limited-slip action.

Pinion Gears: Small bevel gears inside the case involved with the limited-slip action. The pinion gears react (press) against the side gears during vehicle operation, causing the clutch cones or discs to hold the case and axles firmly together.

Preload Springs: Coiled or waved springs that tension the side gears outward, squeezing the

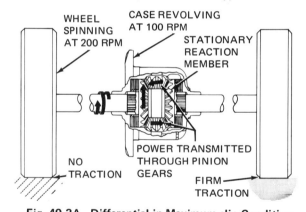

Fig. 49-3A. Differential in Maximum-slip Condition

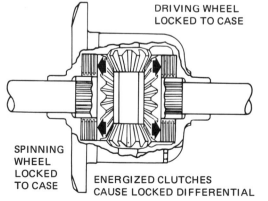

Fig 49-3B. Side Thrust Applies Force to Clutch Packs

315

cone or discs against the case. This tends to cause both side gears to turn with the case, providing a limited-slip function.

Shim: Spacer used in certain models to maintain the desired clearance between the side gears and the pinion gears. Variable thicknesses may be available. Located between the side gears and brake cone on some models, or between the clutch discs and differential case on others.

Splined Discs: Multiple-disc clutch components splined internally to the side gears or over a special hub on single-pack types.

Spring Retainer (Plate, Block): Steel part that locates and retains the coiled-type preload springs between the side gears.

In the following exercises, indicate the best answer by inserting in the blanks the appropriate number, letter, word(s), or calculation, as required.

PICTORIAL REVIEW

A. Identify the limited-slip differential components in figure 49-4 by writing their correct names on the blanks.

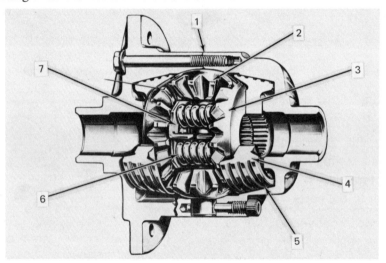

Fig 49-4. Limited-slip Differential Case Assembly

1. _____ 5. _____
2. _____ 6. _____
3. _____ 7. _____
4. _____

SUMMARY REVIEW

____ 1. Spiral lubrication grooves are machined into the

    a. side gears.   c. differential case.
    b. steel clutch discs.   d. brake cones.

____ 2. If a shim is used, it may be located between the discs and the

    a. ring gear.   c. side gear.
    b. case.   d. spring retainer.

____ 3. The number of coiled preload springs used in popular applications ranges from

    a. 1 to 3.   c. 5 to 10.
    b. 4 to 6.   d. 8 to 12.

____ 4. Fixed clutch discs are splined to the

    a. hub.   c. case.
    b. axle shaft.   d. side gear.

____ 5. Most limited-slip differentials require

    a. periodic adjustments.   c. frequent lubricant changes.
    b. a special lubricant.   d. frequent repair.

6. How do the differential pinion gears assist in the limited-slip action during vehicle operation? _____
_____

7. List two things that may occur if the wrong lubricant is used in a limited-slip differential.

    a. _____
    b. _____

8. Insert the correct numbers of the matching terms or definitions in the blanks.

    a. ____ brake cone   1. spring block
    b. ____ spring retainer   2. clutch disc ear
    c. ____ shim   3. smaller bevel gear
    d. ____ disc tab   4. larger bevel gear
    e. ____ differential pinion gear 5. cone clutch
    f. ____ side gear   6. spacer

REFERENCE REVIEW

____ 1. Limited-slip differential action tends to keep both the axle shafts turning at

    a. different speeds.   c. the drive pinion speed.
    b. the differential case speed. d. none of these.

____ 2. With the rear wheels jacked up and the transmission in neutral, turning one rear wheel forward will cause the other wheel to

    a. turn forward.   c. lock in position.
    b. turn backward.   d. turn in either direction.

Section 8 Power Train

___ 3. Rotational torque of a limited-slip differential, as checked with one rear wheel jacked up and the transmission in neutral, using a torque wrench is near

    a. 10 pound inches.   c. 5 pound feet.
    b. 50 pound inches.   d. 40 pound feet.

___ 4. The most limited-slip action occurs during

    a. acceleration.   c. freeway driving.
    b. deceleration.   d. stops.

___ 5. The tapered surface of a clutch cone wedges against the

    a. case.   c. side gear.
    b. clutch discs.   d. carrier.

___ 6. The number of multiple-disc clutch packs (assemblies, groups) used in the various brands is

    a. always one.   c. one or two.
    b. always two.   d. three or more.

7. Is the *multiple-disc clutch type* or the *cone clutch type* or limited-slip differential more likely considered serviceable (repairable)? _____

8. What is likely to happen if one wheel of a car having a limited-slip differential is jacked up, in gear, with the motor running?
_____

9. What may be used to align accurately the cone clutch with the side gear during case assembly? _____

SECTION 9 Air Conditioning and Cooling

UNIT 50 AIR CONDITIONING PRINCIPLES

RELATED AUTOMOTIVE TERMS

Air Conditioning (A/C) Principles: Operational characteristics of an air conditioning (refrigeration) system.

Btu (British Thermal Unit): An English system of measure which is defined as the quantity of heat absorbed, or given off, while changing the temperature of one pound of water one degree Fahrenheit.

Calorie: A unit of measure defined as the quantity of heat absorbed, or given off, while changing the temperature of one gram of water one degree Celsius (formerly centigrade).

Compression: The process of squeezing a vapor (gas) into a smaller space. The compression process raises the temperature of the refrigerant and concentrates its heat.

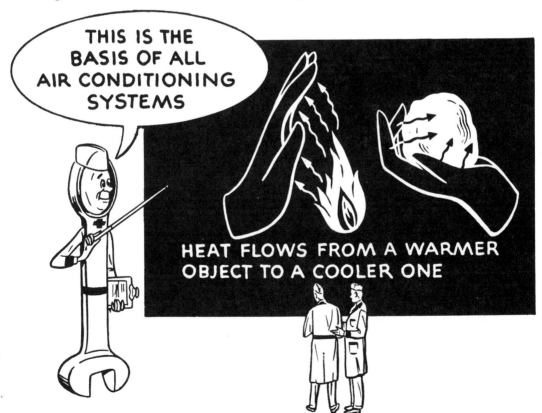

Fig 50-1. Heat Transfer, Hot to Cold

Section 9 Air Conditioning and Cooling

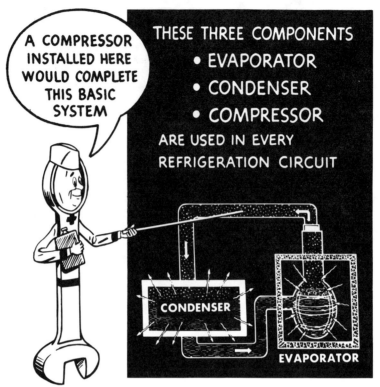

Fig 50-2. Basic Refrigerant Cycle

Condensation: The process of a substance changing state from a vapor (gas) to a liquid.

Dehumidification: The process of removing water vapor from air. The air becomes drier.

Evaporation: The process of a substance changing state from a liquid to a gas. This occurs primarily on the surface of a liquid.

Heat Quantity: Amount of heat contained in an object, measured in Btu's or calories.

Heat Transfer: Movement of heat by any of three methods: conduction, such as direct contact of R-12 with the air conditioner condenser or evaporator tubing; convection, such as cold air circulating downward from the air conditioner evaporator fins; and radiation, such as heat waves leaving the hot air conditioner condenser fins. Heat moves from a warmer to a colder object.

High-pressure (Discharge) Side: Internal section of a refrigeration system that has a

Fig 50-3. Liquid Boiling Points at Sea Level

relatively high pressure (over 125 psi). Compressor outlet side.

High-pressure Vapor: Reference to R-12 leaving the compressor, then entering the condenser. Hot R-12 condenses as its heat radiates into air flowing past condenser.

Unit 50 Air Conditioning Principles

°F	Pressure (psi)	°F	Pressure (psi)
-40	11.0*	+ 50	46.7
-35	8.3*	+ 55	52.0
-30	5.5*	+ 60	57.7
-25	2.3*	+ 65	63.7
-20	0.6	+ 70	70.1
-15	2.4	+ 75	76.9
-10	4.5	+ 80	84.1
- 5	6.8	+ 85	91.7
0	9.2	+ 90	99.6
+ 5	11.8	+ 95	108.1
+10	14.7	+100	116.9
+15	17.7	+105	126.2
+20	21.1	+110	136.0
+25	24.6	+115	146.5
+30	28.5	+120	157.1
+32	30.1	+125	167.5
+35	32.6	+130	179.0
+40	37.0	+140	204.5
+45	41.7	+150	232.0

*Inches of Vacuum

Fig 50-4. Refrigerant-12 Temperature-pressure Relationships

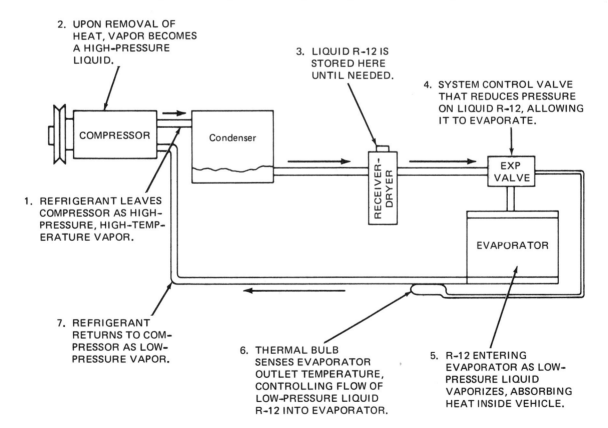

Fig 50-5. Basic Air Conditioning Cycle

Latent (Hidden) Heat: Heat consumed or given off when a substance changes state while remaining at the same temperature, can not be felt or measured with a thermometer. Seventy Btu's per pound are absorbed by R-12 when it changes from a liquid to a gas (inside the car within the system). These seventy Btu's are hidden (latent) heat in the R-12 gas. Seventy Btu's also are given off when R-12 condenses from a gas to a liquid (outside the car within the system).

Low-pressure Liquid: Reference to R-12 entering the evaporator. Low-pressure liquid R-12 boils in evaporator, absorbing quantities of heat.

Low Pressure (Suction) Side: Internal section of a refrigeration system that has a relatively low pressure (under 35 psi). Compressor inlet side.

Low Pressure Vapor: Reference to R-12 leaving the evaporator, then entering the compressor, where its pressure and temperature are raised.

Pressure: Force per unit area, usually measured in psi.

Refrigerant (R-12)(Freon-12): The cooling agent that circulates inside an automotive air conditioning system as a liquid and/or gas. Properties include being colorless, odorless, noncorrosive, nontoxic, nonflammable, having a boiling point of −21.7°F at sea level, and a latent heat value of 70 Btu per pound.

Sensible heat: Heat consumed, or given off, when the temperature of a substance is changed without changing its state; can be felt or measured with a thermometer.

State of a Substance: Refers to whether something is present as a solid, a liquid, or a gas (vapor).

Temperature-pressure Relationship: The known relationship between the temperature and pressure of, for example, R-12 in a confined area. As the temperature of R-12 goes up, more liquid evaporates, further saturating the vapor and raising the pressure.

Use Precautions: Certain refrigerant safety and service procedures for the technician such as to: wear goggles, avoid contact with skin, store in cool place, ventilate area of use, avoid breathing R-12 fumes that have contacted a flame, keep R-12 away from moisture, etc.

Vaporization: The process of a liquid, such as R-12 or water, changing state from a liquid to a gas by boiling throughout and/or surface evaporation.

In the following exercises, indicate the best answer by inserting in the blanks the appropriate number, letter, word(s), or calculation, as required.

PICTORIAL REVIEW

A. Follow the special instructions for the basic refrigeration cycle exercise in figure 50-6, to indicate certain system components, the direction of R-12 flow and areas of high or low pressure.

  1. Identify six system components by writing the correct names in the blanks on the picture.

  2. Place four arrows along the lines to indicate direction of R-12 flowing in an operating system.

Unit 50 Air Conditioning Principles

3. Label the four "key" blocks at the right side of the picture, which correspond to similarly marked lines, to indicate which system area contains *low-pressure liquid, low-pressure gas, high-pressure liquid,* and *high-pressure gas.*

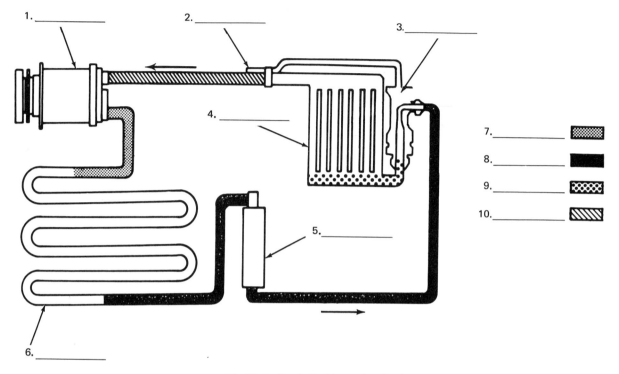

Fig 50-6. Basic Refrigeration Cycle

SUMMARY REVIEW

____ 1. Temperature is a measurement of heat

    a. calories.   c. intensity.
    b. Btu's.   d. quantity.

____ 2. The process of changing the surface of a liquid to a gas is known as

    a. dehumidification.   c. boiling.
    b. condensation.   d. evaporation.

____ 3. The "hidden" heat required to change the state of a substance without changing its temperature is known as

    a. sensible heat.   c. specific heat.
    b. latent heat.   d. relative heat.

____ 4. The heat required to raise the temperature of a substance without changing its state is known as

    a. saturated heat.   c. latent heat.
    b. sensible heat.   d. specific heat.

Section 9 Air Conditioning and Cooling

____ 5. The pressure inside an R-12 storage container at 90°F will be about

   a. 70 psi.   c. 100 psi.
   b. 89 psi.   d. 125 psi.

____ 6. Heat quantity is measured in calories or

   a. degrees.   c. psi.
   b. Btu.   d. inches of vacuum.

____ 7. The process of removing water vapor from air is called

   a. purification.   c. vaporization.
   b. dehumidification.   d. evaporation.

8. Does heat move *from a cold to a hot* substance or *from a hot to a cold* substance? _____

9. Name three methods by which heat may be transferred.

   a. _____ b. _____ c. _____

10. Refrigerant 12 boils at _____ sea level, and has a latent heat value of _____ Btu per pound when vaporized.

11. Define a calorie as referred to in air conditioning. _____
    _____

12. Insert the correct numbers of the matching terms or definitions in the blanks.

   a. ____ Btu   1. vapor
   b. ____ psi   2. pressure measurement
   c. ____ gas   3. R-12
   d. ____ thermometer   4. refrigerant leaving condenser
   e. ____ refrigerant   5. heat quantity measurement
   f. ____ high-pressure liquid   6. refrigerant entering evaporator
   g. ____ low-pressure liquid   7. checks heat intensity

REFERENCE REVIEW

____ 1. Whenever a substance changes state from a liquid to a vapor it

   a. absorbs heat.   c. absorbs moisture.
   b. gives off heat.   d. dehumidifies.

____ 2. Heat is radiated (given off) from the air conditioner condenser fins because

   a. of humidity.   c. of pressure.
   b. of vaporization.   d. the surrounding air temperature is cooler.

Unit 50 Air Conditioning Principles

_____ 3. The vaporized R-12 inside an evaporator is normally
   a. moisture laden.   c. under high pressure.
   b. very cold.   d. very hot.

_____ 4. R-12 returns to the compressor as a
   a. low-pressure liquid.   c. high-pressure gas.
   b. high-pressure liquid. d. low-pressure gas.

_____ 5. Liquid R-12 that contacts an exposed area of skin is likely to
   a. cause no discomfort. c. cause a burn.
   b. cause frostbite.   d. evaporator slowly.

_____ 6. A properly operating air conditioning system will have a low-pressure gage reading between
   a. 0 and 15 psi.   c. 35 and 125 psi.
   b. 15 and 35 psi.   d. 150 and 200 psi.

_____ 7. A one ton air conditioner has a cooling capacity of _____ per hour.
   a. 100 Btu.   c. 12,000 Btu.
   b. 1000 Btu.   d. 120,000 Btu.

8. List six precautions to observe concerning R-12.
   a. _____   d. _____
   b. _____   e. _____
   c. _____   f. _____

9. Explain how an air conditioning system dehumidifies air. ____
   _____
   _____

10. Does a high relative humidity reading make an air conditioner's job *harder* or *easier*? _____

11. Explain how an air conditioning system purifies air. _____
    _____
    _____

12. What should be done with the air conditioning system before a servicing procedure is attempted that raises the system temperature, such as adjacent welding, steam cleaning, or paint baking?
    _____

UNIT 51 AIR CONDITIONING SYSTEMS

RELATED AUTOMOTIVE TERMS

Automatic Temperature Control System: System controlled by an adjustable thermostat inside certain vehicles to blend hot air from the heater and cold air from the air conditioner to automatically maintain the selected temperature.

Automotive Air Conditioning: The process of transferring heat from inside to outside the passenger compartment. The cooled air is also dehumidified, purified, and circulated.

Charging (Filling): Service procedure of adding the correct amount of R-12 to the system. R-12 usually is added to system as a vapor into the low-pressure side.

Compressor (Pump): Component that pressurizes heat laden R-12 vapor. High pressure concentrates the heat, allowing the hot vapor to give up heat to outside air more easily; increased pressure assists process of condensing R-12 vapor back to a liquid. Compressor is driven by a belt from the crankshaft pulley.

Compressor Shaft-seal Assembly: Parts that prevent refrigerant oil and R-12 leakage past the rotating crankshaft or mainshaft bearing. Located at front of compressor. Its useful life is extended by periodic operation the year around. The seal assembly is replaceable.

Condenser: Component having finned tubing, inside which the high-pressure, high-temperature R-12 vapor discharged from the compressor is cooled, changing its state to a high-pressure liquid. Usually located in front of radiator.

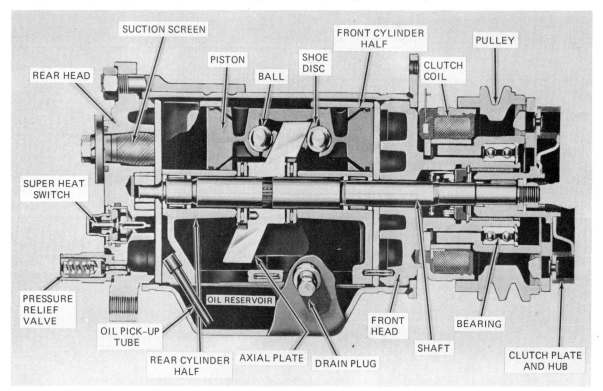

Fig 51-1. Air Conditioning Compressor, Six-cylinder type

Unit 51 Air Conditioning Systems

Desiccant: Drying agent inside the receiver-drier. Usually activated silica alumina or silica gel. Absorbs any moisture contained in circulating R-12; loses effectiveness quickly if exposed to moisture laden atmospheric air.

Discharge (Purge): Service procedure that involves removing (draining) refrigerant from the system.

Electromagnetic Clutch: Electrically operated device allowing the compressor drive pulley and compressor mainshaft or crankshaft to be coupled or uncoupled, according to system or operator demand for compressor operation.

Evacuate: Service procedure using a vacuum pump to remove all atmospheric air and moisture from inside the system. A high vacuum causes moisture to vaporize, allowing it to be drawn out.

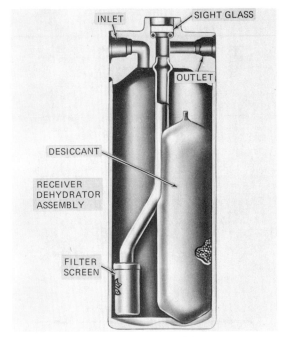

Fig 51-2. Receiver-drier

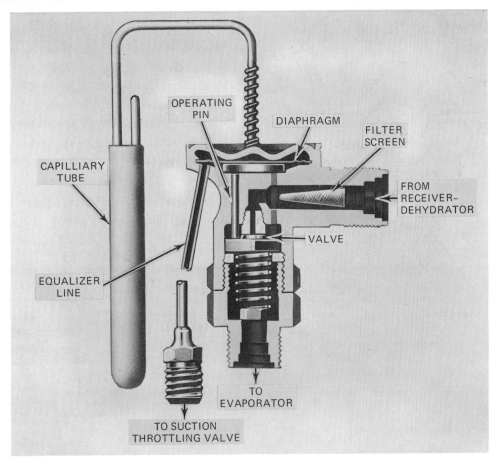

Fig 51-3. Expansion Valve

Section 9 Air Conditioning and Cooling

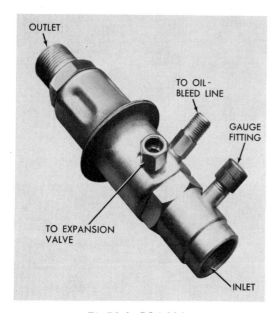

Fig 51-4. POA Valve

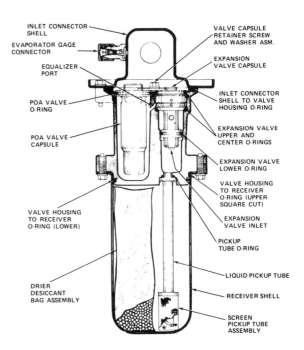

Fig 51-5. VIR Assembly

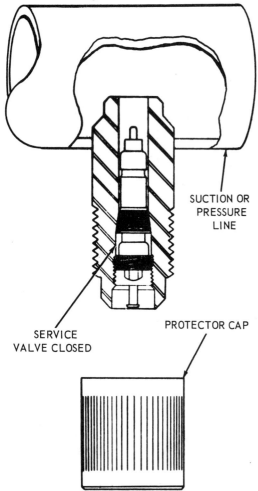

Fig 51-6A. Service Valve, Schrader Type

Evaporator: Component inside which the R-12 liquid, under reduced pressure after leaving the expansion valve, vaporizes (boils/or evaporates) absorbing heat from inside the vehicle. Electrically operated blower circulates air over the evaporator's finned tubing. Moisture condenses on cold evaporator fins, dehumidifying the air.

High-pressure Relief Valve: Safety valve that opens automatically, venting system pressure

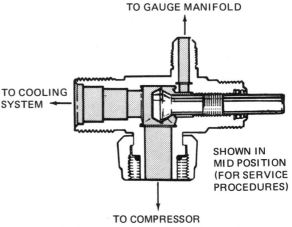

Fig 51-6B. Service Valve, Manual Type

Unit 51 Air Conditioning Systems

above a predetermined amount. Located on the compressor.

Muffler: Device incorporated into certain systems to reduce noise level of compressor surges (pumping action). Located in the high-pressure vapor line between the compressor and the condenser.

POA (Pilot Operated Absolute) Valve: Special valve incorporated into certain automobile air conditioning systems for maintaining pressure inside the evaporator at a predetermined level during various system and vehicle operating conditions. Located in the evaporator outlet line.

Receiver-drier (Dehydrator): Component that stores high-pressure liquid refrigerant received from the condenser until needed by the evaporator. Contains a desiccant (drying material) to absorb any moisture present in the refrigerant. It may contain a sight glass and a fine-mesh screen for R-12 to pass through.

Refrigerant Lines: Specially designed hoses reinforced with woven metal mesh and fabric capable of withstanding the high temperatures and pressures of the system.

Refrigeration Oil: A specially formulated non-foaming mineral oil with all impurities and moisture removed. Used to lubricate the air conditioner compressor.

Service Valves: Special valves that allow connecting manifold gage hoses to the air conditioning system during servicing procedures. Located on the compressor POA valve, or refrigerant lines. Valves may be manually operated type or Schrader-valve type.

Sight Glass: Special viewing glass that helps indicate when the system contains an insufficient amount of refrigerant. Lack of refrigerant is shown if bubbles pass by the sight glass during normal operation. Often located on receiver-drier. Not featured on all new car A/C systems.

Thermostatic Expansion Valve: System control valve that meters the amount of liquid R-12 entering the evaporator. High-pressure liquid R-12 flowing into the valve leaves as low-pressure liquid. Valve operation is controlled by a temperature sensing bulb clamped to the evaporator outlet line.

Thermostatic Switch: Device that controls compressor operation by switching the electromagnetic clutch on or off as required for desired system operation. Switch is actuated by pressure inside a capillary tube. A temperature-sensitive bulb at end of tube is located in the evaporator outlet airstream.

Valves in Receive (VIR) Assembly: A unit that combines the expansion valve, POA valve, and receiver-drier into one integral assembly. Used on certain models only.

In the following exercises, indicate the best answer by inserting in the blanks the appropriate number, letter, word(s), or calculation, as required.

PICTORIAL REVIEW

A. Identify the compressor components or areas in figure 51-7 by writing their correct letters in the blanks.

1. ____ crankshaft
2. ____ service valve
3. ____ cylinder head
4. ____ crankcase body
5. ____ front seal retainer plate

Section 9 Air Conditioning and Cooling

6. ____ compressor mounting hole
7. ____ gage attachment port
8. ____ oil check plug (CAUTION: high pressure, read service instructions)
9. ____ system hose port
10. ____ manual valve dust cap
11. ____ clutch coil mounting hole

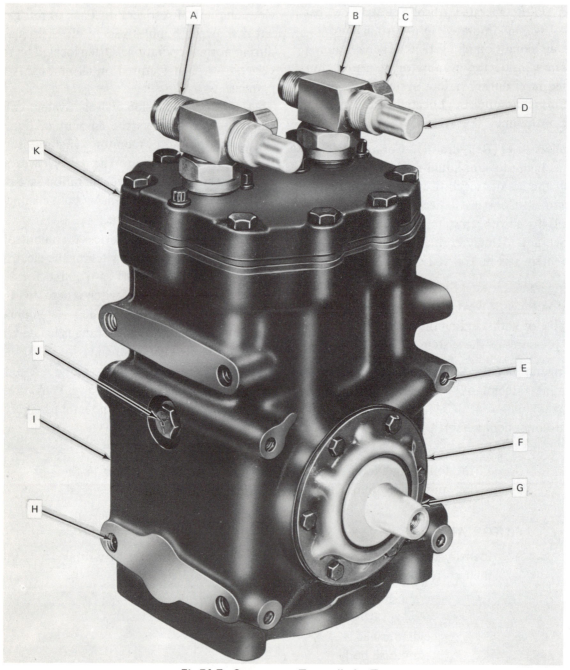

Fig 51-7. Compressor, Two-cylinder Type

Unit 51 Air Conditioning Systems

B. Identify the various system components in figure 51-8 by writing their correct names in the blanks.

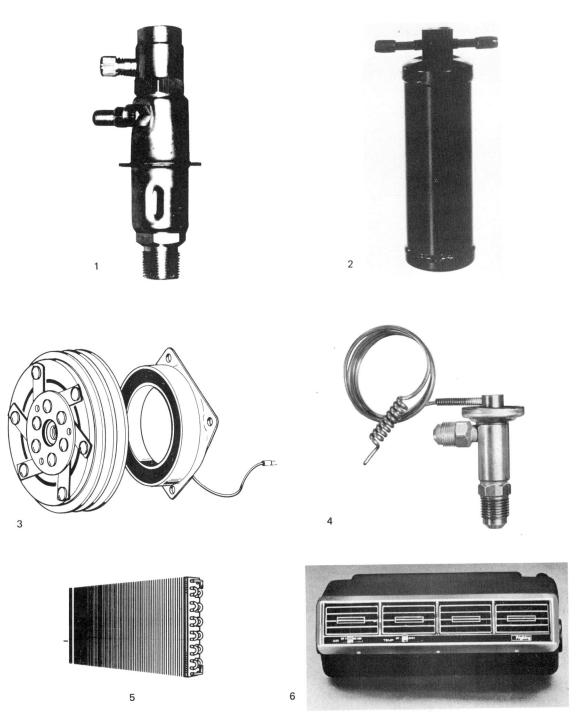

Fig 51-8. Air Conditioning System Components

1. _____ 2. _____ 3. _____
4. _____ 5. _____ 6. _____

331

Section 9 Air Conditioning and Cooling

SUMMARY REVIEW

____ 1. One purpose of the compressor is to
   a. vaporize the R-12.
   b. pressurize R-12 liquid.
   c. concentrate R-12 heat.
   d. pump R-12 vapor through entire A/C system.

____ 2. A special valve on certain air conditioning systems that controls evaporator pressure is known as the
   a. POA valve.
   b. expansion valve.
   c. magnetic control.
   d. service valve.

____ 3. One device that controls operation of the compressor clutch is called the
   a. thermal bulb valve.
   b. pressure relief switch.
   c. expansion valve.
   d. thermostatic switch.

____ 4. A leaking compressor shaft seal usually means the
   a. compressor is worn out.
   b. seal needs replacement.
   c. compressor must be replaced.
   d. system contains excess oil.

____ 5. High-pressure R-12 vapor cools and changes state back to a liquid as it travels through the
   a. condenser.
   b. expansion valve.
   c. compressor.
   d. evaporator.

____ 6. R-12 liquid boils and absorbs heat inside the
   a. condenser.
   b. compressor.
   c. evaporator.
   d. receiver-drier.

____ 7. The amount of R-12 entering the evaporator is controlled by the
   a. throttle suctioning valve.
   b. thermostatic expansion valve.
   c. service valve.
   d. POA valve.

____ 8. The sight glass is usually located in the
   a. low-pressure vapor hose.
   b. compressor.
   c. high-pressure vapor hose.
   d. receiver-drier.

____ 9. All automotive air conditioning systems contain
   a. a muffler.
   b. an electromagnetic clutch.
   c. a POA valve.
   d. all of these.

10. Operation of the expansion valve is controlled by a _____ that is located at the _____.

11. Insert the correct numbers of the matching terms or definitions in the blanks.

   a. ____ desiccant
   b. ____ discharge
   c. ____ evaporator drain
   d. ____ charging
   e. ____ electric blower location
   f. ____ compressor component
   g. ____ evacuate

   1. purge
   2. remove air and moisture
   3. high-pressure relief valve
   4. near evaporator
   5. drying agent
   6. rubber hose
   7. filling

REFERENCE REVIEW

____ 1. Evaporator outlet air temperature depends on the
   a. humidity.
   b. surrounding air temperature.
   c. vehicle speed.
   d. all of these.

____ 2. If the receiver-drier is cold or frosty during operation, the system is usually
   a. undercharged.
   b. operating normally.
   c. clogged at that point.
   d. overcharged.

____ 3. If a new receiver-drier is left uncapped for over an hour during installation, it should be
   a. evacuated.
   b. pressurized.
   c. discarded.
   d. blown out with air.

____ 4. During evacuation, the maximum amount of vacuum obtainable is near _____ inches.
   a. 10
   b. 17
   c. 20
   d. 28

____ 5. The compressor magnetic clutch may consume near _____ amperes.
   a. three
   b. six
   c. eight
   d. eleven

____ 6. A refrigerant leak in the condenser is usually serviced by
   a. component replacement.
   b. welding.
   c. brazing.
   d. soldering.

____ 7. A few bubbles at the sight glass when the compressor magnetic clutch cycles on and off or when outside air temperature is below 70°F means the system is operating
   a. normally.
   b. without refrigerant.
   c. with a defective expansion valve.
   d. with a lack of oil.

Section 9 Air Conditioning and Cooling

8. A low refrigerant charge inside the air conditioning system may be diagnosed by manifold gage readings that are _____.

9. List three causes of both manifold gages reading too high.

   a. _____ b. _____ c. _____

10. Why do most air conditioner manufacturers recommend system discharge, evacuation, and then complete recharge rather than a partial charge, if the system is low on R-12? _____
    _____

11. Name three methods or tools used for locating refrigerant leaks.

    a. _____
    b. _____
    c. _____

12. The system component that stores high-pressure liquid R-12 until needed in the evaporator is called the _____.

UNIT 52 COOLING SYSTEM

RELATED AUTOMOTIVE TERMS

Air Cooling: Simple method of engine cooling that relies on forced airflow over extended metal fins on cylinder head and block to maintain proper operating temperature. Air cooling is popular on small one-cylinder engines.

Antifreeze: A chemical solution added to the coolant (water) to prevent freezing. Usually ethylene glycol.

Antirust: Solution added to coolant to retard rust formation inside cooling system.

Automotive Cooling System: The several components that operate to absorb and dissipate heat developed in the combustion process, thus maintaining the desired engine operating temperature.

Bypass: Passageway that allows water pump to circulate coolant throughout cylinder head and engine block before thermostat opens. It may be holes between head and block or small hose behind water pump.

Coolant: Liquid circulating throughout a liquid cooling system. The coolant may be water or an antifreeze and water solution. Coolant temperature increases in engine and decreases in radiator.

Coolant Circulation: Movement of liquid throughout cooling system. That is caused primarily by water pump operation. Coolant heated by engine combustion area moves on to upper radiator section.

Coolant Recovery (Closed) System: Cooling system that has a semisealed pressure cap, with radiator overflow hose leading into separate plastic reservoir, thus saving coolant during hot operation and returning it to the radiator when the system cools. A special procedure is required to remove the radiator cap.

Fan: Rotating component having pitched blades to pull air past the radiator finned tubing. The fan may have four to seven steel or flexible fiberglass blades, sometimes spaced unevenly to reduce noise. Required mainly at lower speeds. Usually mounted on the water-pump shaft hub.

Fan Belt: Flexible drive belt that transfers power from the crankshaft pulley to the water pump and fan. The same belt often drives the alternator.

Fan Shroud: Thin plastic or metal housing inside which the fan rotates, on certain vehicles in which fan is positioned a considerable distance behind radiator. Allows fan to pull more air past radiator finned tubing and prevents air recirculation. Attached behind and against radiator.

Heat Transfer: Movement of heat from a hotter to a colder area by various methods, such as conduction, radiation, and convection.

Liquid Cooling: Method of engine cooling that relies on coolant circulation through water jackets inside cylinder head and block, then on to radiator to maintain proper operating temperature.

Pressure Cap: Radiator cap that seals in pressure from hot expanding coolant until a predetermined limit is reached, then valve opens, allowing excess pressure to escape. Also contains a vacuum-relief valve that opens after engine is shut off and cools down to permit air (or coolant on closed systems) to re-enter the system. Cap raises coolant boiling point

Section 9 Air Conditioning and Cooling

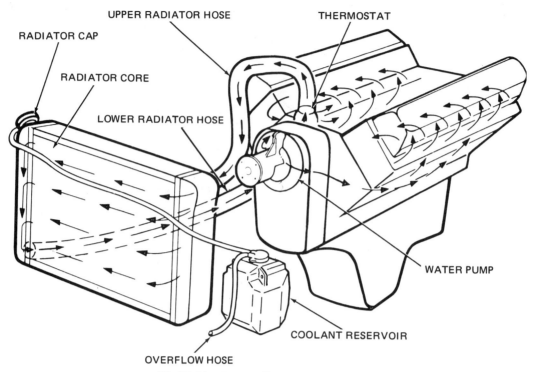

Fig 52-1A. Coolant Flow Reciprocating Engine

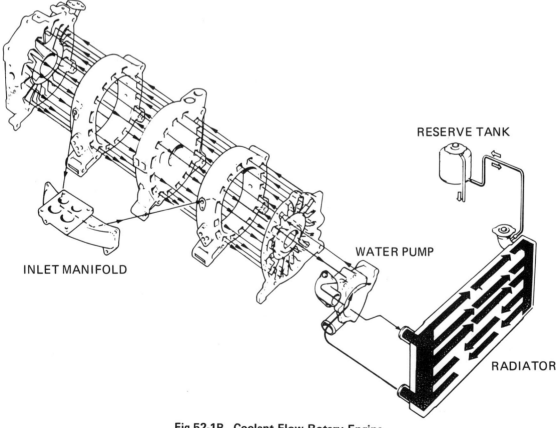

Fig 52-1B. Coolant Flow Rotary Engine

Unit 52 Cooling System

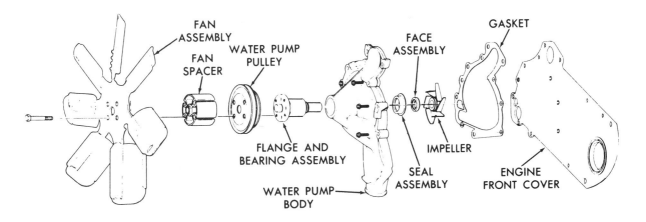

Fig 52-2. Water Pump

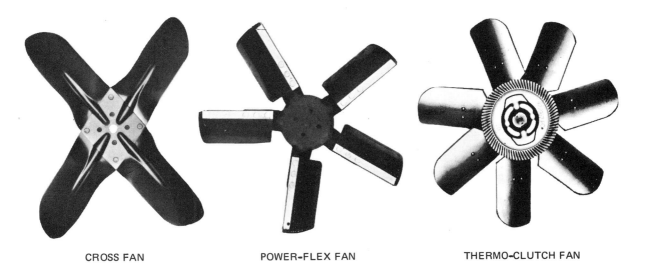

Fig 52-3. Engine Fans

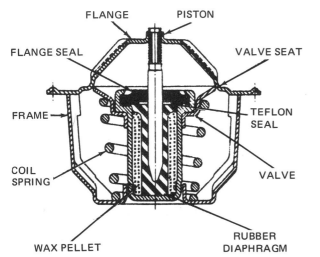

Fig 52-4. Thermostat

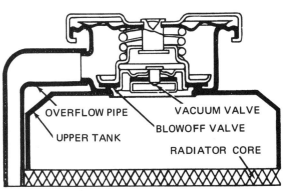

Fig 52-5. Pressure Radiator Cap

Section 9 Air Conditioning and Cooling

approximately 3 1/4°F. for each pound of pressure, increases cooling efficiency, and reduces coolant loss.

Radiator: Component through which excess coolant heat is radiated into atmospheric air. Usually contains vertical or horizontal finned copper tubing connected between two brass end tanks.

Radiator Hoses: Rubber hoses that connect radiator to the thermostat outlet housing and water pump inlet housing. Lower hose contains spiral-wound wire or other special reinforcement to prevent hose collapse from pump suction.

Temperature Sending Unit: Device that sends information relative to engine coolant temperature to dash gage or light. Dash gage may be actuated by electrical or mechanical means.

Thermal Clutch Fan: Fan that has a special driving mechanism that engages during hot operation or low speed, and disengages during cold operation or high speed. This saves power and reduces noise.

Thermostat: Temperature sensitive component that restricts coolant flow to radiator as required to maintain desired engine operating temperature. It begins to open at stamped temperature and is fully open about 20° higher.

Transmission Oil Cooler: Heat exchanger located in radiator outlet end section through which transmission fluid flows for cooling purposes on most automatic transmission cars.

Water Jacket: Hollow passage inside cylinder head and engine block through which coolant flows.

Water Pump: Belt driven component that circulates coolant by causing it to move from the lower radiator outlet section into engine. Water is moved by centrifugal action of finned impeller on pump shaft.

In the following exercises, indicate the best answer by inserting in the blanks the appropriate number, letter, word(s), or calculation, as required.

PICTORIAL REVIEW

A. Identify the water pump component parts in figure 52-6 by writing their correct names in the blanks.

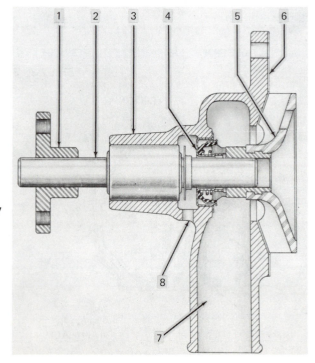

Fig 52-6. Water Pump Assembly

Unit 52 Cooling System

1. _____   5. _____
2. _____   6. _____
3. _____   7. _____
4. _____   8. _____

B. Label each picture in figure 52-7 as to which radiator pressure cap illustrates *vacuum relief* and which *pressure relief*.

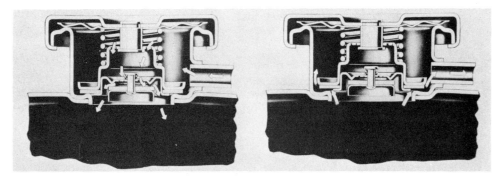

Fig 52-7. Pressure Cap Operation

1. _____   2. _____

C. Identify the type of fan shown in figure 52-8 (thermal-clutch fan, power-flex fan or cross fan); then write the correct answer in the blank.

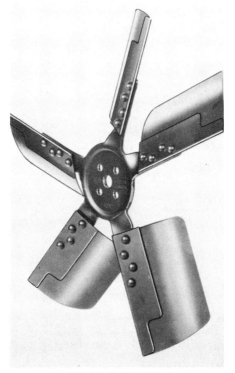

Fig 52-8. Fan Blade

1. _____

Section 9 Air Conditioning and Cooling

SUMMARY REVIEW

____ 1. Most radiator heat that is transferred to atmospheric air leaves by

    a. radiation.   c. combustion.
    b. convection.   d. conduction

____ 2. The main purpose of the thermostat bypass is to allow coolant circulation inside the engine

    a. after pressure cap opens.   c. and radiator.
                                  d. after thermostat opens.
    b. before thermostat opens.

____ 3. The thermostat opens fully _____ its stamped temperature.

    a. above   c. within three degrees of
    b. below   d. any of these

____ 4. The main purpose of the thermostat is to

    a. keep engine hot.
    b. maintain desired engine temperature.
    c. keep engine cool.
    d. increase coolant circulation.

____ 5. A standard pressure cap contains a _____ valve.

    a. bypass   c. vacuum
    b. pressure and a vacuum   d. pressure

____ 6. The main intended purpose of the fan is to

    a. pull air past radiator.   c. circulate coolant.
    b. blow air over engine.   d. support fan belt.

____ 7. After leaving the engine, the coolant moves to the

    a. upper radiator.   c. lower radiator.
    b. water pump.   d. bypass.

    8. Why must the lower radiator hose contain special reinforcement? _____

    9. Explain why fan blades may be spaced unevenly. _____
_____

   10. Is the transmission oil cooler located in the radiator *inlet* or *outlet* end tank? _____

   11. Insert the correct numbers of the matching terms or definitions in the blanks.

Unit 52 Cooling System

a. ____ radiator used as
b. ____ air cooling
c. ____ liquid coolant circulation
d. ____ closed system
e. ____ fan
f. ____ shroud
g. ____ engine block

1. requires water pump
2. coolant recovery system
3. plastic housing around fan
4. heat exchanger
5. contains water jackets
6. small engine cooling method
7. belt driven

REFERENCE REVIEW

____ 1. Heat transfers from the engine metal to the coolant inside the water jacket by

    a. convection.
    b. conduction.
    c. vacuum.
    d. radiation.

____ 2. A water pump may be considered defective if the

    a. seal leaks.
    b. bearings are noisy.
    c. bearings are loose.
    d. any of these.

____ 3. A used fan belt should be adjusted until a belt tension gage reads between _____ pounds on most cars.

    a. 10 and 30
    b. 40 and 60
    c. 70 and 90
    d. 130 and 160

____ 4. A 16-pound pressure cap raises the coolant boiling point about _____ degrees F.

    a. 5
    b. 20
    c. 35
    d. 50

____ 5. Most radiators that leak should be

    a. removed for soldering.
    b. soldered on vehicle.
    c. repaired using stopleak.
    d. operated under reduced pressure.

____ 6. The first component of the cooling system to check, if there is repeated loss of coolant, is the

    a. water pump.
    b. thermostat.
    c. pressure cap.
    d. heater core.

____ 7. The hydraulic fluid inside a thermal fan clutch is usually

    a. water.
    b. antifreeze.
    c. motor oil.
    d. silicone oil.

8. Should the thermostat bellows or pellet be installed *toward the engine* or *toward the radiator*? _____

Section 9 Air Conditioning and Cooling

9. List eight causes of engine overheating.

   a. _____ e. _____
   b. _____ f. _____
   c. _____ g. _____
   d. _____ h. _____

10. List four ways an engine may be affected by driving a car without a thermostat.

    a. _____ c. _____
    b. _____ d. _____

11. The thermostat housing usually attaches to the _____ on inline cylinder engines and the _____ on V-8 engines.

Acknowledgments

The author wishes to thank his wife, Ardis F. Fill, for the many hours she devoted to the preparation of the manuscript.

In addition the author would like to express his appreciation to the following companies for the technical assistance and illustrations they provided.

AC Spark Plug Division, General Motors Corporation: Figs. 26-5, 26-6

American Motors Corporation: Figs. 9-1, 9-2, 9-3, 9-4, 9-5, 14-4, 15-4, 28-1, 32-3, 38-3, 44-6

Audi NSU Auto Union: Fig. 7-5

The Bendix Corporation: Figs. 11-1, 11-5, 11-6

Buick Motor Division, General Motors Corporation: Figs. 6-5, 9-7, 9-8, 10-1, 13-1, 16-8, 17-4, 21-3, 21-5, 27-5, 27-7, 27-8, 30-4, 31-5, 33-3, 40-1, 45-1, 48-1, 51-2

Cadillac Motor Car Division, General Motors Corporation: Figs. 6-1, 6-2, 8-1, 8-2, 19-2, 19-3, 22-7, 26-8 27-1, 29-3, 31-1, 31-4, 32-2, 35-4, 37-5, 37-7, 38-2, 38-6, 44-2, 44-4, 44-9, 44-12, 44-13, 46-1, 46-3, 52-1A, 52-2

Champion Spark Plug Company: Figs. 15-1, 15-3, 15-5

Chevrolet Motor Division, General Motors Corporation: Figs. 1-2, 10-4, 13-3, 14-1, 14-2, 14-3, 16-5, 16-6, 19-4, 20-2, 20-3, 20-6, 21-1, 21-2, 23-1, 23-6, 23-7C, 24-1A, 24-2, 24-3, 24-5, 25-1, 26-1, 27-6, 31-3, 31-8, 32-1, 32-4, 33-2, 33-4, 35-1, 35-3, 35-6, 36-1, 37-1, 37-4, 38-1, 38-7, 41-3, 41-4, 42-2, 42-3, 45-4, 46-4, 48-2, 48-3, 48-5, 48-6, 49-1, 49-2, 49-3, 50-1, 50-2, 50-6, 51-4, 52-4

Chrysler Motors Corporation: Figs. 3-3, 4-3, 4-4, 10-4, 16-1, 16-2, 16-3, 16-4, 16-7, 22-5, 24-8, 26-2, 28-4, 29-1, 34-6, 37-3, 39-1, 39-7, 41-1, 41-2, 44-11, 46-2, 47-1, 47-3, 48-4, 49-4

Curtiss-Wright Corporation: Figs. 7-1, 7-2, 7-6.

Dana Corporation: Figs. 31-6, 31-7

Ford Customer Service Division: Figs. 1-4, 3-1, 3-4, 4-1, 5-1, 5-2, 6-4, 10-2, 13-4, 17-2, 17-3, 19-1, 20-1, 22-2, 22-3, 22-6, 23-2, 23-4, 23-7A, 23-7B, 23-7D, 23-7F, 25-3; 27-2, 28-3, 29-4, 31-2, 38-5, 39-3, 39-5, 43-1, 43-4, 44-1, 44-3, 45-2, 51-6, 52-8

Fram Automotive Division, Fram Corporation: Fig. 39-6

Frigiking, Inc.: Figs. 51-8B, 51-8C, 51-8D, 51-8E, 51-8F

General Motors Corporation: Figs. 22-4, 25-4

Globe Battery Division, Globe-Union Inc.: Fig. 18-3

The Goodyear Tire and Rubber Company: Figs. 35-2, 35-5, 35-7, 35-8

Gould Inc.: Figs. 26-4, 26-7

Jacobsen Manufacturing Company: Figs. 1-3, 15-2

Kelsey-Hayes: Fig. 28-2

Mazda Motors of America, Inc.: Figs. 7-3, 7-4

Mercedes-Benz of North America, Inc.: Figs. 11-2, 11-3, 11-4

Mobil Oil Corporation: Figs. 39-2, 51-1B

Monroe Auto Equipment Company: Figs. 33-1, 33-5, 33-6

Oldsmobile Division of General Motors Corporation: Figs. 23-5, 23-7E, 25-3, 44-5, 44-7, 44-8, 51-1, 51-3, 52-7

Pontiac Motor Division, General Motors Corporation: Figs. 1-1, 9-6, 9-9, 9-10, 13-2, 14-5, 17-1, 20-4, 20-5, 20-7, 20-8, 21-6, 22-1, 24-1B, 27-3, 29-2, 30-1, 30-2, 30-3, 37-6, 39-4, 39-8, 41-1, 43-2, 43-3, 43-5, 44-10, 45-3, 47-2, 51-5, 51-8A, 52-3, 52-5

Sealed Power Corporation: Fig. 4-2

Snap-on Tools Corporation: Figs. 34-1, 34-2, 34-3, 34-4, 34-5

Sun Electric Corporation: Fig. 2-4

Tecumseh Products Company: Fig. 51-7

TRW Inc.: Figs. 37-2, 52-6

United Delco: 21-4, 23-3, 24-4, 24-6, 24-7

Walker Manufacturing: Figs. 26-3, 26-9

Mark Tyszka (Photographer): Figs. 10-3, 40-2

Cover photographs were supplied by:

Pontiac Motor Division, General Motors Corporation (1-1) (14-5)

Ford Customer Service Division (1-4)

Mazda Motors of America, Inc. (7-3)

American Motors Corporation (9-1)

Chevrolet Motor Division, General Motors Corporation (21-1)

Delmar Staff

Director of Publications: Alan N. Knofla

Source Editor: Marjorie A. Bruce

Technical Editors: Fred W. Smith; Roger L. Stern

Director of Manufacturing/Production: Frederick Sharer

Illustrators: Anthony Canabush, George Dowse, Michael Kokernak

Production Specialists: Sharon Lynch, Patti Manuli, Jean LeMorta, Betty Michelfelder, Debbie Monty, Margaret Mutka, Lee St. Onge

INDEX

A

Absolute pressure, 63
AC. *See* Alternating current
Accelerator pump, 44
Accelerator pump nozzle, 44
Accelerator pump system, 51
Accumulator piston, 282
Active plate material, 108
Adjustable shock absorber, 207
After-run. *See* Dieseling
Air bleed, 44
Air cleaner thermostat, 135
Air conditioning principles 319-322
Air conditioning systems, 326-339
Air cooling, 335
Air cooling systems, 1
Air filter, 186
Air-fuel ratio, 44
Air gap, 94
Air injection system, 147-149
Air injector pump, 147
Air-injector system, 147
Air manifold, 148
Air shocks, 207
Air valve, 44
Alignment adjustment method, 213
Alternating current, 114
Alternator
    defined, 114
    related automotive terms, 114-116
Altitude-compensating carburetor, 44, 135
Aluminum heat dissipator, 153
AMA horsepower. *See* SAE horsepower
Ambient sensor, 102
Ambient temperature switch, 141
Ampere, 70
Amplifier, 94
Annular gear. *See* Internal gear
Antifreeze, 335
Antifriction bearing, 255
Antiskid control, 180
Antistall dashpot, 44
Antirust, 335
Applied hydraulic pressure, 174
Applying position, 186
Armature, 120
Armature servicing, 120
Atomization, 50
Atmospheric pressure, 186
Atmospheric suspended, 186
Atmospheric valve, 186
Automatic-choke housing, 44
Automatic level control, 207
Automatic temperature control system, 326
Automatic transmissions
    hydraulic control systems, 282-286
    planetary gears, 291-293
    torque converter, 276-278
Automobile exhaust system controls, 159
Automotive air conditioning, 326
Automotive cooling system, 335
Automotive power brakes, 186
Available voltage, 76
Axle gears. *See* Side gears
Axle shaft, 303

B

Backflow, 129
Backing plate, 167
Backlash, 308
Bail, 180
Balance weight, 37
Balancing (crankshaft assembly), 13
Balancing preliminary steps, 227
Ballast resistor, 94
Ball bearing, 269
Ball joint, 192
Ball joint centerline, 213
Ball joint free-play, 192
Ball joint inclination. *See* Steering axis inclination
Ball joint lubrication, 192, 255
Ball joint preload, 194
Ball joint seal, 194
Band, 282
Base metals, 159
Base valve. *See* Compression valve
Basic ignition timing, 82
Battery, 76, 108-110
Battery capacity test, 108
Battery cell, 108
Battery charger, 108
Battery maintenance, 108
Battery rating methods
    cold-cranking-power rating, 109
    reserve capacity rating, 109
    twenty-four rating, 108-109
Battery water, 109
BDC, 7
Bead, 219
Bearing preload, 308
Bearings, 114
Bed-type converter, 159
Bell housing. *See* Clutch housing
Bench bleeding, 180
Bendix folo-thru drive, 120
Bevel gear, 308
Bhp, 7
Bias-ply belted tire, 219
Bleeding brakes, 167
Block, 1. *See also* Fuse panel
Blow-by, 19, 129
Booster battery, 109
Booster venturi, 50
Bore, 7
Bottom dead center. *See* BDC
Brake cone, 314
Brake drum, 167-168
Brake feel, 186
Brake fluid, 168
Brake horsepower. *See* Bhp
Brake line tubing, 168
Brake lining, 168
Brake system
    disc brakes, 174
    drum brakes, 167-170
    master cylinder and line controls, 180-182
    power brakes, 186-188
Breaker cam, 76
Breaker plate, 82
Breaker-plate ground wire, 82
Breaker-point alignment, 82
Breaker-point gap, 82
Breaker points, 76
Breaker-point spring tension, 83
Breathing port. *See* Intake port
British thermal unit. *See* Btu
Brush, 114
Brushes, 120
Brush holder, 120
Btu, 319
Bubble balancer, 227
Buildup time, 76
Bulkhead connector, 102
Bushing, 120
Butterfly valve. *See* Exhaust manifold heat control valve
Bypass (cooling system), 335
Bypass valve. *See* Diverter valve

C

Caliper, 174
Calorie, 319
Cam, 25
Cam angle. *See* Dwell angle
Cam base circle, 25
Camber angle, 213
Cam ground piston, 19
Cam-lobe face and nose taper, 25
Cam-lobe grind, 25
Cam-lobe lift, 25
Camshaft, 25
Camshaft assembly, 25-27
Camshaft bearings, 25
Camshaft eccentric, 57
Camshaft sprocket, 25
Canister filter, 153
Canister purge line, 153
Capacitor, 114. *See also* Condenser
Capacitor-discharge ignition system, 94
Carbon monoxide. *See* CO
Carburetor, 44
Carburetor circuits, 50
Carburetor deceleration valve, 135
Carburetor emission controls, 135-137
Carburetor emission devices, 135
Carburetor internal vents, 153
Carburetors, 44-46
Carburetor systems
    accelerator pump system, 51
    choke system, 52
    float system, 50
    idle and low-speed system, 50
    main system, 50

345

Index

Carburetor systems (cont.)
    pump system, 51
    related automotive terms, 50-52
Carburetor vacuum, 141
Carrier housing, 303
Case, 109, 269
Caster angle, 213
Catalyst, 159
Catalytic converter, 159
Cell connectors, 109
Center bearing, 37
Center electrode, 88
Centering ball and seat, 297
Centrifugal advance (mechanical), 83
Centrifugal-advance weights, 83
Centrifugal filter, 148
Centrifugal force, 227
Ceramic, 159
Ceramic insulator, 88
Charcoal canister, 153-154
Charging, 326
Chassis dynamometer, 7
Chassis lubrication, 255
    abbreviations, 257
Check valve, 148, 154
Choke piston, 44
Choke plate, 44
Choke valve. *See* Choke plate
CID, 7
Circuit, 70
Circuit breaker, 70
Clearance volume, 7
Clogged filter (fuel system), 57
Closed circuit, 70
Closed-loop EFI systems, 63
Closed PCV system, 129
Clutch disc, 262, 282
Clutches, 262-264
Clutch housing, 262
Clutch hub, 314
Clutch pedal, 262
Clutch purpose, 262
Clutch release bearing, 262
Clutch release fork, 262
Clutch shaft, 262. *See also* Input shaft
CO, 128
Coil, 70, 76
Coil polarity, 76-77
Coil spring, 194
Coil-spring clutch, 262-263
Coil spring seats, 200
Coil spring suspension, 194
Coil tower, 77
Cold-start valve, 63
Collapsible spacer, 308
Collapsible steering column. *See* Energy-absorbing steering column
Color-code chart, 102
Combination valve, 180
Combustion chamber, 7
Combustion recess, 37
Common point, 70

Commutator, 120
Compensating port, 180
Compound planetary gear set, 291
Compression, 319
Compression pressure, 1
Compression ratio, 7
Compression ring, 19
Compression valve, 207
Compressor, 326
Compressor shaft-seal assembly, 326
Condensation, 320
Condenser, 77, 326. *See also* Capacitor
Conductor, 70
Cone clutch. *See* Brake cone
Cone lubrication grooves, 314
Conformability (crankshaft assembly), 13
Connecting rod, 19
Connecting-rod cap, 19
Connections, 70
Connector, 102
Constant mesh, 291
Constant purge line, 154
Constant ratio steering gear, 240
Construction, 219
Contact-controlled ignition system, 94
Continuity, 70
Contour ground shoes, 168
Control arms, 200
Control unit (electronic ignition system), 94
Control valve, 240
Conventional distributors. *See* Distributors, conventional
Converter
    catalytic, 159
    dual-bed, 159
    monolithic, 161-162
    three-way catalytic converters, 162
Converter check valve, 276
Converter cooling, 276
Converter drain plug, 276
Converter pump. *See* impeller
Coolant, 335
Coolant circulation, 335
Coolant recovery system, 335
Cooling system, 335-338
Cord material, 219
Corrosion, 109
Countergear, 269
Counterweight (crankshaft assembly), 13
Coupling link. *See* Coupling yoke
Coupling point, 276
Coupling yoke, 297
Crankcase, 129
Crankcase emissions, 129
Crankcase fumes, 130
Crankcase ventilation, 130
Crankcase ventilation filter, 130
Cranking motor. *See* Starter
Crankshaft, 13
Crankshaft assembly, 13-15
Crankshaft end-play, 13
Crankshaft main journals, 13
Crankshaft oil passage, 13
Cross and roller joint, 297
Cross shaft. *See* Pitman shaft
Cubic-inch displacement. *See* CID

Curb-idle discharge port, 51
Curb-idle metering restriction, 51
Curb-idle screw, 44
Current, 70
Current-draw test, 120
Current regulation, 114
Cushioning springs, 263
Cycle, 1
Cylinder, 1
Cylinder arrangement, 1
Cylinder assembly. *See* Clutch drum assembly
Cylinder bleeder screw, 168
Cylinder numbering, 1
Cylinder pressure, 1

D

Dampening ball joint, 194
Dampening effect, 207
Dampening springs, 263
DC. *See* Direct current
Decel valve. *See* Carburetor deceleration valve
Defective shock absorber, 207
Defective vacuum advance, 83
Dehumidification, 320
Dehydrator. *See* Receiver-drier
Delta-connected stator, 115
Deoxidation. *See* Reduction
Dessicant, 327
Detent ball, 269
Diaphragm, 57
Diaphragm booster. *See* Tandem
Diaphragm-return spring. *See* Piston-return spring
Diaphragm spring, 57
Diaphragm-spring clutch, 263
Diaphragm support plate, 187
Diaphragm-type power unit, 187
Dieseling, 135
Differential, 303
Differential case, 308
Differential cover, 303
Differentials. *See* Conventional differential; Limited-slip differential
Diode, 94, 115
Diode testing, 115
Direct-acting shock absorber. *See* Telescoping shock absorber
Direct battery power, 102
Direct current, 109
Direct drive, 291
Disc. *See* Rotor
Disc-brake fluid, 174
Disc-brake operation, 174
Disc brakes, 174-176
Discharge, 327
Discharge side. *See* High pressure side
Disc lathe, 174
Disc-pad adjustment, 174
Distributor, 77
Distributor cap, 77
Distributor control systems, 141

Index

Distributor holddown, 83
Distributor housing, 83
Distributors, conventional, 82-84
Distributor shaft, 84
Diverter valve, 149
DOHC. *See* Dual overhead camshaft
Double acting shock absorber, 207
Double cardon universal joint. *See* Universal joint, Constant Velocity
Downdraft carburetor, 44
Drilled oil passage, 247
Drive lines, 297-299
Drive pinion flange, 308
Drive shaft, 297
Drive shaft runout, 297
Drive shaft speed fluctuation, 297
Drop center rim, 219
Drum brake fade, 168
Drum brakes, 167-170
Drum diameter, 168-169
Dry-charged battery, 109
Dual-action vacuum, 141
Dual ballast resistor, 94
Dual-bed converter, 159
Dual master cylinder, 181
Duo-Servo Action. *See* Self-energizing action
Dwell angle, 77
Dwell meter, 84
Dwell variation, 84
Dynamically balanced, 227-228
Dynamometer, 7

E

Eccentric, 37
EFI. *See* Electronic fuel injection
EGR, 159
EGR valve, 159-161
Electrical circuits, 70-72
Electrical fuel pump, 58
Electrically assisted choke, 135
Electrical symbols, 70-72
Electrical systems
 alternators, 114-116
 batteries, 108-110
 conventional distributors, 82-84
 electrical circuits and symbols, 70-72
 ignition system, conventional, 76-78
 starting systems, 120-123
 wiring diagrams, 102-105
Electric fuel pump, 57
Electrode gap, 88
Electrolyte, 109
Electromagnetic clutch, 327
Electromagnetic induction, 115
Electronic control unit, 63
Electronic fuel injection
 defined, 63
 related automotive terms, 63-66
Electronic ignition, 96
Electronic ignition system
 defined, 94
 light beam type, 95

Electronic ignition system (cont.)
 related automotive system, 94-96
Electronic ignition system coil, 95
Electronic module. *See* Control unit
Electronic spark control system, 141
Electronic speed sensor, 141
Electronic voltage regulator, 115
Element, 109
Embedability, 14
Emission controls
 air injection system, 147
 carburetor, 135-137
 distributor control system, 141-143
 evaporative controls, 153-155
 exhaust system controls, 159-163
 positive crankcase ventilation, 128-130
End frame, 115
End housing, 37
Energy-absorbing steering column, 233
Engine displacement, 37-38
Engine dynamometer, 7
Engine lubrication systems, 247-250
Engine measurements, 7-9
Engines
 external combustion, 1
 internal combustion, 1
 reciprocating, 1-4
 rotary engines, 37-40
 stratified-charge, 1
Evacuate, 327
Evaporation, 320
Evaporative controls, 153, 154
Evaporator, 328
Exhaust-gas oxygen sensor, 63-66
Exhaust gas recirculation system, 159
Exhaust manifold heat control valve, 161
Exhaust port, 38
Exhaust system controls, 159
Exhaust valve, 31
Extension housing, 269
External combustion engine, 1

F

Fan, 335
Fan (alternator), 115
Fan belt, 335
Fan shroud, 335
Fast charge, 109
Fastener tightness, 174
Fast idle, 44
Fast-idle cam, 44
Fast-idle screw, 44
Fatigue strength, 14
Fhp, 77
Field coils, 120
Field current, 115
Field housing, 120
Fill control system, 154
Filling. *See* Charging
Filter bypass, 247
Filter element material, 247

Filter material, 58
Firing order, 1
Fixed caliper, 175
Fixed discs, 314
Flame travel, 38
Fleming's right-hand rule. *See* Right-hand rule for motors
Flex drive plate, 276
Flexible brake hose, 168-169
Flexible fuel line, 57
Flex stone, 84
Float, 44
Float bowl, 44
Float circuit, 51
Float hinge pin, 51
Floating caliper, 175
Fluid cooler, 240
Flywheel, 14, 263
Four-barrel carburetor, 44
Four-speed transmission, 269
Freon-12. *See* Refrigerant
Fresh air inlet tube, 135
Friction, 247
Friction horsepower, 7
Front end geometry, 213
Front pump, 282
Front suspension system, 194
Front wheel alignment, 213
Fuel burned, 1
Fuel filter, 57
Fuel filter spring, 57
Fuel injection, 58
Fuel line, 58
Fule-line manifold, 66
Fuel-pressure regulator, 66
Fuel pump eccentric, 25
Fuel pump pressure, 58
Fuel pump vacuum, 58
Fuel pump vapor lock, 58
Fuel pump volume, 58
Fuel supply system
 electric fuel pump, 58
 mechanical fuel pump, 57
 related automotive terms, 57-59
Fuel systems
 carburetors, 44-46
 carburetor systems, 50-52
 electronic fuel injection, 63-66
Full-floating axle, 303
Full-floating pin, 19
Full-flow filter, 247-248
Fuse, 70
Fuse panel, 102
Fusible link, 102

G

Gap bridging, 88
Gasket, 88
Gas transfer velocity, 38
Gear oil, 255
Gear ratio, 269, 308
Gear reduction, 120-121
Gear-type pump, 248

347

Index

Governor, 282
Grease, 255
Grease fitting, 255
Grease plug, 255
Grease seal, 255
Grommet, 102
Ground circuit, 70
Ground electrode, 88
Ground wire, 102
Group injection, 66

H

Harmonic balancer. *See* Vibration damper
Harness clip, 102
HC, 128
Heated-air system. *See* Thermostatically controlled-air cleaner
Heat exchanger. *See* Heat stove
Heat quantity, 320
Heat range, 88
Heat shield. *See* Heat stove
Heat sink, 95, 115
Heat stove, 136
Heat transfer, 320, 335
Helical gear, 269
Hidden heat. *See* Latent heat
High gear, 291
High-mounted coil spring suspension, 194-195
High-pressure relief valve, 328-329
High-pressure side (air conditioning), 320
High pressure vapor, 320
High-speed circuit, 51
High speed nozzle. *See* Main gas nozzle
Holding position, 187
Honeycomb, 161
Horsepower. *See* Hp
Hot-air duct, 136
Hotchkiss drive, 297
Hot-idle compensator, 51
Hot post, 110
Hot wire, 104
Housing breather, 303
Hp, 7
Hydraulically operated clutch, 263
Hydraulic lifter, 31
Hydraulic line pressure, 282
Hydraulic pressure, 169
Hydraulic system, 282
Hydrocarbon emissions, 130
Hydrocarbons. *See* HC
Hydrogen gas, 109
Hydrometer, 109
Hypoid gear set, 308-309
Hypoid lubricant, 255

I

Idle air bleed, 51
Idle and low-speed circuit, 51
Idle-mixture needle, 51
Idle-mixture screw, 44
Idle-mixture screw limiter caps, 136
Idle-passage restriction, 136
Idler arm, 233
Idle-stop solenoid, 136
Ignition resistor bypass, 122
Ignition switch, 77
Ignition switch power, 104
Ignition system, conventional, 76-78
Ignition systems
   capacitor-discharge, 94
   contact-controlled, 94
   magnetically controlled, 95. *See also* Electronic ignition systems
I-head, 1
Ihp, 8
Impeller, 276
Impulse trigger, 66
In-carburetor filter, 58
Included angle, 213
Indicated horsepower. *See* Ihp
Inertia weight, 297
Initial lubrication (camshaft assembly), 25
Injector nozzle, 66, 149
In-line filter, 58
Inner shaft, 195
In-pump filter, 58
Input shaft. *See* Clutch shaft; Turbine shaft
Inside-vehicle lubrication services, 255
Insulation, 104
Insulator, 70
Insulator ribs, 88
Intake-manifold vacuum, 141
Intake port, 38
Intake valve, 31
In-tank filter, 58
Integral-carrier differential, 303
Integral charging system, 116
Integral-type, 240
Interference angle, 31
Intermediate gear, 291
Intermediate steering rod, 233
Internal combustion engine, 1
Internal gear, 291
Internal vent (carburetor), 46

J

Jackknife position, 29-30
Journal size, 14-15
Junction box, 104

K

Knuckle arm, 233

L

Latent heat, 322
Lateral runout, 219
Lead-acid storage battery, 109
Lead sulfate, 110
Leaf spring, 200
Leaf spring center bolt, 200
Leaf spring hanger, 200
Leaf spring shackle, 200
Leaf tip inserts, 201
Lean mixture, 136
Lean roll, 137
Left-hand rule for coils, 122
Left-hand rule for current-carrying conductor, 122
L-head, 1
Limited-slip differential
   defined, 314-315
   related automotive terms, 314-316
Limited-slip differential gear oil, 255
Limited-slip gear oil, 315
Limiter gap, 46
Line static pressure, 180
Linkage, 46
Linkage-type, 240
Liquid cooling, 335
Liquid cooling systems, 1
Liquid-vapor separator, 58, 154
Load-carrying ball joint, 195
Load-carrying capacity (of a bearing), 15
Load-leveler shock absorber, 207-208
Load range, 219
Long planet pinions, 292
Lower control arm, 195
Low gear, 292
Low-mounted coil spring suspension, 196
Low-pressure liquid, 322
Low pressure side, 322
Low pressure vapor, 322
Low-speed discharge port, 51
Lubricating felt, 84
Lubrication
   chassis lubrication, 255-258
   engine lubrication system, 247-250
Lubrication guidebook, 255
Lubrication gun adapters, 255
Lubrication interval, 257

M

Magnetically controlled ignition, 95
Magnetic field, 70
Magnetic field collapse, 77
Magnetic pickup coil, 95
Main bearing material, 15
Main bearings, 15
Main gas nozzle, 46
Main metering jets, 46
Main shaft, 38. *See also* Output shaft
Main-shaft bearings, 38
Manifold vacuum, 51
Manual control valve, 282
Manual operation, 240
Manufacturer's code (tire), 219
Master cylinder
   and line controls, 180-182
   defined, 180
Master leaf. *See* Main leaf
Mechanical fuel pump, 58
Mechanically operated secondary, 52
Metering rod, 46, 52
Metering valve, 180
Microfarad, 77
Modulator valve, 282
Momentum, 15

Index

Monolithic converter, 161-162
Motor oil functions, 248
Mounting grommets, 208
Muffler, 329. *See also* Silencer
Multileaved spring, 201
Multiple-disc clutch, 263, 315
Multipurpose grease, 257
Multiviscosity oil, 248

N
Needle bearing, 269, 292
Needle valve and seat, 46
Negative plate, 110
Negative terminal, 70, 110
Neutral (planetary gear), 292
No_x, 128
Noble metals, 162
No-load test, 122
Nonconductor, 70

O
Off-the car spinning balancer, 228
OHC, 25
Ohm, 70
Ohm's Law, 70
Oil additives, 248
Oil classifications, 248
Oil clearance (crankshaft assembly), 15
Oil cooler, 248
Oil filter, 249
Oil gallery, 249
Oil intake screen, 249
Oil pour point, 249
Oil pressure, 249
Oil pressure sender unit, 249-250
Oil pump, 249
Oil reservoir, 208
Oil ring, 19
Oil sludge, 250
Oil-squirt hole, 19
Oil strainer, 282
Oil viscosity rating, 250
On-the-car spinning balancer, 228
Open circuit, 70
Open PCV system, 130
Oscilloscope, 77
Output current, 116
Output shaft, 269. *See also* Main shaft
Outside-vehicle lubrication services, 257
Overflow valve. *See* Fuel-pressure regulator
Overhead camshaft. *See* OHC
Overhead valve, 31
Overlubrication, 257
Overrunning clutch drive, 122-123
Oversize drum, 169
Oversize shoes, 169
Oversize valve stem, 31
Oxidation, 162
Oxidation catalyst, 162
Oxides of nitrogen. *See* No_x

P
Pad, 175
Parallel circuit, 72
PCV hoses, 130
PCV system, 130
PCV valve, 130
Pedal clearance, 180
Pedal free play, 263
Percolation, 52
Permanently lubricated joint, 257
Phases, 38
Pictorial diagram, 104
Pilot operated absolute valve. *See* POA valve
Pinion gears, 309, 315
Pinion gear shaft, 309
Pinion pin, 292
Pinion seal, 309
Piston, 19, 175
Piston assembly, 19-21
Piston boss, 19
Piston cups, 181
Piston markings, 19
Piston material, 19
Piston pin, 19
Piston-pin bushing, 20
Piston removal, 175
Piston return spring, 181, 186
Piston rod, 208
Piston rod adjustment, 187
Piston rod seal, 208
Piston seal, 175-176
Piston skirt, 20
Piston-skirt clearance, 20
Piston slap, 20
Piston temperature, 20-21
Piston-type power unit, 187
Piston valve. *See* Rebound valve
Pitman arm, 233
Pitman shaft, 233
Pivot bushings, 196
Planetary gear set, 292
Planet pinion carrier, 292
Planet pinions, 292
Plate grid, 110
Plies, 219
Ply rating, 219
POA valve, 329
Point metal transfer, 84
Polarity, 72, 116
Polarizing, 116
Poles, 116
Pole shoes, 123
Pollution, 130
Port injection, 66
Positive crankcase ventilation system. *See* PCV system
Positive crankcase ventilation, 128-130
Positive plate, 110
Positive terminal, 72, 110
Power brakes, 186
Power circuit, 52
Power cylinder, 187, 240-242
Power piston, 52, 242
Power piston assembly, 187
Power steering, 242
Power steering fluid, 242
Power system, 51
Power trains
    automatic transmission, 276-278
    clutches, 262-264
    conventional differentials, 308
    drive lines, 297-299
    limited-slip differentials, 314
    rear axle assembly, 303
    standard transmissions, 269
Power unit operational check, 187
Power unit runout, 187-188
Power valve, 52
Precision insert bearing, 15
Preignition, 90
Preliminary alignment checks, 213-214
Preload springs, 315-316
Press fit, 21
Pressure (air conditioning), 322
Pressure cap, 335-336
Pressure differential warning switch, 181
Pressure hose, 242-243
Pressure lubrication, 250
Pressure plate assembly, 263
Pressure plate cover, 263
Pressure regulator, 282
Pressure relief valve, 52, 149, 250
Pressure sensor, 66
Pressure vacuum tank fill cap, 154
Primary brake shoe, 169
Primary circuit, 78
Primary coil winding, 72
Primary idle-transfer circuit, 52
Primary piston assembly, 181
Primary resistance, 77
Primary resistance bypass, 78
Printed circuit, 104
Projected core-nose plug, 90
Prony brake, 7
Propeller shaft. *See* Drive shaft
Proportioning valve, 181
Pulley, 116
Pump, 243. *See also* Compressor
Pump air bleed, 59
Pump-discharged check valve, 46
Pumping brakes, 181
Pump link, 59
Pump reservoir, 243
Pump valves, 59
Purge. *See* Discharge
Purge valve, 154
Pushrod, 31, 59, 181

Q
Quick disconnect, 72

R
R-12. *See* Refrigerant
Rack-and-pinion steering gear, 233-235
Radial-ply belted tire, 219
Radial runout, 219
Radiator, 338
Radiator hoses, 338

Index

RC 2-60, 39
RC engine, 39
Rear axle assembly, 303-309
Rear axle housing, 303-304
Rear axle seal, 304
Rear camshaft plug, 25
Rear-end torque, 201
Rear seal and bushing, 269
Rear suspension, 200-202
Rear suspension rebound stop, 208
Rear wheel bearing, 304
Rebound clips, 201
Receiver-drier, 329
Reciprocating, 1
Reciprocating engines, 1-4
Recirculating ball steering gear, 235
Rectifier, 116
Reduction, 162
Reduction catalyst, 162
Refrigerant, 322
Refrigerant lines, 329
Refrigeration oil, 329
Relay, 104
Release levers, 264
Releasing position, 188
Reluctor, 95
Removable carrier differential, 304
Required voltage, 78
Reservoir diaphragm cover seal, 181
Resistance, 72
Resistor, 72
Resistor spark plug, 90
Restrictor, inline, 154
Return hose, 243
Return springs. *See* Shoe-retracting springs
Reverse gear, 292
Reverse idler gear, 269
Revolutions per minute. *See* Rpm
Right-hand rule for motors, 123
Rim safety ridge, 219
Ring expander, 21
Ring gap, 21
Ring gear. *See* Internal gear
Ring gear and drive pinion set, 309
Ring grooves, 21
Ring land, 21
Ring ridge, 21
Road feel, 243
Rocker arm, 32, 59
Rocker-arm return spring, 59
Rocker-arm shaft, 32
Rocker-arm stud, 32
Rod bearing, 21
Rod press fit, 21
Roller bearings, 309
Roller clutch, 276
Roller lifter, 32
Rotary, 1
Rotary combustion engine. *See* RC engine
Rotary diesel, 39

Rotary (Wankel) engine, 37-40
Rotary oil flow, 276-277
Rotor, 39, 78, 116, 176
Rotor apex seals, 39
Rotor cooling, 39
Rotor face, 39, 176
Rotor-face parallelism, 176
Rotor housing, 39
Rotor radius, 39
Rotor runout, 176
Rotor side, 39
Rotor side groove, 39
Rotor side seals, 39
Rotor-type pump, 250
Rotor width, 39
Rpm, 8
Rubber bumpers, 196, 201
Rubbing block, 84
Run-on. *See* Dieseling

S

SAE horsepower, 8
Scavenger deposits, 90
Schematic diagram, 104
Scored piston, 21
Sealed battery, 110
Sealed bearing, 257
Sealed fuel pump, 59
Sealed torque converter, 277
Secondary brake shoe, 169
Secondary circuit, 78
Secondary coil winding, 72
Secondary flashover, 78
Secondary piston assembly, 181
Secondary piston stop screw, 181
Secondary wire crossfiring, 78
Sector shaft. *See* Pitman shaft
Self-adjusting mechanism, 169
Self discharge, 110
Self-energizing action, 169-170
Semicentrifugal clutch, 264
Semiconductor, 116. *See also* Diode
Semiconductor material, 96
Semifloating axle, 304
Sensible heat, 322
Sensors. *See* Pressure sensor; Speed sensor; Throttle-position sensor
Separators, 110
Series circuit, 72
Series-parallel circuit, 72
Service valves, 329
Servo, 282
Shell, 90, 188
Shifter fork, 269
Shift rail, 269
Shift valve, 282
Shim, 316
Shock absorber
    defined, 209
    related automotive terms, 207
Shock compression, 209
Shock fluid, 209
Shock hydraulic principles, 209

Shock mounting position, 209
Shock operational check, 209
Shock piston, 209
Shock rebound, 209
Shoe hold-down springs, 170
Shoe-retracting springs, 170
Short circuit, 72
Shroud. *See* Hot-air duct
Shunt field winding, 123
Side bearing adjuster, 309
Side bearing cap, 309
Side flanges, 13
Side gears, 309
Side-terminal battery, 110
Sight glass, 329
Silencer, 149
Single-barrel carburetor, 46
Single-leaf spring, 201
Single-wire circuit, 104
Slip angle, 214
Slip rings, 116
Slip yoke, 299
Slow charge, 110
Slow-closing throttle device. *See* Antistall dashpot
Smog, 130
Snap ring, 269
Sodium-cooled valve, 32
Solenoid, 104
Solid-state device, 96
Solid wire, 104
Spark advance, 84, 141
Spark delay valve, 143
Spark plug, 78, 88-90
Spark plug fouling, 90
Spark-plug gage, 90
Spark-plug wires, 78
Spark retard, 143
Specific gravity, 110
Speedometer drive gear, 269
Speed sensor, 66
Spherical joint. *See* Ball joint
Spindle. *See* Steering knuckle
Spinning balancer, 228
Spiral bevel gear set, 309
Splash lubrication, 250
Splash shield, 176
Splice, 104
Splined discs, 316
Sprag clutch, 277
Spring eye, 201
Spring leaf, 202
Spring oscillation, 209
Spring rate, 202
Spring retainer, 316
Spring steel, 202
Spring windup, 202
Sprung weight, 196
Spur gear, 269
Stabilizer bar, 196, 202
Stage valve. *See* Purge valve
Stall-torque test, 123

Index

Standard differential, 310
Standard transmission, 269
Starter, 123
Starter neutral switch, 123
Starter relay, 123
Starter ring gear, 277
Starter solenoid, 123
Starting circuit, 123
Starting systems
    related automotive terms, 120-123
    starting circuit, 122
Star-wheel adjusting screw, 170
State of a substance, 322
Statically balanced, 228
Stationary gear, 39
Stator, 116, 277
Steering
    and linkage, 233-236
    power steering, 240-243
    wheel alignment angles, 213-215
Steering column, 235
Steering gearbox, 235
Steering-gear ratio, 235
Steering knuckle, 196
Steering linkage, 235
Steering lock, 235
Steering shaft, 235
Steering universal joint, 235
Steering wheel centering, 214
Stoplight switch, 181
Stranded wire, 104
Stratified-charge engine, 1, 39
Stroke, 8
Strut rod, 196
Substrate, 162
Suction side. *See* Low pressure side
Sun gear, 292
Suspension
    front suspension, 192-196
    rear suspension, 200
    shock absorbers, 207
Swept volume, 37
Switch, 72
Synchronizer, 269

T

Tab guides. *See* Clutch pack ear guides
Tandem, 188
Tandem master cylinder, 181
Tank pressure and vacuum relief system, 154-155
Tank vapor space, 155
Tapered seat, 90
Tappet, 32
TDC, 8
Telescoping shock absorber, 209
Temperature correction, 110
Temperature-pressure relationships, 322
Temperature sending unit, 338
Temperature sensors, 66
Terminal, 104
Test lamp, 72
Thermal clutch fan, 338
Thermal reactor, 162
Thermal switch, 104
Thermal vacuum control valve, 143
Thermostat, 338
Thermostatically controlled air cleaner, 137
Thermostatic choke spring, 46
Thermostatic expansion valve, 329
Thermostatic switch, 329
Thread reach, 90
Thread size, 90
Three phase (stator), 116
Three-way catalytic converter, 162
Throttle body, 46, 66
Throttle plate, secondary, 46
Throttle plate valves, primary, 46
Throttle-position sensor, 66
Throttle solenoid. *See* Idle-stop solenoid
Throttle valve. *See* Modulator valve
Throw out bearing. *See* Clutch release bearing
Thrust block, 310
Thrust washer, 271
Tie rod, 236
Tie rod coupling, 236
Tie rod end, 236
Tilt and telescoping steering column, 236
Time-port injection, 66
Timing chain, 26
Timing-chain slack, 26
Timing gears, 39
Timing light, 84
Tire balancing, 228
Tire centerline, 228
Tire functions, 219
Tire inflation, 219
Tire rotation, 221
Tires, 219-222
Tire sidewall, 221
Tire size, 221
Tire trueing, 221
Tire unbalance, 228
Tire weight-mass centerline, 228
Toe-in, 214-215
Toe-out turns, 215
Tooth coast pattern, 310
Tooth coast side, 310
Tooth drive side, 310
Top dead center. *See* TDC
Torque, 8
Torque converter, 277
Torque multiplication, 271, 277
Torsion bar, 196
Torsion bar suspension, 196
Total volume, 8
Track bar, 202
Transistor, 96
Transistorized regulator. *See* Electronic voltage regulator
Transmission. *See* Four-speed transmission; Standard transmission; Three-speed transmission
Transmission-controlled spark advance, 143
Transmission controlled spark solenoid, 143
Transmission oil cooler, 338
Treads distortion, 221
Tread wear indicators, 221
Trickle charger, 110
Trim height. *See* Curb height
Trochoid, 39
Tubeless tire, 221
Tube seats, 181
Turbine, 277
Turbine shaft, 277
Two-piece drive shaft, 299

U

U-bolts, 202
Under-hood lubrication services, 257
Under-vehicle lubrication services, 257
Unicast rotor, 176
Universal joint, Constant Velocity, 297-299
Universal joint operating angle, 299
Unloader, 46
Unsprung weight, 196
Upper body, 46
Upper control arm, 196
Use precautions (air conditioning), 32
Utilized bodies, 195
Utilized distributor, 96

V

Vacuum, 188
Vacuum advance, 143
Vacuum-advance line, 84
Vacuum-advance unit, 84
Vacuum booster pump, 59
Vacuum break, 46
Vacuum check valve, 188
Vacuum modulator, 282-286
Vacuum motor, 137
Vacuum-operated secondary, 52
Vacuum operated sensing valve, 143
Vacuum-retard unit, 84
Vacuum suspended, 188
Valve arrangement, 1
Valve body assembly, 286
Valve clearance, 32
Valve face, 32
Valve grinding, 32
Valve guide, 32
Valve head, 33
Valve keeper, 33
Valve key. *See* Valve keeper
Valve lapping, 33
Valve lift, 33
Valve margin, 33
Valve overlap, 26
Valve refacing. *See* Valve grinding
Valve retainer. *See* Valve keeper
Valve rotator, 33
Valves, 31-33
Valve-seat angle, 33

351

Index

Valve-seat grindings, 33
Valve-seat insert, 33
Valve-seat width, 33
Valves in receive assembly, 329
Valve-spring pressure tester, 33
Valve stem, 33, 221
Valve-stem seal, 33
Valve temperature, 33
Valve timing, 26
Valve trains, 31-33
Vanes, 277
Vaporization, 52, 322
Vapor return line, 59
Variable purge line, 155
Variable rate spring, 202
Variable-ratio steering gear, 243
Variable resistor, 72
Ventilated rotor, 176
Venturi, 46
Vibration damper, 15
VIR assembly. *See* Valves in receive assembly

Viscosity index, 250
Volt, 72
Voltage, 72
Voltage-drop test, 123
Voltage regulator, 116
Volumetric efficiency, 8
Vortex oil flow, 277

W

Wankel, Dr. Felix, 39
Wankel engine. *See* Rotary (Wankel) engine
Water jacket, 338
Water pump, 338
Wear pattern, 221-222
Weight mass, 228
Wet-charged battery, 110
Wheel alignment angles, 213-215
Wheel balancing, 227-229
Wheel-bearing retaining collar, 304
Wheel centerline, 215
Wheel cylinder, 170
Wheel-cylinder cup, 170

Wheel-cylinder housing, 170
Wheel-cylinder piston, 170
Wheel-cylinder spring, 170
Wheel nuts, 222
Wheel shimmy, 228
Wheel tramp, 228
Wheel weights, 228
Wire color code, 104
Wire gage, 104
Wire placement, 105
Wiring diagram
    defined, 104
    related automotive terms, 102-105
Wiring harness, 104
With tracer, 105
Worm shaft, 236
Worn cam, 26

Y

Y- (Wye) connected stator, 116

Z

Zener diode, 96
Zinc inner liner, 202